BRITANNICA
ALL NEW
KIDS'
ENCYCLOPEDIA

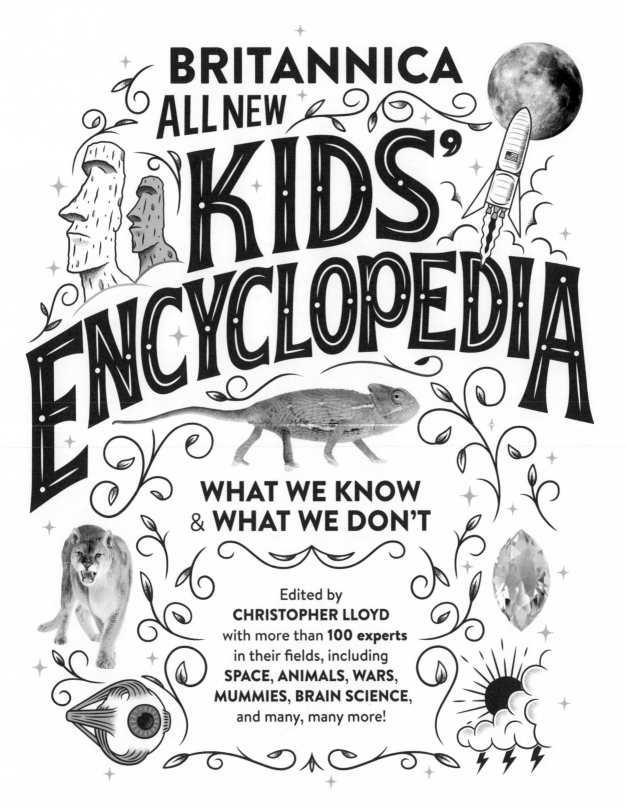

BRITANNICA
ALL NEW
KIDS' ENCYCLOPEDIA

WHAT WE KNOW & WHAT WE DON'T

Edited by
CHRISTOPHER LLOYD
with more than **100 experts**
in their fields, including
**SPACE, ANIMALS, WARS,
MUMMIES, BRAIN SCIENCE,**
and many, many more!

**BRITANNICA
BOOKS**

CONTRIBUTORS

WRITERS

Michael Bright has worked as a producer with the BBC's Natural History unit, based in Bristol, UK. He is an author and ghostwriter, and a member of the Royal Society of Biology.

John Farndon has written hundreds of books on science and nature. He's been shortlisted for the Royal Society's Young People's Book Prize five times. He lives in London, UK.

Dr. Jacob F. Field is an author, historian, and teacher. He studied history at the University of Oxford and got his Ph.D. writing about the impact of the Great Fire of London.

Abigail Mitchell is a modern and medieval historian with degrees from the University of Cambridge and the University of Southern California. She has contributed writing for several books, including *The Vietnam War*, and Scholastic's *Book of World Records*.

Cynthia O'Brien has lived and worked in England and Canada. Her books include *Amazing Brain Mysteries*, *Women Scientists*, and *Encyclopedia of American Indian History and Culture*.

Jonathan O'Callaghan is a freelance space and science journalist based in London, UK. He writes for several publications including *Scientific American*, *Forbes*, *New Scientist*, and *Nature*.

ILLUSTRATORS

Mark Ruffle has been an illustrator and designer for 20 years. He loves drawing animals, people, and anything to do with science.

Jack Tite is an illustrator and children's book author from Leicester, UK. When he's not drawing, Jack likes to birdwatch in his local wildlife parks.

EXPERT CONSULTANTS

Roma Agrawal, Structural Engineer, London, UK; **Tal Avgar**, Utah State University, Logan, UT, US; **A. Jean-Luc Ayitou**, Illinois Institute of Technology, Chicago, IL, US; **Michael D. Bay**, Ph.D., East Central University, Ada, OK, US; **Tracy M. Becker**, Southwest Research Institute, San Antonio, TX, US; **John Bennet**, British School at Athens, Athens, Greece; **Kristin H. Berry**, Western Ecological Research Center, U.S. Geological Survey, Riverside, CA, US; **Alicia Boswell**, University of California, Santa Barbara, CA, US; **Shauna Brail**, University of Toronto, Toronto, ON, Canada; **Monika Bright**, University of Vienna, Vienna, Austria; **Dr. Toby Brown,** McMaster University, Hamilton, ON, Canada; **Cynthia Chestek**, University of Michigan, Ann Arbor, MI, US; **Jeremy Crampton**, Newcastle University, Newcastle upon Tyne, UK; **Dr. Clifford Cunningham**, University of Southern Queensland, Toowoomba, Qld, Australia;

Lewis Dartnell, University of Westminster, London, UK; **Duncan Davis**, Ph.D., Northeastern University, Boston, MA, US; **Pablo De León**, University of North Dakota, Grand Forks, ND, US; **Ivonne Del Valle**, University of California, Berkeley, CA, US; **Paul Dilley**, University of Iowa, Iowa City, IA, US; **Etana H. Dinka**, Oberlin College, Oberlin, OH, US; **Michelle Duffy**, University of Newcastle, Callaghan, NSW, Australia; **Brian Duignan**, Encyclopaedia Britannica, Chicago, IL, US; **Dave Ella**, Catholic Education Office, Broken Bay Diocese, Pennant Hills, NSW, Australia; **Cindy Ermus**, Ph.D., University of Texas at San Antonio, San Antonio, TX, US; **Abigail H. Feresten**, Simon Fraser University, Burnaby, BC, Canada; **Paolo Forti**, Italian Institute of Speleology, University of Bologna, Bologna, Italy; Professor **Kevin Foster**, University of Oxford, Oxford, UK; Chef **Suzi Gerber**, Executive Chef of Haven Foods, Medical Researcher for Inova Medical System, Somerville, MA, US; **Elizabeth Graham**, University College London, London, UK; **Charlotte Greenbaum**, Population Reference Bureau, Washington, DC, US; **Erik Gregersen**, Encyclopaedia Britannica, Chicago, IL, US; **David Hannah**, University of Birmingham, Birmingham, UK; **Nicholas Henshue**, Ph.D., The State University of New York at Buffalo, Buffalo, NY, US; **Katsuya Hirano**, University of California, Los Angeles, CA, US; **Yingjie Hu**, The State University of New York at Buffalo, Buffalo, NY, US; **Professor Alexander D. Huryn**, University of Alabama, Tuscaloosa, AL, US; **Keith Huxen**, The National WWII Museum, New Orleans, LA, US; **John O. Hyland**, Christopher Newport University, Newport News, VA, US; **Salima Ikram**, American University in Cairo, Cairo, Egypt; **Joseph E. Inikori**, University of Rochester, Rochester, NY, US; **Kimberly M. Jackson**, Ph.D., Spelman College, Atlanta, GA, US; **Mike Jay**, Author and Medical Historian, London, UK; **Laura Kalin**, Princeton University, Princeton, NJ, US; **Duncan Keenan-Jones**, University of Queensland, St Lucia, Qld, Australia; **Patrick V. Kirch**, University of California, Berkeley, CA, US; **Dr. Erik Klemetti**, Denison University, Granville, OH, US; **Rudi Kuhn**, South African Astronomical Observatory, Pretoria, South Africa; **Dr. Jaise Kuriakose**, University of Manchester, Manchester, UK; **Nicola Laneri**, University of Catania, Sicily, and School of Religious Studies, CAMNES, Florence, Italy; **Cristina Lazzeroni**, University of Birmingham, Birmingham, UK; **Daryn Lehoux**, Queen's University, Kingston, ON, Canada; **Miranda Lin**, Illinois State University, Normal, IL, US; **Jane Long**, Roanoke College, Salem, VA, US; **Janice Lough**, Australian Institute of Marine Science, Townsville, Qld, Australia; **Ghislaine Lydon**, University of California, Los Angeles, CA, US; **Henry R. Maar III**, University of California, Santa Barbara, CA, US; **Dino J. Martins**, Mpala Research Centre, Nanyuki, Kenya; **Michael Mauel**, Columbia University, New York, NY, US; **Professor Karen McComb**, University of Sussex, Falmer, UK; **Richard

Meade, Lloyd's List, London, UK; **Ian Morison**, 35th Gresham Professor of Astronomy, Macclesfield, UK; **Brendan Murphy**, St. Francis Xavier University, Antigonish, NS, Canada; **Robtel Neajai Pailey**, London School of Economics and Political Science, London, UK; **Matthew P. Nelsen**, The Field Museum, Chicago, IL, US; **Gregory Nowacki**, U.S. Forest Service, Milwaukee, WI, US; **Mike Parker Pearson**, University College London, London, UK; **Bill Parkinson**, The Field Museum; University of Illinois, Chicago, IL, US; **Melissa Petruzzello**, Encyclopaedia Britannica, Chicago, IL, US; **Martin Polley**, International Centre for Sports History and Culture, De Montfort University, Leicester, UK; **John P. Rafferty**, Encyclopaedia Britannica, Chicago, IL, US; **Michael Ray**, Encyclopaedia Britannica, Chicago, IL, US; **Dr. Gil Rilov**, National Institute of Oceanography, Israel Oceanographic and Limnological Research, Haifa, Israel; **Kara Rogers**, Encyclopaedia Britannica, Chicago, IL, US; **Margaret C. Rung**, Roosevelt University, Chicago, IL, US; **Eugenia Russell**, Independent Scholar, UK; **Mark Sapwell**, Ph.D., Archaeologist and Archaeology Editor, London, UK; **Joel Sartore**, National Geographic Photo Ark, Lincoln, NE, US; **Dr. Benjamin Sawyer**, Middle Tennessee State University, Nashville, TN, US; **Mark C. Serreze**, National Snow and Ice Data Center; University of Colorado Boulder, Boulder, CO, US; **Pravina Shukla**, Indiana University, Bloomington, IL, US; **Professor Michael G. Smith**, Purdue University, West Lafayette, IN, US; **Dr. Nathan Smith**, Natural History Museum of Los Angeles County, Los Angeles, CA, US; **Jack Snyder**, Columbia University, New York, NY, US; **Hou-mei Sung**, Cincinnati Art Museum, Cincinnati, OH, US; **Heaven Taylor-Wynn**, The Poynter Institute, St. Petersburg, FL, US; **Silvana Tenreyro**, London School of Economics and Political Science, London, UK; **Lori Ann Terjesen**, National Women's History Museum, Alexandria, VA, US; **Dr. Michelle Thaller**, NASA Goddard Space Flight Center, Greenbelt, MD, US; **David Tong**, University of Cambridge, Cambridge, UK; **Sarah Tuttle**, University of Washington, Seattle, WA, US; **Paul Ullrich**, University of California, Davis, CA., US; **Javier Urcid**, Brandeis University, Waltham, MA, US; **Lorenzo Veracini**, Swinburne University of Technology, Melbourne, Vic, Australia; **Lora Vogt**, National WWI Museum and Memorial, Kansas City, MO, US; **Jeff Wallenfeldt**, Encyclopaedia Britannica, Chicago, IL, US; **Dr. Linda J. Walters**, University of Central Florida, Orlando, FL, US; **David J. Wasserstein**, Vanderbilt University, Nashville, TN, US; **Dominik Wujastyk**, University of Alberta, Edmonton, AB, Canada; **Man Xu**, Tufts University, Medford, MA, US; **Taymiya R. Zaman**, University of San Francisco, California, CA, US; **Alicja Zelazko**, Encyclopaedia Britannica, Chicago, IL, US; **Gina A. Zurlo**, Center for the Study of Global Christianity, Gordon-Conwell Theological Seminary, Boston, MA, US

FOREWORD

Encyclopaedia Britannica has been inspiring curiosity and the joy of learning since 1768. This book continues that tradition. It will take you on an amazing journey through all of history and across the Universe. You'll have the opportunity to dive into a black hole (and emerge unscathed!) and take a tour of a medieval castle. You'll also be given the power to peer into the future and learn about what might matter most to us here on Earth. Each time you turn a page, you'll find something new to explore—and, maybe, you'll even be a bit alarmed, like I was, when you run across the section on creepy crawlies ...

But as surprising and fascinating as each page is, everything we are sharing with you is always subject to change. And that is something that we embrace: watch for sections that describe Known Unknowns. The scholars, researchers, and other brilliant minds who have helped us create this book are the ones who, in their day-to-day lives, are shaping the boundaries of knowledge. They're driven by their passion and their dedication to accuracy and, because of that, they're helping all of us better understand the world. And that includes understanding what we don't know yet.

We believe that facts matter, and we strive for accuracy through rigorous fact-checking of all the information we share, including on every page of this book. Through its more than 250 years of existence, Encyclopaedia Britannica has been committed to inquiry and exploration, working with experts and driving innovation. That's why it's a great honor to be launching Britannica Books, a collaboration between Britannica and What on Earth Publishing, with Christopher Lloyd and this brand-new encyclopedia.

J. E. Luebering
Editorial Director
Encyclopaedia Britannica

CONTENTS

INTRODUCTION

Are you a morning person? Some people find it easy to jump out of bed, while for others it can take several alarms clocks. I used to be like that. But not any more!

You might be surprised to hear that my leaping out of bed all started when I began writing books. Why? The more I realized what I didn't know, the more excited I became about discovering new things. That feedback loop has never stopped. I now wake up bursting with curiosity about whom I might meet and what new stories I might discover. Everyday life is just so bizarre, so amazing!

Imagine a substance that, when you heat it up, just disappears into thin air. Is it a conjuring trick? No, it's just called water.

Or think about looking up at the night sky. The stars you see are not as they are today but as they were at all different times in the past—some as long as 15,000 years ago! That's how long it's taken the light from many of those stars to reach planet Earth.

I started writing books after seeing how my two daughters just loved learning about things they found interesting. The older one, Matilda, adored penguins. You can find out more about them on page 185! The other, Verity, preferred anything to do with food. For that, see page 208.

What I realized is that to capture everyone's interests, we needed to find some way of joining all of the fascinating subjects together. We've done that in this book by including cross-references on the bottom of each left-hand page. If you are interested in topics on a particular page, the cross-references will tell you where else to go to find out more.

Feel free to hop around in this book. That's what we made it for. But if you're the kind of person who likes to read things in order, you can do that, too. You'll be taken on a journey that starts at the big bang, through the story of our planet and how life in all its glorious forms emerged, and on to the history of humans. Toward the end, you'll arrive in today's world and even peer over the horizon to ponder what might happen next.

I bet you've noticed that the subtitle of this book is "What We Know & What We Don't." One thing I have learned in all my research is that each answer leads to a series of new questions. I now think of all answers as twists and turns on a yellow-brick road of discovery, around which there are dozens of new questions that I never knew existed. And many of those new questions are yet to have definitive answers. We call these mysteries Known Unknowns, and it's been so much fun learning about them for this book.

But I'm not the only researcher who's been involved in making the *Britannica All New Kids' Encyclopedia*. In addition to all of the research done by the authors of each chapter, we have been lucky to be able to work with more than 100 expert consultants. Their names are at the bottoms of the pages, plus I'm very excited that you'll be able to meet some of them in the book itself.

Will you be one of the experts of tomorrow? Which are the topics—from space to nature, archaeology to technology—that you like best? The beauty of life is that we are all intrigued by different things, so together we can figure out a tremendous amount about the world around us. And I have one particular hope: that after spending some time with this book, you might have a new spring in your step, sparked by the knowledge that there are still so many exciting twists and turns in the story of life on Earth, just waiting for us to discover.

Christopher Lloyd
What on Earth Publishing

The Sun is a massive plasma fireball of atoms so hot that it has no fixed surface. The huge quantities of heat and light generated by the Sun power most of the processes on Earth, even though it is some 93 million miles away from us.

CHAPTER 1
UNIVERSE

Buckle up for an incredible journey through our Universe. At this moment you are riding on an enormous ball of rock. That rock is soaring through space at thousands of miles an hour in a swirling galaxy of billions of giant balls of fire. That rock, of course, is our Earth. And the giant balls of fire are stars, including our own Sun. I hope that fact alone is enough to convince you that reality is so much more amazing than anything you can make up.

In this chapter, we begin with an unimaginably tiny speck of infinite energy from which the Universe exploded into existence 13.8 billion years ago and finish with a Known Unknown: how, when, or if the Universe will come to an end. Which is a reminder that for every answer we find, there are dozens more questions: is there intelligent life somewhere else in the Universe? Why is there more matter than antimatter? What would happen if an astronaut fell into a black hole? There's lots to discover, even about the unknown.

THE BIG BANG

The big bang is the moment we think the Universe was born 13.8 billion years ago. It describes how a teeny-tiny dot suddenly expanded faster than the speed of light, creating the entire Universe. Belgian astronomer Georges Lemaître, who first proposed the theory in 1931, called the dot the primeval atom. All matter in the Universe began in this tiny dot and eventually became everything you see around you today.

What happened in the big bang?

The big bang took place in a split second. Scientists think it was an expansion rather than an explosion. Everything started out incredibly hot, billions of degrees in temperature, but then cooled. When it cooled to thousands of degrees Fahrenheit, atoms joined together and formed matter. This eventually clumped together to make stars, galaxies, solar systems, and planets.

1

The beginning
The Universe begins as a tiny dot with all known matter and energy squeezed into it

2

Massive expansion
In a split second, the dot rapidly expands, from being smaller than an atom to about 20 light-years across

3

Key elements
Three minutes after the big bang, the Universe cools enough for hydrogen and helium atoms to form

4

Traveling light
Eventually, 300,000 years after the big bang, light travels freely through the Universe

5

Taking shape
The hydrogen and helium form clouds of gas that lead to the first stars and later to galaxies

6

Today's Universe
The stars explode and produce new elements, which make the planets, moons, and everything that lives on Earth

1 SECOND

3 MINUTES

300,000 YEARS

1 BILLION YEARS

13.8 BILLION YEARS

EXPERT CONSULTANT: Sarah Tuttle **SEE ALSO:** Galaxies, p.6–7; Stars, p.10–11; Nebulae, p.12–13; Watching Space from Space, p.16–17; Black Holes, p.18–19; End of the Universe, p.46–47; The Atom, p.100–01; Elements, p.102–03; Energy, p.122–23; Electricity, p.126–27; Gravity, p.134–35

Evidence for the big bang

Our best proof for the big bang comes from something called the Cosmic Microwave Background (CMB), seen in this photo of the night sky. The picture shows heat left over from the big bang that spread thinly all over the Universe. The image was taken by scientists using NASA's Wilkinson Microwave Anisotropy Probe (WMAP).

Places where matter has clumped together, forming galaxies, appears hotter in the CMB

There are fewer galaxies where matter hasn't clumped together

Colors show differences in the heat of the Universe. Cooler areas are blue and hotter areas are red

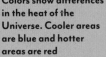

FACTastic!

Hydrogen and helium were the only elements at the start of the Universe. They formed huge stars. In the core of these stars, new elements formed. When the stars exploded, they released those new elements into space.

H 75%

He 25%

Pigeon interference

In 1965, American astronomers Arno Penzias and Robert Wilson were using a radio telescope to study the Universe when they saw a lot of static interference (like a bad connection on a video call). They thought it might be caused by pigeon droppings, as there were two pigeons nesting in their telescope. But when they caught the pigeons the noise didn't stop. Eventually, the two men realized they were hearing the echo of Cosmic Microwave Background radiation—evidence for the big bang!

KNOWN UNKNOWN

Why is there more matter than antimatter in the Universe?

The opposite of matter (stuff) is antimatter. When matter and antimatter collide, they are both destroyed, leaving only energy. Scientists think these were created in equal quantities in the big bang, so why didn't antimatter cancel out the matter that made the Universe and everything in it? Scientists still don't know the answer.

NOTE from the expert!

SARAH TUTTLE
Astronomer

Professor Sarah Tuttle specializes in the observation of nearby galaxies. She loves the fact that she can look at the night sky with a telescope and see back toward the beginning of the Universe. She likes to ponder how the Universe came about—what existed before the Big Bang?

66 *Are we traveling through time? Or space? Or both?* 99

GALAXIES

Most of the visible Universe is made up of galaxies—vast collections of stars, dust, and gas held together by gravity. Scientists think there could be 100 billion galaxies in the Universe. Many of them, including our Milky Way, are nearly as old as the Universe itself.

What does a galaxy look like from Earth?

Almost all the stars we can see with the naked eye belong to our own Milky Way, though Andromeda, the nearest galaxy to Earth, can be seen without a telescope from the Northern Hemisphere (north of the equator). In the Southern Hemisphere, stargazers can sometimes see the Magellanic Clouds, two galaxies that orbit the Milky Way.

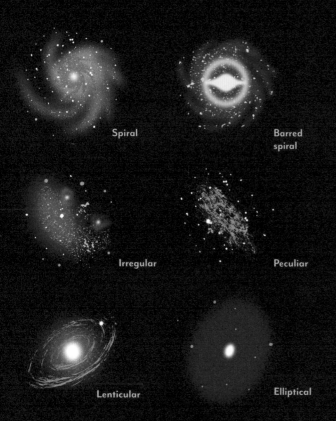

Spiral

Barred spiral

Irregular

Peculiar

Lenticular

Elliptical

Types of galaxies

Astronomers sort galaxies according to their shape. A spiral galaxy spreads out from the center. A barred spiral like our Milky Way is similar but has a bar of stars near the center. Irregular and peculiar galaxies are less defined, while a spiral galaxy with no arms is called a lenticular galaxy. Elliptical galaxies are shaped like eggs.

The dusty band of stars at the top of the picture is the main disk of our Milky Way galaxy

Andromeda galaxy, the nearest galaxy to our own

Venus setting over Dinosaur National Park, Alberta, Canada

EXPERT CONSULTANT: Toby Brown **SEE ALSO:** The Big Bang, p.4–5; The Milky Way, p.8–9; Stars, p.10–11; Watching Space from Space, p16–17; Exoplanets, p.20–21; End of the Universe, p.46–47; Gravity, p.134–35

When galaxies collide

Everything in the Universe is moving. This picture shows Galaxy NGC 6052, a new galaxy formed from two colliding galaxies. In about 4.5 billion years, our own Milky Way will merge with Andromeda galaxy. They will form what scientists have nicknamed Milkomeda.

GAME CHANGER

HENRIETTA SWAN LEAVITT

Astronomer, lived 1868–1921
US

Until the 20th century, most scientists thought our Milky Way was the whole Universe. But in 1912, American astronomer Henrietta Leavitt discovered a new way to calculate the distance to stars that eventually helped prove that some are too far away to be in our own galaxy. In 1924, Edwin Hubble used Leavitt's method to prove that Andromeda was a separate galaxy.

KNOWN UNKNOWN

Will we find intelligent life elsewhere in the Universe and what will it look like?

The sheer number of galaxies, stars, and solar systems in the Universe, and the laws of physics mean there must be other planets like Earth where intelligent life could have evolved. For many scientists, the biggest question is not whether there is intelligent life elsewhere in the Universe, but what it might look like and how we can find it.

THE MILKY WAY

Our own solar system belongs to a galaxy called the Milky Way, which we can see as a starry band across the sky on a dark night. The Milky Way we know today was formed from many smaller galaxies colliding and interacting over the last 13.5 billion years. A huge spiral galaxy, it has two major rotating arms of stars and two minor arms extending from its center.

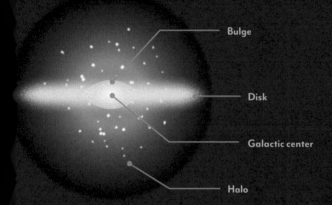

Bulge

Disk

Galactic center

Halo

A central bulge of light

The shape of our galaxy—and its central bulge—can be more easily understood when looked at from the side. Most of its billions of stars are in the flat disk around the bulge, but some are farther out in a halo around the galactic center.

The Scutum-Centaurus Arm fades away at a distance of 55,000–60,000 light-years from Earth

The Outer Arm is thought to be the outer part of the Norma Arm

A halo of dark matter surrounds the Milky Way and makes up about 90 percent of its mass

The Milky Way in Numbers
LISTIFIED.

1. **1.12 trillion years:** The time it would take a car traveling at 60 mph (96 km/h) to cross the Milky Way.
2. **13.5 billion years:** The number of years since the Milky Way formed in the early Universe.
3. **25,000 light-years:** Our solar system's distance from the center of the Milky Way.
4. **100–400 billion:** The number of stars scientists think are in the Milky Way. The precise figure is impossible to calculate, say NASA scientists.
5. **Hundreds of billions:** The number of planets in the Milky Way if each star hosts one or several planets.
6. **240 million years:** The time it takes for the Milky Way to rotate.
7. **4.5 billion years:** The number of years before the Milky Way is set to collide with a neighboring galaxy called Andromeda.

An astronomer
discovered the Far
3kpc Arm in 2008

Mapping the Milky Way

Because we live inside the Milky Way galaxy, we can't see its spiral shape, but we can build an impression like this one. Infrared images from NASA's Spitzer Telescope taught us about its structure, and data from the Cerro Tololo Inter-American Observatory in Chile revealed a new spiral arm that astronomers have called the Far 3kpc Arm. Like other minor arms, it is filled with gas and pockets of young stars.

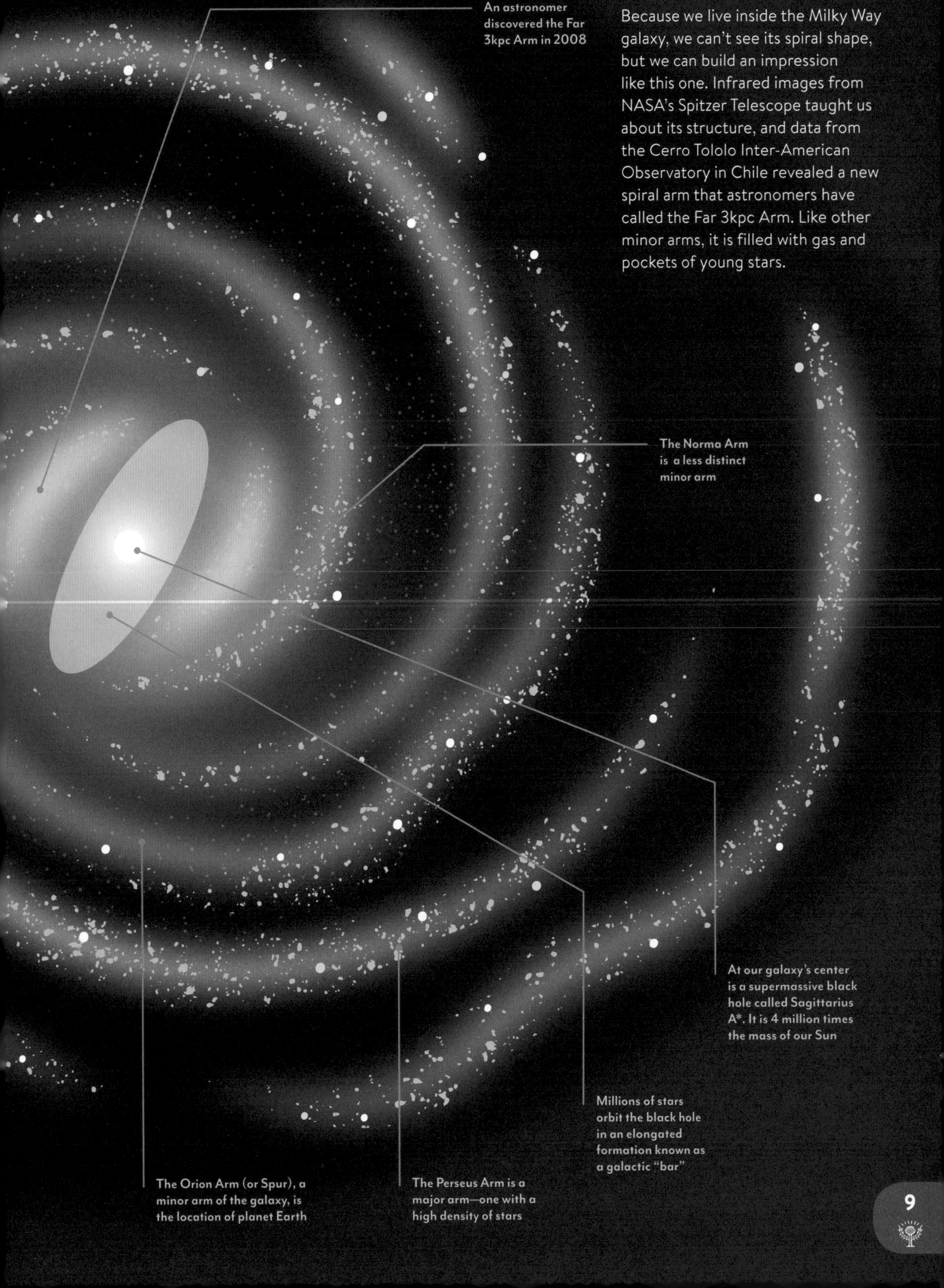

The Norma Arm
is a less distinct
minor arm

At our galaxy's center
is a supermassive black
hole called Sagittarius
A*. It is 4 million times
the mass of our Sun

Millions of stars
orbit the black hole
in an elongated
formation known as
a galactic "bar"

The Orion Arm (or Spur), a
minor arm of the galaxy, is
the location of planet Earth

The Perseus Arm is a
major arm—one with a
high density of stars

STARS

Stars are giant balls of gas. There are vast numbers of stars in the known Universe. A process called nuclear fusion takes place in the core of these gas balls, producing huge amounts of energy in the form of light and heat. The brightness of a star depends on the amount of energy it creates and where the star is in its life cycle. Most stars, like our Sun, are orbited by planets.

Telescopes help us to see far more stars than the few thousand that can be seen with the naked eye

The eyepiece can be changed to alter the level of magnification

Why do stars twinkle?

Stars twinkle because of our atmosphere. As the light from distant stars reaches our planet, it is bent (refracted) by the changes in temperature and density of the atmosphere. When we look at a star it appears to "twinkle," but this is just the zigzagging passage of light as it travels toward us.

Italian scientist Galileo Galilei was the first to use a telescope to view objects in space in 1609

Stargazing

To study stars in more detail, we need a telescope. The refracting telescope collects light from stars by using lenses (curved pieces of glass) and a long tube. When rays of light from a star enter the tube, lenses bend them to a focal point, producing an image of the star. Another lens called the eyepiece then magnifies this image.

EXPERT CONSULTANT: Ian Morison **SEE ALSO:** The Big Bang, p.4–5; Galaxies, p.6–7; Nebulae, p.12–13; Constellations, p.14–15; The Sun, p.24–25; End of the Universe, p.46–47; The Atmosphere, p.86–87; Solids, Liquids & Gases, p.110–11; Light, p.128–29; Gravity, p.134–35; Pressure, p.136–37

Life cycle of a star

Stars can live for millions or even billions of years. How long depends on how much matter a star contains. The bigger a star is, the faster it uses its fuel, and the shorter its life will be. Our Sun, which is a yellow dwarf, will expand to a red giant in about five billion years and then explode, leaving behind a dense object called a white dwarf.

Stars are formed in clouds of dust and gas, called nebulae, which are pulled together by gravity

If there is a lot of dust and gas, an extremely massive star can form

If there is less dust and gas, smaller dwarf stars may form instead

Our Sun is a yellow dwarf, a fairly average kind of star

One of the biggest types of stars in the Universe is called a supergiant

At the end of our Sun's life, it will expand into a red giant

When a supergiant reaches the end of its life, it may explode as a supernova

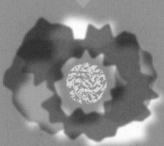

Our Sun will then cast off its outer layers, leaving its core behind in a nebula of gas

If the supergiant was really big, it will leave a black hole behind after it becomes a supernova

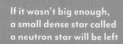

If it wasn't big enough, a small dense star called a neutron star will be left

The remaining core of our Sun will be a white dwarf that will shine as a star for trillions of years

FACTastic!

When we look at stars, we look back in time. This is because the light from stars travels at the speed of light and takes time to reach us. Our nearest star, Proxima Centauri, 4.2 light-years away, is 4.2 years older than the age we see it now. The Andromeda galaxy is 2.5 million light-years away, so it is 2.5 million years older than what we see now.

NOTE from the expert!

IAN MORISON
Astronomer

Professor Ian Morison became interested in the Universe at the age of 12, when he made a telescope. He writes books for amateur astronomers and has contributed to Project Phoenix—a search for extraterrestrial life.

❝ *Stars create the elements such as carbon, oxygen, silicon, and iron that enable planets and life to form.* ❞

NEBULAE

In interstellar space—the areas between the stars of a galaxy—swirling dust and gases like helium and hydrogen form clouds called nebulae. Sometimes this gas and dust simply clumps together under the force of gravity, and sometimes it is ejected by dying stars. Some of the biggest, most impressive nebulae form from exploding supernovae—an event that can lead to the creation of brand-new stars.

Winds from nearby stars shape the towers of gas and dust

Older stars

Gas

Dust

New stars

Star nursery

The nebula RCW 49 in the southern constellation Carina is a nursery for more than 2,000 new stars. Normally, dark dust hides the nebula, but this infrared image taken by NASA's Spitzer Space Telescope picks up matter sending out infrared radiation (a type of light that we feel as heat) that can pass through dust and gas. It shows old stars (in the center) and many new stars.

The Pillars of Creation

One of the most famous nebulae is the Eagle Nebula, especially a section called the Pillars of Creation. About 6,500 light-years from Earth in the Orion spiral arm of the Milky Way, this amazing mass of dust and gas forms pillar-shaped clouds that are five light-years long. The entire Eagle Nebula is approximately 70 light-years across.

Different colors indicate the chemical elements that are present in a nebula. Red indicates sulfur

Different types of nebulae

Scientists classify nebulae according to their appearance and how they formed. They can be very large—a few hundred light-years across—and fantastically shaped, though planetary nebulae, which expand from the center, are often small (about two light-years across) and evenly shaped. Nebulae are broadly divided into bright and dark nebulae.

Planetary nebulae, formed from dying stars but not supernovae, are often round.

Hydrogen atoms in an emission nebula are excited by ultraviolet light from very hot stars, giving out red light.

The dust in a reflection nebula scatters the blue light from very hot stars nearby. It doesn't produce much light itself.

The Horse's Head nebula in the Orion constellation is a dark nebula, in which dense dust absorbs light.

A supernova

Stars are maintained by a balance of forces—the inward force of gravity and the outward pressure of heat and gas from the inner core. When a big star runs out of fuel, it can no longer support itself and gravity wins, causing the star to collapse. When the outer shell hits the star's core, it rebounds out again like a trampolinist. This powerful and very bright explosion is called a supernova. All the dust and gas that is thrown out into space may form a nebula, and sometimes they leave behind a really dense object—a black hole.

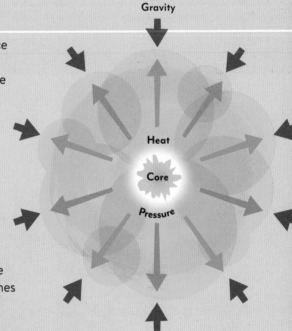

Gravity

Heat

Core

Pressure

FACTastic!

A nebula cloud the size of Earth would weigh the same as a small sack of potatoes! This is because all the dust and gas in a nebula is really light. However, when the dust and gas stretches over many light-years, there is enough mass and gravity for the nebula to collapse and form new stars.

CONSTELLATIONS

A constellation is a group of stars that forms a pattern in the sky. Ancient cultures named the shapes they could see after things like animals and mythological figures. The shapes most of us use today come from the ancient Greeks. Which constellations we see depends on whether we live north or south of the equator and where Earth is in its orbit around the Sun.

Northern Hemisphere

Constellations that are easy to spot if we live north of the equator are Cassiopeia, which forms a W shape, Orion (look for three stars that form Orion's belt), and Cygnus, the Swan, in the form of a cross.

Pisces · Cetus · Pegasus · Aquarius · Aries · Taurus · Delphinus · Andromeda · Triangulum · Cassiopeia · Perseus · Orion · Cygnus · Camelopardalis · Auriga · Aquila · Polaris · Gemini · Lyra · Ursa Minor · Lynx · Ophiuchus · Hercules · Draco · Cancer · Ursa Major · Boötes · Corona Borealis · Coma Berenices · Leo

Mythical creatures

The Great Bear (Ursa Major) constellation is one of the brightest in the Northern Hemisphere. The ancient Greeks saw Ursa Major as Callisto, a nymph transformed into a bear in one of their myths. It incorporates the Big Dipper.

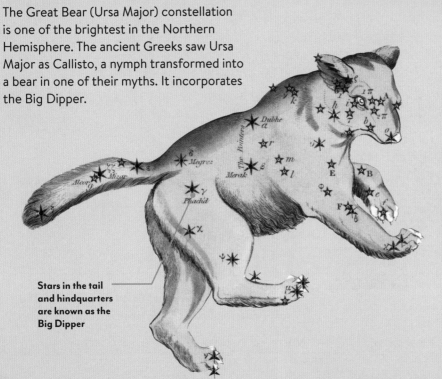

Stars in the tail and hindquarters are known as the Big Dipper

Some of the best and darkest places to view a clear night sky

Death Valley National Park, US
Teide Observatory, Tenerife
Gobi Desert, Mongolia
Atacama Desert, Chile
NamibRand Nature Reserve, Namibia
Mauna Kea, Hawaii, US
Aoraki Mackenzie, New Zealand

EXPERT CONSULTANT: Ian Morison **SEE ALSO:** Galaxies, p.6–7; The Milky Way, p.8–9; Stars, p.10–11; Age of Exploration, p.298–99

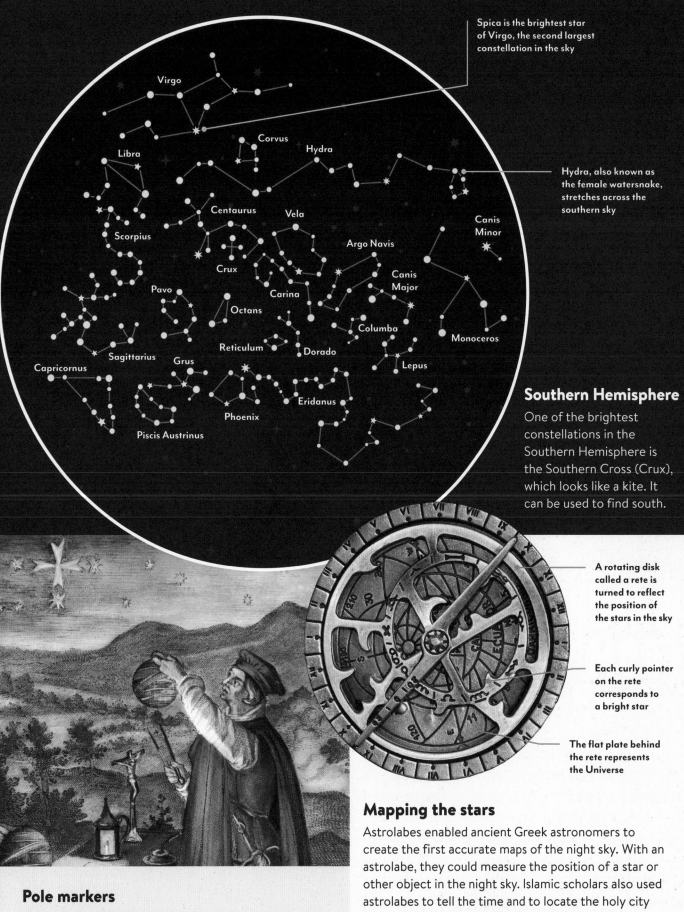

Spica is the brightest star of Virgo, the second largest constellation in the sky

Virgo

Corvus

Hydra

Hydra, also known as the female watersnake, stretches across the southern sky

Libra

Canis Minor

Scorpius

Centaurus

Vela

Argo Navis

Crux

Carina

Canis Major

Pavo

Octans

Columba

Monoceros

Sagittarius

Grus

Reticulum

Dorado

Lepus

Capricornus

Piscis Austrinus

Phoenix

Eridanus

Southern Hemisphere

One of the brightest constellations in the Southern Hemisphere is the Southern Cross (Crux), which looks like a kite. It can be used to find south.

A rotating disk called a rete is turned to reflect the position of the stars in the sky

Each curly pointer on the rete corresponds to a bright star

The flat plate behind the rete represents the Universe

Pole markers

Early sailors and explorers used the Pole Star (Polaris), above Earth's North Pole, to point the way north and the Southern Cross (Crux), shown here, in the Southern Hemisphere, to help them find south.

Mapping the stars

Astrolabes enabled ancient Greek astronomers to create the first accurate maps of the night sky. With an astrolabe, they could measure the position of a star or other object in the night sky. Islamic scholars also used astrolabes to tell the time and to locate the holy city of Mecca, so that they knew in which direction to pray. In the Age of Discovery, from the 15th century, the early navigators used astrolabes to find their way across the oceans.

This secondary mirror focuses infrared light from the primary mirror into the telescope. From there, it will be transmitted back to Earth as data

A large shield the size of a tennis court allows the JWST to observe the Universe without being blinded by the Sun or getting too hot

WATCHING SPACE FROM SPACE

What secrets do the stars hold? Today, thanks to the latest telescope technology, we can study the Universe in great detail. The best-known space telescope is NASA's Hubble Space Telescope (HST), launched in 1990. Now a new generation of super space telescopes is set to probe even farther into the Universe. The first of these, the James Webb Space Telescope (JWST), has a giant gold-coated mirror and will look at the Universe in infrared—that is, by detecting the heat that objects give off.

EXPERT CONSULTANT: Clifford Cunningham **SEE ALSO:** The Big Bang, p.4–5; Black Holes, p.18–19; Exoplanets, p.20–21; Our Solar System, p.22–23; the Sun, p.24–25; Rocky Planets, p.28–29; Gas Giants, p.30–31; Moons, p.32–33; Artificial Satellites, p.40–41; Space Probes, p.44–45

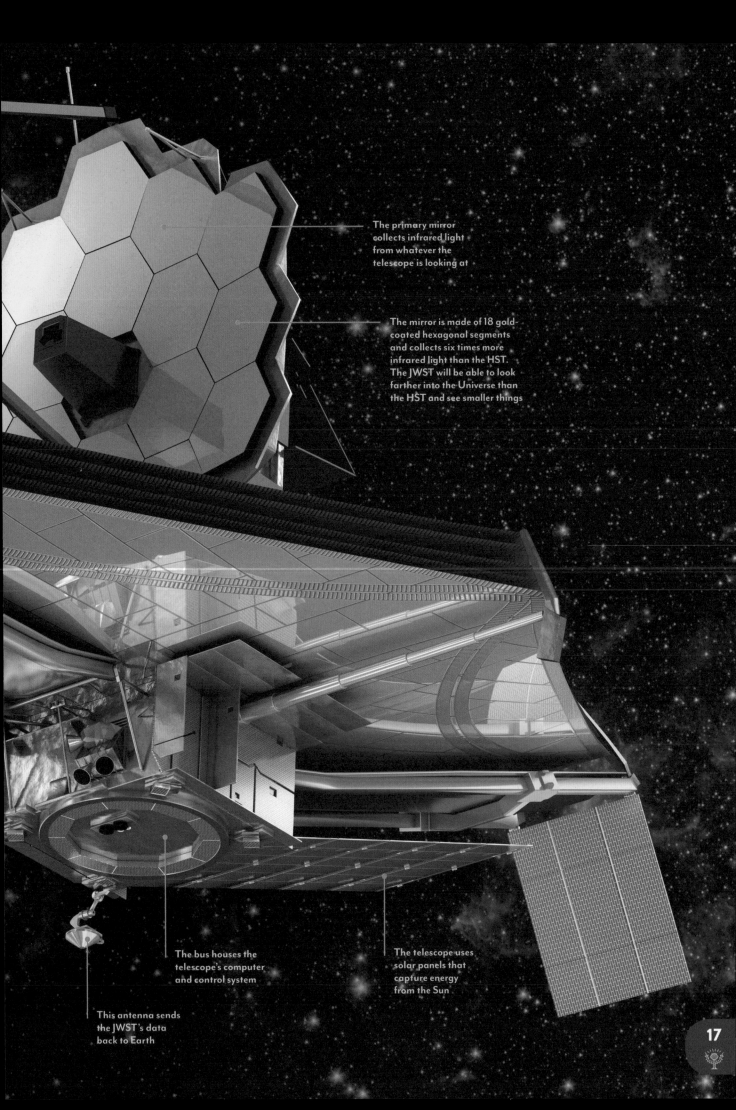

The primary mirror collects infrared light from whatever the telescope is looking at

The mirror is made of 18 gold-coated hexagonal segments and collects six times more infrared light than the HST. The JWST will be able to look farther into the Universe than the HST and see smaller things

The bus houses the telescope's computer and control system

The telescope uses solar panels that capture energy from the Sun

This antenna sends the JWST's data back to Earth

17

BLACK HOLES

A black hole is an object in space with gravity so strong that nothing can escape from it. One often forms when a massive star dies and some of its matter is squashed into an extremely dense object. Black holes may range from mini black holes the size of an atom but with the mass of a mountain to supermassive black holes at the center of galaxies.

First image of a black hole

Not even light can get out of a black hole, so they are invisible. But in 2019, astronomers saw bright gases around a black hole at the center of galaxy M87. They used a network of radio telescopes to create a super telescope called the Event Horizon Telescope (EHT). Until then, scientists had detected black holes by their gravitational pull on stars and hot gas.

EXPERT CONSULTANT: Michelle Thaller **SEE ALSO:** The Big Bang, p.4–5; Nebulae, p.12–13; Earth in Space, p.54–55; The Atom, p.100–01; Energy, p.122–23; Electricity, p.126–27; Light, p.128–29; Forces, p.132–33; Gravity, p.134–35

Anatomy of a black hole

The gravity of a black hole increases toward its center. On the outskirts, dust and gas form an accretion disk that heats up to 180 million °F (100 million°C) as it spins around the black hole. Inside this is the event horizon, where nothing can escape the black hole's pull. The very center of the black hole may be a singularity—a point where matter is squashed so tightly that it has infinite density—or it may be that matter at such densities behaves in ways we can't yet imagine.

Supermassive black holes are at the center of almost all galaxies. The one at the center of the Milky Way is called Sagittarius A*

Dust and gas form a superhot accretion disk that spins around the black hole at high speed, producing electromagnetic radiation

The spherical event horizon is the point of no return, where nothing can escape the black hole's gravity. At its center is the singularity, a tiny point of infinite density

GAME CHANGER

STEPHEN HAWKING
**Physicist, lived 1942–2018
UK**

British physicist Stephen Hawking expanded our understanding of black holes. He suggested that something might be able to escape from a black hole. He called this Hawking radiation, a type of light. He thought that the escape of such radiation would eventually reduce the energy of black holes. So far, scientists haven't found this radiation, but they are still looking.

Weird physics

Gravity is so strong in the center of black holes that strange things might happen there—things that upset the laws of physics that govern the Universe. Such gravity could make time stand still or even produce "wormholes" (tunnels) to other places in the Universe.

KNOWN UNKNOWN

What would happen if an astronaut fell into a black hole?

Scientists think that a body pulled over the event horizon of a black hole would be spaghettified—stretched out like spaghetti by the black hole's gravity. However, it is not known what would happen to the astronaut in the very center of the black hole.

19

EXOPLANETS

Our Sun is not the only star to be orbited by planets. There are billions of stars in our galaxy, and almost all of them are thought to have planets. We call planets that are outside our solar system exoplanets. So far, scientists have found more than 4,000 of them. They range in size from smaller than Earth to much bigger than Jupiter. Scientists hope to find out whether some of these exoplanets could have life.

Kepler telescope

NASA's Kepler telescope found the vast majority of exoplanets discovered so far. This telescope trailed Earth on its orbit around the Sun from 2009 to 2018, when it ran out of fuel. It found planets by watching for a dip in light of distant stars as planets passed in front of them. This is known as the transit method of detection.

A comet is a chunk of ice and rock left over after the formation of a solar system

Every solar system has a star at its center. The Sun is the star at the center of our solar system

Newly formed planets carve out paths in the dusty disk of their star

Gas giants tend to form farther from their star, where they can collect more dust and gas

Asteroids are rocky bodies that failed to form into planets. Sometimes they collide with planets

How does a solar system develop?

A solar system develops when a star forms at the center of a disk of dust and gas. As the star spins, some of the dust and gas clumps together, forming objects that grow larger over time. Over millions of years, this can lead to the creation of planets. Many smaller objects form during this time, too, such as asteroids and comets.

EXPERT CONSULTANT: Tracy M. Becker and Erik Gregersen **SEE ALSO:** Galaxies, p.6–7; The Milky Way, p.8–9; Stars, p.10–11; Watching Space from Space, p.16–17; Our Solar System, p.22–23; The Sun, p.24–25; Planetary Exploration, p.26–27; Rocky Planets, p.28–29; Gas Giants, p.30–31

FACTastic!

A year on exoplanet NGTS-10b is only about 18 hours long!
Discovered in 2019, NGTS-10b orbits so close to its star that it completes an orbit every 18 hours. We think such planets, which are similar to Jupiter, form farther out in a solar system before being pushed inward. Nicknamed "hot roasters," they reach thousands of degrees in temperature. Eventually their star rips them apart.

Exoplanet Firsts
TIMELINE

1984 Discovery of the first planetary disk surrounding another star.

1992 Confirmation of the first planets known to be in orbit around another star.

1995 Astronomers find the first planet known to orbit a star like our Sun (51 Pegasi b).

2004 Astronomers take an image of an exoplanet for the first time, a world called 2M1207b.

2009 Launch of NASA's Kepler telescope; it goes on to find thousands of new planets.

2015 Discovery of the Kepler-452b planet, thought to be potentially habitable, like Earth.

2016 Discovery of Proxima Centauri b, a planet orbiting the nearest star to our Sun.

2017 Scientists learn that the Kepler-90 system has as many planets as our solar system; they also discover that the TRAPPIST-1 system has seven planets roughly the size of Earth.

2018 Launch of NASA's new exoplanet-hunting telescope, TESS.

KNOWN UNKNOWN

Is there an Earth 2.0?

Thousands of exoplanets have been found, but none has been identified as "Earth 2.0." In other words, scientists haven't found a planet just like Earth orbiting a star just like our Sun. Such a planet might have life, like our own planet. Astronomers look for planets orbiting a star in the habitable zone—at just the right distance from a star for conditions to be right for life to survive.

NOTE *from the expert!*

ERIK GREGERSEN
Astronomy editor

Gregersen is Britannica's expert on astronomy and space exploration. He loves astronomy because there is always some new and astonishing discovery.

66 *The ever-growing number of exoplanets is one of the most exciting developments in astronomy right now.* **99**

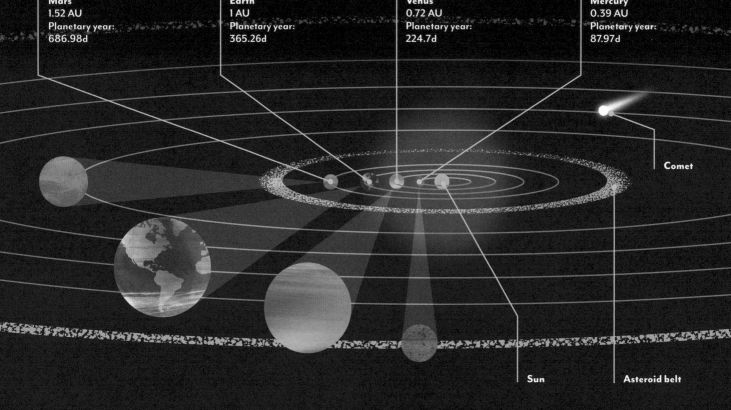

| **Mars** 1.52 AU Planetary year: 686.98d | **Earth** 1 AU Planetary year: 365.26d | **Venus** 0.72 AU Planetary year: 224.7d | **Mercury** 0.39 AU Planetary year: 87.97d |

Comet

Sun

Asteroid belt

OUR SOLAR SYSTEM

Our solar system is the place we call home. It contains the Sun, the planets, dwarf planets such as Pluto, asteroids, and many other objects that orbit the Sun. There are eight major planets, the smallest being Mercury and the largest being Jupiter. Between Mars and Jupiter is the asteroid belt, a vast region full of asteroids. Beyond Neptune is a belt of comets and asteroids named the Kuiper Belt. Farther still is a distant ring of comets, the Oort cloud.

AU = Astronomical Unit—
1AU is the average distance
from Earth to the Sun

m = one Earth minute

h = one Earth hour

d = one Earth day

y = one Earth year

One rotation

The time it takes for a planet to rotate once on its own axis (shown as a yellow dotted line) is measured against one Earth day. An average Earth day is just short of 24 hours at 23h 56m 4s. Jupiter's day is the shortest at less than half an Earth day.

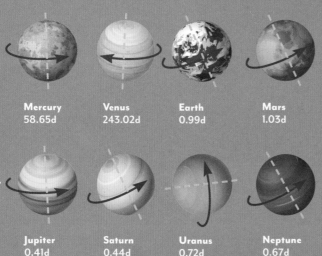

Mercury 58.65d

Venus 243.02d

Earth 0.99d

Mars 1.03d

Jupiter 0.41d

Saturn 0.44d

Uranus 0.72d

Neptune 0.67d

FACTastic!

The computer in each Voyager spacecraft has only about 70 kb of memory, as much as a very low-res Internet picture. With that, they've explored the solar system and beyond for more than 40 years.

EXPERT CONSULTANT: Rudi Kuhn **SEE ALSO:** The Milky Way, p.8–9; Stars, p.10–11; Exoplanets, p.20–21; The Sun, p.24–25; Planetary Exploration, p.26–27; Rocky Planets, p.28–29; Gas Giants, p.30–31; Moons, p.32–33; Asteroids, p.34–35; The Kuiper Belt, p.36–37

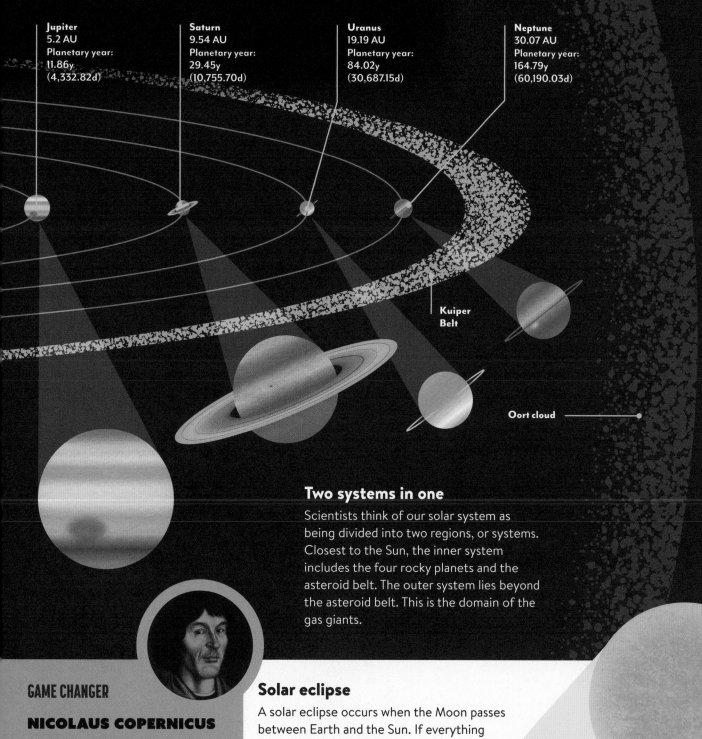

Jupiter
5.2 AU
Planetary year:
11.86y
(4,332.82d)

Saturn
9.54 AU
Planetary year:
29.45y
(10,755.70d)

Uranus
19.19 AU
Planetary year:
84.02y
(30,687.15d)

Neptune
30.07 AU
Planetary year:
164.79y
(60,190.03d)

Kuiper
Belt

Oort cloud

Two systems in one

Scientists think of our solar system as being divided into two regions, or systems. Closest to the Sun, the inner system includes the four rocky planets and the asteroid belt. The outer system lies beyond the asteroid belt. This is the domain of the gas giants.

NICOLAUS COPERNICUS

Astronomer, lived 1473–1543
Poland

For centuries, most Europeans thought that Earth was the center of the Universe. In the 16th century, Nicolaus Copernicus suggested Earth and the other planets orbited the Sun. His ideas changed our understanding of the Universe.

To know that we know what we know, and to know that we do not know what we do not know, that is true knowledge.

Solar eclipse

A solar eclipse occurs when the Moon passes between Earth and the Sun. If everything lines up just right, the Moon blocks the light from the Sun and casts a shadow at a specific location on Earth. While it is dangerous to look directly at the Sun, it is possible to watch an eclipse from Earth using special eclipse glasses.

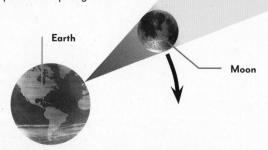

Sun

Earth

Moon

THE SUN

The Sun is the star that powers our solar system. It formed from a nebula of dust and gas about 4.5 billion years ago and is now a giant ball of gas known as a yellow dwarf. It is 865,000 miles (1.4 million km) across and mostly made of hydrogen and helium, although it has heavier metals at its core. The temperature of the core can reach 27,000,000°F (15,000,000°C)!

Life-giver

The Sun's energy is created in its core, where nuclear fusion converts hydrogen into helium to release vast amounts of energy. The light and heat produced are radiated throughout the solar system. On Earth, we depend on this radiation to survive, but the Sun also has effects elsewhere. Its heat makes Venus far too hot for life, and its rays even touch the surface of Pluto in the outer solar system.

Sun Rays
LISTIFIED.
....

1. **Light radiation** Most of the light emitted by the Sun is visible light, but it emits ultraviolet and infrared (heat) rays too.
2. **Solar wind** The Sun constantly emits streams of particles, called solar wind, from its surface. These particles interact with atoms in a planet's atmosphere, causing aurorae (luminous streamers of light) on Jupiter and Saturn as well as over Earth's poles. On Earth, the aurorae are known as the northern and southern lights.
3. **Solar flares** Bright bursts of radiation on the Sun known as solar flares release huge amounts of energy into space.
4. **Coronal Mass Ejections** The Sun ejects large amounts of material into space in giant "burps" called Coronal Mass Ejections. If they reach Earth, they jostle the planet's magnetic field. Like solar flares, they can disrupt technology, such as communication systems and power grids.

The surface of the Sun is about 9,900°F (5,500°C), but its outer atmosphere, called the corona, is millions of degrees. No one is sure why the atmosphere is so much hotter

This is a solar prominence, an arc of material thrown into the atmosphere by the Sun's magnetic field

EXPERT CONSULTANT: Ian Morison **SEE ALSO:** Galaxies, p.6–7; The Milky Way, p.8–9; Watching Space from Space, p.16–17; Our Solar System, p.22–23; End of the Universe, p.46–47; The Atmosphere, p.86–87; The Atom, p.100–01; Solids, Liquids & Gases, p.110–11; Energy, p.122–23

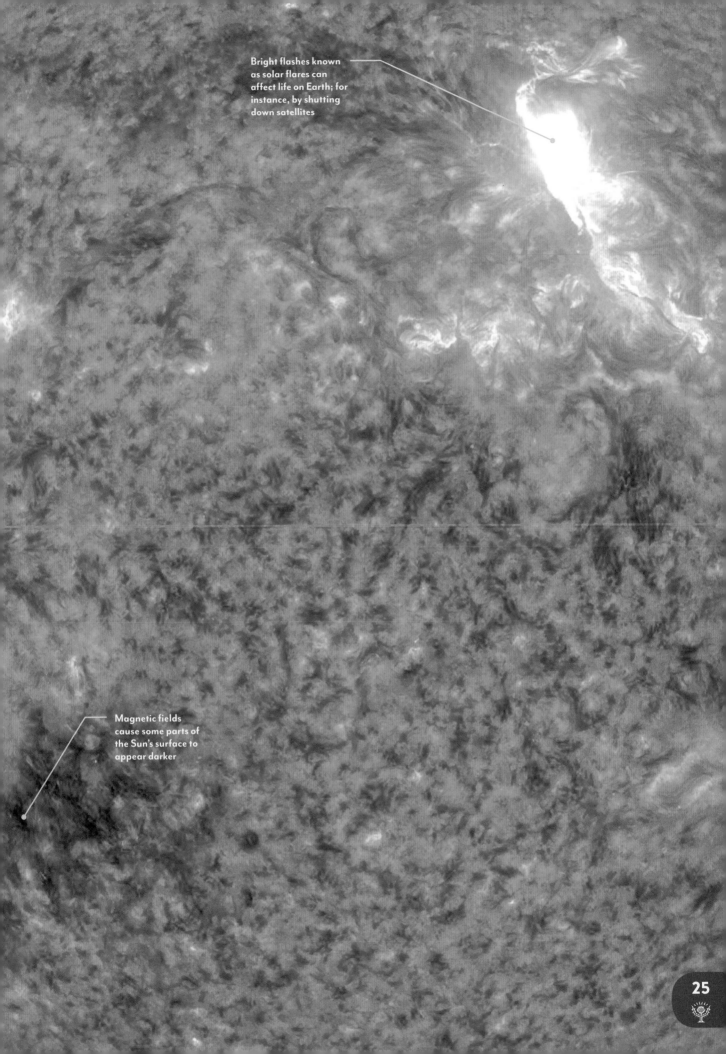

Bright flashes known as solar flares can affect life on Earth; for instance, by shutting down satellites

Magnetic fields cause some parts of the Sun's surface to appear darker

25

PLANETARY EXPLORATION

Since the 1960s, scientists have launched missions that have landed on other worlds. Several countries have sent probes to Venus, with Russia successfully landing many of them. These survived only briefly, but they sent back amazing images. The US, Russia, China, Japan, India, and Europe have all sent missions to the Moon. We've even sent rovers to Mars, searching for signs of life.

Curiosity on Mars

NASA's Curiosity rover landed on Mars on August 6, 2012. It has been trundling across the surface ever since, looking for signs of ancient life. The rover discovered that its landing site, Gale Crater, once hosted a lake. It has also found pebbles, evidence of Martian streams that existed billions of years ago.

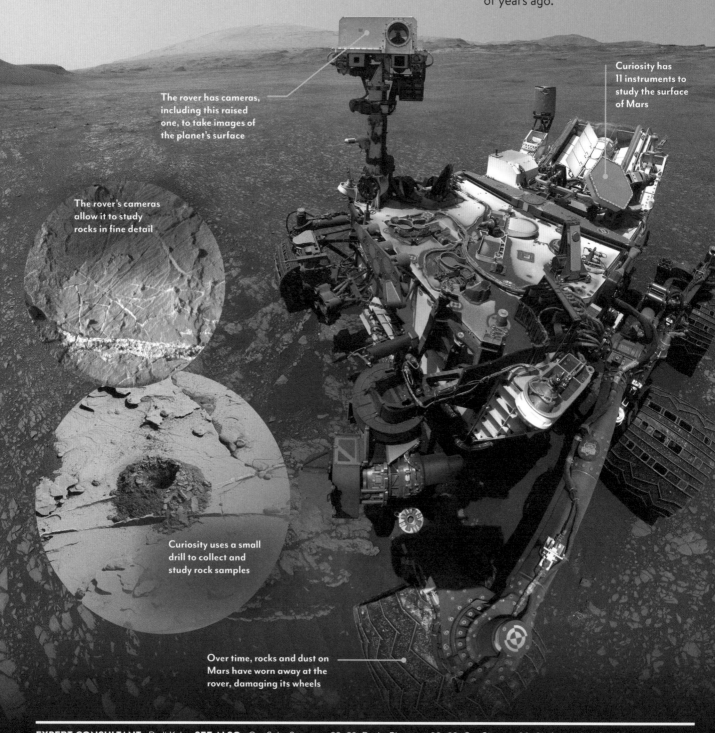

The rover has cameras, including this raised one, to take images of the planet's surface

Curiosity has 11 instruments to study the surface of Mars

The rover's cameras allow it to study rocks in fine detail

Curiosity uses a small drill to collect and study rock samples

Over time, rocks and dust on Mars have worn away at the rover, damaging its wheels

EXPERT CONSULTANT: Rudi Kuhn **SEE ALSO:** Our Solar System, p.22–23; Rocky Planets, p.28–29; Gas Giants, p.30–31; Asteroids, p.34–35; The Kuiper Belt, p.36–37; Nuclear Power, p.376–77

Huygens is thought to have landed in a dried-up riverbed

The Huygens probe lasted just over an hour on Titan's surface

FACTastic!

Saturn's moon Titan has lakes and seas. Titan is the only place we know of, apart from Earth, to have bodies of liquid on its surface. However, on Titan, these are substances similar to gasoline, not water. In 2005, NASA and the European Space Agency (ESA) sent a lander to Titan, called the Huygens probe, that took the first images of the Moon's surface as it parachuted in.

Solar System Landings
LISTIFIED.

Humans have landed probes on multiple worlds in the solar system, including asteroids, comets, planets, and moons. Some of the missions were very short-lived, while others are still operational today. We've left humanity's mark all over the solar system, with the following destinations among them.

1. The Moon Six crewed missions have visited our Moon.

2. Mars Multiple landers and rovers have landed on Mars, including Curiosity. Exploration continues.

3. Venus Most landers on Venus survive less than an hour, because the temperature and pressure are so high.

4. Titan The Huygens probe is the only landing so far.

5. Asteroids Several craft have landed on asteroids, some of them returning samples to Earth.

6. Comet In 2014, the European Space Agency (ESA) landed a probe—called Philae—on a comet for the first time.

NOTE *from the expert!*

RUDI KUHN
Astronomer

Dr. Rudi Kuhn works as an observational astronomer for one of the largest telescopes in the world—the Southern African Large Telescope (SALT). His current research focuses on detecting exoplanets.

❝ *I am often the first person ever to see some of the most amazing things in space—like planets orbiting distant stars, exploding stars, or colliding galaxies.* ❞

KNOWN UNKNOWN

Are there live volcanoes on planet Venus?

Venus's atmosphere is really thick, so we can't see through it. But using infrared and radar images, scientists have been looking for signs of active volcanoes on its surface that they think might be there. If they are, this would make Venus more like Earth than we had thought.

Infrared and radar images of Venus let us study its surface

ROCKY PLANETS

A rocky planet consists mostly of rock. In our solar system, the four inner planets are rocky planets: Mercury, Venus, Earth, and Mars. Each has a solid surface and is made of metals and types of rocks called silicates, such as quartz. Each has a mostly metal center. A blanket of gases sometimes surrounds a rocky planet. This is referred to as the planet's atmosphere.

Planet cross sections (to scale)

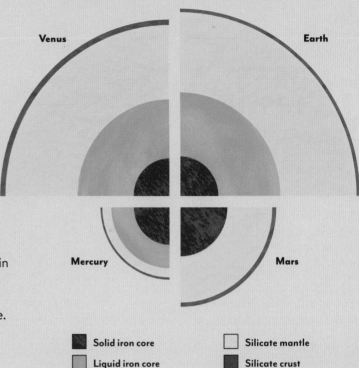

Venus

Earth

Mercury

Mars

■ Solid iron core

■ Liquid iron core

□ Silicate mantle

■ Silicate crust

Rocky interiors

Rocky planets form when fragments of dust and gas join together over time. This creates a ball, and if it is big and hot enough, the ball separates into layers of rock and metal. The planet's metallic center is called its core. Next comes a rock layer called the mantle. The rocky outer layer of the planet is called its crust.

FACTastic!

The object that formed the Caloris Basin smacked Mercury so hard that hills popped out on the other side of the planet. The impact occurred as long as four billion years ago. It left a crater measuring 950 miles (1,525 km) across.

Caloris Basin

Venus's stifling atmosphere

Venus has the thickest atmosphere of the rocky planets. Its gases trap a lot of heat, making Venus the hottest planet in our solar system. Venus's atmosphere is poisonous, too, containing dangerous sulfuric acid.

Most sunlight is reflected by thick clouds of sulfuric acid

Sunlight that gets through is trapped by the clouds and stays on the planet's surface

The clouds also trap gases such as carbon dioxide, making the planet even hotter

EXPERT CONSULTANT: Tracy M. Becker **SEE ALSO:** The Milky Way, p.8–9; Stars, p.10–11; Exoplanets, p.20–21; Our Solar System, p.22–23; The Sun, p.24–25; Planetary Exploration, p.26–27; Gas Giants, p.30–31; Moons, p.32–33; Asteroids, p.34–35; The Kuiper Belt, p.36–37

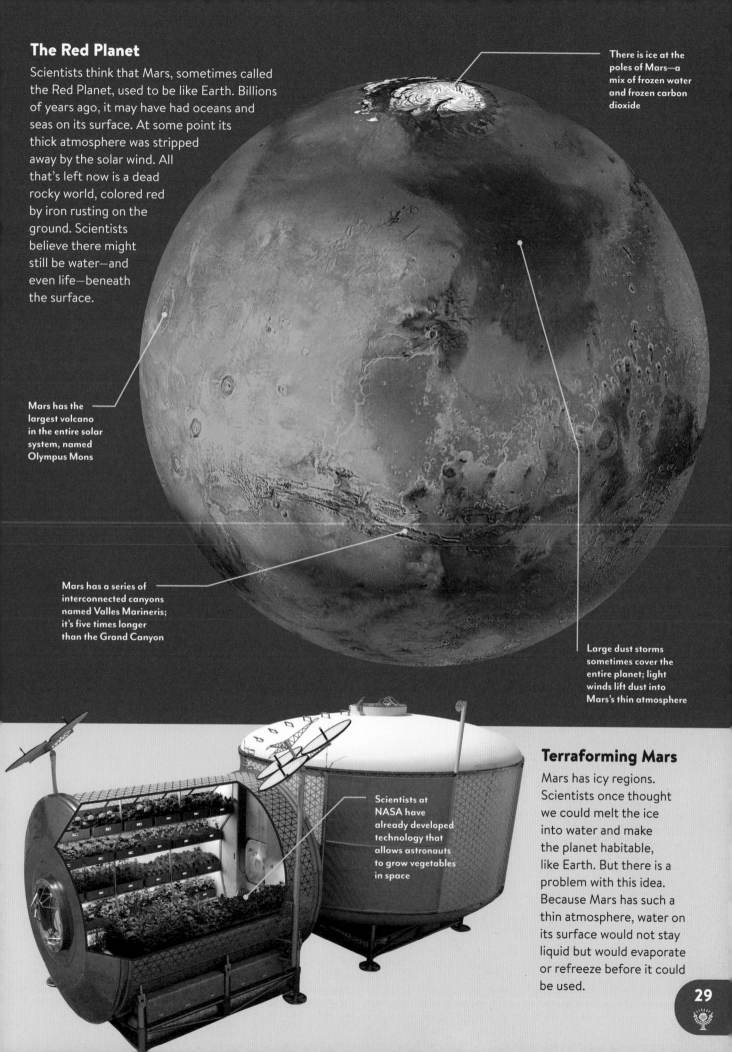

The Red Planet

Scientists think that Mars, sometimes called the Red Planet, used to be like Earth. Billions of years ago, it may have had oceans and seas on its surface. At some point its thick atmosphere was stripped away by the solar wind. All that's left now is a dead rocky world, colored red by iron rusting on the ground. Scientists believe there might still be water—and even life—beneath the surface.

There is ice at the poles of Mars—a mix of frozen water and frozen carbon dioxide

Mars has the largest volcano in the entire solar system, named Olympus Mons

Mars has a series of interconnected canyons named Valles Marineris; it's five times longer than the Grand Canyon

Large dust storms sometimes cover the entire planet; light winds lift dust into Mars's thin atmosphere

Scientists at NASA have already developed technology that allows astronauts to grow vegetables in space

Terraforming Mars

Mars has icy regions. Scientists once thought we could melt the ice into water and make the planet habitable, like Earth. But there is a problem with this idea. Because Mars has such a thin atmosphere, water on its surface would not stay liquid but would evaporate or refreeze before it could be used.

29

GAS GIANTS

A gas giant is a planet made almost entirely of helium and hydrogen. The temperature and pressure inside the planet turn the gas into a liquid. In our solar system, the gas giants are Jupiter, Saturn, Uranus, and Neptune. Gas giants tend to have thick bands of clouds in their upper atmospheres. Unlike rocky planets, they have no surface, but may have huge weather systems, such as giant hurricanes or massive lightning storms.

Birth of a gas giant

Gas giants form when clouds of dust and gas draw together to make a larger object. The immense size of a gas giant produces huge pressures inside the planet. This results in liquids such as metallic hydrogen surrounding what's thought to be a rocky center, or core.

Planet cross sections (to scale)

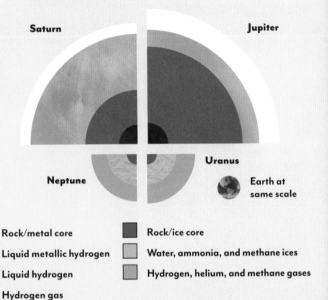

Saturn

Jupiter

Neptune

Uranus

Earth at same scale

- ■ Rock/metal core
- ■ Liquid metallic hydrogen
- ■ Liquid hydrogen
- □ Hydrogen gas

- ■ Rock/ice core
- ■ Water, ammonia, and methane ices
- ■ Hydrogen, helium, and methane gases

Saturn

The second-largest planet in our solar system (after Jupiter), Saturn is most famous for its huge ring system. The main rings extend to about 87,000 miles (140,000 km) from the planet's center. You can see them from Earth using a telescope. The planet has more than 80 moons. It also has a hexagonal-shaped storm at its north pole that scientists can't quite explain.

Vast bands of storms encircle the planet, as winds roar through its atmosphere

Saturn's rings are made up of water ice particles that range in size from small pieces of dust to huge boulders the size of houses

Other gas giants have rings, but Saturn's are particularly impressive

EXPERT CONSULTANTS: Tracy M. Becker and Erik Gregersen **SEE ALSO:** The Milky Way, p.8–9; Stars, p.10–11; Exoplanets, p.20–21; Our Solar System, p.22–23; The Sun, p.24–25; Planetary Exploration, p.26–27; Rocky Planets, p.28–29; Moons, p.32–33; Asteroids, p.34–35; The Kuiper Belt, p.36–37

Jupiter's Great Red Spot

Jupiter (below) plays host to the biggest storm in the solar system. A huge cyclone called the Great Red Spot (close-up pictured right) has been raging for more than 400 years. At one point it was bigger than Earth. The storm has been getting smaller in recent years, but is not thought to be dying just yet.

Axis of rotation

NOTE from the expert!

Colorful giants

Neptune is particularly noticeable for its blue color, which is caused by a gas called methane in its atmosphere. We've only ever seen Neptune up close once, with the *Voyager 2* spacecraft in 1989. It is possible to spot vast storms and winds in its blue atmosphere using powerful telescopes on Earth.

TRACY M. BECKER
Planetary research scientist

In Tracy Becker's work as a planetary scientist, she enjoys being able to pursue her questions about planets, moons, and asteroids. One of her first science projects was to study the icy particles that make up Saturn's rings, and she now wants to discover how they formed.

66 *The in-depth study of Saturn's rings has answered many science questions, but also sparked dozens more.* 99

EARTH
(1 moon)

Moon

The diameter
of Earth's Moon
is 2,159 miles
(3,474 km)

MARS
(2 moons)

Phobos

Deimos

JUPITER
(79 known moons)

Io

Europa

Ganymede

Callisto

SATURN
(82 known
moons)

Mimas

Enceladus

Tethys

Dione

Rhea

Titan

Hyperion

Iapetus

Phoebe

URANUS
(27 known
moons)

Puck

Miranda

Ariel

Umbriel

Titania

Oberon

NEPTUNE
(14 known
moons)

Proteus

Triton

Nereid

FACTastic!

The Moon is moving away from Earth by about 1½ inches (3.8 cm) every year. That is about the same speed at which our fingernails grow!

Planet Earth shown
at the same scale as
the moons

The planets' main moons

There are at least 214 moons in our solar system, orbiting every planet except Mercury and Venus. Scientists recently discovered that Saturn has 20 more moons than previously thought, bringing its total to 82—more than any other planet.

MOONS

The moons of our solar system come in all shapes and sizes. Many are spherical, like Earth's moon. Some, like Pan, Daphnis, and Atlas that orbit Saturn, are shaped a bit like ravioli. There are also some very small moons, such as Mars's Deimos, which is just 9 miles (15 km) across. Jupiter's moon Ganymede is larger than the planet Mercury.

Exploring Earth's moon

Earth's moon is the only place in space where humans have landed. Between 1969 and 1972, the US landed six Apollo missions on the Moon. However, lots of uncrewed probes visit it. They include China's Chang'e 4 mission, sent to explore the Moon's far side in 2019.

EXPERT CONSULTANT: Tracy M. Becker **SEE ALSO:** Our Solar System, p.22–23; The Sun, p.24–25; Rocky Planets, p.28–29; Asteroids, p.34–35; Rockets, p.38–39; Elements, p.102–03; Gravity, p.134–35; The Origin of Life, p.148–49; Future Humans, p.382–83

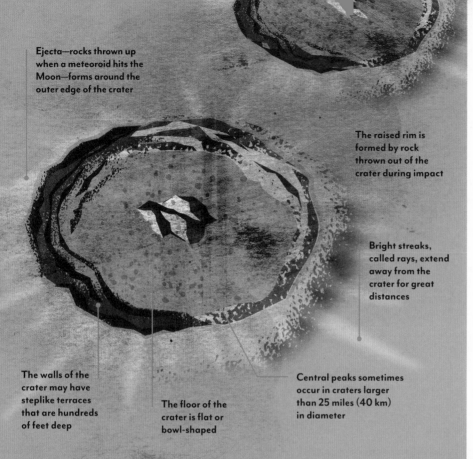

Ejecta—rocks thrown up when a meteoroid hits the Moon—forms around the outer edge of the crater

The raised rim is formed by rock thrown out of the crater during impact

Bright streaks, called rays, extend away from the crater for great distances

The walls of the crater may have steplike terraces that are hundreds of feet deep

The floor of the crater is flat or bowl-shaped

Central peaks sometimes occur in craters larger than 25 miles (40 km) in diameter

Anatomy of a crater

Our Moon is covered in craters—circular indentations made when space rocks such as asteroids or meteoroids hit its surface. The biggest crater is the South Pole-Aitken basin, at 1,600 miles (2,575 km) across. Scientists think that bits of the asteroid that formed this crater may lie under the surface.

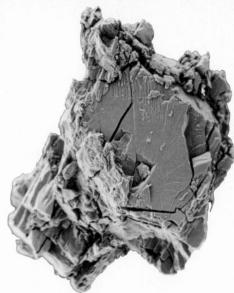

A grain of Moon dust

Moon dust, called regolith, seen here through an electron microscope, is the result of meteoroids from space breaking down lunar rocks over billions of years. Astronauts who have gone to the Moon say that it smells like gunpowder.

KNOWN UNKNOWN

Could humans live on the Moon?

Scientists in the US and Europe are working on plans to build bases on the Moon. They think water could be extracted from ice under the Moon's surface. However, life would be harsh, with temperatures ranging from -208°F to 250°F (-133°C to 121°C). Imagine a lunar day lasting 14 Earth days, followed by an equally long lunar night.

Structure of our Moon

Our Moon has different layers, just as Earth does. It has a metallic core at its center that is made of iron and nickel. This is enclosed by a fluid outer core and then a solid mantle layer. The crust, or surface, is about 22 miles (35 km) thick on average. It has mountains, craters, and flat areas called seas, such as the Sea of Tranquillity.

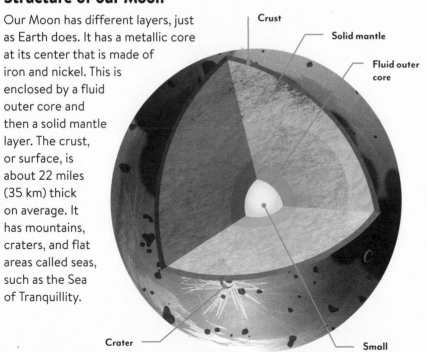

Crust

Solid mantle

Fluid outer core

Crater

Small metallic core

ASTEROIDS

Asteroids are pieces of rock. They date from the early solar system, about 4.6 billion years ago, and are bits of rock that didn't quite manage to form into planets. Today there are millions of asteroids in the solar system. They range in size from a few feet to hundreds of miles across. Most are found in the asteroid belt, a vast region that lies between the planets Mars and Jupiter. Asteroids that come close to Earth's orbit are called near-Earth objects (NEOs).

Rocky remnant

Sometimes asteroids enter Earth's atmosphere and hit the ground. They leave a crater or pieces of rocks called meteorites. Scientists study the rocks to work out where the asteroid came from.

Extinction event

Scientists believe that a few times in Earth's history, a large asteroid from space has hit our planet. The most notable collision saw the extinction of the dinosaurs (other than birds) 66 million years ago. The impact of the asteroid formed the Chicxulub crater in Mexico. It is thought to have killed 75 percent of all life on Earth.

EXPERT CONSULTANT

Meteor, meteoroid, or meteorite?

These three terms might sound similar, but they actually refer to different things. Here's what they all mean, and how to tell them apart.

An asteroid is a small rocky body found in space; it is not big enough to form a planet

A meteoroid is a piece of rock that is less than 3 feet (1 meter) across

A meteor is any meteoroid that burns up in Earth's atmosphere, producing a streak of light (a shooting star)

A meteorite is any part of a meteoroid that reaches the ground intact

FACTastic!

Earth is hit by around 500 meteorites every year. Most of them fall in uninhabited areas—the middle of the ocean, for example. Occasionally meteorites fall near humans, although no one has ever been killed by one.

KNOWN UNKNOWN

Did life travel on asteroids and comets?

Some scientists believe that life came to Earth on board an asteroid or comet. The suggestion is that types of microscopic life, such as bacteria, could survive a journey through space on a rock. When reaching Earth, such life would have thrived in our habitable environment.

Ingredients for life, such as amino acids, could have traveled through space

This could have led to the evolution of DNA-based life, such as humans, on Earth

Asteroid missions

Scientists have sent several missions to study asteroids. In 2019, the Japanese spacecraft *Hayabusa2* picked up some rocks from an asteroid called Ryugu to return them to Earth. NASA's OSIRIS-REx mission is picking up rocks from an asteroid called Bennu.

KUIPER BELT

Beyond the orbit of Neptune in our solar system lies the Kuiper Belt. Like the asteroid belt, this region is full of rocks left over from the early solar system. Kuiper Belt Objects (KBOs) are so far from the Sun, they tend to be icy. If they get pushed into the inner solar system, they sublimate (the ice turns into gas) and are known as comets.

Neptune

Scientists believe that there are millions of objects in the Kuiper Belt—thousands of them larger than 60 miles (100 km) across.

Pluto has a vast frozen lake of nitrogen on its surface, called Sputnik Planitia. Its surface layer vaporizes by day and refreezes at night

The big heart-shaped feature on Pluto is called Tombaugh Regio

Pluto has five moons. The largest is Charon. It is around 750 miles (1,200 km) across, roughly half the size of Pluto

Some parts of Pluto appear red because of materials called tholins, which form in the atmosphere and fall onto the planet's surface

Dwarf planet Pluto

Pluto orbits in the Kuiper Belt and is smaller than our Moon. Once considered a true planet, Pluto lost its "planet" status in 2006. In more than 200 years, Pluto's orbit will bring it temporarily inside Neptune's orbit. Pluto has a noticeable atmosphere and mountains on its surface.

EXPERT CONSULTANT: Tracy M. Becker **SEE ALSO:** Our Solar System, p.22–23; Planetary Exploration, p.26–27; Rocky Planets, p.28–29; Gas Giants, p.30–31; Moons, p.32–33; Asteroids, p.34–35

What is a comet?

Comets are different from asteroids in that they contain large amounts of ice. This ice surrounds a rocky core, called the nucleus. Comets were born in the outer solar system but sometimes get pushed inward toward the Sun. When this happens, the solid ice turns to gas, producing a fantastic tail.

The comet's tail is made of gas and dust. Because the Sun repels the gas, the tail will be in front of the comet when the comet is moving away from the Sun

The coma is a cloud of gas and dust that surrounds the comet

The center of a comet is called its nucleus. It is mostly ice and dust

Together, the coma and the nucleus are known as the head of the comet

A small planet that shares its orbit with other objects is called a dwarf planet. Most known dwarf planets orbit in the Kuiper Belt.

1. Ceres The biggest object in the asteroid belt, Ceres is 587 miles (945 km) across. NASA's *Dawn* spacecraft visited it in 2015.

2. Pluto In 2006, astronomers decided that Pluto shared its orbit with too many other objects to be a true planet.

3. Eris Eris is located within the Kuiper Belt in a scattered disk of objects.

4. Haumea Found in the Kuiper Belt, Haumea is about 770 miles (1,240 km) across. It has both rings and moons.

5. Makemake Also found in the Kuiper Belt, Makemake is slightly bigger than Haumea, at around 888 miles (1,430 km) across.

Distant flyby

In July 2015, NASA's *New Horizons* became the first spacecraft to fly past Pluto. But the mission didn't end there. *New Horizons* went on to study another object in the Kuiper Belt, called Arrokoth. This strange object, with two parts stitched together, looks a little like a snowman.

Oort cloud

Beyond the Kuiper Belt is a place called the Oort cloud. It begins nearly 70 times farther from the Sun than Neptune, and extends one-quarter of the way to the next closest star. The Oort cloud is thought to contain more than one trillion icy objects that surround our solar system.

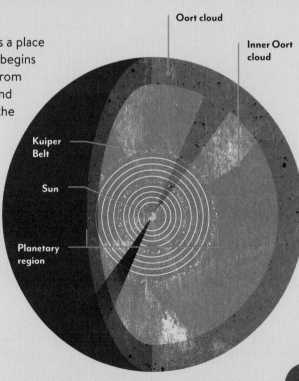

Oort cloud

Inner Oort cloud

Kuiper Belt

Sun

Planetary region

ROCKETS

To travel into space, you need a rocket to overcome the pull of Earth's gravity. Space agencies use rockets to launch satellites and space probes and to send spacecraft containing astronauts to the International Space Station. All rockets have several parts, or stages, stacked on top of each other. As each part uses up all its fuel, it is discarded and falls back to Earth. Eventually, the spacecraft reaches orbit.

FACTastic!

The first rockets were made by the Chinese using bamboo tubes. The tubes were packed with gunpowder and attached to arrows fired by bows. During the Battle of Kai-Keng in 1232, the Chinese used "arrows of flying fire" to repel the Mongols.

How rockets work

Rockets turn fuel into gas by mixing it with oxygen and igniting it. Early rockets often used solid fuel, while modern rockets mainly use liquid fuel like liquid hydrogen. The engines push this gas out of the rocket's base to produce thrust, which makes the rocket rise. Because Earth's gravity is so strong, rockets have to be very big to store enough fuel.

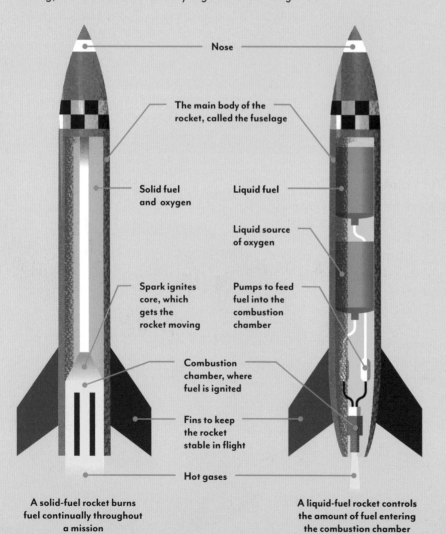

Nose

The main body of the rocket, called the fuselage

Solid fuel and oxygen

Liquid fuel

Liquid source of oxygen

Spark ignites core, which gets the rocket moving

Pumps to feed fuel into the combustion chamber

Combustion chamber, where fuel is ignited

Fins to keep the rocket stable in flight

Hot gases

A solid-fuel rocket burns fuel continually throughout a mission

A liquid-fuel rocket controls the amount of fuel entering the combustion chamber

The First Rockets
TIMELINE

Around 1200 The Chinese make the first solid-fuel rockets.

1903 Russian Konstantin Tsiolkovsky works out the amount of fuel needed for different-sized rockets to reach space.

1926 American scientist Robert Goddard launches the first liquid-fueled rocket. It reaches a height of 41 feet (12.5 meters).

1942 In Germany, the Nazis develop the V2, the first rocket that can eventually reach space. They first use it as a weapon against London in World War II.

1957 The Soviet Union launches the first artificial satellite into orbit, *Sputnik 1*.

1961 Soviet Yuri Gagarin becomes the first human to travel into space and orbit Earth.

1969 In the US, the *Apollo 11* mission to the Moon launches on a Saturn V rocket. Astronauts Neil Armstrong and Buzz Aldrin become the first people to walk on the Moon.

EXPERT CONSULTANT: Michael G. Smith **SEE ALSO:** Planetary Exploration, p.26–27; Moons, p.32–33; Combustion, p.108–09; Solids, Liquids & Gases, p.110–11; Energy, p.122–23; Forces, p.132–33; Gravity, p.134–35; World War II, p.324–25; The Cold War, p.326–27

Mega rockets

The most powerful rocket ever flown was the US's Saturn V rocket. As tall as a 36-story building, and as heavy as 400 elephants, this type of rocket was used to take humans to the Moon from 1969 to 1972. Now new "mega rockets" are being built, such as SpaceX's Starship rocket and NASA's Space Launch System (SLS). These rockets may eventually take humans to Mars, perhaps in the 2020s or 2030s.

The crew sit in the top of the rocket

Black panels help ground crew assess how much the rocket is rotating

The lowest stage of the rocket is the first to separate

Reusable rockets

Most rockets burn up after use, and their debris falls into Earth's oceans. But some rockets are reusable like planes. The company SpaceX has built rockets like this one (above) that use some of their fuel to land back on the ground. This means they can be reused, making space exploration less expensive and more sustainable.

KNOWN UNKNOWN

How can we launch rockets from other planets?
We've launched rockets from Earth and the Moon for decades, but we've never launched one from another planet. Scientists want to figure out how to do this so that they can use rockets to bring rocks and soil back to Earth to study. Eventually, they want to use rockets to bring back planetary explorers, too.

ARTIFICIAL SATELLITES

Satellites are any objects that orbit something else in space. There are natural satellites, such as our Moon, and artificial satellites that are built by humans and launched into orbit around planets to do specific jobs. Thousands of artificial satellites orbit Earth. Some of them are the size of buses, others are smaller than a toaster.

Orbiting Earth

Satellites are launched using rockets. But if they were sent upward in a straight line, they would fall back down again because of the pull of Earth's gravity. To send satellites into an orbit—a path around a planet—they are launched upward and sideways at the same time. This gives them a speed of more than 16,800 mph (27,000 km/h), so they constantly "fall" toward our planet but never reach it, resulting in an orbit.

SORCE

The Solar Radiation and Climate Experiment satellite (SORCE) measures energy from the Sun to help scientists understand how it affects long-term climate change on Earth.

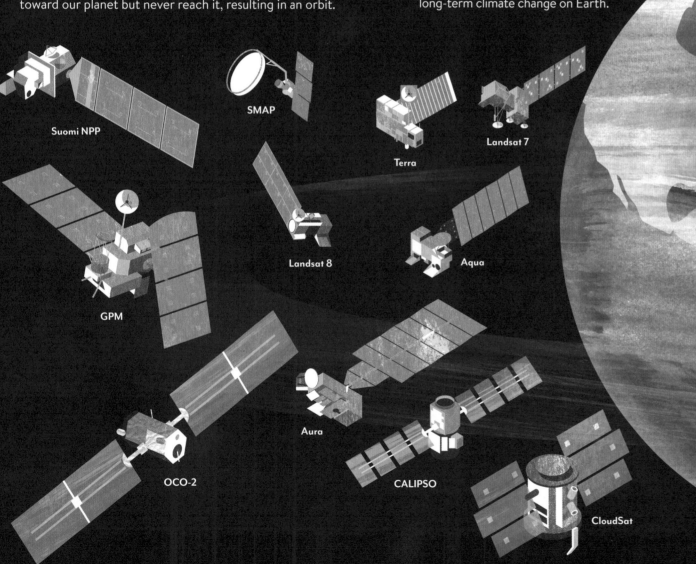

Suomi NPP

SMAP

Terra

Landsat 7

Landsat 8

Aqua

GPM

Aura

OCO-2

CALIPSO

CloudSat

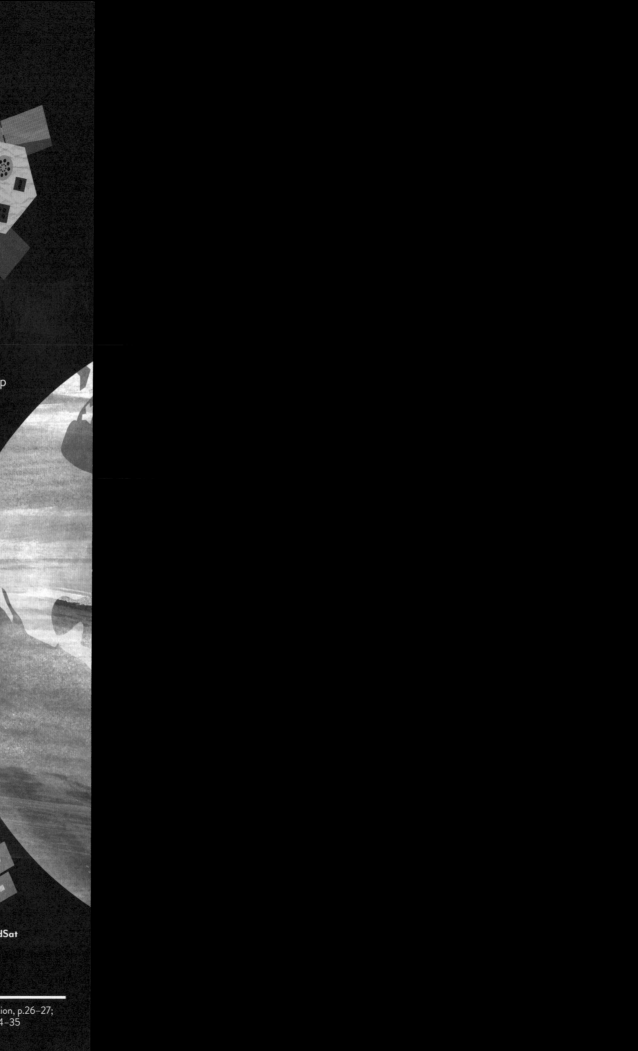

EXPERT CONSULTANT: Clifford Cunningham **SEE ALSO:** Watching Space from Space, p.16–17; Our Solar System, p.22–23; Planetary Exploration, p.26–27; Moons, p.32–33; Measuring Earth, p.56–57; The Atmosphere, p.86–87; Weather, p.88–89; Mega Storms, p.90–91; Forces, p.132–33; Gravity, p.134–35

Jobs That Satellites Do
LISTIFIED.

1. Observe the Universe Scientific satellites like the Hubble Space Telescope observe other planets and the distant Universe. They send amazing photographs back to Earth.

2. Send communications Some satellites have dishes like giant mirrors that bounce signals from one place on Earth to another. This enables us to make phone calls around the world, use the Internet, and beam TV shows into our homes.

3. Spy on other countries Military satellites monitor activities in other countries, such as the movement of troops.

4. Monitor weather and climate Satellites can tell us when and where it is going to rain and how much the planet is warming due to climate change.

5. Help us navigate GPS (Global Positioning System) satellites can help us pinpoint any place on Earth. By bouncing a signal off multiple satellites, they can work out exactly where you are located.

FACTastic!

There is a spacecraft cemetery in the Pacific Ocean! At the end of their mission, many satellites and rockets are deliberately crashed into the Pacific Ocean, at a place known as Point Nemo. Located east of New Zealand, it is the farthest point from land on the planet. Hundreds of spacecraft have ended up there.

Point Nemo is more than 1,550 miles (2,500 km) from the nearest land

CubeSats

Rockets can carry miniature satellites called CubeSats (left) along with bigger satellites. Scientists use these small, inexpensive satellites to carry out experiments and take measurements. Several CubeSats can be fitted together to perform various tasks. Because they are small, CubeSats burn up when they are pulled back into Earth's atmosphere.

Space junk

About 3,000 old satellites that no longer work orbit Earth, along with millions of bits of machinery. If this space junk collided with active satellites, it could destroy them. Scientists are trying to remove defunct satellites from orbit. In 2025, the European Space Agency (ESA) plans to launch ClearSpace-1, the first mission to remove a piece of space junk from orbit.

ClearSpace-1 will capture a large chunk of a rocket left in orbit about 500 miles (800 km) above the ground

The spacecraft will use robotic arms to capture the space junk

NOTE *from the expert!*

CLIFFORD CUNNINGHAM
Planetary scientist

Dr. Clifford Cunningham is interested in the history of astronomy, especially the discoveries of ancient Greeks and Romans. He believes that if you can advance knowledge or civilization, what you are doing is worthwhile.

❝ *Satellites carry with them the intelligence of humanity into space.* ❞

The International Space Station

If you look at the night sky, you can sometimes spot the International Space Station (ISS) about 240 miles (400 km) above Earth. Up to six astronauts at a time live aboard the station, carrying out experiments and research. It has lots of rooms, including a kitchen, laboratories, and a toilet. There's also a room with seven large windows, where the astronauts can gaze down at Earth.

The walls have many layers to keep out tiny meteors and space debris

Solar panels make energy by collecting heat from the Sun. In a single day the ISS experiences 16 sunrises and 16 sunsets as it orbits Earth every 90 minutes

This central module, called Zarya, was the first part of the ISS launched in 1998

The Japanese Kibo module is the largest of the station's modules

CREWED SPACECRAFT

Humans have been traveling into space since 1961, on rockets and space shuttles. In the near future, new spacecraft may take humans beyond Earth's orbit. In the US, a rocket company called SpaceX is already working on a new spacecraft called Starship, designed to take 100 people at a time on trips to Mars.

Eating in space

In space, where the pull of gravity can be weaker, everything floats around, including food. Because of this, astronauts use pouches instead of plates. But space food is not that different from food on Earth. Astronauts get to eat pizza and tacos, and fresh fruit and bread are delivered to the ISS by cargo spacecraft.

EXPERT CONSULTANT: Pablo De Leon **SEE ALSO:** Exoplanets, p.20–21; Our Solar System, p.22–23; Planetary Exploration, p.26–27; Moons, p.32–33; Rockets, p.38–39; The Atmosphere, p.86–87; Gravity, p.134–35

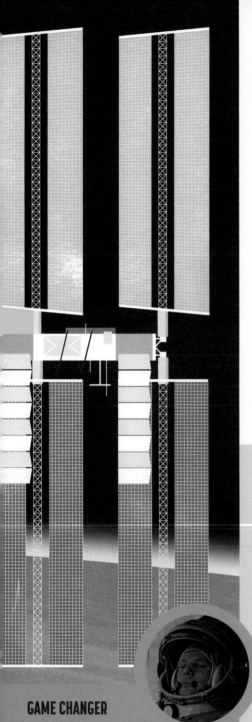

KNOWN UNKNOWN

What are the long-term effects of being in space for months or years?

Even after a short time in space, astronauts grow an average of 2 inches (5 cm) taller because of the weaker gravity. But we don't know how the body will cope with long-term space travel. Some astronauts at the ISS stay for a year. Studying the long-term effects on their health will help scientists prepare astronauts for multiyear missions to Mars.

Space work

Sometimes astronauts have to go outside the spacecraft to fix things. In 2019, American astronauts Christina Koch and Jessica Meir completed the first space walk by an all-women team. They replaced a piece of hardware connected to the solar panels that is used to charge the International Space Station's batteries.

Robot hotel

In December 2019, NASA sent a new habitat to the ISS—for robots instead of humans. Astronauts attached the Robotic Tool Stowage (RiTS) to the exterior of the ISS on a space walk—a mission outside the spacecraft. Sensors and instruments attached to the unit allow robotic helpers to perform vital measurements in the cold vacuum of space. One of their jobs is to sniff out gases.

Astronauts have to pee into a nozzle like this

FACTastic!

One space toilet cost $19 million! Why was it so expensive? Well, space toilets are like super-special vacuum cleaners. They need a complex series of pipes and vacuum tubes to suck up waste and dry it out. The extracted water is recycled, and the waste is stored. Eventually, it is sent back into Earth's atmosphere, where it burns up like shooting stars.

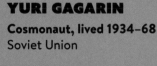

GAME CHANGER

YURI GAGARIN

Cosmonaut, lived 1934–68
Soviet Union

On April 12, 1961, Russian cosmonaut Yuri Gagarin became the first person to travel into space. He completed one orbit of Earth on the *Vostok 1* spacecraft and returned safely to the ground. The orbit took him one hour and 29 minutes. The mission brought him worldwide fame and led to a race between the Soviet Union and the US to be the first to send humans to the Moon. The US won the race in 1969.

SPACE PROBES...
LISTIFIED.

SPACECRAFT STUDYING THE SOLAR SYSTEM RIGHT NOW
(in order from the Sun)

1. **Parker Solar Probe** Orbiting close to the Sun to observe solar wind, the magnetic field, and how the energy flows at the outer edges of the Sun.
2. **Akatsuki** Studying the atmosphere of Venus, including how the clouds work.
3. **ARTEMIS 1/P2** Studying how the solar wind affects the Moon.
4. **Chandrayaan-2** Studying the Moon and looking for water-ice on or below its surface.
5. **Chang'e-4 (lander)** exploring the far side of the Moon for the first time in history.
6. **BepiColombo** On its way to study Mercury, arriving in 2025.
7. **Mars Reconnaissance Orbiter** Studying landforms, minerals, and ice on Mars.
8. **Curiosity Rover (lander)** Searching for evidence of life on Mars and exploring Mars's Gale Crater, where it landed.
9. **Mangalyaan** Developing technologies for future space missions while orbiting Mars.
10. **MAVEN** Studying how Mars's atmosphere has been lost over time.
11. **Trace Gas Orbiter** Studying gases in Mars's atmosphere.
12. **InSight (lander)** Studying the deep interior of Mars, including looking for "marsquakes" and working out the structure of the planet.
13. **Hayabusa 2** Studying asteroid 162173 Ryugu, including gathering samples.
14. **OSIRIS-REx** Studying asteroid 101955 Bennu, including gathering samples.
15. **Juno** Studying Jupiter to figure out what it is made of and how it formed.
16. **New Horizons** Studying Pluto and exploring the outer edges of the solar system.

The Juno spacecraft has been orbiting Jupiter since 2016

This is Juno's large antenna. It is used for communication with Earth

Juno is the farthest spacecraft from the Sun to operate using solar power

EXPERT CONSULTANT: Clifford Cunningham **SEE ALSO:** Watching Space from Space, p.16–17; Our Solar System, p.22–23; The Sun, p.24–25; Planetary Exploration, p.26–27; Rocky Planets, p.28–29; Gas Giants, p.30–31; Moons, p.32–33; Asteroids, p.34–35; Crewed Spacecraft, p.42–43

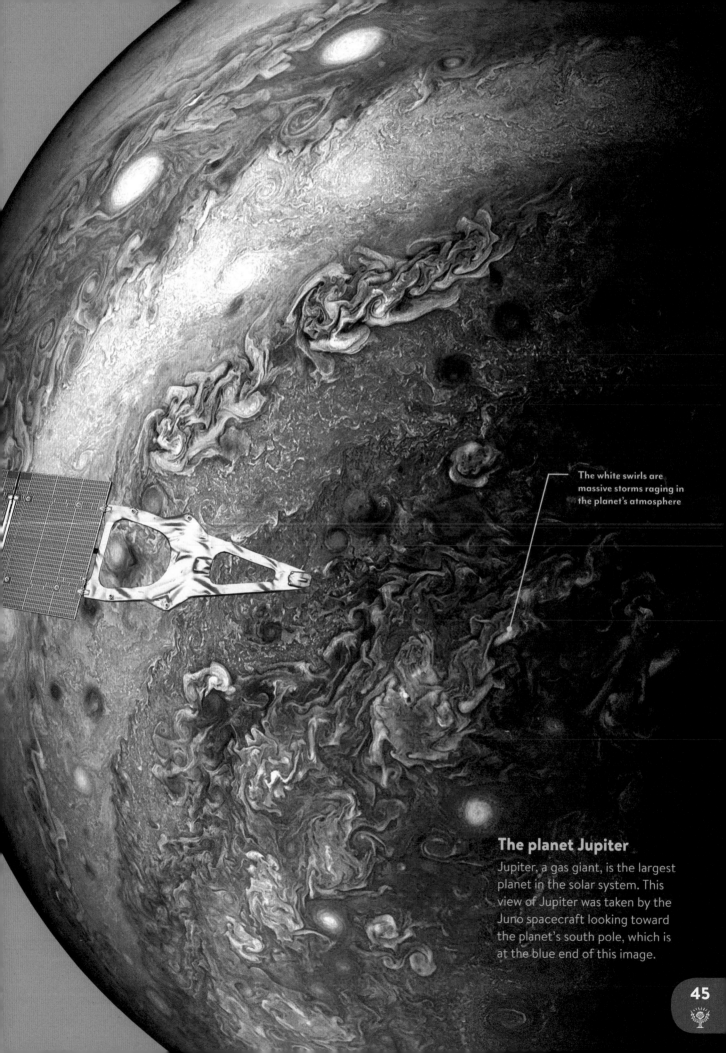

The white swirls are
massive storms raging in
the planet's atmosphere

The planet Jupiter

Jupiter, a gas giant, is the largest
planet in the solar system. This
view of Jupiter was taken by the
Juno spacecraft looking toward
the planet's south pole, which is
at the blue end of this image.

END OF THE UNIVERSE

In about five billion years, our Sun's energy will begin to run down and it will expand into a red giant star that will consume Earth. But what will happen to the Universe? Most scientists think it will die but they disagree on how and when. One theory is that the Universe will continue to expand at an ever faster rate. Eventually everything will be so spread out that nothing new can form.

Hubble findings

Everything in the Universe is moving. By studying the Universe with telescopes like Hubble, scientists can see that galaxies are expanding away from each other more rapidly than in the past. This means the expansion is speeding up.

HOW WILL THE UNIVERSE END?

There are three competing theories for how the Universe might end—the Big Crunch, the Big Rip, and the Big Freeze. Most scientists now think the Big Freeze, also known as Heat Death, is the most likely.

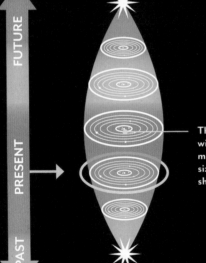

FUTURE
PRESENT
PAST

The Universe will reach a maximum size before shrinking again

The Universe's energy will spread out forever

The Big Rip will tear everything in the Universe apart, leaving nothing

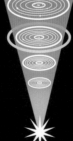

The Big Crunch

The expansion of the Universe will slow down and then reverse, leading to a Big Crunch. At this point, a new big bang will take place and the Universe will begin again!

The Big Freeze

The Universe will continue to expand. Eventually, the energy of the Universe will be so spread out that no new stars or planets can form. This state is known as the Big Freeze or Heat Death.

The Big Rip

The expansion of the Universe will accelerate so fast that it will tear everything apart—starting with galaxies and going on to destroy stars, planets, and even atoms.

EXPERT CONSULTANT: Michelle Thaller **SEE ALSO:** The Big Bang, p.4–5; Stars, p.10–11; Nebulae, p.12–13; Watching Space from Space, p.16–17;

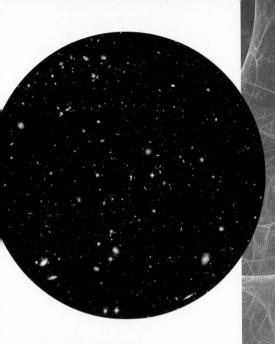

KNOWN UNKNOWN

What is dark energy?

Because the expansion of the Universe is getting faster, we know there must be a force causing it to accelerate. Scientists think that this is a strange force called dark energy, which is the opposite of gravity. They think it makes up 68 percent of the Universe, but they haven't been able to detect it yet!

GAME CHANGER

EDWIN HUBBLE
Astronomer, lived 1889–1953
US

Edwin Hubble was the first astronomer to realize that the Universe is expanding. In the 1920s, he noticed that all galaxies were moving away from each other at a certain speed. He came up with something called Hubble's Law, which explained how galaxies farther away were moving faster than those closer to us. His findings support the big bang theory for the start of the Universe.

The multiverse

Some scientists believe our Universe is not the only universe. They think there could be an infinite number of parallel universes that all exist alongside each other like bubbles! We call this the multiverse. Each bubble would be its own expanding universe, with all of them stuck together like Bubble Wrap.

ASK THE EXPERTS!

MICHELLE THALLER
Astronomer

What made you want to study astronomy?
I decided to study stars when I found out that they are responsible for making all the atoms of our body, except the very simplest ones that were formed in the big bang. Our blood is red because of a tiny amount of iron in it, and the only thing that makes iron in the Universe is a dying star, violently exploding.

What is an exciting development in your field?
I think we may be very close to discovering life outside Earth! The first life we find will likely be fairly simple stuff. It will probably be like our bacteria or very simple cells. There are several places in our own solar system that have the right conditions: places such as Mars, or the moons of Jupiter and Saturn.

What do you enjoy about your work?
I love working at observatories. There's something magical about being up all night, usually on top of a mountain, with a giant telescope: this huge yet delicate piece of technology shows you completely new things about the Universe.

MICHAEL G. SMITH
Space historian

What makes your work exciting?
I enjoy discovering the mysteries of history. In my job as a historian, this happens in libraries and archives when I'm leafing through documents buried in old files and find evidence from the past. Sometimes it's an amazing fact or idea. At other times, it's a detail that makes sense only later. It is always fun and inspiring to discover a piece of a puzzle that fits with others to complete a bigger picture of the past.

What is a challenge in your field?
How to make space exploration, colonization in places like space stations, and new planetary homes, cost less and last longer. We know that Earth is vulnerable as a planet, so we need to find a way to live in outer space, rather than just visiting space periodically or exploring it with spacecraft robots.

TOBY BROWN
Astrophysicist

What do you want to discover most?
How do galaxies evolve? is the question at the heart of my research. Uncovering the origins of galaxies, including our own Milky Way, is fundamental to understanding humankind's own story.

What is an unsolved problem in your field?
Why do galaxies stop forming stars? In most cases, galaxies are either actively forming stars or stopped forming them billions of years ago. Understanding why this is sits right at the heart of my field. And despite a huge amount of effort over the last few decades, we are still a long way from fully understanding the answer.

Universe
THE QUIZ

1) **Which of the following elements were the only two that existed soon after the Universe formed?**
   a. Hydrogen and helium
   b. Hydrogen and oxygen
   c. Carbon and hydrogen
   d. Helium and oxygen

2) **In 1965, American astronomers Arno Penzias and Robert Woodrow Wilson thought readings from their radio telescope had been disrupted by:**
   a. Vandals
   b. A nearby pop concert
   c. Aliens
   d. Pigeon droppings

3) **What is the opposite of matter?**
   a. Negative matter
   b. Antimatter
   c. Zeromatter
   d. No matter

4) **Planet Earth is located in which spiral arm of the Milky Way galaxy?**
   a. The Orion Arm
   b. The Perseus Arm
   c. The Major Arm
   d. The Norma Arm

5) **Approximately how long does one complete rotation of the Milky Way take?**
   a. 24 years
   b. 240 years
   c. 24,000 years
   d. 240 million years

6) **Which of these constellations cannot be seen from the Northern Hemisphere?**
   a. Orion
   b. Cassiopeia
   c. The Great Bear
   d. The Southern Cross

7) **What scientific instrument was first used by ancient Greek astronomers to map stars in the night sky?**
   a. Telescope
   b. Astrolabe
   c. Orrery
   d. Oracle

8) **In which year was the Hubble Space Telescope launched?**
   a. 1980
   b. 1990
   c. 2000
   d. 2010

9) **What evidence did NASA's Curiosity Rover find that suggests there was once running water on Mars?**
   a. Ice crystals
   b. Pebbles
   c. Seashells
   d. Drainpipes

10) **The asteroid belt lies between which two planets?**
   a. Jupiter and Saturn
   b. Mars and Saturn
   c. Saturn and Neptune
   d. Mars and Jupiter

11) **Saturn's moon Titan has liquid running over its surface. This liquid is similar to:**
   a. Water
   b. Slime
   c. Ectoplasm
   d. Gasoline

12) **Up to how many people at a time live on the International Space Station?**
   a. 3
   b. 6
   c. 12
   d. 24

13) **Which of the following is NOT the name of a theory about how the Universe will end?**
   a. The Big Crunch
   b. The Big Freeze
   c. The Big Dipper
   d. The Big Rip

14) **Astronomer Edwin Hubble is famous for discovering that the Universe is:**
   a. Expanding
   b. Contracting
   c. Heating up
   d. Cooling down

49

ANSWERS: 1) a, 2) d, 3) b, 4) a, 5) d, 6) d, 7) b, 8) b, 9) b, 10) d, 11) d, 12) b, 13) c, 14) a

Earthrise, photographed by astronaut Bill
Anders as he orbited the Moon in the *Apollo 8*
spacecraft. After capturing this iconic
image, Anders said: "We came all this way
to explore the Moon, and the most important
thing is that we discovered the Earth."

CHAPTER 2
EARTH

For thousands of years people have seen the sunrise and the moonrise, but it was only in 1968 that we were first given a glimpse of the *earth*rise. Imagine our giant, beautiful blue planet climbing upward against the black void of deep space. How incredible it must have been for *Apollo 8* astronaut Bill Anders. He photographed earthrise for the very first time! Our Earth was wrapped in a glowing blanket of air, with much of the surface glistening blue. Streaky-white clouds revealed patches of green-brown land beneath.

In this chapter you'll find out how our planet's collision with another planet gave birth to our beautiful seasons. You'll discover that our rocky, watery home spins on its axis at more than 1,000 miles (1,600 km) per hour. And if that isn't enough to make you dizzy, then dive into some of Earth's Known Unknowns, such as whether animals can predict earthquakes. Or meet ancient Greek genius Eratosthenes. He worked out the circumference of the planet using just a well, a stick, and the shadow cast by the Sun.

Be inspired by our planet's stunning natural wealth of fossils, minerals, gems, and crystals. And marvel at the awesome power of nature's volcanoes, earthquakes, hurricanes, and tsunamis.

EARTH IS BORN

Scientists think Earth formed 4.6 billion years ago as a tiny hard ball that came together in the debris whirling around the newborn Sun. The heavier elements collected to form a superdense core. But collisions with other debris left the early Earth's surface a sea of boiling hot magma. Eventually the magma cooled to form a rocky crust and water began to condense to form Earth's first ocean.

Why is Earth a sphere?

A planet's gravity is the force that pulls everything to its center. Because gravity pulls equally in every direction, the distance from the center to the edge is the same in all directions. This makes a sphere.

Earth was still hot and half-melted like a giant ball of lava when Theia crashed into it

Scientists think Theia formed in an orbit around the Sun that was very close to Earth's orbit

Bits of Theia and Earth flew off and eventually gathered together to form the Moon

How Earth got its tilt

In the early solar system, rocky chunks smashed into each other all the time. The craters on the surface of planets and moons are scars from these collisions. Early on, a giant rock the size of Mars, which scientists call Theia, smashed into Earth. The collision may have helped give Earth the tilt it has today. This tilt is responsible for Earth's seasons.

EXPERT CONSULTANT: Lewis Dartnell **SEE ALSO:** The Big Bang, p.4–5; Exoplanets, p.20–21; Our Solar System, p.22–23; Rocky Planets, p.28–29; Moons, p.32–33; Inside Earth, p.58–59; Mountains, p.68–69; Rocks & Minerals, p.70–71

FACTastic!

The Moon is egg-shaped! The Moon looks round but that's only the end we can see. It is actually shaped more like an egg. Scientists think Earth's gravity pulled the Moon out of shape when the Moon's thin crust floated on hot molten rock. Even today, Earth's gravity tugs on the Moon, causing it to bulge.

Mythical beginnings

Ancient cultures created stories about how Earth began. In Chinese myth, Pan Gu, the first man, placed the Sun, Moon, stars, and planets in their positions, separated Earth's oceans, and shaped the land according to the idea of yin-yang—that there are two sides to everything. Another Chinese legend says that Earth was made from Pan Gu's gigantic corpse. His eyes became the Sun and Moon, his blood formed rivers, and his hair grew into trees and plants.

Mythical creator Pan Gu holds the yin-yang symbol

The world's earliest rocks

Why are there no rocks dating from Earth's earliest years? Rock samples from meteorites and the Moon prove that Earth is 4.6 billion years old. So why is the oldest rock on Earth just 4.28 billion years old? One theory is that Earth's own tectonic activity has destroyed the planet's original crustal rocks.

Canada's Acasta gneiss rocks are roughly 4 billion years old; also from Canada, Nuvvuagittuq greenstone is 4.28 billion years old

NOTE from the expert!

LEWIS DARTNELL
Astrobiologist

Professor Lewis Dartnell studies how different features of Earth have affected life on our planet. He supports the theory that water was delivered to Earth during collisions with water-bearing asteroids and comets after the collision with Theia.

❝ *Earth is a wonderfully active and dynamic planet. It is constantly changing its face through time. Its personality can be very unpredictable.* ❞

53

EARTH IN SPACE

Of all the planets in our solar system, Earth is the only one that supports life. It is unique in that much of its surface is rocky, temperatures are neither too hot nor too cold, and it has lots of water, which is necessary for life. More than 3.5 billion years ago, a microbe that scientists call LUCA (Last Universal Common Ancestor) emerged somewhere on Earth, and all Earth's varied life descended from it!

Earth from space

Satellites and spacecraft send back photographs to show what Earth looks like from a distance. Satellites can't show the whole of Earth in a single image because they orbit too close, so pictures like this are put together from separate shots. Space agencies boost the colors to make Earth look more beautiful.

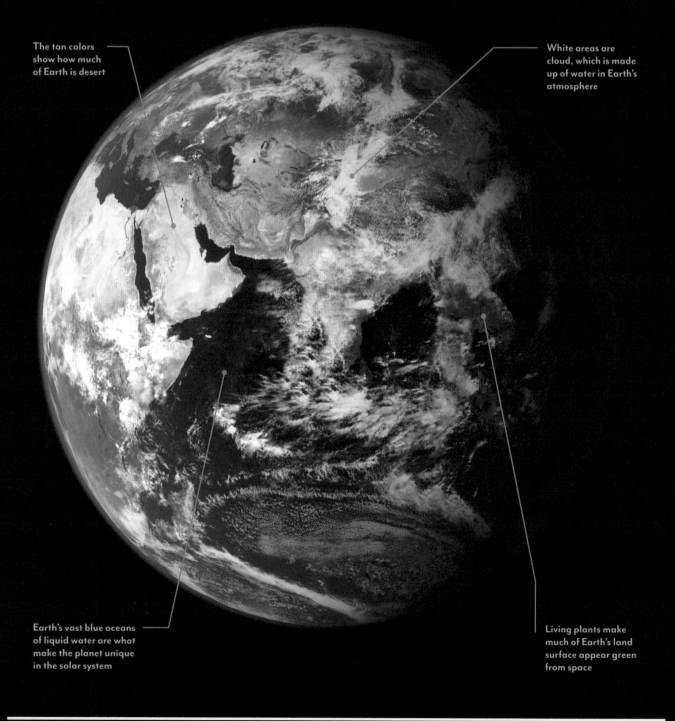

The tan colors show how much of Earth is desert

White areas are cloud, which is made up of water in Earth's atmosphere

Earth's vast blue oceans of liquid water are what make the planet unique in the solar system

Living plants make much of Earth's land surface appear green from space

Goldilocks zone

Earth sits in just the right place—not too hot or too cold—for liquid water to lie on the surface and make life possible. Some scientists call this place the Goldilocks zone after the fairy tale. The scientific name for it is the circumstellar habitable zone (CHZ).

Jupiter, Saturn, and the planets beyond are too far from the Sun and too cold to be habitable.

Mars is within the habitable zone, and is most like Earth, but it is too small to have a protective atmosphere.

Mercury and Venus and their moons are near the Sun and too hot to be habitable.

Saturn

Jupiter

Mars

Earth

Venus

Mercury

Sun

Reasons for seasons

The polar regions are cold, and the tropics (the bands just north and south of the equator) are warm. In the area between the polar regions and the tropics, the year has four noticeable seasons—spring, summer, fall, and winter. This is because our planet tilts, and the angle at which sunlight hits Earth changes as we orbit the Sun. When the northern half of Earth tilts toward the Sun, it is summer there and winter in the south. Six months later, the southern half tilts toward the Sun, and the opposite is true.

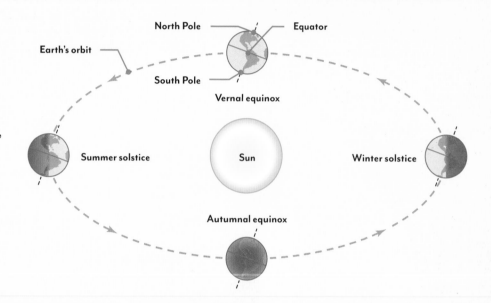
North Pole • Equator • Earth's orbit • South Pole • Vernal equinox • Summer solstice • Sun • Winter solstice • Autumnal equinox

Earth's magnetosphere

Nuclear reactions in the Sun send out a stream of high-energy particles called the solar wind. Earth's magnetic field (magnetosphere), which extends into space, acts like a shield, protecting it from this deadly force.

Why do Earth's oceans have tides?

Earth's oceans are pulled by the gravity of the Sun and the Moon, resulting in the rise and fall of the tides. There are two high tides and two low tides a day. When both the Sun and Moon are positioned on the same side of Earth, high tides are even higher than when the Sun and Moon are positioned on opposite sides of Earth.

Earth in Numbers
LISTIFIED.

1. Earth zooms around the Sun at 67,000 mph (107,000 km/h).

2. It takes 365.2564 days for Earth to orbit the Sun (not 365 days). That's why February has 29 days every four years. We call such years leap years. They keep our calendar on track.

3. More than 90 percent of Earth's mass is made of iron, oxygen, silicon, and magnesium.

4. Earth is the densest planet in the solar system. The average cubic inch of Earth weighs 3.19 ounces (90.4 g).

5. Earth's atmosphere weighs 5,500 trillion tons (5,000 trillion tonnes).

6. Earth spins on its axis at 1,036 mph (1,674 km/h) every 24 hours. But our planet is slowing down! In about 140 million years from now, one full spin (currently 24 hours) will last about 25 hours.

MEASURING EARTH

Earth is a giant ball of rock. It's round, but not quite perfectly round, and scientists now describe its shape as "geoid," which just means Earth-shaped. It's a little flatter at the poles and fatter at the equator, which is 24,870 miles (40,024 km) in circumference (all the way around). Satellite images also show that Earth has tiny bumps here and there. These imperfections are so small they can only be detected by accurate measuring.

How much does Earth weigh?

Earth weighs more than 13 trillion trillion pounds (about 6 trillion trillion kg). Of course, we can't weigh Earth, so how do scientists know this? They can work it out from how much Earth's gravity pulls on neighboring planets. The gravity of an object is in proportion to its mass—the amount of material that makes up that object.

Latitude and longitude

The location of any place on Earth can be pinpointed precisely using a grid of lines of latitude and longitude. Lines of latitude are imaginary circles that are drawn around Earth parallel to the equator, which is why they are often called parallels. Lines of longitude are circles that are drawn between the North and South poles, which divide Earth like the segments of an orange. Lines of longitude are called meridians.

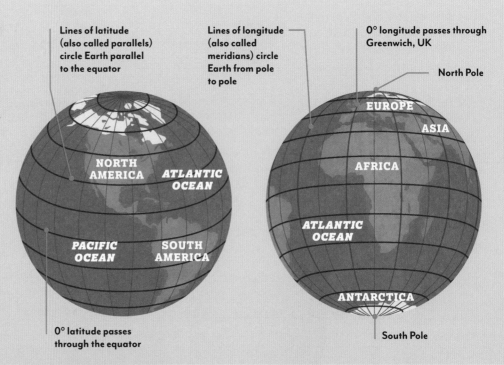

Lines of latitude (also called parallels) circle Earth parallel to the equator

Lines of longitude (also called meridians) circle Earth from pole to pole

0° longitude passes through Greenwich, UK

North Pole

NORTH AMERICA

ATLANTIC OCEAN

PACIFIC OCEAN

SOUTH AMERICA

EUROPE

ASIA

AFRICA

ATLANTIC OCEAN

ANTARCTICA

South Pole

0° latitude passes through the equator

Measuring by satellite

Satellites in space can detect tiny differences in height on Earth's surface. They can even make a map of the seafloor by detecting little bumps and dips in the ocean surface (averaged out to ignore waves). Because of the varying pull of gravity, these bumps and dips mirror the seafloor. In this satellite map (left), orange and red indicate areas of the seafloor where gravity is strongest—ridges and mountains.

EXPERT CONSULTANT: Paolo Forti **SEE ALSO:** Artificial Satellites, p.40–41; Earth in Space, p.54–55; Inside Earth, p.58–59; The Earth, p.60–61; Light, p.128–29; Gravity, p.134–35; Calendars, p.224–25

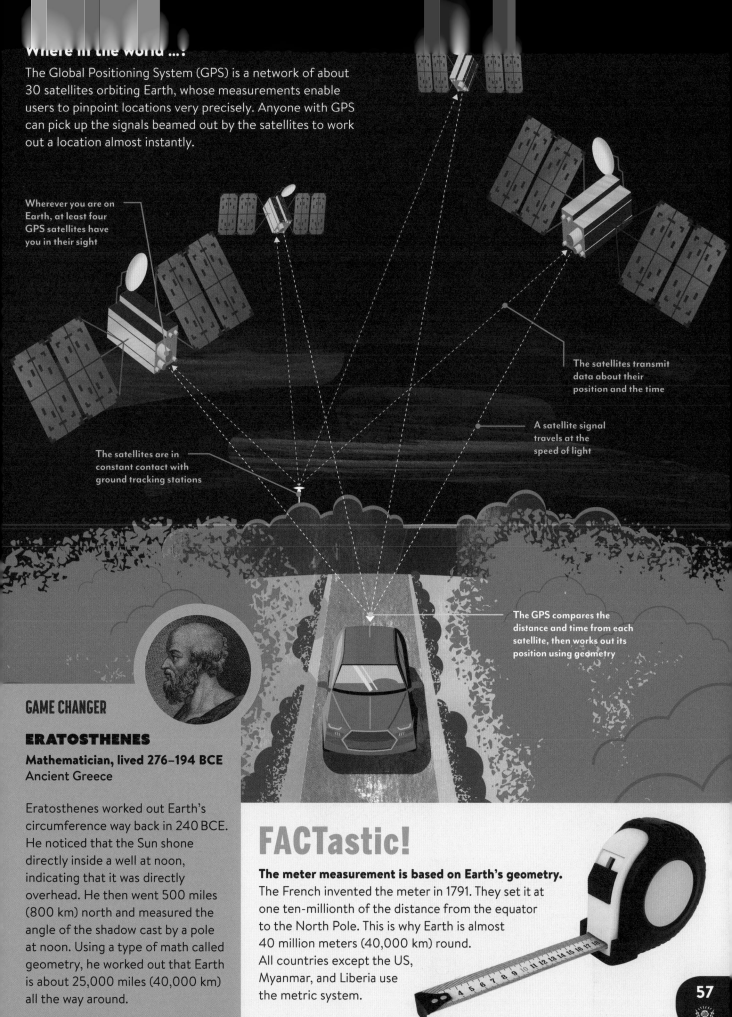

Where in the world ...?

The Global Positioning System (GPS) is a network of about 30 satellites orbiting Earth, whose measurements enable users to pinpoint locations very precisely. Anyone with GPS can pick up the signals beamed out by the satellites to work out a location almost instantly.

Wherever you are on Earth, at least four GPS satellites have you in their sight

The satellites transmit data about their position and the time

A satellite signal travels at the speed of light

The satellites are in constant contact with ground tracking stations

The GPS compares the distance and time from each satellite, then works out its position using geometry

GAME CHANGER

ERATOSTHENES

Mathematician, lived 276–194 BCE
Ancient Greece

Eratosthenes worked out Earth's circumference way back in 240 BCE. He noticed that the Sun shone directly inside a well at noon, indicating that it was directly overhead. He then went 500 miles (800 km) north and measured the angle of the shadow cast by a pole at noon. Using a type of math called geometry, he worked out that Earth is about 25,000 miles (40,000 km) all the way around.

FACTastic!

The meter measurement is based on Earth's geometry.
The French invented the meter in 1791. They set it at one ten-millionth of the distance from the equator to the North Pole. This is why Earth is almost 40 million meters (40,000 km) round. All countries except the US, Myanmar, and Liberia use the metric system.

INSIDE EARTH

Earth has three major layers: crust, mantle, and core. Each of these has layers of its own. Scientists discovered this by listening to the vibrations from earthquakes. Earth's crust is the thin outer shell of rock. Its mantle is a thick belt of partly melted rock. The core, Earth's center, has two parts—inner and outer. The inner core contains incredibly dense metals as hot as the surface of the Sun!

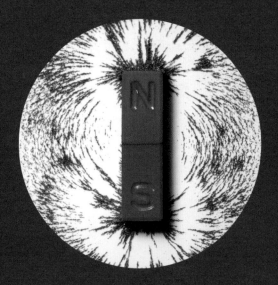

The planet's layers

Only Earth's outer crust is cool. Below the surface, temperatures rise the deeper you get. Intense heat keeps the rock in the mantle partly melted and slowly churning, like boiling soup. The even hotter outer core is liquid metal, but the inner core is solid. The core contains up to 90 percent of all Earth's iron.

Magnetic Earth

As Earth spins, the swirling metal of the outer core turns the planet into a giant magnet. The magnetic force is strongest near the poles. That's why compasses always point to a place near the North Pole, called magnetic north.

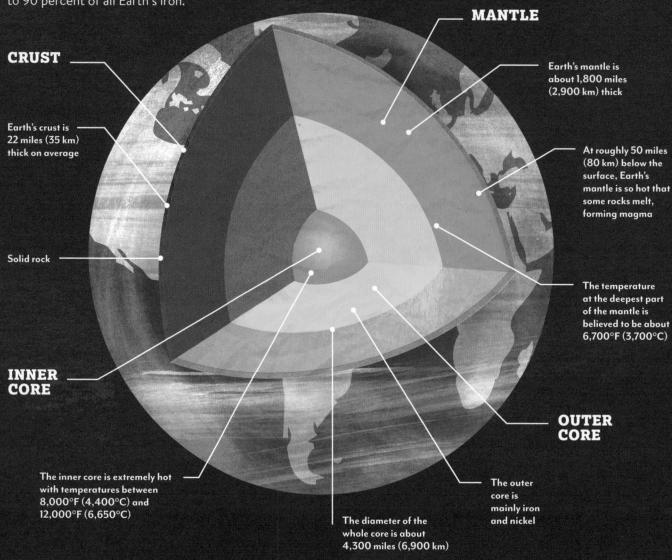

MANTLE

Earth's mantle is about 1,800 miles (2,900 km) thick

CRUST

Earth's crust is 22 miles (35 km) thick on average

At roughly 50 miles (80 km) below the surface, Earth's mantle is so hot that some rocks melt, forming magma

Solid rock

The temperature at the deepest part of the mantle is believed to be about 6,700°F (3,700°C)

INNER CORE

OUTER CORE

The inner core is extremely hot with temperatures between 8,000°F (4,400°C) and 12,000°F (6,650°C)

The outer core is mainly iron and nickel

The diameter of the whole core is about 4,300 miles (6,900 km)

EXPERT CONSULTANT: Lewis Dartnell **SEE ALSO:** Earth in Space, p.54–55; Plate Tectonics, p.62–63; Volcanoes, p.64–65; Earthquakes & Tsunamis, p.66–67; Mountains, p.68–69; Rocks & Minerals, p.70–71; Earth's Riches, p.74–75; Elements, p.102–03; Metals, p.114–15; Electricity, p.126–27

Earth's crust and mantle

There are two kinds of crust: Earth's outer layer, a thick "continental" crust that forms the land, and a thin, newer "oceanic" crust that forms the seabed. The top layer of the mantle is fused to the crust, forming the rigid lithosphere. Below it, at depths of 60 miles (100 km) to 450 miles (700 km), is the more fluid asthenosphere.

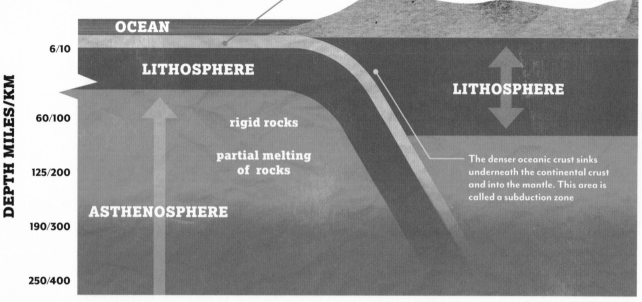

The oceanic crust is 3–6 miles (5–10 km) thick—much thinner and denser than the continental crust

Continental crust is 15–40 miles (25–70 km) deep. It floats higher on the mantle because its rocks are less dense than those that make up the oceanic crust

OCEAN

LITHOSPHERE

LITHOSPHERE

DEPTH MILES/KM

6/10

60/100 — rigid rocks

125/200 — partial melting of rocks

190/300 — ASTHENOSPHERE

250/400

The denser oceanic crust sinks underneath the continental crust and into the mantle. This area is called a subduction zone

UPPER MANTLE

Underground mountains

Using earthquake data and a technique called seismic tomography (similar to ultrasound, which we use to look at unborn babies), scientists have made astonishing discoveries. They think the mantle is layered, with marked breaks 255 miles (410 km) and 410 miles (660 km) down. At the 410-mile mark, they think there is a mountain range with peaks that may be taller than Mount Everest.

Buried treasure

Diamonds are made deep down in Earth's mantle, 100 miles (160 km) from the surface. They form under extreme pressure. The diamonds we mine were spewed up long ago by very deep volcanic eruptions that solidified in pipes of rock called kimberlites. There may be more than a quadrillion tons of diamonds still in the mantle, far out of reach.

KNOWN UNKNOWN

What else is in Earth's core?

The heart of our planet is a mystery. Scientists used to believe that iron and the metal nickel made up the whole of Earth's innermost layer. But the core is lighter than it would be if it was just metal. Scientists think the main missing ingredient might be silicon.

THE EARTH

From a distance, Earth looks as smooth as a marble. But its surface is actually quite rough. Oceans cover nearly 71 percent of Earth's surface, but even under the sea, there are mountains and valleys. There are about 65,000 feet (20,000 meters) between the highest point, the top of Mount Everest, and the lowest, the bottom of Challenger Deep in the Pacific Ocean. In between come all the ups and downs that make Earth so varied.

ARCTIC OCEAN

Arctic Circle

NORTH ATLANTIC OCEAN

NORTH AMERICA

The Ring of Fire is a belt of active volcanoes and an earthquake epicenter

Rocky Mountains

The Mid-Atlantic Ridge is one the major ridges of the huge oceanic ridge system that spans the globe

Tropic of Cancer

PACIFIC OCEAN

Equator

SOUTH AMERICA

Tropic of Capricorn

Andes Mountains

SOUTH ATLANTIC OCEAN

Scale at the Equator

| 0 | 1000 | 2000 | 3000 | 4000 | 5000 kilometer |
| 0 | 500 | 1000 | 1500 | 2000 | 2500 | 3000 miles |

Antarctic Circle

Physical Extremes
LISTIFIED.

Our planet has extraordinary heights, lows, and extremes.

1. The Sahara is the world's largest hot desert, with an area of 3,320,000 sq. miles (8,600,000 sq km).

2. The oceanic ridge system, a series of volcanic mountains underneath the sea, is Earth's longest range. It's about 50,000 miles (80,000 km) in length and encircles the planet.

3. The Himalayas is the world's highest mountain range. More than 110 peaks are taller than 24,000 ft (7,300 meters).

4. The Great Barrier Reef is the largest collective structure of living things—coral, algae, and tiny moss animals. Its 2,000 reefs cover an area of around 135,000 sq. miles (350,000 sq. km).

5. Challenger Deep is the deepest ocean point—36,070 feet (10,994 meters) deep.

EXPERT CONSULTANT: Lewis Dartnell **SEE ALSO:** Earth in Space, p.54–55; Volcanoes, p.64–65; Earthquakes & Tsunamis, p.66–67; Mountains p.68–69; The Rain Forest, p.164–65; The Taiga & Temperate Forests, p.166–67; Grasslands, p.168–69; Mount Everest, p.170–71; Ends of the Earth, p.184–85

NORTH AMERICA

ASIA

Magnetic Pole + (2019)
North + Pole

Arctic Circle

EUROPE

SOUTH AMERICA

Antarctic Circle

South + Pole

ARCTIC OCEAN

Alps

EUROPE

The Himalayas, the highest range, includes Mount Everest, the world's tallest mountain

Arctic Circle

ASIA

PACIFIC OCEAN

Tropic of Cancer

AFRICA

Mariana Trench, the deepest ocean trench, includes Challenger Deep, the deepest known point in Earth's oceans

Equator

INDIAN OCEAN

AUSTRALIA

Tropic of Capricorn

The Great Rift Valley runs from Jordan in the Middle East to Mozambique in southeastern Africa

The Sahara Desert spans 11 countries in North and Central Africa

The Nullarbor Plain is a vast limestone plateau covering 100,000 sq. miles (260,000 sq. km)

The Great Barrier Reef stretches for more than 1,250 miles (2,000 km) off the northeastern coast of Australia

SOUTHERN OCEAN

Antarctic Circle

Height in meters
over 5000 5000 4000 3000 2000 1000 500 200 0

land below sea level

ANTARCTICA

0 -200 -1000 -2000 -3000 -4000 -5000 below -5000
Depth in meters

PLATE TECTONICS

Earth's rigid outer layer is made up of giant slabs of rock called tectonic plates. Some of these are much bigger than continents, while others are much smaller. These plates float on a weak, soft (like Play-Doh) layer of rock called the asthenosphere, typically 60–420 miles (100–700 km) below the surface, and jostle against one another, causing earthquakes and volcanoes. Plate movement is very slow—on average about 1 inch (2.5 cm) a year. Over millions of years, it causes oceans to widen and mountains to form.

FACTastic!

Earth's continents were once joined up in one vast supercontinent, surrounded by a giant ocean. This was about 335 million years ago. Geologists call this supercontinent Pangea. About 180 million years ago, Pangea began to break apart, creating the Atlantic Ocean and eventually forming the modern continents.

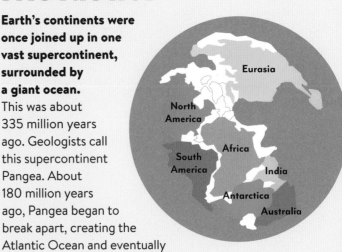

Dynamic Earth

Most volcanoes and earthquakes occur near where tectonic plates meet—the plate margins. Different kinds of margins exist. At diverging margins, plates pull apart, allowing molten rock (magma) to rise through the gap. At converging margins, plates collide, forcing one under the other (subduction). At transform margins, the plates slide past each other.

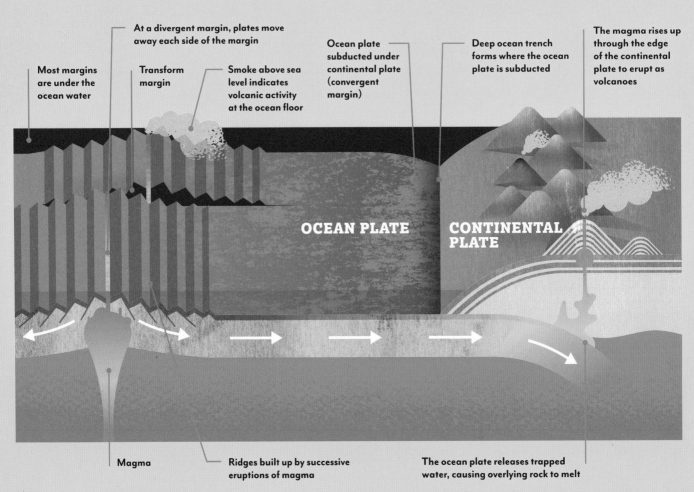

At a divergent margin, plates move away each side of the margin

Most margins are under the ocean water

Transform margin

Smoke above sea level indicates volcanic activity at the ocean floor

Ocean plate subducted under continental plate (convergent margin)

Deep ocean trench forms where the ocean plate is subducted

The magma rises up through the edge of the continental plate to erupt as volcanoes

OCEAN PLATE

CONTINENTAL PLATE

Magma

Ridges built up by successive eruptions of magma

The ocean plate releases trapped water, causing overlying rock to melt

EXPERT CONSULTANT: Brendan Murphy **SEE ALSO:** Earth Is Born, p.52–53; Inside Earth, p.58–59; The Earth, p.60–61; Volcanoes, p.64–65; Mountains, p.68–69; Rocks & Minerals, p.70–71; Solids, Liquids & Gases, p.110–11; Energy, p.122–23; Pressure, p.136–37

Islands rise up

In 1963, a new island began to spring out of the sea off Iceland. Named Surtsey, after the Norse fire god Surtur, it formed during a volcanic eruption on the seabed that lasted almost four years. Surtsey (below) sits on a split in the seafloor where the plates under the Atlantic Ocean are moving apart. The volcanic material erupting through such gaps has formed the Mid-Atlantic Ridge along the ocean floor.

Lava balls

All along the dip at the margins of diverging plates, hot magma (molten rock) continually erupts up from beneath the ocean floor (becoming lava). As soon as it hits the chilly water of the deep ocean, the lava freezes into solid balls. The seafloor here is littered with balls of lava, called pillow lavas, because they look like piles of cushions.

Current tectonic plates

There are seven major plates—one giant plate under the Pacific Ocean and six others that sit under land and ocean. Between the major plates, there are also 15 minor plates. Microplates, which are even smaller, line the gaps between the major and the minor plates. Some tectonic plates can be up to 124 miles (200 km) thick and are composed of solid rock. As the rock is denser and heavier under oceans, it sits lower than continents.

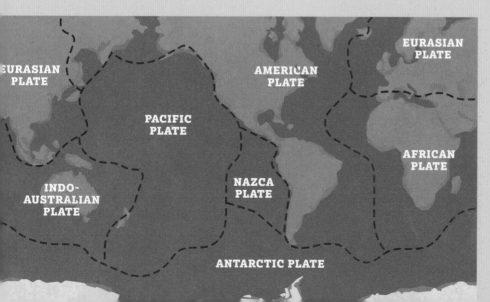

EURASIAN PLATE

EURASIAN PLATE

AMERICAN PLATE

PACIFIC PLATE

AFRICAN PLATE

INDO-AUSTRALIAN PLATE

NAZCA PLATE

ANTARCTIC PLATE

Proof of Plate Tectonics
LISTIFIED.

We know Earth's plates have shifted and are still moving because:

1. Land-dwelling fossils that are similar to one another have been found on different continents, as groups of living things separated when the continents divided.

2. Coal deposits in eastern North America were deposited 300 million years ago, when North America lay across the equator.

3. Glaciers have left traces in India, Africa, Australia, and Antarctica, pointing to a time when Africa was near the South Pole.

4. Many earthquakes and volcanoes result from plate tectonic forces.

5. Satellite laser ranging uses laser light from space to detect movement in GPS receivers, indicating movement of continents.

NOTE *from the expert!*

BRENDAN MURPHY
Geologist

Specializing in Earth sciences, Brendan Murphy is curious about the supercontinent cycle. He wants to know why continents collide to form vast mountains, then move apart, only to gather together again some 400 million years later.

❝ *I like to think about what I would see if I could take a journey to the center of the Earth.* ❞

VOLCANOES

We know where most volcanoes are in the world but not when they will erupt. Some lie inactive for thousands of years before erupting suddenly and violently. Volcano experts—volcanologists—look for clues, such as movement in the rocks of the volcano and unusual gases coming from its vent. Drones can be flown in to measure this gas and spot other signs of dangerous activity.

Stromboli blasts

Volcanoes erupt in different ways. Strombolian eruptions, named after this volcano in Italy (Stromboli), spray hot molten rock called lava in a "fire fountain." Others ooze gently year after year. Still others explode suddenly, propelling gas, volcanic ash, and fragments of bubbly solidified lava called pumice high into the air.

Fire fountains shoot hot lava thousands of feet into the air

The gases are a mix of mostly water vapor, carbon dioxide, and sulfur gases

Craters and cracks eject spectacular lava fountains

Vent through which the magma flows out

Fire fountains can be a series of short bursts or a continuous jet

Clouds of ash and debris cover the volcano's slopes

EXPERT CONSULTANT: Erik Klemetti **SEE ALSO:** Inside Earth, p.58–59; Plate Tectonics, p.62–63; Earthquakes & Tsunamis, p.66–67; Rocks & Minerals, p.70–71; Solids, Liquids & Gases, p.110–11; Energy, p.122–23; Forces, p.132–33; The Origin of Life, p.148–49

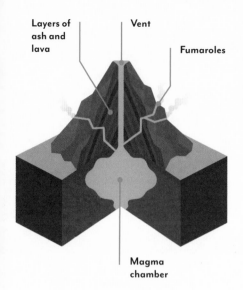

Layers of ash and lava

Vent

Fumaroles

Magma chamber

Inside a volcano

Beneath most mountain volcanoes, there is a reservoir of molten rock called magma. Gases may leak from the magma chamber to the surface through cracks called fumaroles. Over time, magma wells up from underneath the magma chamber and pressure builds. Eventually, the magma is driven out through the vent. At this point, it becomes lava. The temperature of lava can be up to 2,300°F (1,250°C).

FACTastic!

Ash and lava can travel up to 430 mph (700 km/h). When Mount Vesuvius, in Italy, erupted in 79 CE, it buried the towns of Pompeii and Herculaneum under 20 feet (6 meters) of ash, killing people instantly. When the ash cooled, it became solid, preserving the positions the people were in when they died.

KNOWN UNKNOWN

When will Yellowstone blow?

The steam shooting out of cracks called geysers in Yellowstone National Park in the US is one of the reasons that scientists think a lot of magma lies under the park. The Yellowstone volcano erupts about every 600,000 years, and the last time it erupted was 640,000 years ago. That time it produced enough lava to fill up the Grand Canyon. Another eruption could cover much of the western half of the US in ash at least 3 feet (1 meter) deep.

Ring of Fire

Three-quarters of Earth's volcanoes—more than 450—are situated around the Pacific Ocean in what's called the Ring of Fire. This is where vast tectonic plates under the Pacific Ocean slam into each other, forcing the bottom plate into Earth's hot interior. As the rock melts, blobs of magma shoot up as volcanoes.

Three-quarters of all the world's active volcanoes lie in the Ring of Fire

Hawaii (US)

Yellowstone (US)

Vesuvius (Italy)

Stromboli (Italy)

ASIA

EUROPE

ASIA

NORTH AMERICA

ATLANTIC OCEAN

AFRICA

PACIFIC OCEAN

SOUTH AMERICA

Indonesia's volcanoes are the most active in the world. Other countries with several active volcanoes include Japan and the US

AUSTRALIA

ATLANTIC OCEAN

Japan

ANTARCTICA

EARTHQUAKES & TSUNAMIS

If you feel the ground really shaking, it could be an earthquake. There are about 50,000 earthquakes every year. Most are so small you can only pick them up on a special instrument called a seismometer. Some, however, are so violent they do real damage, bringing buildings tumbling down and killing many people. An earthquake under the sea can also cause a tsunami, a mighty wave that brings even more destruction.

An aerial view of the San Andreas Fault in California. It is more than 800 miles (1,300 km) long

Tsunami—monster wave

Tsunamis are giant waves that can rise 100 feet (30 meters)—one-third as high as a house—apparently out of nowhere. A tsunami is set off when an earthquake or erupting volcano shifts a lot of water under the sea. The pulses of water then surge along the seabed, out of sight, at up to 500 miles per hour (800 kph)—as fast as a jet plane. When the tsunami reaches the shallows, it grows into a great wall of water, washing away everything in its path.

Crack and smash

Nearly all big earthquakes happen along giant cracks known as faults, like the one above. A fault can form anywhere where stress is felt by rock that is too cold or hard to bend. They occur between tectonic plates, the giant slabs of rock that make up Earth's crust—its skin. The slabs can get stuck as they grind past each other. Big earthquakes happen when the pressure builds up and the slabs shudder past each other, sending out shock waves.

The sudden shift in the seabed during an undersea earthquake can move a huge amount of water

The movement sends powerful pulses of water, about 60–120 miles (100–200 km) apart, along the seabed

The racing pulses are no more than 2 feet (60 cm) high—hardly noticeable from the surface of the sea

Pulses race along the seabed at up to 500 mph (800 km/h)

EXPERT CONSULTANT: Erik Klemetti **SEE ALSO:** Inside Earth, p.58–59; Plate Tectonics, p.62–63; Volcanoes, p.64–65

Shock waves

Earthquakes send out massive, fast-moving shock waves called seismic waves. The first waves to reach you are superfast P, or Primary, waves, which stretch and squeeze as they roar along at 3.7 miles (6 km) a second. Slower S, or Secondary, waves strike seconds later, shaking the ground from side to side. A third type, called surface waves, cause the most shaking and do the most damage. These waves travel on Earth's surface, rather than deep underground.

KNOWN UNKNOWN

Can animals predict earthquakes?

People have reported seeing fish, birds, reptiles, and insects acting strangely before an earthquake—sometimes weeks before. Scientists are trying to figure out if they can use these animals to predict an earthquake in time to help keep people safe. So far, however, there is no scientific evidence that animals can work as an earthquake early warning system.

FACTastic!

In 2011, one of the biggest earthquakes to ever hit Japan pushed Honshu, its main island, 8 feet (2.4 meters) east. That's more than the length of a small car! The earthquake sank 250 miles (400 km) of Japan's coastline by 2 feet (0.6 meters) and killed thousands of people. And it lasted only six minutes. Land is always moving, but not usually that fast.

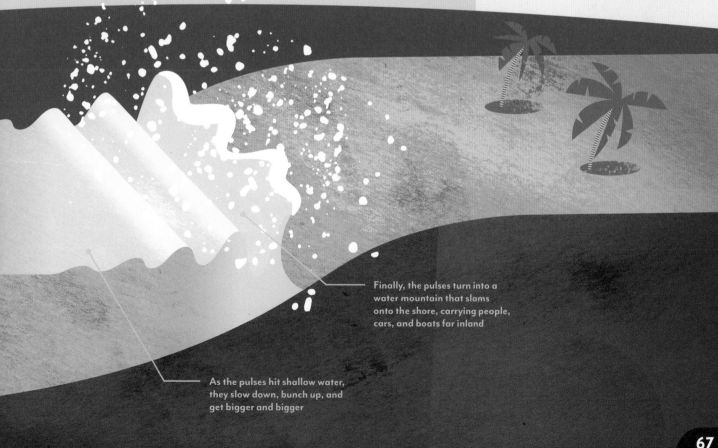

Finally, the pulses turn into a water mountain that slams onto the shore, carrying people, cars, and boats far inland

As the pulses hit shallow water, they slow down, bunch up, and get bigger and bigger

MOUNTAINS

There are mountains on every continent. A few are isolated peaks made by volcanoes, like Mount Kilimanjaro in Kenya and Mount Fuji in Japan. But most mountains form part of great chains like the Andes in South America and the Rockies in North America. Because temperature decreases the higher you go, the very highest mountains are always capped with snow above a certain level called the snow line. The snow line gets lower the farther you go from the equator.

FACTastic!

You can calculate the height of a mountain by boiling a kettle! The boiling point of water reduces by 1.8°F (1°C) every 1,000 feet (304 meters) you climb. This is because the boiling point of water depends on pressure, and pressure drops as you climb. The higher you climb, the faster water boils.

Which is the highest peak?

We measure a mountain from sea level to the mountain's peak, so Mount Everest in the Himalayas is classified as the highest mountain. Mauna Kea, on the island of Hawaii, is actually taller when measured from its base to its peak, but much of it lies underwater. The farthest peak from Earth's center is Chimborazo in Ecuador. This is because Earth, which is not a perfect sphere, is fatter at this point.

Mount Everest, in the Himalayas, is the world's highest mountain at 29,035 feet (8,850 meters)

Two-thirds of Mauna Kea lies under the sea

MOUNT EVEREST

Mauna Kea is only 13,803 feet (4,207 meters) but it's a whopping 33,474 feet (10,203 meters) if you count the part under the ocean

MAUNA KEA

EXPERT CONSULTANT: Erik Klemetti **SEE ALSO:** Inside Earth, p.58–59; The Earth, p.60–61; Plate Tectonics, p.62–63; Volcanoes, p.64–65; Rocks & Minerals, p.70–71; Fossils, p.76–77; Pressure, p.136–37; Mount Everest, p.170–71

Types of mountains

Some mountains are pushed up by volcanoes or earthquakes, but most of the world's great mountain ranges, such as the Alps in Europe and the Caucasus, straddling Europe and Asia, are fold mountains. These are forced up gradually by the slow shifting of tectonic plates.

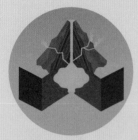

Volcanic mountains
These form when molten rock from inside Earth erupts through the crust and piles up.

Block mountains
Stresses within the tectonic plates cause cracks and force up blocks of rock.

Dome mountains
These form when magma inside Earth pushes the crust into a dome and hardens.

Fold mountains
Movements of Earth's tectonic plates squeeze layers of rock, causing them to rise and crumple.

Major mountain belts

The biggest mountain ranges, shaded brown on this map, have formed along the boundaries of tectonic plates, the sliding slabs of rock that make up Earth's surface. These include the mountain ranges and chains of volcanoes that line the western coasts of North and South America (the Rockies and the Andes), the the Alps and Caucasus ranges in Europe, and the Himalayas, which rise up north of India.

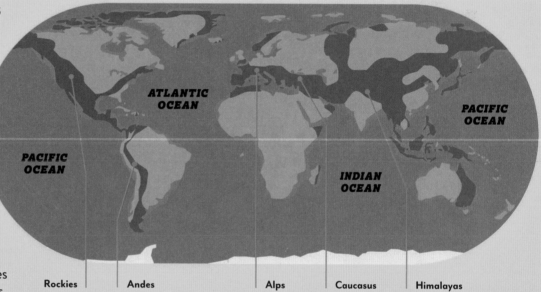

ATLANTIC OCEAN

PACIFIC OCEAN

PACIFIC OCEAN

INDIAN OCEAN

Rockies | Andes | Alps | Caucasus | Himalayas

Mount Chimborazo's peak is 20,702 feet (6,310 meters) but it is the farthest peak from Earth's center

Mount Kilimanjaro is 19,340 feet (5,895 meters). It has the longest climb from base to summit

MOUNT CHIMBORAZO

MOUNT KILIMANJARO

ROCKS & MINERALS

Rocks are the building blocks of Earth's surface.
Most are combinations of one or more minerals
that are cemented or fused together. Although
there are thousands of different minerals—from
hard sparkly diamonds to soft gypsum—only 40
are common in rocks. The hundreds of varieties
of rocks can be divided into three basic groups—
igneous, sedimentary, and metamorphic.

FACTastic!

Soil starts out as rock! Crumbled into powder
by the weather and mixed with plant and animal
matter, it can support plants and their roots.

The rock cycle

Rocks change gradually over millions of years.
At the surface, they crumble and are deposited
to form sedimentary rock. Inside Earth,
they are squashed and scorched to form
metamorphic rock. Or they partially
melt and solidify to form igneous rock,
which rises toward the surface. When
exposed at the surface, the rocks
crumble and the cycle repeats.

Volcanic eruptions extrude
igneous rock as lava and
expose it to the weather

Solidification

Tiny bits of broken down rock
and dead organisms settle on
the seabed. Over millions of
years sediment hardens and
becomes rock

Weather, flowing water,
and plant roots break
down rocks

**IGNEOUS
ROCKS**
(EXTRUSIVE)

Uplift exposes
sedimentary rock
to the weather

Uplift exposes
metamorphic
and igneous rock
to the weather

Over time,
the sediment
is buried under
more layers
of sediment

**SEDIMENTARY
ROCKS**

IGNEOUS ROCKS
(INTRUSIVE)

The layers above it press the
sediment into sedimentary rock

Heat and
pressure squash
igneous rock into
metamorphic rock

Igneous
rock melts
to become
magma

METAMORPHIC ROCKS

Heat and pressure squash
sedimentary rock into
metamorphic rock

Magma cools and
crystallizes to
become igneous rock

Metamorphic rock melts
to become magma

MAGMA

EXPERT CONSULTANT: Brendan Murphy **SEE ALSO:** Rocky Planets, p.28–29; Inside Earth, p.58–59; Plate Tectonics, p.62–63; Volcanoes p.64–65;
Mountains, p.68–69; Giant Crystals!, p.72–73; Earth's Riches, p.74–75; Fossils, p.76–77; Fossil Fuels, p.80–81; Elements, p.102–03, Compounds, p.106–07

Types of rocks

We classify rocks into three types, according to the forces and substances that made them.

Igneous rocks
Super hot, molten magma rises up from deep within Earth and cools to form igneous rock. If it reaches the surface as lava, it is called extrusive. If it solidifies before it reaches the surface, it is called intrusive.

Sedimentary rocks
Mud, sand, or the remains of dead organisms that settle on the bed of a sea or lake form sedimentary rocks. New sediments later pile on top like a layer cake. Over millions of years, the sediment hardens into layers of solid rock.

Metamorphic rocks
Minerals in rocks become unstable if they are cooked by hot magma or squeezed when tectonic plates (giant slabs of Earth's surface) collide. New stable minerals crystallize and the rocks that form are called metamorphic rocks.

Minerals

Each mineral has a certain chemical makeup. Some, such as gold (left), are made from just one chemical element. Most are compounds—a chemical combination of two or more elements. Tiny traces of other chemicals can make minerals look very different. Traces of copper make minerals blue or green, for example.

How hard is it?

The Mohs scale was devised in 1812 by German geologist Friedrich Mohs. He chose ten minerals of increasing hardness to use as testers. The full list is below. To figure out how hard an unknown rock is, you first try to scratch it with talc, a very soft mineral. If that doesn't work, try gypsum, and so on—all the way up to diamond— stopping at the rock type that scratches your sample. For example, if you can scratch your sample using topaz but not with quartz, you know that the rock sample is harder than quartz but softer than topaz.

1. Talc
2. Gypsum
3. Calcite
4. Fluorite
5. Apatite
6. Orthoclase
7. Quartz
8. Topaz
9. Corundum
10. Diamond

How crystals form

Left free to grow, minerals form crystals with perfect shapes. Geodes are hollow rocks with space for crystals to grow inside them. Cracked open, they often reveal beautiful minerals like this glittering amethyst (right). Geode crystals grow from mineral-rich fluids trapped in a bubble inside the rock. Most geode crystals are tiny, but larger ones can grow, and a few rare ones are classed as gemstones.

Sparkling amethysts inside a geode rock

71

EXPERT CONSULTANT: Paolo Forti **SEE ALSO:** Plate Tectonics, p.62–63; Volcanoes, p.64–65; Rocks & Minerals, p.70–71; Earth's Riches, p.74–75; Compounds, p.106–07; Solids, Liquids & Gases, p.110–11

GIANT CRYSTALS!

In 2006, scientists studied giant crystals inside a hot and steamy cave at the Naica Mine in Chihuahua, Mexico. Up to 39 feet (12 meters) long and 3 feet (1 meter) wide, the crystals are made from sulfide chemicals in water that seeps into the cave. The cave sits on top of a magma chamber—an underground pocket of molten rock. A constant temperature of around 131°F (55°C) allowed the crystals to form very slowly over the course of 250,000 years. Miners had drained the cave for exploration, and water has since been allowed to flood the cave once more.

The crystals are a form of gypsum called selenite

The air temperature in the drained cave was 122°F (50°C). It was so hot that scientists had to wear special suits in order to work in the cave, and no one stayed inside for more than 90 minutes

EARTH'S RICHES

Earth's rocks are our true buried treasure. They provide the materials to make steel for cars, rare minerals for computers and cell phones, and even most of the salt we put on our food. All elements are dispersed in Earth's crust, and this includes metals such as iron, aluminum, copper, and tin. Natural processes lead to concentrations of metals forming in special rocks called ores.

Blowing up hot!

We have to heat and process ores to extract metals from rock. Iron is a super-tough metal. We use it to make many things, from bridges to saucepans. To get the iron out of the rock, we have to heat the iron ore to a high temperature in a giant blast furnace that blasts air in to raise the temperature. This process is called smelting.

Mines

Getting iron ore out of the ground is difficult. We dig some of it out in huge pits called open-pit mines (below). Some of the world's biggest iron ore mines are in Australia, where the Rio Tinto mines alone produce more than 330 million tons (300 million tonnes) every year.

EXPERT CONSULTANT: Brendan Murphy **SEE ALSO:** Inside Earth, p.58–59; Rocks & Minerals, p.70–71; Giant Crystals!, p.72–73; Fossil Fuels, p.80–81; Metals, p.114–15; Plastics, p.118–19; Environmental Challenges, p.366–67

Commonly Mined Materials
LISTIFIED.

We extract billions of tons of materials from our planet every year.

1. Coal 8.7 billion tons (7.8 billion tonnes). Coal is the most mined material in the world. China is the biggest producer.

2. Iron ore 1.7 billion tons (1.5 billion tonnes). Iron is by far the most widely used metal. Much of it is made into steel.

3. Bauxite 414 million tons (370 million tonnes). Bauxite is an earthy ore rather than solid rock. It is the main ore used to make aluminum.

4. Phosphate rock 269 million tons (240 million tonnes). Phosphate is the source of the fertilizer phosphorus. Around half of it comes from China.

5. Gypsum 157 million tons (140 million tonnes). Gypsum is used in construction materials, such as wallboard and cement.

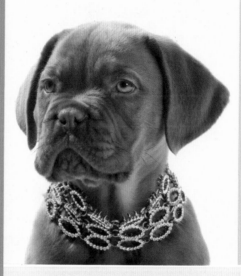

GAME CHANGER

HENRY BESSEMER
Inventor, lived 1813–98
UK

In 1856, English inventor Henry Bessemer created a furnace that could turn iron into steel, a strong substance that can be used to make a huge range of things, from skyscrapers to knives and forks. Inside the Bessemer converter, air is blown into molten iron to take away impurities. The operator then adds other elements, depending on what the steel is going to be used for.

Precious gems

Sparkling colored crystals are rare and valuable. If they are hard enough to cut and shape into jewels, they are called gemstones, or gems. Diamonds, rubies, emeralds, and sapphires are all gems. Gems form only in very unusual conditions, which is why they are so rare. Earth has around 2,000 different minerals, but fewer than 100 form gems, and only 50 of these are used in jewelry.

95%

5%

Recycle cans!

Aluminum is a useful metal because it is very light and doesn't rust. Drinks cans are made from it. Recycling old aluminum uses just 5 percent of the energy and emits only 5 percent of the greenhouse gases compared to mining aluminum. Recycling cans is vital!

The screen is aluminum oxide and silicon dioxide glass with an ultrathin layer of indium tin oxide

Elements such as gold, copper, and silver are used in the phone's wires

The circuitry contains the metals platinum and tungsten

Batteries contain the rare metal lithium cobalt oxide and carbon graphite

What's a cell phone made of?

Cell phones contain special, rare materials. Yet we throw away more than 100 million cell phones every year. Just 1 million of those discarded cell phones contains 17.5 tons (16 tonnes) of copper and 75 pounds (34 kg) of gold, not to mention valuable rare metals such as lithium and platinum. This is a lot of waste!

FOSSILS

Fossils are the remains or molds of ancient life that have been preserved in rock. Usually, only the hard bits of animals—shells, bones, and teeth—are preserved or imprinted as fossils. Some of the most common fossils are of shellfish. They are so common that some rocks are made almost entirely of shellfish. Fossils of large animals are much rarer.

FACTastic!

Fossil hunters have found fossilized dinosaur poop! They call fossilized lumps of poop coprolites. By looking at the shape and size of coprolites, as well as where they were found, experts can work out what kind of animal the droppings came from. Coprolites may also contain clues about an animal's diet.

HOW A FOSSIL IS MADE

Most animals never become fossils. Their bodies just rot away or get eaten. They are only fossilized if sediment covers their bodies quickly after their death.

1

Buried whole

A creature such as a dinosaur dies and is buried by sediment. Sometimes that sediment is carried by a river, and other times the animal dies in mud and sinks into it.

A dinosaur dies on the edge of a lake

Layers of muddy sediment lie at the bottom of the lake

2

Bones turn to rock

Even though the dinosaur's flesh rots away, the mud protects its bones. Over a long time, the skeleton gets buried deeper. Minerals in the groundwater fill empty spaces in the bones and replace the original minerals in the bones, turning them to rock.

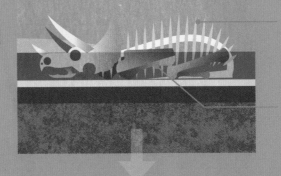

The flesh rots away, leaving only bones and teeth

The skeleton sinks into the mud

3

Hidden for millions of years

The minerals filling and replacing the bones retain the original shapes of the bones. Over millions of years, the mud turns to rock, encasing the fossil. When the rock is broken the fossil is revealed.

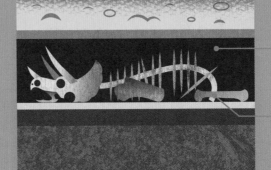

Sometimes, the weight of the mud flattens or breaks the skeleton

The fossil is as old as the rock in which it is buried. This is how scientists date fossils

---

EXPERT CONSULTANT: Nathan Smith **SEE ALSO:** Rocky Planets, p.28–29; Asteroids, p.34–35; Inside Earth, p.58–59; Rocks & Minerals, p.70–71; Finding Dinosaurs, p.78–79; Fossil Fuels, p.80–81; The Micro World, p.154–55

The mighty *Triceratops*

Triceratops was a plant-eating dinosaur that lived 68–66 million years ago. It was 29 feet (9 meters) long and had one of the biggest skulls of any animal that ever lived. The skull had three horns and a large frill up to 3 feet (1 meter) across. *Triceratops* may have used its horns to fend off attacks from predatory dinosaurs such as *Tyrannosaurus rex*, in combat, or to signal with other *Triceratops*.

The Oldest Fossil Types
LISTIFIED.

Fossils help us understand how life on Earth evolved. These are some of the oldest known types of fossils.

1. Plants The oldest plant fossils date back 1 billion years. They were found in China in 2019.

2. Shelled animals Brachiopods were among the first shelled animals. Their fossils, which look like clams, date back 550 million years.

3. Fish Rocks from about 530 million years ago contain fossils of the first known fish. They show long, thin, jawless creatures similar to eels.

4. Insects The 400-million-year-old Rhynie chert in Scotland, UK, contains the fossilized remains of tiny creatures similar to springtails. They are the oldest insects ever found.

5. Dinosaurs *Nyasasaurus*, a small, long-necked creature, may be the oldest dinosaur. Paleontologists (people who study fossils) found its remains in 243-million-years-old rocks in Tanzania. So far, fossil hunters have found about 800 types of dinosaurs in the fossil record, but there may be many more that they haven't yet found.

6. Mammals The oldest mammal fossil is from a tiny shrewlike creature called *Ambondro mahabo*. It was discovered in rocks in the Mahajanga Basin in northwestern Madagascar. The fossil is around 167 million years old.

NOTE from the expert!

Big feet

Dinosaurs have left footprints all over the world, like these in Torororo National Park, Bolivia. The footprints were made in soft mud that then baked hard in the sun before turning to rock. The footprints of sauropods, some of the biggest dinosaurs, can be 5.6 feet (1.7 meters) across. Experts cannot tell the species of a dinosaur from its footprint alone, but they can tell what group of dinosaurs it belonged to—and sometimes even how fast it was moving.

NATHAN SMITH
Paleontologist

Dr. Nathan Smith is a curator at the Natural History Museum of Los Angeles County. He uses many tools and techniques to answer questions about the history of life. He is especially interested in what made dinosaurs so successful.

66 *There's less time separating you and Tyrannosaurus (66 million years), than there is separating Tyrannosaurus and Allosaurus (84 million years)!* 99

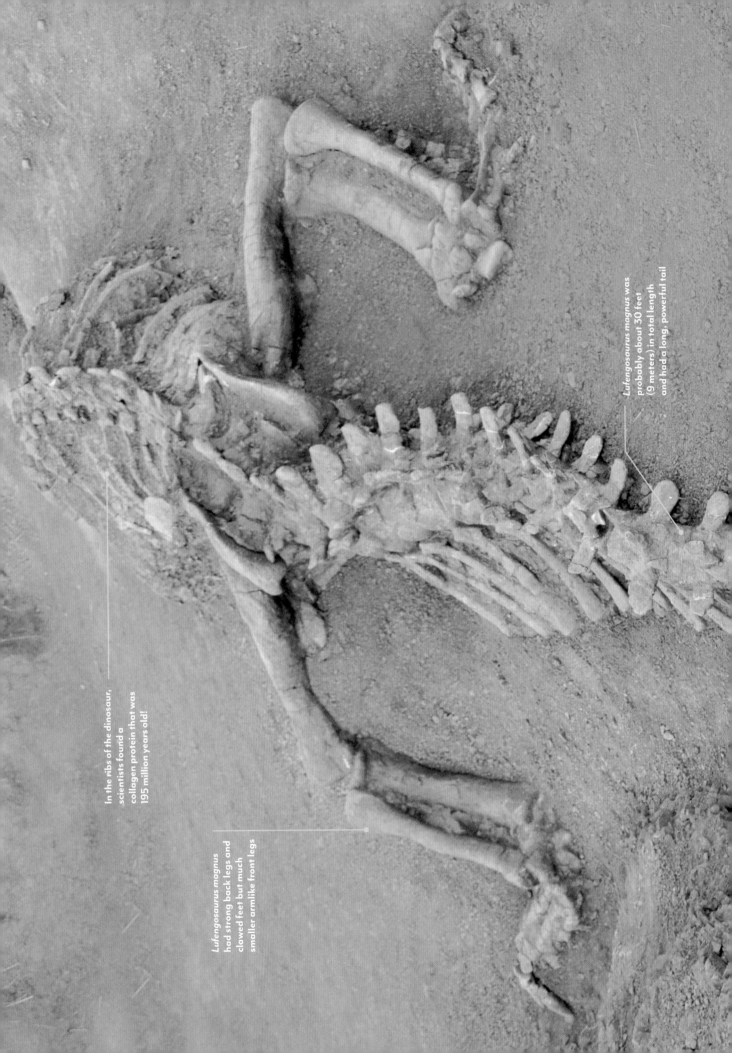

In the ribs of the dinosaur, scientists found a collagen protein that was 195 million years old!

Lufengosaurus magnus had strong back legs and clawed feet but much smaller armlike front legs

Lufengosaurus magnus was probably about 30 feet (9 meters) in total length and had a long, powerful tail

FINDING DINOSAURS

Workers building a road in China stumbled on this massive fossil of a plant-eating dinosaur in 2015. It represents a new species of *Lufengosaurus magnus* (large Lufeng lizard), named for Lufeng County in Yunnan Province where it was found. Minerals in groundwater turn dinosaur bones into fossils like these over millions of years. We are finding more dinosaurs today than ever before—around 50 new species a year. This is because new places are being excavated.

Lufengosaurus magnus was probably a plant-eater. Like a giraffe, it would have used its long neck to reach high leaves on trees

Lufengosaurus magnus

By looking at the fossil remains of *Lufengosaurus magnus*, paleontologists (scientists who study fossils) can work out what the dinosaur looked like, how much it would have weighed, and what it would have eaten. They know that it had a long tail and also a long neck and believe that it weighed about 1.9 tons (1.7 metric tonnes).

EXPERT CONSULTANT: Nathan Smith **SEE ALSO:** Mountains, p.68–69; Fossils, p.76–77; Animals, p.158–59; Ecology, p.162–63; The Taiga & Temperate Forests, p.166–67

FOSSIL FUELS

Fuels such as coal and oil are made of fossils—the squashed carbon-rich remains of plants or single-celled animals that lived millions of years ago. Most of the energy we use comes from burning fossil fuels taken from under Earth's crust. Fossil fuels have powered the world for hundreds of years, but using them harms the environment and one day, they will run out.

How fossil fuels formed

Coal formed from the remains of trees that grew in tropical swamps between about 360 and 300 million years ago, long before the dinosaurs. Meanwhile, tiny aquatic organisms were buried and changed by bacteria into a substance called kerogen, which Earth's heat turned into oil or gas. We call the time when fossil fuels formed the Carboniferous Period.

One of the most common plants in the Carboniferous Period was the scale tree

Plants remove carbon from the air

Types of fossil fuels

There are three major types of fossil fuels: coal, oil, and natural gas.

Coal
A lot of coal lies deep underground. We get it out by digging mines. Coal nearer the surface can be scooped out of huge pits. Coal is solid and very bulky. Trains or ships transport it to where it is needed.

Oil
Also known as petroleum, oil is a liquid. Oil workers dig wells with giant drills and then pump it out, though some oil shoots up on its own. Pipes take it to where it is needed; ships called tankers transport it around the world.

Natural gas
Sometimes found with coal or oil deposits, and sometimes on its own, natural gas is stored in tanks and transported by pipelines around the world.

EXPERT CONSULTANT: John P. Rafferty **SEE ALSO:** Plate Tectonics, p.62–63; Rocks & Minerals, p.70–71; Earth's Riches, p.74–75; Fossils, p.76–77; Chemistry of Life, p.120–21; Pressure, p.136–37; The Origin of Life, p.148–49; The Effects of Climate Change, p.372–73

What is fracking?

Shale rock contains tiny holes like a sponge, in which oil can become trapped. The only way to get the oil out is by fracking, another name for hydraulic fracturing. Water, sand, and chemicals are pumped into the rock at high pressure to force the oil or gas out. Fracking is widely used in North America, but it is controversial because it can poison freshwater sources and cause small earthquakes.

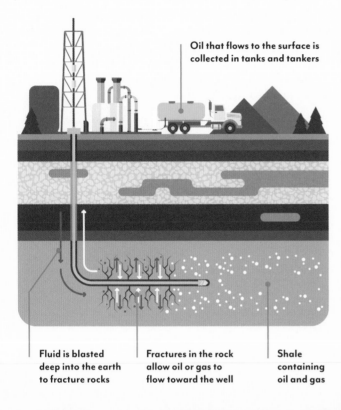

Oil that flows to the surface is collected in tanks and tankers

Fluid is blasted deep into the earth to fracture rocks

Fractures in the rock allow oil or gas to flow toward the well

Shale containing oil and gas

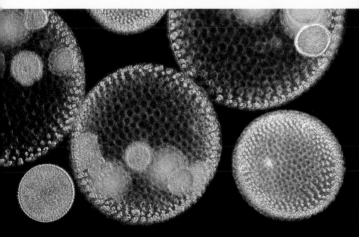

FACTastic!

A drop of oil is like a battery charged by sunlight. It was charged up millions of years ago when the Sun shone on land plants and tiny sea organisms called phytoplankton. These life-forms used the Sun's energy to change chemicals into food—a process called photosynthesis. When they died and turned into oil, the trapped energy became super concentrated, making oil a source of energy.

Consequences of Using Fossil Fuels
LISTIFIED.

Fossil fuels are an important source of power, but they can harm the environment in many ways.

1. Damaged landscapes Mining, extracting, processing, and transporting oil, gas, and coal deposits alter the land's surface and disrupt wildlife.

2. Less clean water Extracting fossil fuels can spoil drinkable freshwater sources such as groundwater (underground water), which accounts for 30 percent of the world's freshwater.

3. Health risks The extraction of fossil fuels often releases toxic chemicals into the air. These chemicals can cause illness, disease, and death.

4. Global warming Burning fossil fuels releases huge amounts of carbon dioxide. This increases global warming and adds to the climate crisis.

5. Toxic emissions Power stations that burn coal give off poisonous chemicals, including mercury and sulfur.

6. Smog Gasoline- and diesel-powered cars, trucks, and boats cough up poisonous carbon monoxide and nitrogen oxide, creating a combination of smoke and fog, called smog, on hot days.

7. Acid oceans Burning fossil fuels changes the sea's chemistry, making it much more acidic and destroying corals and other sea life.

KNOWN UNKNOWN

When will fossil fuels run out?

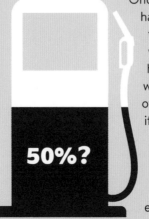

50%?

Once all fossil fuels underground have been dug up or drained, there will be no more. And we don't know how much we have left. Some experts think we have gobbled up nearly half of the planet's fossil fuels. Even if we keep using fossil fuels at the same rate as we do today, we could run out of oil and gas by the end of the 21st century and coal by the early part of the 22nd.

WATER WORLD

Oceans, lakes, and rivers cover three-quarters of Earth's surface. But you can't drink much of this. Roughly 97 percent is saltwater in the oceans, about 2 percent is glaciers and ice sheets, and half a percent is underground. Only a tiny fraction is surface freshwater that we can drink, yet human activities such as building, industry, and farming, are impacting this supply.

The water cycle

The tiny amount of freshwater in the world is constantly recycled by nature. Evaporation from oceans, lakes, and from the leaves of plants adds water vapor to the air. The vapor cools and condenses into tiny droplets of water that form clouds. These droplets join together, and when they get too big, water falls back to the ground as rain or snow.

FACTastic!

The water you're drinking now may have been drunk by dinosaurs and other prehistoric creatures! Water has been on Earth since the beginning of our planet—4.6 billion years ago. Much of our water is ancient water that has been used over and over again.

When the drops of water and the ice crystals grow too big, they fall to the ground as rain or snow

Rainwater and melted snow run off over the land into rivers and streams that carry it back to the sea

Frozen water can be stored as snow and glaciers

Clouds are made from drops of water and crystals of ice so tiny they float in the air

As water vapor rises, the air cools, and the vapor condenses into cloud droplets

In cities, where land is covered with buildings and roads, less rainwater is absorbed into the ground. People create wastewater in their homes and businesses

Water evaporates from the surface of leaves. This is called evapotranspiration

Some rainwater soaks into the ground. Plants absorb some of it through their roots

Some groundwater—the water from both rain or snow that is held in soil or rock crevices—filters into streams

EXPERT CONSULTANT: David M. Hannah **SEE ALSO:** Asteroids, p.34–35; Earth Is Born, p.52–53; Earth's Ice, p.84–85; The Atmosphere, p.86–87; Weather, p.88–89; Mega Storms, p.90–91; Climate, p.92–93; Natural Climate Change p.94–95

KNOWN UNKNOWN

Where did Earth's water come from?

Earth is unique among the rocky planets of our solar system because it has oceans of liquid water on its surface. Many scientists think that Earth's surface water came from icy asteroids, like this one, that crashed into our planet in its very early days. That's because the water in Earth's oceans and in asteroids has the same proportion of a kind of hydrogen called deuterium. But there's also water deep inside Earth that was locked in when Earth formed, so maybe much of our water was here right from the start.

The World's Longest Rivers
LISTIFIED.

Measuring rivers is tricky, as experts can disagree on where they start and end. This list includes river systems.

1. The Nile is about 4,132 miles (6,650 km) long and has two branches, the White Nile and the Blue Nile. It runs through northeast Africa into the Mediterranean Sea.

2. The Amazon flows for 4,000 miles (6,400 km) through South America and into the Atlantic. It carries more water than any other river.

3. The Yangtze is 3,915 miles (6,300 km) long and is the longest river to flow entirely within one country, China. It empties into the East China Sea.

4. The Mississippi-Missouri system is 3,710 miles (5,971 km) long and flows through 31 American states and two Canadian provinces. It empties into the Gulf of Mexico.

5. The Yenisey-Angara-Selenga system is 3,442 miles (5,540 km) long. It rises as the Selenga in Mongolia, flows into the Angara, on into the Yenisey, and north across Russia to the Arctic Ocean.

6. The Huang or Yellow River is 3,395 miles (5,464 km) long. It flows through China and empties into the East China Sea near Beijing.

7. The Ob-Irtysh river system is 3,362 miles (5,410 km) long. It rises in northwestern China and flows across Kazakhstan and Russia into the Kara Sea of the Arctic Ocean.

Why do rivers bend?

All rivers wind. As they get closer to the sea, they flow over wide soft plains of silt (soil and grains of rock). They form S-shaped loops called meanders, as they wear away the banks on the outside of bends, where the flow of water is faster, and deposit silt on the inside of bends, where the flow is slower.

NOTE from the expert!

DAVID M. HANNAH
Hydrologist

Professor David M. Hannah is fascinated by the water cycle: where does water come from, where does it go, and what happens to it along the way? He believes our biggest future challenge will be water security—having enough water for everyone on the planet.

66 We need to understand how people interact with the water cycle to manage the sustainability of this precious resource. 99

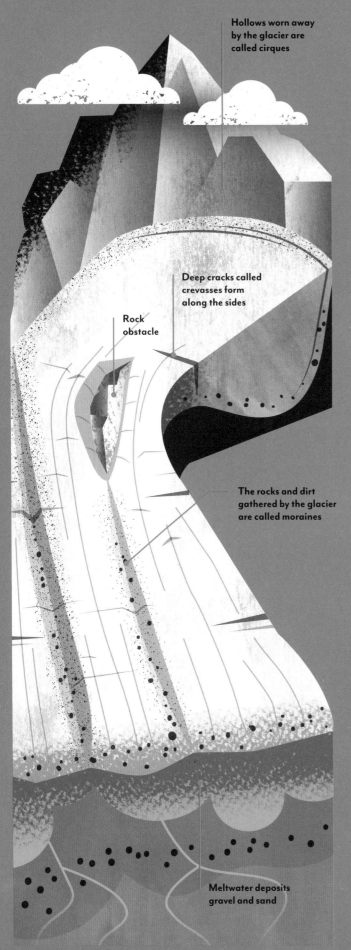

Hollows worn away
by the glacier are
called cirques

Deep cracks called
crevasses form
along the sides

Rock
obstacle

The rocks and dirt
gathered by the glacier
are called moraines

Meltwater deposits
gravel and sand

EARTH'S ICE

Two-thirds of the world's freshwater is frozen.
Some of this is snow, and some is locked up in
glaciers. But most of Earth's frozen water lies
in two vast ice sheets near the poles. It wasn't
always like this. At several points in Earth's
history, the planet had almost no ice. At other
times, Earth may have been a "snowball,"
entirely frozen over. During long periods of very
cold weather called ice ages, ice sheets covered
one-third of the land for thousands of years.
Right now, Earth's ice sheets are shrinking.

Valley glaciers

Glaciers form when snow piles up in mountain valleys and
compacts into solid ice. The ice eventually starts sliding
down the mountains as a glacier—a slow-moving river of
ice, moving about 10 inches (25 cm) a day. The immense
weight of ice in glaciers gives them the power to carve
out deep U-shaped valleys.

KNOWN UNKNOWN

Why are some icebergs green?

Most icebergs are bluish in color but some in the
Antarctic are green (called jade bergs because they look
like the stone jade). Scientists don't know why these
icebergs are green, but one theory is that yellowish-red
iron oxide minerals scraped up by glaciers mix with the
normal blue color of icebergs and make them green.

EXPERT CONSULTANT: Mark C. Serreze **SEE ALSO:** Earth's Surface, p.60–61; Water World, p.82–83; Weather, p.88–89; Climate, p.92–93;
Natural Climate Change, p.94–95; Ends of the Earth, p.184–85; Shrinking Ice, p.186–87

Ice sheets

Areas of ice spreading over 20,000 square miles (50,000 sq. km) or more are called ice sheets. They form where heavy snow falls in winter and does not melt in summer. The two big ice sheets that cover Greenland and Antarctica hold much of the world's freshwater. If the Antarctic ice sheet melted, the level of the world's oceans would rise by about 200 feet (60 meters), transforming the face of the planet.

Vast chunks of ice can break off the edges of ice sheets, making icebergs; this is called calving

Ice sheets look blue if the ice is dense. Ice sheets that look white are packed with air bubbles

Sea ice

The North Pole is in the middle of the Arctic Ocean rather than on land like the South Pole. The Arctic Ocean is covered in floating ice, the outer edges of which grow in winter and melt in summer. Global warming has caused sea ice to shrink dramatically, and 95 percent of old ice—ice that has lasted more than four years—has melted. Old ice is thick and glues the rest of the ice together. Without it, the ice breaks up and melts even more.

Seals need ice to rest, give birth, and nurse their pups

THE ATMOSPHERE

Earth is wrapped in a thick blanket of invisible gases called the atmosphere. Without the atmosphere, life on Earth would not be possible. It provides the air we breathe and the water we drink. It holds the Sun's warmth in, and it protects Earth from the Sun's harmful rays and from meteoroids. The atmosphere has five different layers, each with its own gas density and temperatures. The atmosphere is 78 percent nitrogen and 21 percent oxygen. All of the other gases make up only 1 percent.

EXOSPHERE 372–6,200 MILES (600–10,000 KM) ABOVE EARTH'S SURFACE

THERMOSPHERE 53–372 MILES (85–600 KM) ABOVE EARTH'S SURFACE

MESOSPHERE 31–53 MILES (50–85 KM) ABOVE EARTH'S SURFACE

STRATOSPHERE 9–31 MILES (14.5–50 KM) ABOVE EARTH'S SURFACE

TROPOSPHERE EXTENDS 5–9 MILES (8–14.5 KM) ABOVE EARTH'S SURFACE

Meteors
These are lumps of rock that start to glow as soon as they impact Earth's atmosphere; most burn up in the mesosphere

Aurora
When high-energy particles from the Sun crash into the gases of the thermosphere, polar skies fill with colored lights

Weather
Earth's weather occurs in the troposphere, with the most extreme tropical storm clouds reaching the edge of the stratosphere

Noctilucent clouds
These "night-shining" clouds of ice can sometimes be seen in the mesosphere just after the Sun goes down in summer

EXPERT CONSULTANT: Paul Ullrich **SEE ALSO:** Our Solar System, p.22–23; Rockets, p.38–39; Artificial Satellites, p.40–41; Crewed Spacecraft, p.42–43; Water World, p.82–83; Weather, p.88–89; Climate, p.92–93; Natural Climate Change, p.94–95

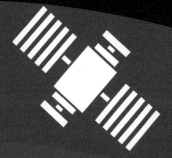

Geosynchronous satellites
For TV and weather
forecasting, these stay in
the same position above
Earth, orbiting at a height of
22,500 miles (36,000 km)

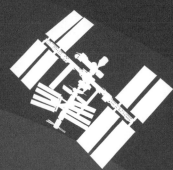

ISS
The International Space
Station, where astronauts live
and work, orbits Earth in the
thermosphere, at a height of
250 miles (400 km)

Spacecraft
These can orbit Earth in
a Low Earth Orbit (LEO),
which is between 100
and 1,000 miles (160 and
1,600 km) above the ground

Skydiver
In the US, Alan Eustace
set the world record for the
longest free fall jump in
2014 when he leapt from
135,890 feet (41.4 km)

Passenger planes
To avoid bumpy turbulence
caused by air currents in
the lower atmosphere,
passenger planes fly up to
7 miles (11 km) high

High-altitude balloons
These monitor the weather
from heights of 23 miles
(37 km). In 2002, BU60-1
reached a record altitude of
33 miles (53 km)

Fighter jets
In 1977, a Soviet MIG-25M,
piloted by Aleksandr
Fedotov, reached 23.4 miles
(37.7 km) high

WEATHER

The heat of the Sun causes frozen and liquid water on Earth to evaporate. This provides the lowest layer of Earth's atmosphere with moisture. The moisture gives us clouds and rain, and the movement of the air produces winds. Together, day-to-day changes in temperature, air pressure, wind, and moisture in the lower atmosphere produce every kind of weather.

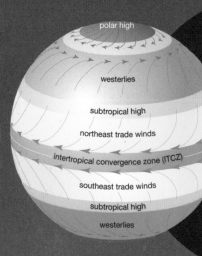

polar high
westerlies
subtropical high
northeast trade winds
intertropical convergence zone (ITCZ)
southeast trade winds
subtropical high
westerlies

Global winds

Wind mostly blows in a typical, or "prevailing," direction. There are three broad prevailing wind zones on either side of the equator: easterlies (coming from the east) in polar regions, westerlies (from the west) in temperate zones, and easterlies again in the tropics.

Cirrus
High, wispy clouds made of ice crystals

Cirrocumulus
Gusty air mixes supercooled water in with ice crystals and piles cirrus clouds into ripples like fish scales

Cirrostratus
Rising air spreads out in a vast, thin veil of ice crystals that can make a halo around the Sun

Cumulonimbus
These vast thunderclouds tower so high they are topped by icy cirrus clouds and bring thunder, lightning, and heavy rain

5 MILES (8 KM) ABOVE THE GROUND

Altocumulus
These small clouds form where the wind stirs the air into waves near mountains

Altostratus
These form when cirrostratus clouds sink, and the ice mixes with water drops

Stratocumulus
These white clumps form sometimes when stratus clouds break up

Nimbostratus
These dark rain clouds form when altostratus clouds thicken

Stratus
These low-lying clouds form when breezes raise moist air over colder land

Cumulus
These fluffy clouds pile up where sunshine warms the ground and causes puffs of warm air to rise into the sky

What are clouds made of?

3 MILES (4.8 KM) ABOVE THE GROUND

While most clouds are made of tiny water droplets, some are made of ice crystals, and others are a mixture of both. There are three main types. Cirrus are wispy clouds of ice crystals. Cumulus are fluffy, heaped clouds that pile up as warm air rises. They can be made of ice crystals, water, or a mixture of both. Stratus—flat, low clouds that cover the sky in a blanket of white or gray—can also be made of both water and ice crystals.

1 MILE (1.6 KM) ABOVE THE GROUND

EXPERT CONSULTANT: Paul Ullrich **SEE ALSO:** Earth in Space, p.54–55; Water World, p.82–83; The Atmosphere, p.86–87; Mega Storms, p.90–91; Solids, Liquids & Gases, 110–11; Ecology, p.162–63; The Open Ocean, 180–81

FACTastic!

An average-sized cumulus cloud weighs the same as 100 elephants! Scientists worked out that there is 0.5 gram of water in every cubic meter of cloud. The size of an average cloud is about a billion cubic meters. So that means it weighs 1.1 million pounds (0.5 million kg).

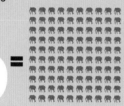

It's raining!

Rain starts when the droplets or ice crystals in clouds grow so big and heavy they can no longer float on the air. In warm tropical clouds, droplets merge as they crowd together, then fall as raindrops. Elsewhere, in icy clouds, ice crystals grow bit by bit, then melt into rain as they fall. Snow is simply small ice crystals that don't melt before they hit the ground.

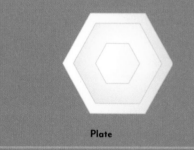
Plate

Column

Capped column

Star   Needle

Dendrite

Irregular

Snowflakes

Every snowflake has its own unique shape, which we can see under a microscope. But most snowflakes have six points or six sides and form one of seven basic shapes: plates, columns, columns capped with plates, stars, needles, dendrites (with branches), and irregular (these are typically damaged snowflakes). The shape a snowflake takes depends on the temperature and the amount of moisture in the cloud.

How to read a weather map

Meteorologists (scientists who study weather and climate) forecast the weather by monitoring conditions such as temperature, wind, pressure, humidity, and rainfall. By comparing this information with past patterns and using computers to simulate the atmosphere, they can tell what the weather is likely to be. They use lines and symbols on weather maps to indicate the kind of precipitation (such as rain or snow), the amount of cloud, and the wind strength and direction.

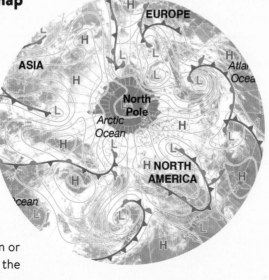

Cold front
Cold air is replacing warm air

Warm front
Warm air is replacing cold air

Occluded front
A cold front is overtaking a warm front

Stationary front
Warm and cold fronts are pushing against each other

H   High-pressure center
An area of cool dry air, leading to clear skies

L   Low-pressure center
An area of warm moist air, leading to cloudy skies

Isobars
The closer these are to each other, the stronger the winds

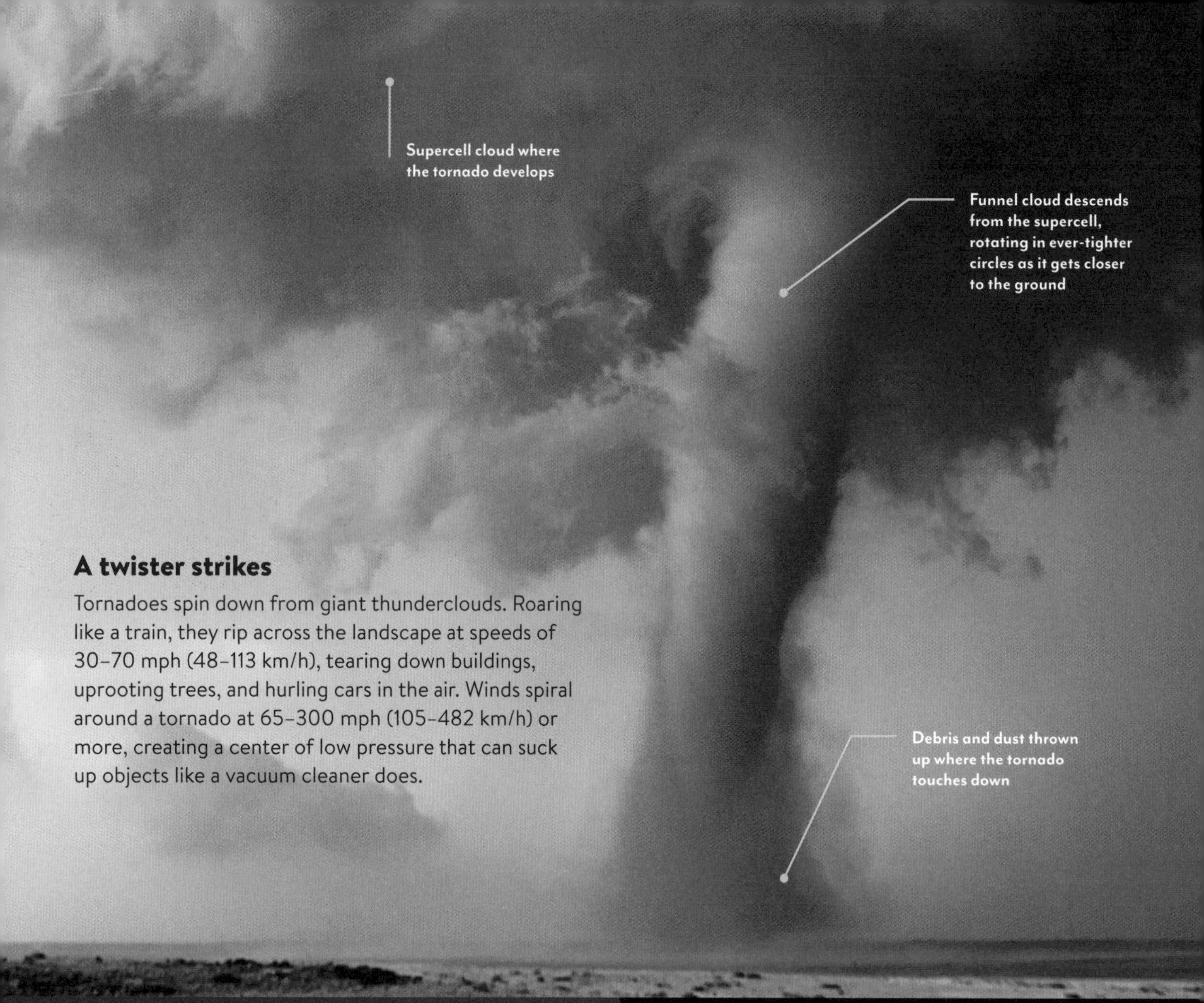
Supercell cloud where the tornado develops
Funnel cloud descends from the supercell, rotating in ever-tighter circles as it gets closer to the ground
Debris and dust thrown up where the tornado touches down

A twister strikes

Tornadoes spin down from giant thunderclouds. Roaring like a train, they rip across the landscape at speeds of 30–70 mph (48–113 km/h), tearing down buildings, uprooting trees, and hurling cars in the air. Winds spiral around a tornado at 65–300 mph (105–482 km/h) or more, creating a center of low pressure that can suck up objects like a vacuum cleaner does.

MEGA STORMS

Hurricanes are huge circular storms hundreds of miles wide that blow into the Gulf of Mexico from the Atlantic, bringing fierce winds, heavy rain, and huge seas. Typhoon and cyclone are the names hurricanes go by in the Indian and Pacific oceans. Tornadoes are different, racing across land for a few miles before dying out.

Hurricane on the way

Weather forecasters use satellites to track hurricanes. Hurricanes begin over the ocean near the equator, sweep westward, then swing away to the northeast. In the Northern Hemisphere, they rotate counterclockwise. In the Southern Hemisphere, they spin clockwise.

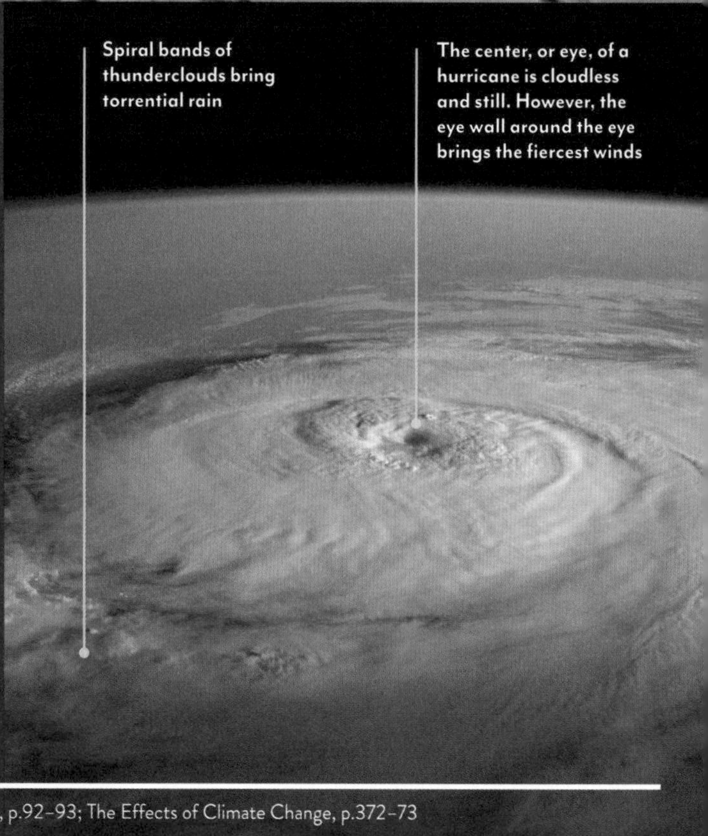
Spiral bands of thunderclouds bring torrential rain
The center, or eye, of a hurricane is cloudless and still. However, the eye wall around the eye brings the fiercest winds

EXPERT CONSULTANT: Paul Ullrich **SEE ALSO:** Weather, p.88–89; Climate, p.92–93; The Effects of Climate Change, p.372–73

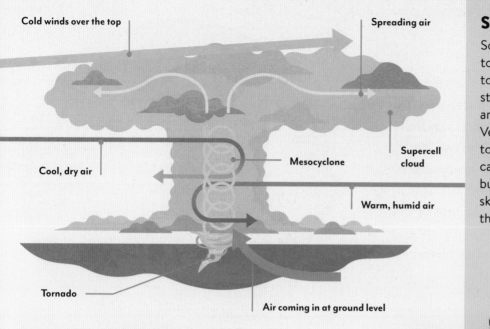

Cold winds over the top

Spreading air

Cool, dry air

Mesocyclone

Supercell cloud

Warm, humid air

Tornado

Air coming in at ground level

How a tornado starts

Most tornadoes form when a strong updraft concentrates into a swirling column of air 6–12 miles (10–20 km) across. This column, called a mesocyclone, rotates weakly at first but gets stronger as inflowing air stretches it upward. It becomes a tornado when its spinning core hits the ground.

Storm chaser

Some people are so fascinated by tornadoes that they risk their lives to see them up close. American storm chaser Sean Casey built two armor-plated Tornado Intercept Vehicles (TIVs) to film inside a tornado for IMAX. The TIV has a camera turret, weather sensors, bulletproof windows, and metal skirts to protect the underside of the vehicle against flying debris.

FACTastic!

A tornado in Dallas, Texas, in 2012 tossed 18-wheel trucks into the air. The powerful tornado swept up the 30-to 40- ton trucks as though they were toys.

Measuring a hurricane's strength

The strength of a hurricane is graded from 1–5 on the Saffir-Simpson scale, based on a hurricane's sustained wind speed. The scale estimates damage to buildings and trees. As hurricanes get their energy from water vapor rising from the sea, they start to lose their strength once they hit land.

1. 74–95 mph (119–153 km/h) Mild damage: mobile homes moved, signs blown over, branches broken.

2. 96–110 mph (154–177 km/h) Moderate damage: mobile homes turned over, roofs lifted.

3. 111–129mph (178–208 km/h) Extensive damage: small buildings wrecked, trees uprooted.

4. 130–156 mph (209–251 km/h) Extreme damage: most trees blown down, widespread structural damage to all buildings.

5. Over 157 mph (252 km/h) Catastrophic damage: most buildings destroyed, roads wrecked.

The World's Worst Tropical Cyclones
LISTIFIED.

Tropical storms can be extremely powerful. Some of them bring deadly rains and winds.

DEADLIEST
The Bhola cyclone
Location: East Pakistan, now Bangladesh
Date: November 1970
Cost in lives: killed up to 500,000 people

STRONGEST WIND GUSTS
Cyclone Olivia
Location: Barrow Island, Western Australia
Date: April 1996
Wind speed: 253 mph (408 km/h)

WETTEST
Cyclone Hyacinthe
Location: Réunion Island, Indian Ocean
Date: January 1980
Total rain: 239.5 inches (6,083 mm)

CLIMATE

Every part of the world has its own climate, though many places share climates that are similar. Climate is not the same as weather. Weather can change from day to day, and extreme weather days happen everywhere. But climate is weather averaged out over long time periods—how warm or cold, wet or dry it is most of the time. Climate also describes how frequently a place will experience abnormal or extreme weather.

The role of oceans

The oceans provide the moisture that determines weather. They also stave off climate change by absorbing heat and carbon dioxide from the atmosphere. But the oceans are running out of room to store heat; this means the atmosphere will store more heat and the world's climates could grow more extreme and stormier.

Earth's climate zones

The five main types of climate are shown on this map. The warmest, tropical climates are on the equator, where the Sun is strong. North and south of this region are subtropical (warm and wet) climates. The coldest climates are at the poles, where the Sun is weak. They include the treeless, frozen tundra. Temperate zones are areas that have moderate, rather than extreme, temperatures. Highland climates have a great range of temperature between day and night.

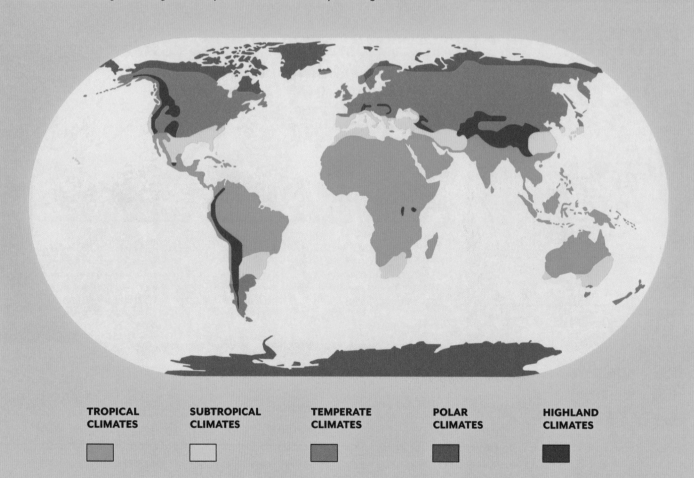

TROPICAL CLIMATES	SUBTROPICAL CLIMATES	TEMPERATE CLIMATES	POLAR CLIMATES	HIGHLAND CLIMATES

EXPERT CONSULTANT: Paul Ullrich **SEE ALSO:** The Sun, p.24–25; Artificial Satellites, p.40–41; The Atmosphere, p.86–87; Weather, p.88–89; Mega Storms, p.90–91; Natural Climate Change, p.94–95; Ecology, p.162–63; Shrinking Ice, p.186–87; Stopping Climate Change, p.374–75

The greenhouse effect

Up in the air, carbon dioxide and other gases gather in a layer that acts like glass in a greenhouse. Like the glass, these gases let light pass through, and they slow the escape of heat back into space. This keeps the world warm. This greenhouse effect happens naturally, but humans have boosted it to harmful levels by burning coal and oil and by raising livestock such as cattle, which produce a gas called methane.

Sunlight hitting Earth is a mix of light rays; some bounce back into space

Greenhouse gases

Sun

Greenhouse gases slow the radiation of heat back into space, trapping much of the warmth they provide in the atmosphere

The ground soaks up some of the Sun's energy, then releases it again as heat

Factors that influence climate

We sort climates according to the average monthly temperature and rainfall of a region. But because climates are so varied, experts often argue about where a particular climate begins and ends. Sometimes areas that are just a short distance apart experience different climates. We call these microclimates. Many different factors can produce microclimates. Hills that block rainy winds can create one, as can buildings that trap heat. These are some of the natural factors that affect climate.

When sunlight hits Earth at a low angle, it spreads over a wider area, and so is weaker than when the Sun is directly overhead, as at the equator.

Clouds block off and reflect sunlight, making it cooler. But they also stop Earth from cooling, reducing variations in temperature.

In temperate regions, prevailing, rain-bearing westerly winds can drop slightly more rain on the western sides of continents.

Mountain ranges can cause rain because they get in the way of rain clouds, forcing them to drop their moisture in order to rise up the slope and over the peak.

Oceans provide moisture, making coastal climates wetter. They also take longer to heat up and cool down than land. This helps makes climates less extreme.

Trees add moisture to the air and shade the ground, helping to moderate climate. They absorb carbon dioxide, reducing the strength of the greenhouse effect.

FACTastic!

Without Earth's natural greenhouse, our whole planet would be like Antarctica—the coldest place on Earth. Temperatures would drop by around 59°F (33°C), and the world would be covered in ice. Life as we know it would not be able to survive.

NATURAL CLIMATE CHANGE

The world's climate never stays the same for very long. All through Earth's history, there have been periods when the weather has been much colder, or hotter, or wetter, or drier, than it is now. Over long time periods, these shifts can be due to little wobbles in Earth's tilt or changes in its orbit. Such changes can swing Earth closer to the Sun or farther away. But the slow movement of land masses, the shrinking of ice sheets, or the activity of living things have affected climate, too.

Snowball Earth

Around 650 million years ago, Earth was so chilly it may have been entirely encased in ice or slush. We call this time Snowball Earth. It was a catastrophe for life, but its end may have led to the evolution of oxygen-breathing animals, and the expansion of life known as the Cambrian explosion.

Mega-desert

About 250 million years ago, all the world's continents were locked together in one giant landmass. The climate was super hot, and the heart of the landmass became a vast sandy desert. Many kinds of animals died out altogether in this scorching world. The remnants of the mega-desert can still be seen in the massive sandstone rocks of Monument Valley in Arizona and Utah in the US.

EXPERT CONSULTANT: Paul Ullrich **SEE ALSO:** Our Solar System, p.22–23; The Sun, p.24–25; Plate Tectonics, p.62–63; Water World, p.82–83;

ASIA

NORTH AMERICA

Bering Land Bridge allowed animals and people to cross from Asia to North America

Changing sea levels

Oceans rise and fall with changing climates. Asia and North America were once connected by land, known as the Bering Land Bridge. This area was flooded when the gigantic ice sheets in Europe and North America melted after the last Ice Age 11,700 years ago, cutting off the land route between continents.

Clues to past climates

Experts who look for clues to Earth's past climates are called paleoclimatologists. They examine valleys scarred by Ice Age glaciers, for example. They also look at ice cores, tree rings, and ancient coral. It is through such evidence that we can understand what the climate was like hundreds of thousands—even millions—of years ago.

Ice cores extracted by drilling down through polar ice that has built up over a long time reveal past changes in conditions.

Differences in the width and pattern of tree rings show the changing weather conditions during a tree's life.

Patterns in ancient coral skeletons can reveal rainfall and temperatures during a single growing season many years ago.

KNOWN UNKNOWN

Did climate change cause the extinction of the megafauna?

Tens of thousands of years ago, many more big animals, or megafauna, roamed Earth. There were wolf-sized otters, rhinoceros-like animals that were twice as big as elephants, and a hefty relative of the giraffe called *Sivatherium giganteum* (above). So what happened to them? Human hunters may have killed off some. But these animals may also have been the victims of climate change, because they could not adapt to rapid changes in their habitats.

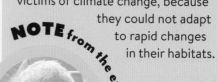

NOTE from the expert!

PAUL ULLRICH
Climate scientist

Professor Paul Ullrich became interested in climate science after designing a space adventure video game and thinking about the atmospheres of different planets. This led him to study planetary atmospheres, and in particular, the atmosphere of Earth.

" *The big unsolved problem in climate science is how can we ensure the long-term survival of our species.* "

95

ASK THE EXPERTS!

PAOLO FORTI
Geomorphologist

What sparked your interest in science?
From an early age, I was interested in any kind of natural phenomena. From the flutter of a butterfly to the sound made by a sea wave—I always wanted to understand each one.

What was your most surprising experience at work?
The most unexpected event I experienced was at the Cave of Crystals in Naica, Mexico. At that time, I was sure it was impossible for giant crystals like these to develop in nature. When I entered the cave, I was astonished by what I saw. I sat down in the center of the cave, not considering the deadly hot temperature, just looking at the giant, perfectly transparent crystals. I stayed there until my colleagues hauled me out.

What do you find exciting about your field?
Caves are the single part of the Earth that is still the most unexplored. My life as a scientific caver was fantastic because I had the privilege to make astonishing explorations in places where no other human being had been before me.

ERIK KLEMETTI
Volcanologist

What do you want to discover most?
I want to know about all the events that happen under a volcano before an eruption, and how rapidly things can change. Figuring this out can help us do a better job getting people to safety before volcanoes erupt. We can't go underground and watch it happen, so we need to infer what's going on by looking at clues from crystals erupted in lava.

What do you love about your work?
The research Earth scientists do can really help us be better prepared for problems like climate change or natural disasters. The study of Earth builds an appreciation for just how long our planet has been around, and the fact that we need to be careful with how we use Earth's natural resources.

MARK C. SERREZE
Climate scientist

What is your special area of research?
I study climate change—this is one of the biggest challenges facing our society.

What misadventures have you experienced in your research?
I've had plenty. Many of them happened while I was working in the Arctic. I've driven snowmobiles into ice cold water that reached my chest, gotten frostbite on my ears and nose, and gotten lost in whiteouts.

What do you like about science?
When you begin to understand science, you start to see the world in new ways that you never thought possible. You expand your mind and become aware of how our planet works, and you understand that we all have a responsibility to help make the world a better place.

Earth
THE QUIZ

1) **How old is Planet Earth?**
   a. 13.8 billion years old
   b. 4.6 billion years old
   c. 4,004 years old
   d. 2,020 years old

2) **What name did scientists give to the planet that smashed into the early Earth and may have given our planet its tilt?**
   a. Gaea
   b. Pangea
   c. Titan
   d. Theia

3) **What name do scientists use to describe the first microbe on Earth?**
   a. ADAM
   b. EVE
   c. LUCA
   d. BORIS

4) **Earth's magnetic field protects the planet from:**
   a. Comets
   b. Meteorites
   c. Acid rain
   d. Solar wind

5) **Which element is most common inside Earth's core?**
   a. Oxygen
   b. Iron
   c. Silicon
   d. Silver

6) **Three-quarters of Earth's volcanoes exist in a chain surrounding which ocean?**
   a. Pacific
   b. Atlantic
   c. Indian
   d. Arctic

7) **About how many earthquakes does Earth experience each year?**
   a. 500
   b. 5,000
   c. 50,000
   d. 500,000

8) ***Nyasasaurus* is famous for being:**
   a. The largest dinosaur
   b. The smallest dinosaur
   c. The oldest dinosaur
   d. The newest dinosaur

9) **Who holds the world record for the longest ever free-fall jump through the atmosphere?**
   a. Felix Baumgartner
   b. Alan Eustace
   c. Eddie the Eagle
   d. Evel Knievel

10) **If the Antarctic ice sheet completely melted, the sea would rise by how much?**
   a. 15 feet (5 meters)
   b. 33 feet (10 meters)
   c. 66 feet (20 meters)
   d. 200 feet (61 meters)

11) **What is the scientific name for fluffy white clouds?**
   a. Cumulus
   b. Cirrus
   c. Stratus
   d. Fluffus

12) **Which of these is NOT a type of mountain?**
   a. Fold mountain
   b. Block mountain
   c. Dome mountain
   d. Blob mountain

13) **The strength of a Category 5 hurricane is more than:**
   a. 88 mph (142 km/h)
   b. 124 mph (200 km/h)
   c. 135 mph (217 km/h)
   d. 157 mph (252 km/h)

14) **About 650 million years ago Earth was covered with ice. This period in our planet's history is known as:**
   a. Snowball Earth
   b. Icicle Earth
   c. Cryogenic Earth
   d. Deep-freeze Earth

ANSWERS: 1) b, 2) d, 3) c, 4) d, 5) b, 6) a, 7) c, 8) c, 9) b, 10) d, 11) a, 12) d, 13) d, 14) a

This lump of iron pyrite is also known as "fool's gold" because sometimes it is mistaken for real gold. Actually, it is formed of iron sulfite—which, even though it glimmers and looks like gold, is almost worthless. Famously, in 1577, a pirate called Martin Frobisher loaded up his ship with 200 tons of what he thought was mineral treasure and sailed from Canada to England. Sadly for him, it contained worthless pyrite, and no gold at all!

CHAPTER 3
MATTER

It's amazing to think that all the gold in the world (and all other metals heavier than iron) were originally forged in the collision of stars before our Sun shone or Earth was formed. So, some of the stuff around us is billions of years old. But plastics were invented only about 150 years ago by a guy who was looking for a cheaper way to play billiards. That's what it's like learning about matter. The stories never end.

The world around us (and we ourselves) are a constantly moving mix of solids, liquids, and gases. All matter is made of molecules, which are made of atoms, which in turn are made of subatomic particles. Some of the smallest of those have very weird names, such as top, down, strange, and charm. Over the last 200 years, more than 14 million different compounds have been described—with millions more new discoveries being made each year. And every compound, from salt to cement, has its own unique characteristics, many of which have defined and changed the world we live in. All of this stuff transforms, too. It can burn or freeze or radioactively decay or be stretched or squashed or ... well, you'll see. Welcome to the world of matter.

Everything of substance in the Universe, from air and water to plants and animals, is made from lots of tiny atoms, each of which is the smallest possible form of a chemical element. There are about 7 million billion trillion atoms in the human body. Atoms are made of the subatomic particles protons, neutrons, and electrons. Protons and neutrons, in turn, are made of quarks and gluons.

Electrically charged

Protons and electrons have an electric charge. Because protons have a positive electric charge (+) and electrons have a negative electric charge (-), they attract each other. This makes the parts of the atom stick together.

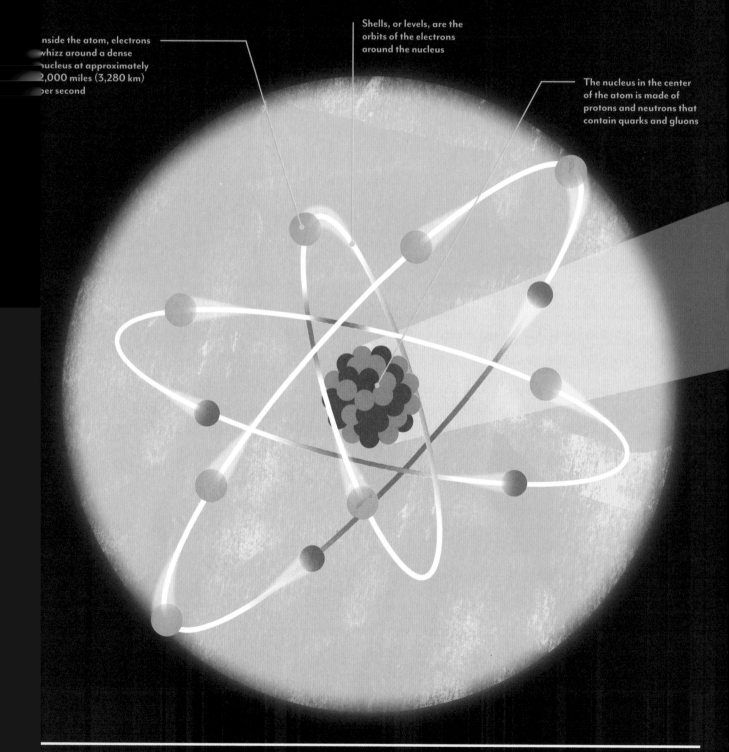

Inside the atom, electrons whizz around a dense nucleus at approximately 2,000 miles (3,280 km) per second

Shells, or levels, are the orbits of the electrons around the nucleus

The nucleus in the center of the atom is made of protons and neutrons that contain quarks and gluons

EXPERT CONSULTANT: Cristina Lazzeroni **SEE ALSO:** The Big Bang, p.4–5; The Sun, p.24–25; Elements, p.102–03; Radioactivity, p.104–05;

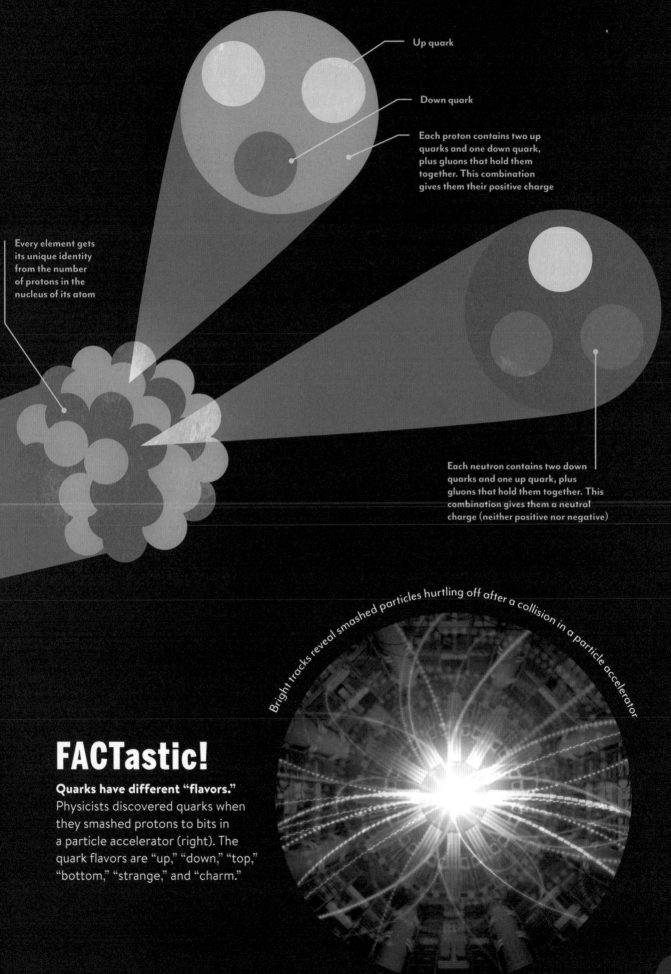

Up quark

Down quark

Each proton contains two up quarks and one down quark, plus gluons that hold them together. This combination gives them their positive charge

Every element gets its unique identity from the number of protons in the nucleus of its atom

Each neutron contains two down quarks and one up quark, plus gluons that hold them together. This combination gives them a neutral charge (neither positive nor negative)

Bright tracks reveal smashed particles hurtling off after a collision in a particle accelerator

FACTastic!

Quarks have different "flavors."
Physicists discovered quarks when they smashed protons to bits in a particle accelerator (right). The quark flavors are "up," "down," "top," "bottom," "strange," and "charm."

What is matter?

Matter is made up of atoms—small particles of elements. At the beginning of the Universe, the only elements were hydrogen and helium, plus a tiny amount of lithium. The other elements have emerged over time through nuclear or atomic fusion. The pressure inside a star was enough to create nitrogen (the main element in air). But it took the incredible might of colliding stars and supernovae— the explosion of giant stars (pictured here)—to forge heavy metals such as gold and uranium.

ELEMENTS

Elements are the Universe's most basic substances—the substances from which all things are made. They cannot be broken down into any other substance. Incredibly, there are just 118 elements. Only 94 of them occur naturally on Earth, including gold, hydrogen, and oxygen. Scientists created the other 24 elements through nuclear fusion in laboratories. The periodic table lists and groups all the known chemical elements.

FACTastic!

A chemist once estimated that the amount of phosphorus in a human body would make 2,200 matches. Dr. Charles Henry Maye also calculated that there was enough iron in the body to make a medium-sized nail.

EXPERT CONSULTANT: A. Jean-Luc Ayitou **SEE ALSO:** The Atom, p.100–01; Compounds, p.106–07; Combustion, p.108–09; Solids, Liquids & Gases, p.110–11; Plasma, p.112–13; Metals, p.114–15; Nonmetals, p.116–17; Plastics, p.118–19; Chemistry of Life, p.120–21

Periodic Table

Legend:
- Alkali metals
- Alkaline-earth metals
- Transition metals
- Other metals
- Other nonmetals
- Halogens
- Noble gases
- Rare-earth elements (21, 39, 57–71) and lanthanoid elements (57–71 only)
- Actinoid elements

Period / Group	1*	2	3	4	5	6	7	8	9	10	11	12	13	14	15	16	17	18
1	1 H																	2 He
2	3 Li	4 Be											5 B	6 C	7 N	8 O	9 F	10 Ne
3	11 Na	12 Mg											13 Al	14 Si	15 P	16 S	17 Cl	18 Ar
4	19 K	20 Ca	21 Sc	22 Ti	23 V	24 Cr	25 Mn	26 Fe	27 Co	28 Ni	29 Cu	30 Zn	31 Ga	32 Ge	33 As	34 Se	35 Br	36 Kr
5	37 Rb	38 Sr	39 Y	40 Zr	41 Nb	42 Mo	43 Tc	44 Ru	45 Rh	46 Pd	47 Ag	48 Cd	49 In	50 Sn	51 Sb	52 Te	53 I	54 Xe
6	55 Cs	56 Ba	57 La	72 Hf	73 Ta	74 W	75 Re	76 Os	77 Ir	78 Pt	79 Au	80 Hg	81 Tl	82 Pb	83 Bi	84 Po	85 At	86 Rn
7	87 Fr	88 Ra	89 Ac	104 Rf	105 Db	106 Sg	107 Bh	108 Hs	109 Mt	110 Ds	111 Rg	112 Cn	113 Nh	114 Fl	115 Mc	116 Lv	117 Ts	118 Og

Lanthanoid series 6

58 Ce	59 Pr	60 Nd	61 Pm	62 Sm	63 Eu	64 Gd	65 Tb	66 Dy	67 Ho	68 Er	69 Tm	70 Yb	71 Lu

Actinoid series 7

90 Th	91 Pa	92 U	93 Np	94 Pu	95 Am	96 Cm	97 Bk	98 Cf	99 Es	100 Fm	101 Md	102 No	103 Lr

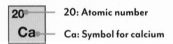

20: Atomic number
Ca: Symbol for calcium

The periodic table

The 118 elements are neatly organized in a chart called the periodic table. They are arranged in rows, called periods, in order of their atomic number (the number of protons in the atom). Atomic number 1, hydrogen (H), is top left; number 118, oganesson (Og), is bottom right. The columns in the table are called groups. Each element has its own name and abbreviation (or symbol)—either one or two letters. So, C is for carbon and Ni is for nickel. Some symbols are abbreviated from Latin. For example, Au comes from the Latin word "aurum" for gold.

DMITRI MENDELEEV

Chemist, lived 1834–1907
Russia

It was Russian chemist Dmitri Mendeleev who, in 1869, created the periodic table. He did so by arranging the elements in seven rows, or periods, according to their atomic weight or number. It was a stroke of genius, for the table revealed a hidden pattern. It turned out that the elements in the same place in each row share similar properties. We now know this is due to the structure of their atoms.

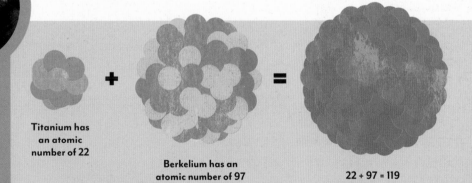

Titanium has an atomic number of 22

Berkelium has an atomic number of 97

22 + 97 = 119

Making new elements

To make new elements, scientists smash atoms together at incredible speeds in a machine called a particle accelerator. Scientists are trying to make element 119 by hurtling titanium and berkelium at one another (above). Even if they do make element 119, it will last only a split second before it breaks up. New elements have no practical use outside the lab, but they further our knowledge of the Universe.

RADIOACTIVITY

Radioactivity is particles splitting off from the nucleus of an atom. With unstable atoms such as uranium, this happens naturally—scientists call it radioactive decay. Most natural particle radiation is low level and does no harm, but long-term exposure to it or bursts from uncontrolled nuclear reactions can kill or cause cancer.

The world's most dangerous toy?

When radioactive materials were first discovered, people wore watches with radium dials that glowed green in the dark. Children were even given atomic energy kits containing uranium to play with—although not enough to cause harm. Still, the idea seems crazy today.

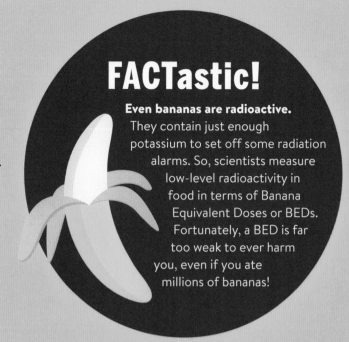

FACTastic!

Even bananas are radioactive.
They contain just enough potassium to set off some radiation alarms. So, scientists measure low-level radioactivity in food in terms of Banana Equivalent Doses or BEDs. Fortunately, a BED is far too weak to ever harm you, even if you ate millions of bananas!

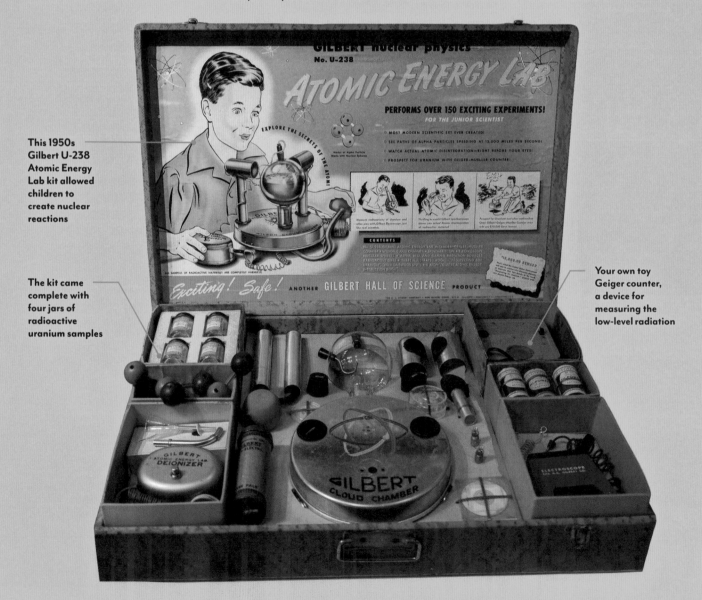

This 1950s Gilbert U-238 Atomic Energy Lab kit allowed children to create nuclear reactions

The kit came complete with four jars of radioactive uranium samples

Your own toy Geiger counter, a device for measuring the low-level radiation

EXPERT CONSULTANT: Cristina Lazzeroni **SEE ALSO:** The Atom, p.100–01; Elements, p.102–03; Electricity, p.126–27; Nuclear Power, p.376–77

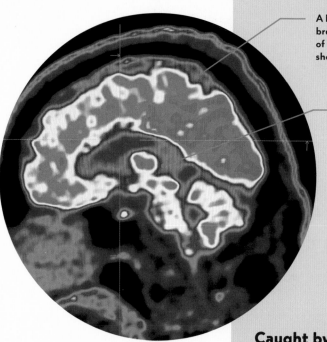

A PET scan of a human brain, where high levels of chemical activity show up as bright spots

High levels of chemical activity can be an indication of a disease, such as cancer

Radioactive scanning

If you are ill, doctors may use radioactivity to find out what's wrong. When patients go for a PET scan, they are injected with a substance that contains atoms, which send out harmless radioactive particles. The atoms gather wherever certain chemical activities are happening in the body. The scanner detects the pattern of particles and gives doctors a picture of what is going on.

Caught by the tusk

A poacher found with a stash of elephant tusks claimed he got them before hunting had been banned. But science caught him! Once a living thing dies, a type of atom called carbon-14 slowly breaks up radioactively. Carbon dating showed the tusks contained so much carbon-14 that the elephants could only have died recently.

Around 100 elephants a day are killed illegally for their ivory tusks

Ivory is prized for making luxury items and souvenirs

Carbon-14 atom

Carbon-14 in tusk at time of death

The rate of decay is very slow

After 5,730 years the carbon-14 reduces by half

Carbon dating

The radioisotope carbon-14 (a kind of carbon atom) is present in all living things. When plants and animals die, particles split off from the carbon-14, causing it to disintegrate slowly. By measuring the proportion of carbon-14 isotopes left in a well-preserved fragment, scientists can tell how long the plant or animal in question has been dead.

105

COMPOUNDS

Only a few elements, such as gold, exist in a pure form at Earth's surface. Most are combination chemicals called compounds. Water, minerals such as salt, and the chemicals that make living things are nearly all compounds. Each compound is made of atoms of two or more elements that join together in a particular way. These atom combinations are called molecules. Water is made of trios of atoms—two hydrogen and one oxygen.

Making explosives

Combining elements into a compound makes them totally different. Mixed in the air, elements of nitrogen pair off into nitrogen gas (N_2) and elements of oxygen pair off into oxygen gas (O_2). Oxygen and nitrogen gas are both harmless, but when they are brought together in a compound called nitroglycerin, they form the basis of dynamite—a powerful explosive.

Dynamite is mainly used in the mining, quarrying, construction, and demolition industries

EXPERT CONSULTANT: Duncan Davis **SEE ALSO:** The Atom, p.100–01; Elements, p.102–03; Combustion, p.108–09; Solids, Liquids & Gases, p.110–11; Plasma, p.112–13; Metals, p.114–15; Nonmetals, p.116–17; Plastics, p.118–19; Chemistry of Life, p.120–21

Bonding molecules

To form molecules, an atom must stick to other atoms. To do this, the atoms share or swap their electrons, the tiny particles that orbit the nucleus (core) to create chemical bonds. Sharing electrons is called covalent bonding. Swapping electrons is known as ionic bonding. Water (H_2O) has its own special bond called a hydrogen bond.

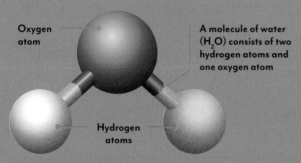

Oxygen atom

A molecule of water (H_2O) consists of two hydrogen atoms and one oxygen atom

Hydrogen atoms

Chemical reactions

When the correct combination of elements or compounds are brought together, they cause chemical reactions. Reactions can be quick or slow. Iron, for example, reacts very gradually with oxygen in the air to make rust—and only if there's moisture to help it.

Building new chemicals

Chemists have discovered tens of millions of compounds in the last two centuries. They continue to discover tens of thousands of new ones every year. Each compound has its own unique qualities, and some chemists look for compounds that will do a particular job better. For example, firefighters need to stop fires quickly. Compounds based on the gas bromine have proved effective at quelling fires.

GAME CHANGER

ANTOINE-LAURENT DE LAVOISIER

Chemist, lived 1743–94
France

In the 1700s, when most scientists misunderstood combustion (how things burn), French scientist Lavoisier made a major discovery. Using a simple experiment, he showed that fuels take oxygen from the air as they burn. Lavoisier named both oxygen and hydrogen and invented letter symbols for chemicals. He is called the father of chemistry.

Making colored glass

The tiniest amount of a substance can completely change the look or effect of a compound. Scientists call these minute amounts traces. Trace elements in the human body keep it healthy. They include zinc and iron. Traces of chromium make rubies red. Traces of compounds of other metals are used to stain glass vivid colors.

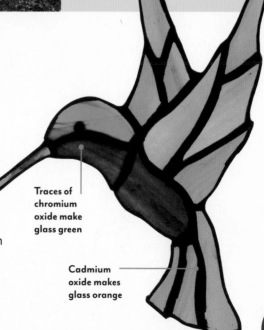

Traces of chromium oxide make glass green

Cadmium oxide makes glass orange

COMBUSTION

When early humans learned to make fire up to 1.7 million years ago, it was a huge breakthrough. Now they could control combustion—the combination of oxygen, heat, and fuel in what is called an oxidation reaction. An oxidation reaction can be just a slow burn or a full-blown firestorm. It has been at the heart of key developments in our history, such as the Industrial Revolution. The invention of the combustion engine in the 1800s took many years to perfect and now provides the power for most automobiles and many other machines from lawn mowers to airplanes.

Scramjet 2004
The X-43A owes its speed to a jet engine with no moving parts. It can fly at almost 7,000 mph (11,265 km/h)

Jet truck 1984
In the US, Les Shockley fits a jet engine to a truck; a later remodeling of the truck hits record-breaking speeds of 376 mph (605 km/h)

Jet engine 1939
German scientist Hans Joachim Pabst von Ohain creates the first successful jet-powered airplane

Rocket engine 1926
American engineer Robert H. Goddard invents the first rocket engine for missiles and later spaceflight

Incinerator 1874
The first superhot "destructor" to burn waste completely is built in Nottingham, UK

Gas boiler 1868
In the UK, Benjamin Maughan invents the "geyser" to heat water for the home

Dynamite 1867
Swedish chemist and inventor Alfred Nobel invents the powerful explosive, dynamite

Combustion needs heat, fuel, and oxygen

The wick carries vapors from the melted wax

Producing a flame

Although you can't always see it, combustion happens in stages. In a candle, vapors from the wax are the fuel. First, you light the wick, so that heat travels down the wick into the wax. Second, the wax melts and sends vapors up through the wick. Finally, the vapors get hot enough to "ignite"—that is, burst into flame.

Internal combustion engine 1859
Belgian Étienne Lenoir makes an engine to burn fuel (gasoline) inside a cylinder.

Bunsen burner 1855
In Germany, Robert Bunsen designs a gas burner with a controllable flame for laboratories.

Limelight 1816
Scottish engineer Thomas Drummond uses white-hot quicklime to make a bright light for use in theaters.

Steam engine 1712
In England, Thomas Newcomen invents the first practical steam engine.

Gas lamp 1792
Scottish inventor William Murdock creates lamps for use in his home and office, burning gas made from coal.

Matches 1805
French chemist Jean Chancel invents matches by dipping splints tipped with potassium chlorate and sugar in sulfuric acid.

Explosives 1000 CE
The ancient Chinese discover the explosive power of gunpowder for fireworks.

Iron 1500 BCE
As iron begins to be worked, it requires furnaces that can create very high temperatures.

Smelting 5000 BCE
Rock containing copper is smelted by heating it to melt out pure copper.

First kiln 6000 BCE
Fires are made hotter and pottery finer by enclosing the fire within a brick kiln or furnace.

Pottery 28,000 years ago
People shape wet clay, then fire it to make figurines.

Cooking 1.7–1 million years ago
No one knows when people began to cook. It could be over 1 million years ago.

Fire 1.7–1 million years ago
Our ancestors, *Homo erectus*, probably begin to control and use fire.

EXPERT CONSULTANT: David Tong **SEE ALSO:** Fossil Fuels, p.80–81; Elements, p.102–03; Solids, Liquids & Gases, p.110–11; Energy, p.122–23; Speed Demons, p.130–31; Food & Cooking, p.208–09; The Industrial Revolution, p.314–15

SOLIDS, LIQUIDS & GASES

Anything that has mass—takes up space—is called matter. There are three main states of matter: solid, liquid, and gas. Matter in the solid state, such as a book, has a set size and shape that does not change easily. In the liquid state, matter changes shape depending on its container. For example, milk changes shape when you pour it from a glass into a bowl. Gases do not have a set size or shape. They can expand to fill a large container or be squeezed into a smaller one.

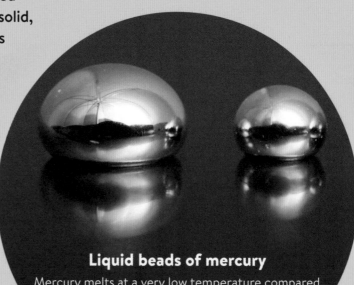

Liquid beads of mercury
Mercury melts at a very low temperature compared to other metals. It is the only metal that is liquid at room temperature. The attraction between its molecules make it roll into liquid beads.

Changing states of matter

How the particles that make up a substance behave determines its state. Matter can change from one state to another. Heat melts a solid by adding energy to its particles' movement. This movement weakens the bonds between its particles, until the solid forms a liquid. Heat turns a liquid into a gas by speeding up the particles, until they break free of one another. Cold condenses a gas by slowing its particles, so that they join together and form a liquid. Cold freezes the liquid by slowing the particles until they join together so strongly that they stay in a certain arrangement, forming a solid.

Solid (ice)

Liquid (water)

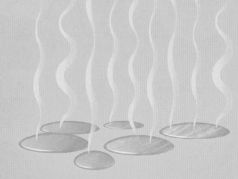

Gas (water vapor)

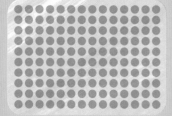

In a solid, atoms and molecules are bonded together to give a fixed shape and volume.

In a liquid, particles lack the order of a solid, and move around one another more freely.

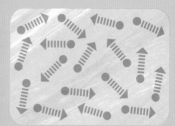

In a gas, particles move randomly, and the gas can expand or shrink to any volume.

EXPERT CONSULTANT: Kimberly M. Jackson **SEE ALSO:** Mountains, p.68–69; Rocks & Minerals, p.70–71; Water World, p.82–83; Earth's Ice, p.84–85; The Atom, p.100–01; Elements, p.102–03; Plasma, p.112–13; Plastics, p.118–19; Pressure, p.136–37; Lighter Than Air, p.138–39

Supercool!

Nitrogen is one of the main gases in the air. It turns into liquid when it is cooled below -320°F (-196°C)—its boiling point. This is done by compressing the nitrogen inside special flasks (below), then letting it slowly expand. Normal freezing damages living tissue. But liquid nitrogen is so cold that it freezes things instantly, without damage. It is also useful for freeze-drying food and for keeping foods cold when they are being transported.

A technician pulls cell samples taken from a human body from a liquid nitrogen storage tank

Gases and pressure

If gases have no shape, how do balloons like this one (above) keep their shape when filled with helium? The answer is that as gas molecules zoom about, they bombard the inside of the inflatable, creating pressure. As the inflatable is filled, there is more pressure, tightening the inflatable until it is firm.

FACTastic!

Not everything that looks solid is solid.
Living things are made mostly of liquids, held in by a slightly more solid wrapper. For example, up to 5 percent of most jellyfish are solid; the rest are water (right). But even the adult human body, which looks solid in shape, is 60 percent water. Children are about two-thirds water, and newborn babies are an amazing 78 percent water.

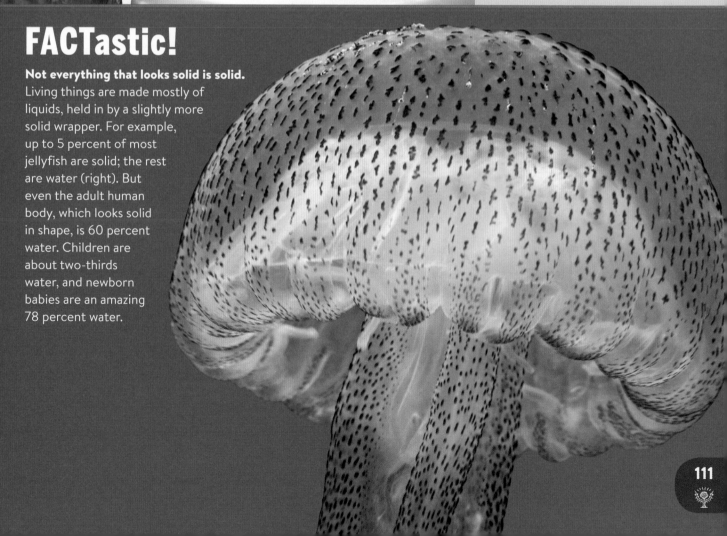

PLASMA

Plasma is sometimes called the fourth state of matter because it has qualities that are not found in the other three states of matter—solids, liquids, and gases. It is light and shapeless like a gas, but it's made of particles with an electrical charge called ions, and electrons that vibrate even more than those of gas. Most of the ordinary matter in the Universe is made of plasma, including the Sun and stars. On Earth, plasma can be found in lightning strikes, plasma TV screens, and plasma lamps like the one pictured.

Nuclear fusion reactors

The Sun and stars are powered by nuclear fusion—the combination of two hydrogen atoms to form helium. If scientists could copy this process efficiently, it would provide a safe, renewable power source. The process involves getting gases so hot that they create a plasma in which fusion takes place. To keep the plasma superhot, it must not come in contact with any other substance. One way to do this is to trap it in a donut-shaped device called a tokamak (below) that uses a system of magnetic fields to hold the plasma in place.

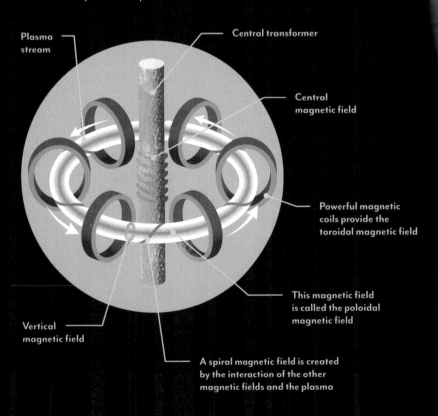

Plasma stream

Central transformer

Central magnetic field

Powerful magnetic coils provide the toroidal magnetic field

This magnetic field is called the poloidal magnetic field

Vertical magnetic field

A spiral magnetic field is created by the interaction of the other magnetic fields and the plasma

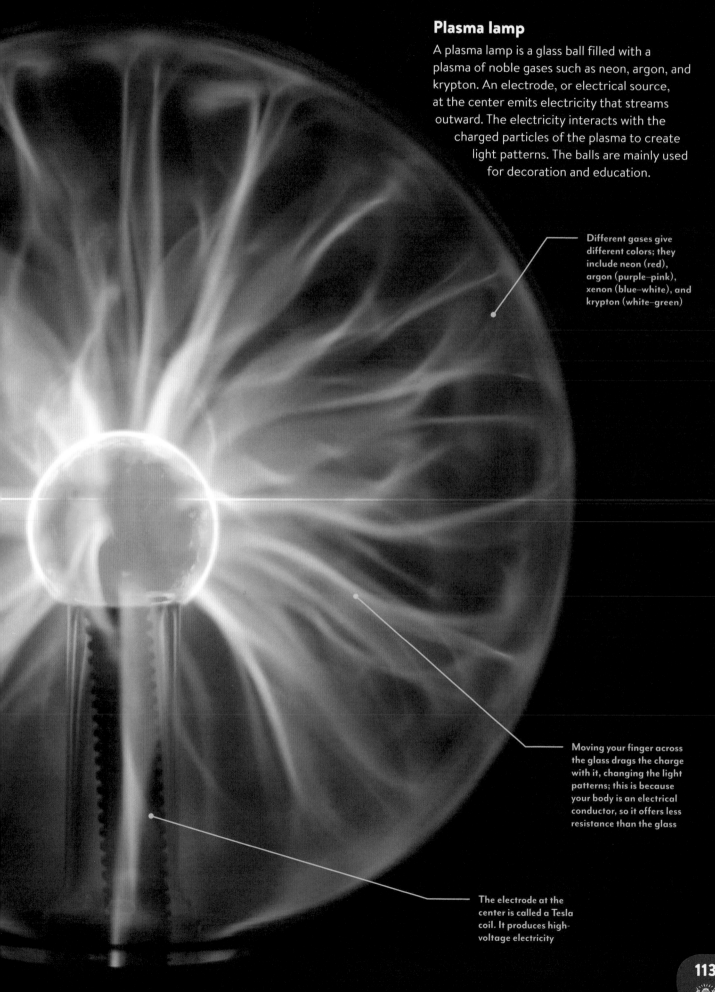

Plasma lamp

A plasma lamp is a glass ball filled with a plasma of noble gases such as neon, argon, and krypton. An electrode, or electrical source, at the center emits electricity that streams outward. The electricity interacts with the charged particles of the plasma to create light patterns. The balls are mainly used for decoration and education.

Different gases give different colors; they include neon (red), argon (purple–pink), xenon (blue–white), and krypton (white–green)

Moving your finger across the glass drags the charge with it, changing the light patterns; this is because your body is an electrical conductor, so it offers less resistance than the glass

The electrode at the center is called a Tesla coil. It produces high-voltage electricity

Gold is a soft metal, which makes it ideal for shaping

METALS

Approximately three-quarters of all known chemical elements in our Universe are metals. All metals share a number of common factors. They are all shiny when cut, for example. They also conduct electricity and heat well—that is, electricity and heat pass through them easily. Most metals are tough solids at room temperatures but melt when they are hot enough.

Glittering gold

Gold has long been used to make precious items, like this plaque from China, dating from around 475–221 BCE. Gold objects can be buried in the dirt, or exposed to the weather, for thousands of years and yet still come out shiny and yellow. That's because gold doesn't change when it is exposed to other elements. In the reactivity series—a table ranking how much different metals react with things like oxygen, water, or acid—gold is at the bottom, along with platinum.

Copper and the Bronze Age

The discovery of copper changed human history. In the Stone Age, humans made tools from stone. Then, 7,000 years ago, people learned to extract copper from rocks by heating them to melting point. They then found they could turn copper into the super-tough metal bronze by adding tin. Bronze Age people were the first to work and use metals extensively. Today, copper is vital for use in electric cables (left) because it conducts electricity very well.

FACTastic!

A silver dollar minted in 1794 is now worth a cool $10 million. Known as the flowing hair silver dollar, the coin (pictured) was the first US dollar ever struck. People no longer make coins from silver or gold, as both became so precious that the metal in silver and gold coins was worth more than the coin value. Today, they use cheaper metals, such as copper and nickel.

EXPERT CONSULTANT: Cristina Lazzeroni **SEE ALSO:** Elements, p.102–03; Compounds, p.106–07; Solids, Liquids & Gases, p.110–11; Nonmetals, p.116–17; Plastics, p.118–19; Electricity, p.126–27; Pressure, p.136–37

Building with steel

Traces of carbon in just the right quantity (less than 2 percent in weight) turns iron into steel. Steel may be the most useful of all metals. Not only is it incredibly tough, but it is cheap to make in huge quantities. We use steel to make many things, from ships and bridges to tools and weapons. Mixing in tiny amounts of other metals can change its properties. Adding 10–30 percent chromium, for example, turns it into stainless steel, which never rusts.

Steel can be shaped to make many useful, strong components, such as girders to support bridges

Explosive metals

We make ships from steel. But certain metals may explode when they come into contact with water. Just a drop or two of water can cause alkali metals, such as sodium, potassium, and cesium, to explode and release toxic gases, while alkaline earth metals, such as magnesium, can burst into flames, releasing toxic gases. For this reason, such metals are internationally recognized as hazardous substances.

Metal fatigue

The gradual weakening of metal over time is called metal fatigue. Small cracks can form in metal. In the early 1950s, this led to three airplanes breaking up in midair. The difference in air pressure between the inside and outside of planes had caused stress on the corners of the square windows. Because of this, the windows of planes are now rounded to distribute such stress. Airlines also carry out strict inspections, using ultrasonic and other equipment to detect even the tiniest cracks in the metal.

Some cracks occurred around the windows

NONMETALS

The nonmetals on the periodic table have different qualities from metals. They tend to be less dense than metals and to melt or boil at lower temperatures. Unlike metals, most nonmetals do not conduct electricity. Nonmetals can be gases, such as hydrogen or oxygen, or solids such as carbon or sulfur. There is one liquid, bromine. By mass, the nonmetals hydrogen and helium make up at least 98 percent of matter in the Universe.

Laser beams do not spread like other lights, so they produce clear lines in the air that can be seen even by airplanes in the sky

Using high-voltage machines, krypton mixed with argon produces a white laser beam. Other noble gases create colored laser beams

Fluorine—the most reactive nonmetal

The nonmetal fluorine is reactive, so it joins up easily with other elements. It is often found as a calcium compound, as in this purple fluorite stone. Elements are most stable when they have a complete number of electrons. Fluorine is more reactive than other nonmetals because it needs one more electron to finish the shell of electrons closest to its nucleus. At room temperature, it is a poisonous yellowish gas.

Noble gases

The nonmetals krypton and argon are used to generate laser beams. Lasers are used in science for precise measuring and in spectacular laser shows like this one at the Burj Khalifa skyscraper in Dubai. You cannot see, smell, or taste these nonmetals. They come from a group of elements known as noble gases. These tend to stay in their pure form, as they don't easily react with other elements.

EMAAR

EXPERT CONSULTANT: Duncan Davis **SEE ALSO:** Elements, p.102–03; Compounds, p.106–07; Metals, p.114–15; Chemistry of Life, p.120–21; Light, p.128–29; Artificial Materials, p.360–61; Smart Tech & AI, p.364–65

Silicon

There is more silicon in Earth's crust than any element apart from oxygen. The nonmetal is often found in rock, sand, and soil, usually as a compound such as silica (silicon dioxide). Silicon has been used for centuries to make glass. Today, it is used to make microchips for computers. It gave its name to Silicon Valley in California, the heart of the computer industry.

The US is a big producer of silica sand. It is made by processing silica-rich rocks, such as quartz, and has many industrial uses

FACTastic!

Scientists grow crystals to make computer chips.
Silicon is the main ingredient in computer chip manufacturing. To ensure the silicon is free from defects, scientists grow huge crystals, called ingots, which are then sliced into thin wafers and processed in hundreds of ways before being cut up to make tiny computer chips.

Acids

Some nonmetals combine with oxygen or other elements to form compounds that are highly acidic. They can corrode, or eat through, metals in the way the acid in this battery has leaked to corrode the metal casing. Many acids, such as hydrochloric acid, can burn human skin. Acid gases, such as sulfur dioxide, are present in the air. These acids dissolve in rainwater, making water so acidic that it can kill trees.

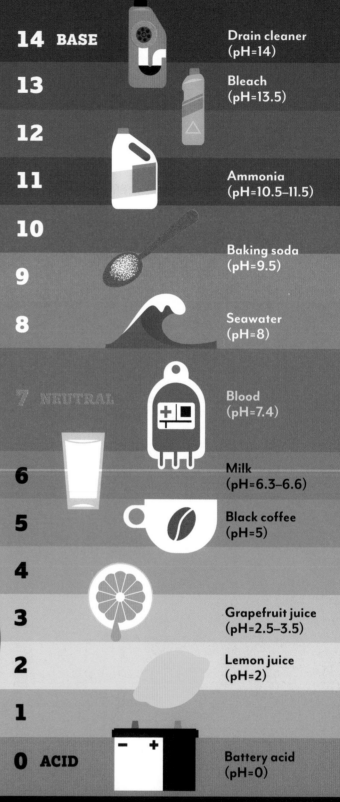

14	BASE	Drain cleaner (pH=14)
13		Bleach (pH=13.5)
12		
11		Ammonia (pH=10.5–11.5)
10		
9		Baking soda (pH=9.5)
8		Seawater (pH=8)
7	NEUTRAL	Blood (pH=7.4)
6		Milk (pH=6.3–6.6)
5		Black coffee (pH=5)
4		
3		Grapefruit juice (pH=2.5–3.5)
2		Lemon juice (pH=2)
1		
0	ACID	Battery acid (pH=0)

The pH scale

Scientists need to know whether substances are acids or bases because they behave differently in chemical reactions. Substances with a pH less than 7 are considered acidic; those with a pH greater than 7 are considered basic (the opposite of acid). Scientists use a special paper that changes color to measure the pH of a substance.

PLASTICS

It is hard to imagine our world without plastics. Plastics are a human-made material that can be formed into almost any shape or color. Most plastics are strong, long-lasting, and lightweight. They resist damage by water, heat, chemicals, and electricity. Often they are cheaper than natural materials. Plastics are artificially manufactured, usually from raw materials like natural gas and petroleum. They are used to make everything from beverage bottles and grocery bags to crash helmets and flooring.

FACTastic!

A gecko's feet can adhere to almost any surface, but they will slip on dry Teflon. This waxy resin, a plastic called polytetrafluoroethylene (PTFE), is so slippery that it is used to make nonstick cooking pans. The attractive forces known as Van de Waals forces are so low in Teflon that other molecules cannot bind to it.

The History of Plastics
TIMELINE

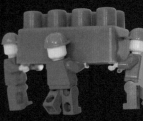
Lego brick and characters

1856 Englishman Alexander Parkes invents Parkesine, the first plastic, as a cheap alternative for ivory in billiard balls.

1872 A machine is invented that injects plastics into molds.

1909 Leo Baekeland, a Belgian-born American chemist, makes Bakelite, the world's first synthetic polymer.

1933 Chemists produce polyethylene, now one of the most common plastics in the world.

1935 American chemist Wallace Carothers develops nylon, the first totally synthetic fiber.

1958 Lego patents toy building bricks that are originally made from cellulose acetate.

1965 American chemist Stephanie Kwolek invents Kevlar, a plastic fiber so strong it is used in bulletproof vests.

1973 The first plastic beverage bottles are made from polyethylene terephthalate.

2009 Plastics make up nearly half of the new Boeing 787 airliner's outer skin.

2016 In Japan, scientists discover a tiny organism living in soil that is capable of eating plastic.

Plastic bottle

The power of polymers

Most plastics are a type of chemical called a polymer. In Greek *poly* means "many" and *mer* means "units." Each polymer is made up of one unit that repeats hundreds, thousands, or millions of times. Think of a polymer as a necklace, with each bead as one unit. Bound tightly, the units make chains that are strong but flexible and can take on different shapes. This quality is called plasticity. Plastic is easy to form into any shape—even this Slinky spring toy (left).

The problem with plastics

Plastics are a major cause of pollution. They break down very slowly—or not at all. It upsets natural ecosystems and harms animals. Some discarded plastic ends up in oceans. In 2019, a diver found a plastic bag when he was 7 miles (11 km) deep in the ocean, in the Mariana Trench.

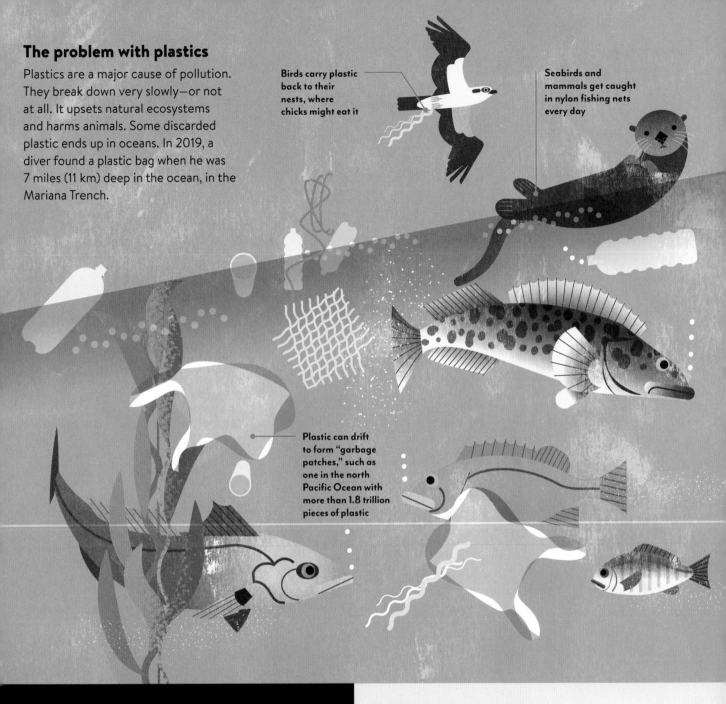

Birds carry plastic back to their nests, where chicks might eat it

Seabirds and mammals get caught in nylon fishing nets every day

Plastic can drift to form "garbage patches," such as one in the north Pacific Ocean with more than 1.8 trillion pieces of plastic

Microplastics

Plastic pollution often comes in pieces so tiny they are barely visible. Microplastics are less than 0.2 inch (5 mm) long, and there are thousands of tons in the ground and in the oceans. Some come from tiny microbeads used in makeup, but others are produced when larger plastics are worn away. Microplastics harm creatures that eat them, including humans.

Do bioplastics live up to their name?

Bioplastics are made from plant material, such as cassava (right). Today, popular objects made from this material include plates and cups, flatware, and straws. The European company IKEA began to manufacture furniture using bioplastics in 2018. Makers of bioplastics claim that they will degrade, or break down, more easily than plastics produced from fossil fuels. While some bioplastics degrade reasonably quickly, this is not true for all of them.

CHEMISTRY OF LIFE

All life on Earth is based on a single chemical element—carbon. Carbon in the air combines with oxygen to make carbon dioxide (CO_2). Plants use CO_2, water, and sunlight to make carbohydrates, food they use to live and grow. They give off oxygen as waste. Animals (including humans) eat plants and breathe in oxygen to get energy from the carbohydrates. Then they release CO_2 back into the air in their breath.

Tufa towers

At Mono Lake, California, carbon has created towers of porous limestone (tufa) over the centuries. They grow up from the lake bed as carbon in the water reacts with calcium to cause a buildup of the compound calcium carbonate, a rock-forming mineral. Scientists study the towers to help them understand the area's climate history.

Spots help a leopard blend in with trees and grass as it hunts. This is called camouflage

Patterns in nature

Chemistry is responsible for animal markings, such as a leopard's spots or a zebra's stripes. Before an animal is born, different chemicals compete to control its biological development. A leopard's spots occur when one chemical signal creates black colors in the skin, but another chemical programs other parts of the skin to create yellow pigment.

EXPERT CONSULTANT: Kimberly M. Jackson **SEE ALSO:** Rocks & Minerals, p.70–71; Giant Crystals, p.72–73; Earth's Riches, p.74–75; The Atmosphere, p.86–87; Elements, p.102–03; Compounds, p.106–07; Solids, Liquids & Gases, p.110–11; Plants & Fungi, p.156–57; Animals, p.158–59; The Human Body, p.198–99

Amino acids

For growth and development, all living things need proteins, which are built from amino acids. All living organisms rely on the same 20 amino acids. We can make 11 of these in our bodies but have to get the other essential nine from foods high in protein, such as meat, fish, eggs, beans, and nuts, which are broken down into amino acids during digestion. In many organisms, including humans, proteins play many crucial roles, such as helping transport nutrients, build muscles, and fight disease.

Tufa towers up to 30 feet (9 meters) high have developed on the lake's shoreline

Mono Lake is a soda lake. The water of such lakes is full of carbonates (CO_2 dissolved in water)

Enzymes

Chemical reactions, such as turning food into energy, occur in plants and animals, allowing them to function. Enzymes are a family of proteins that control these reactions. They speed up a chemical reaction, but they remain unchanged in the process. Such substances are known as chemical catalysts. In bread making, enzymes in yeast react with other ingredients, causing the dough to rise.

GAME CHANGER

DOROTHY HODGKIN
Chemist, lived 1910–94
UK

Dorothy Hodgkin studied the structure of chemicals by firing X-rays at crystals to see the patterns they made. During World War II, she worked out the structure of penicillin, a medicine that heals wounds and fights infections. Her work helped scientists to make new, more effective drugs. She later discovered the structure of vitamin B12 and also insulin, a hormone that controls sugar levels in the body.

FACTastic!

Researchers have made diamonds out of peanut butter! Peanut butter is rich in carbon. Carbon is also the mineral from which diamonds are made. While German scientists were studying how crystals form beneath Earth's surface, they squeezed peanut butter under high pressure to remove any oxygen. A rogue gas upset the experiment, but not before diamonds had emerged.

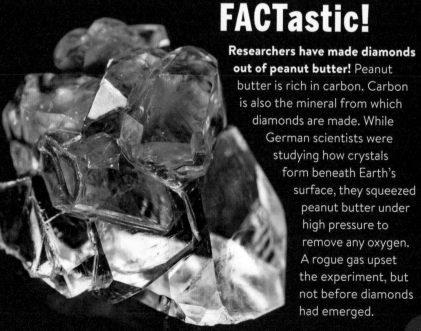

ENERGY

Energy is a fundamental property contained within everything in the Universe. Energy is needed to make anything happen. It's needed to make machines work. Your body cannot move without energy, and it's needed to make all living things grow—from bacteria to redwood trees, sharks to humans.

Kinetic and potential energy

There are two basic kinds of energy. Kinetic energy exists when something moves. The faster it moves, the more kinetic energy it has. Potential energy is stored energy. It can depend on the position or state of parts in a system. A ball that is held up high has a kind of potential energy known as gravitational energy. When you drop the ball, it falls and picks up speed. Its potential energy is turned into kinetic energy.

Heat

Heat is a form of energy. It is generated, or produced, by the movement of atoms and molecules inside a substance. The faster these particles move, the hotter the object. If this energy stays within the object, it is called thermal energy.

ENERGY
Energy is needed to make matter move or change.

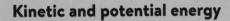

KINETIC ENERGY
The motion, or movement, of an object requires kinetic energy.

POTENTIAL ENERGY
This is stored in an object until it is changed into another energy form.

Thermal energy

Thermal energy is made by moving molecules; this creates heat.

Gravitational energy
This is energy in a gravitational field—the higher up you go, the more there is.

Radiant energy

This is made by the movement of light or electromagnetic radiation.

Nuclear energy
Stored in the nucleus of an atom, this is released when atoms split or join together.

Sound energy

This type of energy appears in vibrations of air or of matter.

Electrical energy
This is energy stored in electric fields. Examples include chemical energy, where the electric fields are responsible for the bonds between atoms and molecules.

EXPERT CONSULTANT: David Tong **SEE ALSO:** The Big Bang, p.4–5; End of the Universe, p.46–47; Sound, p. 124–25; Electricity, p.126–27; Light, p.128–29; Speed Demons, p.130–31; Gravity, p.134–35

Transforming energy

There is a scientific law known as the conservation of energy. This law states that energy cannot be created or destroyed. It can only be transformed into a different type of energy. Take, for example, a water wheel. A stream flowing downhill converts gravitational energy into kinetic energy. The water pushes against the blades, transferring kinetic energy to the wheel. The wheel turns around the hub at its center, rotating an axle in order to power a machine such as a mill.

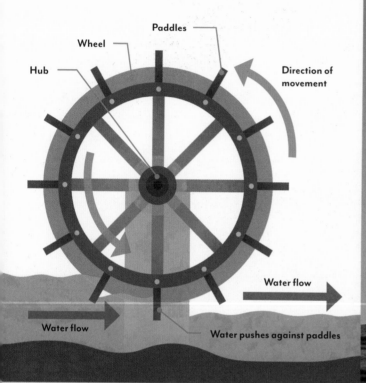

Paddles

Wheel

Hub

Direction of movement

Water flow

Water flow

Water pushes against paddles

When is energy useful?

Although the total amount of energy in the Universe remains the same, not all of it is useful. As things get more disordered and muddled, the energy that can be used decreases. The amount of disorder in the Universe is measured by entropy. A law of physics says that the entropy always increases over time, so the amount of usable energy is always decreasing. For example, when popcorn is heated, it pops. Even on cooling down, the popcorn doesn't go back to its unpopped state. Making popcorn increases the entropy in the Universe.

The 120-foot (36.5 meter) blades are angled to catch the wind

The drive shaft turns the generator to produce electricity

Wind turbines

Kinetic energy from moving air turns the rotor blades in wind turbines, which pick up that kinetic energy. The rotors transfer the energy to drive shafts (devices that make other parts rotate) that turn a generator. The generator changes the kinetic energy into electrical energy. The electricity can be stored and used far away.

Infrasound

All sound waves travel at much the same speed, but the pitch (or level) you hear depends on their frequency, or how many waves come each second. The very lowest frequencies, called infrasound, can't be heard by human ears, but some animals, such as elephants and baleen whales like this humpback, can hear them. Because infrasound waves travel very far through water, whales can communicate even when they are 100 miles (160 km) apart.

SOUND

Sound is the vibrations in the air that we can hear. When a drum beats, a person shouts, or thunder cracks, they're just vibrations causing movement that rhythmically stretch and squeeze the air. These vibrations enter your eardrum and make it vibrate. Nerves then send messages to your brain, which turns it into a sound we understand. The vibrations are called sound waves, and like waves in the sea, they travel through the air without actually moving it much. Sound waves can travel through liquids (water) and many solids (metal, stone, wood), as well as air.

FACTastic!

In the deep emptiness of space there is no sound. This is because sound needs molecules to shake and vibrate, and in space there are none. Even when giant stars explode, they make no sound.

EXPERT CONSULTANT: David Tong **SEE ALSO:** Light, p.128–29; Speed Demons, p.130–31; The Senses, p.206–07; Language & Storytelling, p.216–17

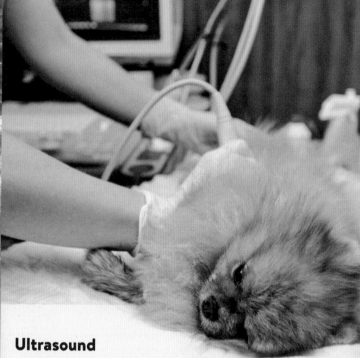

Ultrasound

Ultrasound is sound with too high
a frequency for our ears to hear. Some animals can
emit (make) these sounds. Bats, for example, emit and
hear ultrasound waves. They use ultrasound for locating
prey and navigating. Ultrasound has been harnessed by
humans to diagnose and treat diseases inside a body.
Veterinarians use it on animals. It works even through a
dog's thick fur.

The speed of sound

When an airplane flies fast, it pushes up waves of
pressure in the air in front. These waves travel at the
speed of sound. If the plane flies even faster than sound,
it can "break the sound barrier." This means it catches
up with the waves and scrunches them into a giant
shock wave. People on the ground hear this as a loud,
thundering "sonic boom."

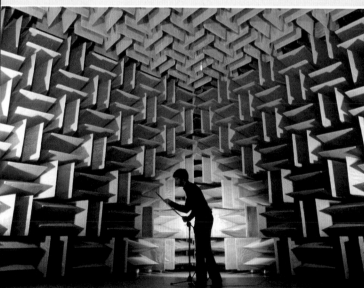

Anechoic chambers

An anechoic chamber (above) is the quietest
place on Earth. It is a space lined with special
foam wedges that soak up, or absorb, sound vibrations.
It is so quiet your heartbeat sounds like thunder. The
silence is so complete that no one can take it for more
than 45 minutes, and people quickly lose their balance.
NASA uses these chambers to prepare astronauts for
the total silence of space.

ELECTRICITY

Electricity is the movement of electrons—the tiny particles in the outer part of an atom—from one atom to the next. There are two kinds of electricity, current electricity and static electricity. Current electricity is the type that powers our lights and machines. It is created in a power plant and flows through wires to reach the outlets in our homes. It can also be stored in batteries. Static electricity occurs naturally, such as when you rub a balloon on your hair and it then sticks to the wall. Static electricity also causes lightning and the little shocks you sometimes get when you take off a wool sweater.

The flash carries electricity to the highest point beneath the cloud

Lightning rods protect tall buildings by carrying electricity safely to the ground

Where lightning comes from

Lightning is a form of static electricity created inside clouds. At high altitudes, drops of water or ice rub together. This creates static electricity. When there is enough electricity, it is released as a flash of lightning. Earth experiences eight to nine million lightning strikes every day.

NEW YORKER

EXPERT CONSULTANT: Cristina Lazzeroni **SEE ALSO:** Weather, p.88–89; Mega Storms, p.90–91; The Atom, p.100–01; Powering the Planet, p.348–49; Med Tech, p.362–63

Conductors and insulators

Materials that allow electricity to flow through them easily are called conductors. They include many metals. Materials that don't allow electricity to pass through easily are called insulators. Birds can stand on a single wire because the electricity bypasses them. However, if a bird stood on two wires at the same time, the electricity would pass through it to get to the other wire. The bird would be electrocuted.

Metal wires conduct electricity

Birds are not shocked because no electricity passes through them

Static electricity

The atoms in most objects have a balance of positive and negative charges, so are neutral. But sometimes electrons, which are negatively charged, can build up. This is called static electricity. The girl in the picture is touching a Van de Graaff static electricity generator. When someone touches the ball, the electrons that make up the static electricity jump into the person's body and move through it to the ends of their hair. Because all the electrons in the static have the same kind of charge, they repel one another, making the hair stand on end.

NOTE *from the expert!*

CRISTINA LAZZERONI
Particle physicist

Professor Lazzeroni studies the physics of subatomic particles, the smallest and simplest objects that exist. The big unsolved problem in her field is understanding the building blocks of the Universe.

❝ Scientists are often represented as people hidden away in laboratories. But I work with people from many countries who do amazing things with computers, electronics, and mechanical systems. ❞

FACTastic!

Electric eels have thousands of cells that store power like mini batteries. The eels stun their prey with a shock twice as powerful as the electricity in a household socket. An eel found in the Amazon basin in South America delivers a whopping 850-volt shock.

127

LIGHT

Light is a form of energy that travels in waves. It comes in different wavelengths. The light that we see is called visible light. Other kinds of light have shorter or longer wavelengths than visible light, so our eyes can't see them. Light from the Sun is called white light, but it gets bent as it passes through water droplets and splits into all the colors: this is a rainbow. Nothing in the Universe travels as fast as light: around 186,000 miles (300,000 km) per second.

Cameras can detect more vivid aurora borealis colors than human eyes can see

The aurora borealis most commonly appears in shades of green

Northern lights

Near the Arctic Circle, the night sky sometimes fills with luminous curtains of colored lights. These are called the aurora borealis, or northern lights. They are caused when waves of energetic particles given off by the Sun meet atoms high in Earth's atmosphere. A similar phenomenon near the South Pole is called the aurora australis, or southern lights.

EXPERT CONSULTANT: David Tong SEE ALSO: Stars p.10–11; Black Holes p.18–19; The Sun p.24–25; Combustion p.108–09; Plasma p.112–13;

Lasers
LISTIFIED.

A laser creates a narrow but intense beam of light. Laser beams don't spread out like light from a flashlight. They can travel long distances and still focus an intense amount of energy. Lasers have many uses in our world.

1. Barcode scanners at supermarket checkouts use a red laser beam. The light from the beam reflects back off the black-and-white stripes of the barcode. This information is turned into a code that a central computer instantly checks against a database to supply the product's price.

2. Laser harps are musical instruments that project a row of laser beams into the air. When a performer's hand interrupts a beam, the instrument plays a particular note. Laser harps are used in spectacular live performances.

3. Cutting diamonds to make them sparkle is not easy because they are the hardest natural substance on Earth. In place of the diamond saws once used, craftsmen now use lasers. Lasers focus extreme heat on a diamond's surface to burn the stone, cutting it very precisely.

4. Surgeons use laser beams to make cuts in body tissue and to seal them again to prevent bleeding. Laser surgery is often used to improve the focus of people's eyes.

5. Telescopes use lasers to give us a sharper view of the deep Universe. Turbulence—winds that churn up the atmosphere—can obstruct the view. The lasers in advanced telescopes reveal turbulence by lighting up a layer of the atmosphere some 60 miles (96 km) above the Earth. The telescopes use this visual information to adjust their focus.

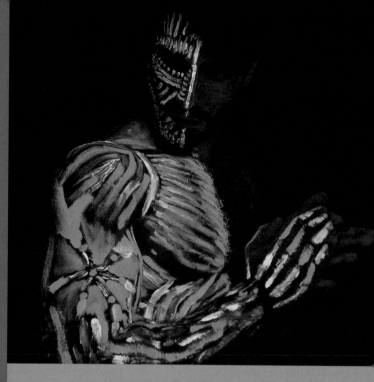

UV light

Ultraviolet (UV) light has a shorter wavelength than visible light. It causes objects to fluoresce, or glow brightly. Artists use fluorescent paints to create body art that glows under ultraviolet lights in nightclubs or at festivals. UV light can penetrate human skin but not as deeply as X-rays.

Bending light

Light usually travels in a straight line at a constant speed. However, its speed changes when it passes from one transparent material to another, such as when passing from air into a glass of water. Because water is denser than air, the light slows down slightly. The slowing down causes the light's path to change angle, seeming to create a bend where the air and water meet. This bend is called refraction.

Light from the pencil is refracted

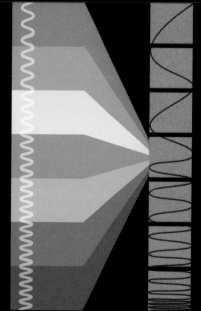

Radio waves
These can be detected by electronic receivers

Microwaves
These are used to cook food

Infrared light
This transmits heat, including from the Sun

Visible light
This is the light we see. It can be split into colors

Ultraviolet light
This light tans skin and can cause sunburn

X-rays
These can pass through human flesh

Gamma rays
The most powerful, these can be used to kill cancer

Electromagnetic spectrum

Visible light is just one type of energy emitted in the form of electromagnetic waves. Others include infrared light, radio waves, and X-rays. They differ from visible light only in their wavelength—the distance between two peaks of the wave. The full range is known as the electromagnetic spectrum.

Bloodhound LSR

The world land speed record is an incredible 763 mph (1,228 km/h), set by Richard Noble's British ThrustSSC in 1997. A race is on to try to beat that record. Contenders include New Zealand's Jetblack, Australia's Aussie Invader A5, and the British Bloodhound LSR, whose original model is pictured below. Unlike ordinary cars, these vehicles are powered by jet engines. Their teams hope to reach speeds of 1,000 mph (1,600km/h).

The friction of the wheels is not enough to keep the Bloodhound LSR on course at high speeds, so it has a huge tail fin to stabilize it, like an airplane

The main power comes from a jet engine. The car has been designed so that a rocket engine can be added, too.

The car has three braking systems: first airbrakes; then parachutes kick in; finally, conventional brakes work on the rear wheels

EXPERT CONSULTANT: David Tong **SEE ALSO:** Rockets, p.38–39; Combustion, p.108–09; Energy, p.122–23; Sound, p.124–25; Light, p.128–29; Forces, p.132–33; Simple Machines, p.142–43

SPEED DEMONS...
LISTIFIED.

THE FASTEST VEHICLES OF ALL TIME

1.   Apollo 10 Top speed: 24,791 mph (39,897 km/h). This speed—the fastest humans have ever moved—was achieved by the crew of the Apollo 10 spacecraft as it zoomed back to Earth after visiting the Moon in 1969.

2.   The DARPA Falcon HTV-2 Top speed: 13,000 mph (20,921 km/h). This speed, achieved on August 11, 2011, is the fastest ever by a plane. The HTV-2 is an unmanned glider, launched high in the air by a rocket. On HTV-2, the flight time from New York City to Los Angeles would be less than 12 minutes—a commercial airliner takes about five hours.

3.   The X-15 Top speed: 4,520 mph (7,274 km/h). The experimental X-15 rocket planes were the fastest ever piloted. They were launched at high altitude by a B-52 bomber and then propelled forward by a rocket engine. This speed was achieved by pilot Pete Knight in 1967, who also reached heights of 65 miles (100 km).

4.   Lockheed SR-71 Top speed: 2,193 mph (3,530 km/h). This plane, nicknamed Blackbird, was the fastest jet plane ever. In 1974, a Blackbird SR-71 flew from New York to London in under two hours.

5.   ThrustSSC Top speed: 763 mph (1,228 km/h). This is the world land speed record achieved by Richard Noble's jet-powered ThrustSSC car. Driven by Andy Green on October 15, 1997, it broke the sound barrier!

6.   Koenigsegg Agera Top speed: 278 mph (447 km/h). This is the fastest verified speed by a production car, a car built for sale to the public, achieved in 2017.

7.   The Shanghai Maglev Average speed: 268 mph (431 km/h). The world's fastest train works through magnetic levitation.

Only a jet engine can give the speed and acceleration to achieve world record speeds

The wheels are solid aluminum for minimum weight and air resistance. They spin at over 10,000 times a minute

FORCES

All objects have a quality called inertia. That means they remain as they are until a force acts on them. A force is like a push or a pull. A still ball remains still until a force pushes it. A rolling ball keeps rolling in the same direction until a force makes it turn or stop. There are two main types of forces. A contact force touches the object, like your hand pushing the ball. A force that acts at a distance doesn't touch the object directly. Gravity is a force that works at a distance. So is magnetism.

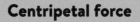

Particle accelerators

Forces shape the tiniest particles inside atoms. Scientists use particle accelerators like the Large Hadron Collider in Geneva (below) to crash protons together at close to the speed of light. Scientists study how the protons break up to learn about the forces that hold them together. They hope this will help them understand the nature of all matter.

Centripetal force

Riders on a carnival ride are spun outward as the ride rotates. They are not thrown off completely because there is a force pulling them in toward the center of the ride. This is called centripetal force. It acts through the chains holding the seats of the ride.

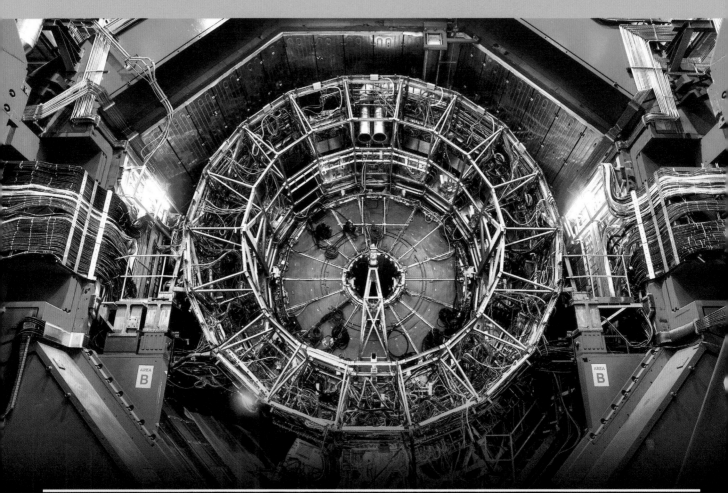

Fundamental Forces
LISTIFIED.

Four fundamental forces keep our universe ticking. Two are familiar: gravity and electromagnetism. The other two are known as the strong and weak nuclear forces. They work inside atoms.

1. Gravity Gravity is a force of attraction. It pulls all matter together. All objects exert gravity on other objects, but those with more mass exert more gravity.

2. Electromagnetism
Electromagnetism is a force that can attract or repel, like a magnet. It holds atoms together but also keeps them apart—which is why the atoms of your body don't combine with those of your chair.

3. The strong force This force holds together the nucleus of an atom. It acts over a short distance but is extremely powerful.

4. The weak force This causes changes inside atomic nuclei. It starts the nuclear reactions that fuel the Sun.

GAME CHANGER

ISAAC NEWTON
**Physicist, lived 1643–1727
UK**

Isaac Newton was one of the most important scientists of all time. He not only came up with the laws of motion, but he also discovered the law of physics that describes gravity—the attraction between all matter, including the Moon and the Earth. Newton also made breakthroughs in mathematics and performed a famous experiment in which he split sunlight into all the colors of the rainbow.

KNOWN UNKNOWN

Is there a fifth force?

The Universe is expanding faster than it should be, considering the amount of matter holding it together with its gravity. A mysterious repulsive force called dark energy seems to be pushing it apart. Scientists are still trying to understand what makes up this dark energy.

THE LAWS OF MOTION

In the 1600s, Sir Isaac Newton discovered that virtually every movement in the Universe obeys three simple rules, known as the laws of motion. Newton's laws explain all the moving things we see every day, from why a ball rolls to why it's difficult to steer a full shopping cart and why a rocket can shoot up into space.

First law

An object won't move unless something forces it to move; it will go on moving at the same speed and in the same direction unless forced to change. This is called inertia.

A ball rolling along a flat horizontal surface won't stop unless something stops it

A ball on a flat surface won't roll unless something pushes it

Second law

The greater the mass of an object, the more force is needed to make it go faster or to slow down or change direction.

A full shopping cart is harder to push, steer, or stop than a lighter, empty one

Third law

For every action, there is an equal and opposite reaction. When something pushes, whatever it pushes against pushes back with equal force in the other direction.

When the exhaust goes out of the back of a rocket, the equal and opposite reaction is that the rocket goes up

GRAVITY

Why is it more difficult to cycle up a hill than down? And why do things fall down and not up if you release them? The answer is Earth's gravity. Gravity is a force that pulls objects toward the center of Earth. Gravity is also what gives an object weight. If someone stands on a scale, gravity pulls that person toward the scale. The scale shows the strength of this force, or the person's weight. Gravity is important in space, too. It's what holds solar systems and galaxies together. Objects with more mass have more gravity.

Galileo's experiment

In the late 1500s, the Italian scientist Galileo Galilei carried out experiments to test how gravity pulls on objects, making them fall. His pupil Vincenzo Viviani claimed that in one experiment, Galileo dropped balls of different weights from the Leaning Tower of Pisa, in Italy, although no one knows if Galileo really did this. Galileo's finding that heavy and light objects released near Earth's surface fall at roughly the same speed upset the idea that heavy objects fall faster, which the ancient Greek philosopher Aristotle had stated 1,900 years earlier. On Earth, slight differences in the speed at which objects fall are due to air resistance, not mass.

Galileo would have climbed nearly 300 steps to reach the top of the Leaning Tower of Pisa to drop the two balls

Gravity makes the balls—one lighter than the other— fall at the same speed

The two balls are the same size but weigh different amounts

The balls hit the ground at almost the same time, despite the difference in their weights

EXPERT CONSULTANT: Roma Agrawal **SEE ALSO:** Nebulae, p.12–13; End of the Universe, p.46–47; Earth in Space, p.54–55; Measuring Earth, p.56–57; Combustion, p.108–09; Forces, p.132–33; Pressure, p.136–37

Free fall

Skydivers can free-fall for minutes before releasing their parachutes. At the start of the jump, they accelerate fast, as gravity pulls them toward the ground. After about 15 seconds, they reach a constant speed. Called terminal velocity, this is the speed at which the pull of gravity is balanced by the resistance of the air. Jumpers can tuck in their limbs to free-fall quicker or, like this skydiver, they can spread them out to fall more slowly.

Flames in space

Gravity even affects fire. When someone lights a match on Earth, gravity pulls on gases in the flame, creating the bottom-heavy shape we are used to seeing. If you change the way you hold the match, the flame shifts, keeping the biggest part closest to the ground. But high above Earth, where the International Space Station orbits, there is very little gravity. There, flames are rounded, and they stay rounded no matter how you hold them.

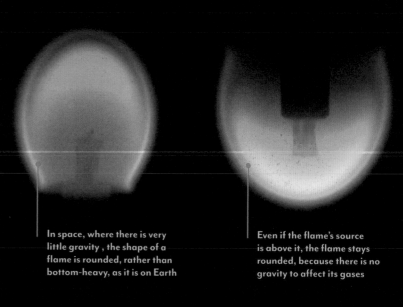

In space, where there is very little gravity , the shape of a flame is rounded, rather than bottom-heavy, as it is on Earth

Even if the flame's source is above it, the flame stays rounded, because there is no gravity to affect its gases

GAME CHANGER

ALBERT EINSTEIN

Physicist, lived 1879–1955
Germany

The scientist Albert Einstein figured out several very important rules about the way the Universe works. One of them is that time is a dimension, just like height, length, and width—the three dimensions we commonly use to measure things. He called this four-dimensional combination space-time and figured out that gravity can bend it. Knowing this helps physicists predict the behavior of the Universe.

KNOWN UNKNOWN

Does life need gravity?

All the living things we know are on Earth. They all exist in gravity. Does that mean plants and animals need gravity to thrive? Plants and animals on the International Space Station (ISS) don't develop as they do on Earth, but maybe they will adapt to life in low gravity. Mice on the ISS continued to be in good health, suggesting that they might.

Mice on one space trip ran in circles, possibly to stimulate fine hairs in the inner ear that aid balance, helping them cope with weightlessness

135

Aerosols

Street artists produce their wall paintings with aerosol spray paints. These work using pressure. The paint manufacturers squeeze a mix of paint and gas (often hydrocarbon) into the can. Usually, the pressure in the can is two to eight times the normal air pressure. Pressing the button releases some of the pressurized gas, carrying paint with it. As the gas swells out, it breaks up the paint into a fine spray.

PRESSURE

Pressure is how much force pushes on an area. It can be measured in pounds per square inch. A strong push on a small area creates high pressure. The same amount of push on a large area creates lower pressure. If you stand on snow in shoes, your weight is focused on a small area so the pressure makes you sink into the snow. If you wear skis, however, your weight is spread over a larger surface, reducing the pressure enough for the snow to support you. Gases, such as air, and liquids, such as water, exert pressure, because their molecules move in every direction, creating a push.

FACTastic!

There are 15 pounds of air pressure pushing in on every square inch of your body ($1kg/cm^2$). That adds up to about a ton, or the weight of a buffalo. So, why don't we feel crushed? It's because all the water in our body pushes back with much the same force.

EXPERT CONSULTANT: Roma Agrawal **SEE ALSO:** The Atom, p.100–01; Elements, p.102–03; Compounds p.106–07; Solids, Liquids & Gases, p.110–11; Lighter than Air, p.138–39; The Deep Sea, p.182–83

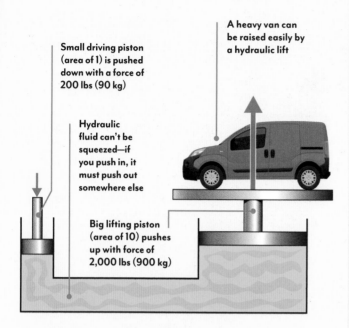

Small driving piston (area of 1) is pushed down with a force of 200 lbs (90 kg)

A heavy van can be raised easily by a hydraulic lift

Hydraulic fluid can't be squeezed—if you push in, it must push out somewhere else

Big lifting piston (area of 10) pushes up with force of 2,000 lbs (900 kg)

How hydraulic machines work

Hydraulic car lifts use the pressure in oil. When you push oil down on one side, it is pushed up on the other side with the same pressure. But because the lifting piston is much bigger, the pressure is spread over a larger area, multiplying the force enough to lift the car. To get the extra force, the smaller pushing piston has to move much farther.

Atmospheric pressure

The atmosphere that surrounds Earth has weight and pushes down on anything below it. Air is heaviest at sea level because the air molecules are compressed by the weight of the air above them. Air becomes lighter farther away from Earth's surface, as the air molecules become separated by more space. Because this thinner air contains less oxygen, airplanes are pressurized—air is pumped into planes as they rise. This pressurization ensures passengers and crew can breathe properly and don't get sick. However, pumping air into the cabin can put too much outward pressure on the body of the airplane and damage it. Pressurization must be carefully controlled.

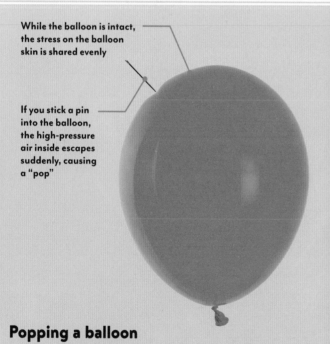

While the balloon is intact, the stress on the balloon skin is shared evenly

If you stick a pin into the balloon, the high-pressure air inside escapes suddenly, causing a "pop"

Popping a balloon

When you blow up a balloon, you force in more air. This increases pressure inside the balloon, which keeps the skin of the balloon stretched tight. If you poke the balloon, the pressure of your finger presses in the rubber. If you poke the balloon with a pin, however, the same force is placed on the tiny pinhead. This creates such high pressure that it pierces the rubber, which splits, or pops and creates a shock wave—the loud bang you hear.

This is a modern suit, but the first atmospheric diving suit was invented in the 1930s

Divers can repair oil rigs and submarines at great depths

Under pressure

The deeper down divers go, the greater the pressure the water places on their bodies. At 33 feet (10 meters) under water, there is twice as much pressure on the air in the lungs as at the surface. Divers must come up slowly to adjust the pressure in their lungs with the pressure in the atmosphere. If they come up too fast, they can get sick. Atmospheric diving suits protect divers from the effects of pressure at depths of up to 2,000 feet (600 meters).

LIGHTER THAN AIR

The first passengers on a hot-air balloon flight on September 19, 1783, were a sheep, a duck, and a rooster. They all survived. Humans took to the air in a balloon two months later. These early pioneering experiments kick-started the history of aviation. They led to the development of the motor-powered flying machine. Hot-air balloons also played a key part in establishing the "ideal gas law," which describes how gas temperature, pressure, and volume affect each other.

The ideal gas law

Three gas laws combine to make the ideal gas law: Boyle's, Charles's, and Gay-Lussac's. Boyle's gas law states that if a gas expands, its pressure drops. Charles's law states that as temperature rises, gases will expand proportionally—as long as the pressure stays the same. Gay-Lussac's law states that if the volume stays the same, pressure will increase as the temperature increases.

EXPERT CONSULTANT: David Tong **SEE ALSO:** Crewed Spacecraft, p.42–43; The Atmosphere, p.86–87; The Atom, p.100–01; Elements, p.102–03; Solids, Liquids & Gases, p.110–11; Gravity, p.134–35; Pressure, p.136–37

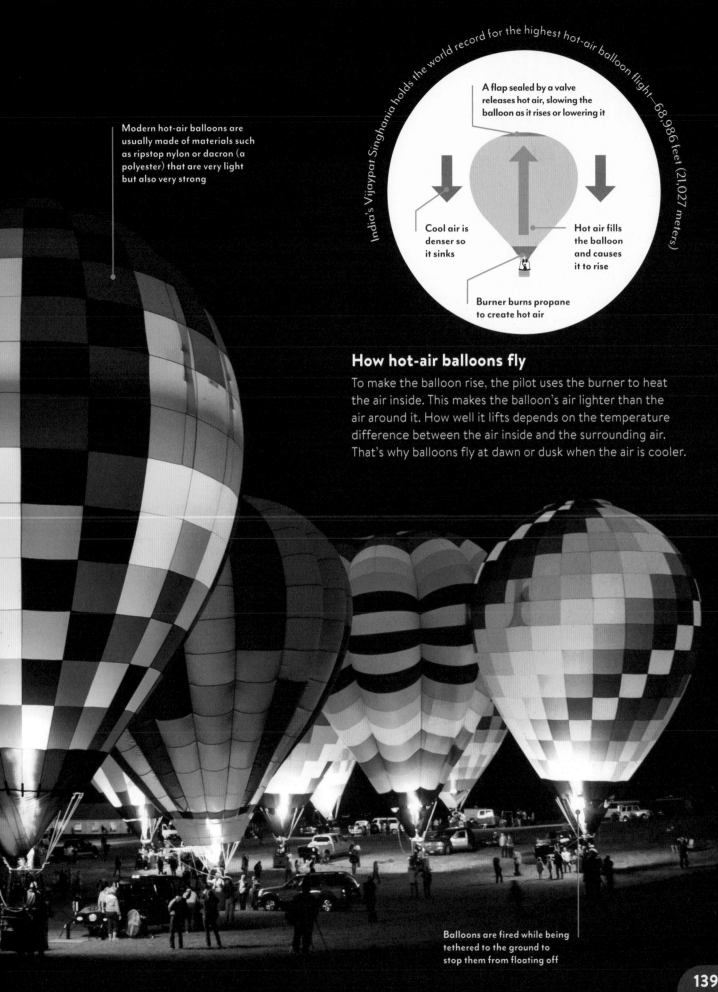

Modern hot-air balloons are usually made of materials such as ripstop nylon or dacron (a polyester) that are very light but also very strong

A flap sealed by a valve releases hot air, slowing the balloon as it rises or lowering it

Cool air is denser so it sinks

Hot air fills the balloon and causes it to rise

Burner burns propane to create hot air

How hot-air balloons fly

To make the balloon rise, the pilot uses the burner to heat the air inside. This makes the balloon's air lighter than the air around it. How well it lifts depends on the temperature difference between the air inside and the surrounding air. That's why balloons fly at dawn or dusk when the air is cooler.

Balloons are fired while being tethered to the ground to stop them from floating off

STRETCHING & SQUASHING

All solids have a definite shape, but they can be pulled and pushed, squeezed and twisted in lots of directions. Some are brittle and break easily. Others are elastic and will bend and stretch a long way. It all depends on how the particles within the material are bonded together. Some metals are relatively elastic because the bonds between their atoms hold them together. Glass, on the other hand, is very brittle. If it is stretched or squeezed even a little out of shape, it shatters.

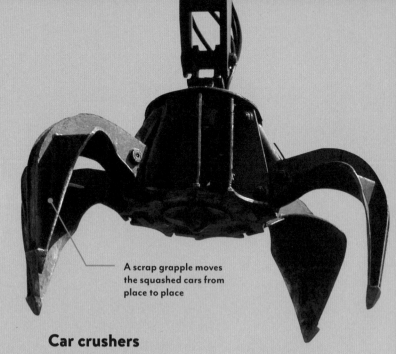

A scrap grapple moves the squashed cars from place to place

Car crushers

Crushers squash old automobiles for scrap metal. The squashed cars are easier to store. The metal bends and folds, but does not break apart. A hydraulic press can squeeze cars flat (below). They can also be squeezed from several directions to make a cube shape.

EXPERT CONSULTANT: Roma Agrawal **SEE ALSO:** The Atom, p.100–01; Elements, p.102–03; Metals, p.114–15; Plastics, p.118–19; Forces, p.132–33; Gravity, p.134–35; Pressure, p.136–37; Artificial Materials, p.360–61

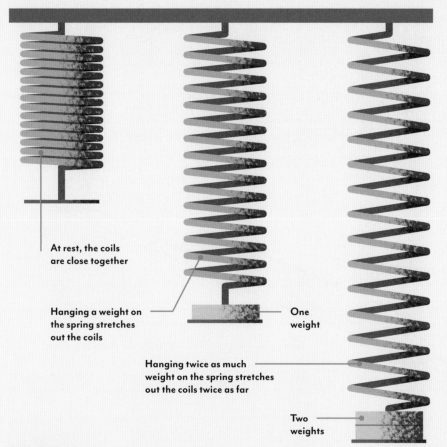

At rest, the coils are close together

Hanging a weight on the spring stretches out the coils

One weight

Hanging twice as much weight on the spring stretches out the coils twice as far

Two weights

Hooke's law

The amount any springy material squeezes or stretches depends on how much force is used. If you apply twice the force when stretching out a coil of wire (above), it stretches twice as far. This is the law of elasticity, also known as Hooke's law because it was discovered in 1660 by English scientist Robert Hooke.

Four Kinds of Force
LISTIFIED.

Stress is a measure of the amount of force being exerted on a material, and strain is a measure of how much the material changes shape under the force. There are four ways force can be applied on structures.

1. Compression crushes a material by squeezing it together. Compressive strength is the compression force something can take, before it breaks or fails.

2. Tension stretches a material by pulling its ends. Tensile strength is the maximum tension a material can take before it pulls apart or snaps.

3. Shear is when a material pulled or pushed from both ends breaks into layers (like two pieces of paper sliding over one another).

4. Torsion is a twist when the ends are turned in opposite directions. Torsion strength is the most twisting a material can take before breaking.

Suspension bridge

Suspension bridges like California's Golden Gate Bridge rely on the high-tensile strength of steel. The giant cables that hang between the towers and the vertical cables that support the road deck are all steel. Steel's tensile strength means that even thin cables can hold huge weights.

The two tall towers carry the bridge's weight

Two steel cables are strung between the two towers

The road deck hangs from the steel cables

NOTE *from the expert!*

ROMA AGRAWAL
Structural engineer

There are so many forces that act on buildings, such as gravity, wind, and earthquakes. Engineers like Agrawal make sure that structures can resist these forces and stand strong. For Agrawal, an important challenge is how to make structures more environmentally friendly.

❝ *Engineering is creative. You get to design something, then watch it become a real thing.* ❞

SIMPLE MACHINES

Machines can be as basic as a hammer or as complex as an airplane. Many machines make physical tasks like lifting or carrying easier. Simple machines are wheels, levers, pulleys, and screws. They help multiply the effort—meaning that a small effort will have a more powerful effect. This provides what is known as mechanical advantage.

A winch motor supplies the effort

Fulcrum

The jib is the long arm that carries the load

Cables run over pulley wheels that help them to pull up the load

A heavy weight called a counterweight balances the load

Cranes

Without very tall cranes to lift building materials, skyscrapers like the Jeddah Tower in Jeddah, Saudi Arabia (shown here), just couldn't be built. Cranes are machines used to lift and move heavy loads. Their lifting power or effort is provided by a winch. The winch is a motor that winds in cables to hoist up the load. The winch is aided by two simple machines: a lever and a pulley. The crane's arm, or jib, is a lever—its length multiplies the effort. The cables run over pulleys, which further multiply the effort.

Archimedes screw

Slopes are simple machines. They help you lift a load gradually, spreading your effort further than lifting the load straight up. A screw is a twisted slope. Archimedes's screw, said to have been invented by the Greek mathematician Archimedes about 2,250 years ago, can lift water from a river to a higher field to irrigate crops. Each time the screw in the tube turns, it lifts water a little higher.

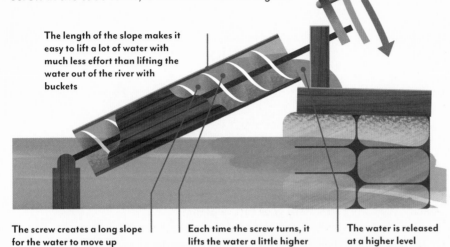

Handle

The length of the slope makes it easy to lift a lot of water with much less effort than lifting the water out of the river with buckets

The screw creates a long slope for the water to move up

Each time the screw turns, it lifts the water a little higher

The water is released at a higher level

Levers

Levers are just bars that give you extra force by turning around an anchor point called a fulcrum. If the load is close to the fulcrum and the effort far away, you get a lot of extra force. There are three types of levers, depending on where the fulcrum is in relation to the load and effort.

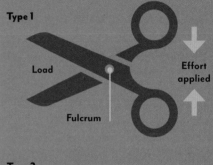

Type 1

Load

Fulcrum

Effort applied

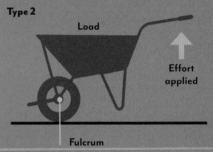

Type 2

Load

Fulcrum

Effort applied

Changing gears

Gears are toothed wheels that fit together in pairs. As one wheel turns, its teeth drive the other wheel around. When wheels are the same size, they turn with the same speed and force. But if they're different sizes, the speed and force change. Bicycles use different-sized gears so that less force is needed to cycle up hills.

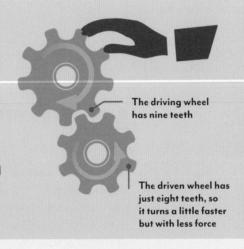

The driving wheel has nine teeth

The driven wheel has just eight teeth, so it turns a little faster but with less force

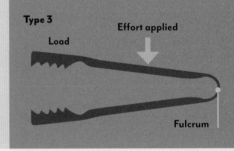

Type 3

Load

Effort applied

Fulcrum

Pulleys

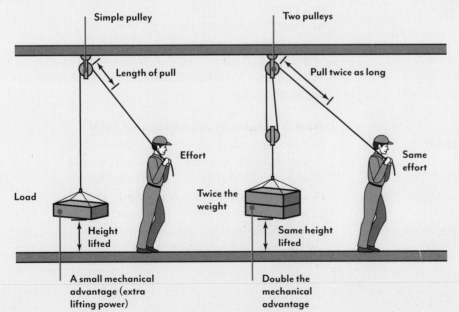

Simple pulley

Length of pull

Two pulleys

Pull twice as long

Effort

Load

Height lifted

Twice the weight

Same height lifted

Same effort

A small mechanical advantage (extra lifting power)

Double the mechanical advantage

A pulley is used for lifting heavy loads, such as a pile of bricks. It is a rope wound around a wheel. One end is attached to a load, and the other end is pulled to raise the load. Pulleys make it easier to lift heavy loads by changing the direction of the effort. The more pulleys there are, the easier it is to lift the load using the same amount of effort.

ASK THE EXPERTS!

KIMBERLY M. JACKSON
Biochemist

What do you find fascinating about your field?
I have always been interested in how proteins fold in the body into these cool functional structures. It's fascinating to know that proteins start in the cell as long chains of amino acids and then fold into complex structures with different jobs in the body.

What is an unsolved problem in your field?
There are several, but one in particular is how to cure cancer. Cancer cells grow uncontrollably, meaning they can divide without stopping and invade other tissues. Since there are so many types of cancer, one treatment does not fit all. I study licorice root as a potential cure for prostate cancer.

What are your future plans?
I love science so much that I want to share what I do on a larger platform. One day I would like to work for a museum so that I can create huge exhibits that intersect art and science.

DUNCAN DAVIS
Chemical engineer

What do you find exciting in your field?
Polymers are amazing! They get a bad rap in society because they are not the most eco-friendly, but they changed the world for the better and are some of the most interesting materials in the world. If you like chemistry and complex systems that are on the cutting edge of science, I highly recommend reading more about polymer science.

Can you tell us something surprising about chemistry?
In polymer chemistry, many of the biggest discoveries were made by accident! Vulcanized rubber, Teflon, vehicle safety glass, and entire branches of polymer chemistry happened because scientists made mistakes. But some mistakes can become new research discoveries.

A. JEAN-LUC AYITOU
Chemist

What do you want to discover most?
Chemists work tirelessly to explore the unknowns of chemical science and solve problems. For example, in my lab, we are currently developing a new technique that mimics Mother Nature. It will allow us to use light to make valuable chemicals in water, just as plants do.

What is a challenge you face in your field?
Accidents do occur in a chemistry lab, even though chemists take many safety precautions. One thing chemists fear most is the sudden rise of temperature in a reaction flask. This may cause explosions or fire. In my research lab, we always perform chemical reactions on a small scale first in order to learn how things will react.

Matter
THE QUIZ

1) **How many elements are on the periodic table?**
   a. 101
   b. 118
   c. 121
   d. 212

2) **Scientists measure levels of radioactivity in food using units called BEDs. This stands for:**
   a. Bicarbonate Equivalent Doses
   b. Biological Equivalent Doses
   c. Banana Equivalent Doses
   d. Becquerel Equivalent Doses

3) **What is the symbol for mercury on the periodic table?**
   a. Hg
   b. Mc
   c. Gl
   d. My

4) **What kind of bond is formed when a compound is made up of elements that share electrons?**
   a. Ionic
   b. Covalent
   c. Molecular
   d. Brooke

5) **A tokamak is a device used to create:**
   a. Electricity
   b. Jet engines
   c. Nuclear fusion
   d. Laser beams

6) **Bronze is created by mixing which two metals?**
   a. Copper and iron
   b. Copper and tin
   c. Tin and iron
   d. Iron and copper

7) **Which element is most abundant in Earth's crust?**
   a. Silicon
   b. Iron
   c. Carbon
   d. Oxygen

8) **In 2019, scientists were shocked to find what at the bottom of the Mariana Trench?**
   a. A living deep sea spider
   b. A hoard of gold coins
   c. A shipwreck
   d. A plastic bag

9) **German researchers became famous for making diamonds out of:**
   a. Soot
   b. Air
   c. Gasoline
   d. Peanut butter

10) **Tufa is a type of:**
   a. Animal
   b. Vegetable
   c. Mineral
   d. Gas

11) **Whales communicate through what kind of sound waves?**
   a. Infrasound
   b. Decisound
   c. Macrosound
   d. Suprasound

12) **About how many lightning strikes occur on Earth each day?**
   a. Eight to nine thousand
   b. Eight to nine hundred thousand
   c. Eight to nine million
   d. Eight to nine billion

13) **Which of the following animals was among those on the first ever hot air balloon flight in 1783?**
   a. Pig
   b. Sheep
   c. Dog
   d. Cow

14) **Heavy metals such as gold were originally created:**
   a. By the big bang
   b. During the formation of Earth
   c. Through forces in Earth's crust
   d. By stars colliding

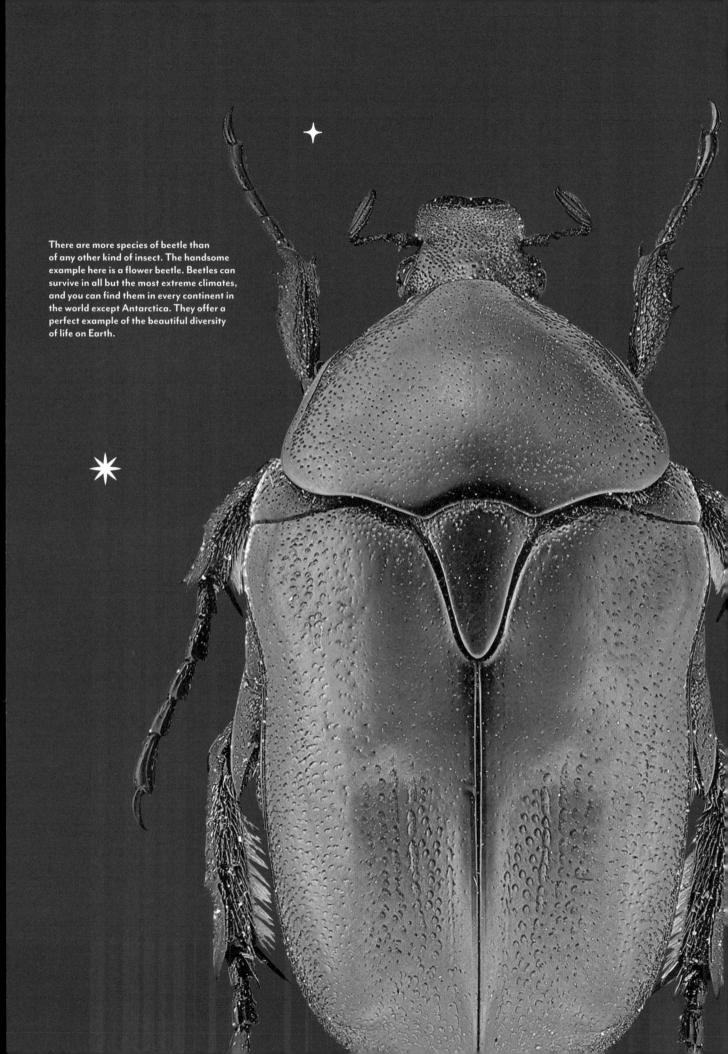

There are more species of beetle than of any other kind of insect. The handsome example here is a flower beetle. Beetles can survive in all but the most extreme climates, and you can find them in every continent in the world except Antarctica. They offer a perfect example of the beautiful diversity of life on Earth.

CHAPTER 4
LIFE

The living world is a treasure trove of surprises. Discover spiders that can walk on water, fish that glow in the dark, plants that eat animals, and even trees that communicate through smells! But there is still so much left to discover. In fact, more is known about the surface of the Moon than about what lies in the deepest oceans. And while scientists have identified 360,000 species of beetle, some think there are more than a million still waiting to be described.

In this chapter, you will see how life thrives on diversity—that means having the greatest possible variety of different living things. It's easy to see why this matters. Even if massive changes happen to our planet, some creatures will be suited to survive and thrive. So, life will persist. But there is a problem. Humans are destroying that diversity. Read about the Great Pacific Garbage Patch and the harm it is doing to ocean life or about the destruction in the great Amazon rain forest. Knowing as much as possible about our living world is key to helping solve these problems. Be inspired by our experts and see what you can do to help life flourish on Earth!

Black and white smokers

One theory for the origin of life is that it started in hot springs called hydrothermal vents that exist at the bottom of the sea. These vents spew out hot water containing minerals from deep inside Earth. The minerals make the water cloudy like smoke. Nonliving molecules may have used the energy in these vents to reproduce themselves and eventually evolve into living cells.

The color of the "smoke"—black or white—depends on the kind of minerals in the hot water

The chimneylike structures form from the minerals that spew out of them

THE ORIGIN OF LIFE

Life on Earth appeared almost 4 billion years ago. Nobody knows for certain how this happened, but it was probably a gradual process over millions of years rather than a single event. Some scientists think that nonliving chemicals gathered together and copied themselves, eventually forming living organisms. Living organisms are defined by the capacity to use energy to grow, reproduce, and change.

FACTastic!

For the first billion years after the formation of Earth, the only living things were single-celled microbes. The evolution of multicelled organisms was a big step forward. Instead of each cell looking after itself, groups of cells shared tasks and resources. Scientists think this occurred at least 2.5 billion years ago.

EXPERT CONSULTANT: Michael D. Bay **SEE ALSO:** Plate Tectonics, p.62–63; Volcanoes, p.64–65; Giant Crystals, p. 72–73; Fossils, p.76–77; Chemistry of Life, p.120–21; Evolution in Action, p.150–51; The Micro World, p.154–55; Animals, p.158–59

Early life on Earth

What is the earliest evidence for life on Earth? For a long time, it was thought to be bacteria-like fossils in rocks that were 3.5 billion years old. In 2016, scientists found fossilized microbes in rocks that were more than 3.7 billion years old. There could be even earlier evidence of life that has not yet been found.

1 billion years ago
Brown and red algae appear

4.6 billion years ago
Earth formed

3.7 billion years ago
Microbial life appears

2.3 billion years ago
The Great Oxidation Event

600 million years ago
Soft-bodied invertebrates evolve

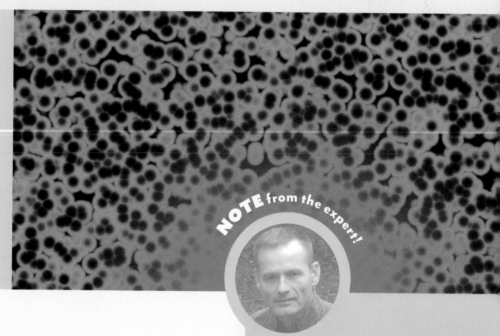

The Great Oxidation Event

For much of the first 2 billion years, Earth had very little oxygen. But then a single-celled algae called cyanobacteria evolved the ability to turn sunlight, nutrients, and water into energy. The process released oxygen as a waste product. Eventually, the atmosphere filled with oxygen, a development known as the Great Oxidation Event. Without this, complex life may not have evolved.

Living rocks

These stromatolites in Hamelin Pool, Western Australia, are made from mats of living cyanobacteria, similar to the cyanobacteria that caused the Great Oxidation Event, and mineral particles in the water. Stromatolites were abundant on Earth between 2.5 billion and 541 million years ago.

NOTE from the expert!

MICHAEL D. BAY
Biologist

Professor Michael D. Bay wants to understand how life evolved on Earth in order to understand life today. He wants to know why some animals are more susceptible to habitat loss while others appear to be able to adapt, and what specifically makes some species more susceptible or less adaptable.

❝ *Studying animal life is fascinating and rewarding.* ❞

EVOLUTION IN ACTION

Evolution is a change in the characteristics of a species that passes from one generation to the next. The features may have been passed on because creatures that had them survived better than those that did not—a process called natural selection. Gradually, useful features become more common in a population, and the species changes.

Brontornis had one of the biggest skulls of any known bird and a beak designed for ripping flesh

Its wings were small and could have been used as stabilizers while running. When flapped, they could have been part of a courtship display

The *Brontornis* stood 9.2 feet (2.8 meters) tall and weighed up to 880 lb (400 kg), making it the third heaviest bird that ever lived

The terror bird

Birds are living dinosaurs. Escaping the mass extinction of dinosaurs that occurred 66 million years ago, some birds evolved into ferocious monsters such as the *Brontornis* terror bird. Taking over places left vacant by their extinct relatives, terror birds were South America's top predators for 60 million years.

Long, powerful legs with formidable claws could kick and hold down prey. *Brontornis* was probably a walking bird rather than a runner

Astrapotherium resembled a cross between an elephant and a tapir, but was related to neither. It lived at the same time as *Brontornis* and could have been its prey

EXPERT CONSULTANT: Michael D. Bay **SEE ALSO:** Fossils, p.76–77; Finding Dinosaurs, p.78–79; The Origin of Life, p.148–49; Classifying Life, p.152–53; Ecology p.162–63; Harnessing Nature, p.190–91; Extinction Event, p.368–69

Newest rocks

Oldest rocks

Time

Understanding prehistoric creatures

By comparing the fossils of ancient creatures in old and young rocks, scientists can see how a species might have evolved. Hard parts of an animal, such as bones, fossilize well, but soft parts, such as flesh, do not. So scientists look at modern species to work out how their extinct ancestors may have looked.

GAME CHANGER

CHARLES DARWIN
Naturalist, lived 1809–82
UK

In 1858, British scientists Charles Darwin and Alfred Russel Wallace shocked the world by claiming that all living things, including humans, had evolved through natural selection. This, they said, explained the diversity of life on Earth. The next year, Darwin published *On the Origin of Species*. The book upset many people who believed that God had created all living things in their present-day form.

Changing color

Evolution didn't just happen millions of years ago. One recent example is the peppered moth in 19th-century Britain. The white moth was hard to see against the white birch trees, where it lived. Sometimes one was born black and was gobbled up by a bird. Then, coal smoke from factories turned the trees black. The white moths stood out and got eaten, while the black ones survived and reproduced. Soon there were mainly black moths and very few white ones!

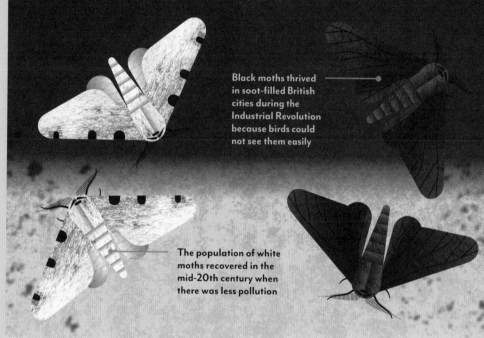

Black moths thrived in soot-filled British cities during the Industrial Revolution because birds could not see them easily

The population of white moths recovered in the mid-20th century when there was less pollution

FACTastic!

More than 99.9 percent of species that ever lived are now extinct. Some disappeared because of competition for food, others because their habitat changed. Volcanic eruptions wiped out some. Others went extinct when an asteroid hit Earth. More recently, human activities have driven animals to extinction.

KNOWN UNKNOWN

Could dinosaurs come back?

If scientists can find dinosaur DNA, they might be able to create a dinosaur. Some thought they might find dinosaur DNA inside ancient blood-sucking mosquitoes preserved in lake sediments. So far, they haven't found any, but some people continue to look for it.

151

CLASSIFYING LIFE

Biologists sort living organisms into groups that share characteristics, a process called classifying. This helps them understand how living things relate to each other and how they evolved. The ancient Greeks simply divided the natural world into animals and plants. Later systems of classification looked at how living organisms reproduce, get oxygen, or process energy. Now scientists use genetics to figure out how creatures are related.

Five kingdoms

One of the main classification systems divides the living world into five kingdoms: animals, plants, fungi (molds, yeast, and mushrooms), protists (such as amoeba and algae), and monerans (bacteria). Some scientists say that archaebacteria, many of which can live in extreme places like ice and boiling water, are different from other bacteria and form a kingdom of their own.

KINGDOM OF PROTISTS

AMOEBA   ALGAE

KINGDOM OF FUNGI

MUSHROOMS

YEAST

MOLD

KINGDOM OF PLANTS

BROAD-LEAVED TREE   CONIFER TREE

FERN   MOSS

KINGDOM OF MONERANS

BACTERIA

KINGDOM OF ANIMALS

INSECT   MOLLUSK

BIRD   MAMMAL

AMPHIBIAN

REPTILE

FISH

EXPERT CONSULTANT: Dino J. Martins **SEE ALSO:** Evolution in Action, p.150–51; The Micro World, p.154–55; Plants & Fungi, p.156–57; Animals, p.158–59; Bugs, p.160–61; Becoming Human, p.196–97; DNA & Genetics, p.200–01

Relative biomass in gigatons of carbon

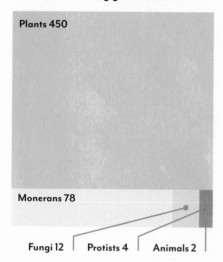

Plants 450

Monerans 78

Fungi 12 | Protists 4 | Animals 2

Measuring biomass

Biomass is the total weight or quantity of living things in an area. It can be measured by how much carbon the organism or group of organisms produces and stores during a year. Bacteria may be more numerous than, say, plants, but plants have a greater biomass because they contain more carbon than all other known life-forms combined.

Taxonomic rank

The classifying of living things is called taxonomy. Taxonomic rank shows how a species fits into bigger groups. For example, the domestic cat species (catus) belongs to the family Felidae (which also includes big cats like lions and tigers). Felidae are mammals (Mammalia), which belong to the phylum (group) Chordata, which have a spinal chord. Chordata belong to the kingdom Animalia.

KINGDOM Animalia
PHYLUM Chordata
CLASS Mammalia
ORDER Carnivora
FAMILY Felidae
GENUS Felis
SPECIES catus

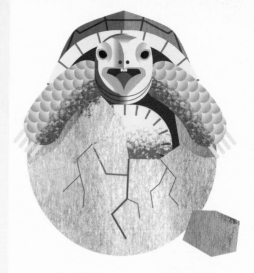

Shared characteristics

One of the reasons a land tortoise is classed as a reptile (class Reptilia) is that it hatches from a soft-shelled egg. Most reptiles have this type of egg. Biologists decide which large group a species belongs to by looking for shared characteristics like this one.

What is a species?

There are now twice as many documented species of lemur than there used to be. This isn't because we have discovered many more kinds of lemur but because we discovered DNA. Some biologists now consider a species to be distinct from a similar one if just 2 percent of its DNA is unique. Biologists now recognize more than 100 species of lemur.

KNOWN UNKNOWN

How many species are there?

No one knows how many species there are on Earth because we are constantly finding new ones, especially when remote areas become more accessible. The latest figure is aboutt 8.8 million but there may be many millions more!

FACTastic!

Greta Thunberg has a beetle named after her! A newly discovered beetle from Kenya has been given the scientific name *Nelloptodes gretae*, for the Swedish activist Greta Thunberg. The scientist who discovered the beetle thought that its antennae looked like Greta's braids.

153

The tubular mouth is used to suck juices from moss and algae

Their stubby legs end in tiny claws

Toughest of the tough

The tardigrade or water bear is smaller than a poppy seed, yet this animal can survive low-oxygen levels and high radiation. It can also stand being frozen, boiled, or completely dried out, and even survived for 10 days in space. Research into tardigrades may help scientists work out how astronauts can be protected on trips to Mars or other planets.

THE MICRO WORLD

Microorganisms—the smallest living things— can be seen only with a microscope. They include some eukaryotes, archaea, bacteria, and viruses. Eukaryotes are organisms whose cells have a control center called a nucleus. Archaea and bacteria cells, Earth's oldest life forms, don't have a nucleus. Viruses do not have cells and survive by invading other living cells. Many microorganisms are extremophiles—they live in conditions that would kill most forms of life.

Archaea

These ancient microorganisms are everywhere on Earth, including in places where other life forms would die. They are found in deep-sea hydrothermal vents and high in Earth's atmosphere. *Archaea methanosarcina* (left) live in the guts of animals, where they produce methane gas.

EXPERT CONSULTANT: Kevin Foster **SEE ALSO:** Exoplanets, p.20–21; Our Solar System, p.22–23; Chemistry of Life, p.120–21; The Origin of Life, p.148–49; Classifying Life, p.152–53; Plants & Fungi, p.156–57; Animals, p.158–59; The Deep Sea, p.182–83

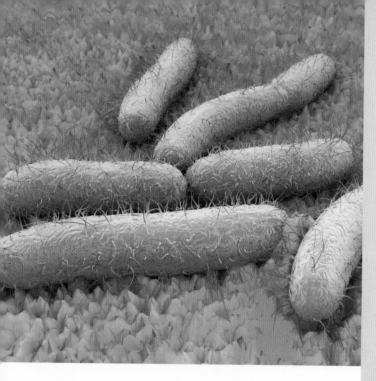

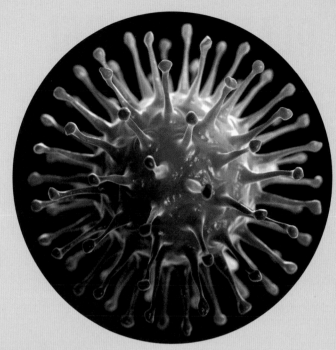

Bacteria

Bacteria are single-celled organisms. They come in many shapes including: spherical, rod (above), spiral, comma, and corkscrew. Most bacteria clump together in biofilms—layers of bacteria that attach to surfaces. Some bacteria are useful, such as those living in our gut and bacteria that eat up oil spills from tankers. Some bacteria cause diseases.

Viruses

Unable to exist on their own, viruses are parasites—they need to enter and take over a host cell in order to thrive and reproduce. Small and light, they multiply easily and spread through the air and in the tiniest water droplets. They are the cause of many diseases such as flu, chickenpox, measles, and Covid-19.

Extremophiles
LISTIFIED.
....

Many types of microbes live in extreme conditions. They are called extremophiles—lovers of extremes. Such conditions may have existed on early Earth. By studying extremophiles, scientists can work out whether there could be life on planets without liquid water.

1. Radiation-resilient Nicknamed Conan the Bacterium, *Deinococcus radiodurans* is a polyextremophile—it can survive multiple extremes and lives in many harsh environments. It can also self-repair, making it able to withstand over 1,000 times more radiation than humans.

2. Acid-resistant *Picrophilus torridusis* is the most acid-tolerant organism on Earth. It was found in sulfur beds on the island of Hokkaido in northern Japan, at temperatures of 149°F (65°C).

3. Salt-loving Bacteria at the bottom of Mono Lake, California, live in an environment that is two to three times saltier than seawater, with no oxygen.

4. Dark-defying Challenger Deep, the deepest part of the Pacific Ocean's Mariana Trench, teems with microbes more than 6 miles (10 km) below the surface of the ocean.

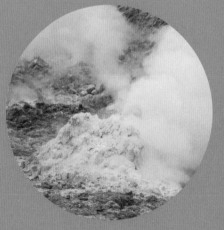

Sulfur bed, Hokkaido, Japan

5. Ice-encased *Chryseobacterium greenlandensis* has been found alive in a 120,000-year-old block of ice 2 miles (3 km) deep inside a Greenland glacier.

6. Heat-seeking *Geogemma barossii* lives in deep-sea vents. It thrives at temperatures of 250°F (121°C), much hotter than the boiling point of water (212°F/100°C).

Mono Lake, California

155

PLANTS & FUNGI

Unlike most forms of life, plants can make their own food. They take carbon dioxide from the air and water from the soil and use the Sun's energy to make sugars in a process called photosynthesis. Because of this, plants form the basis of most food chains. Fungi are more closely related to animals than they are to plants. Many of them rely on plants and animals for nutrients.

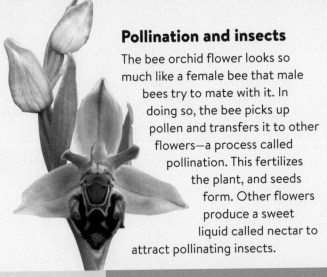

Pollination and insects

The bee orchid flower looks so much like a female bee that male bees try to mate with it. In doing so, the bee picks up pollen and transfers it to other flowers—a process called pollination. This fertilizes the plant, and seeds form. Other flowers produce a sweet liquid called nectar to attract pollinating insects.

Organelle

Cell membrane allows some substances to pass through

Chloroplast, where photosynthesis takes place

Plasmodesmata form bridges with neighboring cells

Cell wall

Vacuole, a fluid-filled space

Mitochondrion

Nucleus

Cytoplasm, a water-based fluid

Organelle

Chromosomes contain the genetic material of the plant

A plant cell

Every plant cell has a cell wall. Inside the wall are a nucleus containing chromosomes made of DNA and structures called organelles ("little organs"). These include chloroplasts, where photosynthesis takes place, and mitochondria, which turn sugar into energy. Channels called plasmodesmata in the cell wall form bridges with other cells.

Seed-spreading
LISTIFIED.

Most plants that produce seeds are rooted in place and cannot move. To occupy new sites and multiply, they must find ways to spread their seeds.

1. Flight Maple and sycamore trees produce seeds resembling helicopter blades that spiral through the air. Dandelion seeds are like feathery parachutes that blow away in the wind.

2. Water Coconuts, the single seed of the coconut palm, float away on ocean currents.

3. Explosive force When ripe, the squirting cucumber bursts and shoots its seeds high into the air.

4. Eaten and expelled Animals eat the seeds of many fruits. After passing though the gut, the seeds are expelled in droppings, complete with their own dollop of fertilizer.

5. Buried by animals When squirrels bury acorns for winter, they sometimes forget. In spring, these acorns take root.

Maple "helicopter" seed

EXPERT CONSULTANT: Matthew P. Nelsen **SEE ALSO:** Classifying Life, p.152–53; Ecology, p.162–63; The Rain Forest, p.164–65; The Taiga & Temperate Forests, p.166–67; Feeding the World, p.346–47; Environmental Challenges, p.366–67

Venus flytrap

In addition to the food they make through photosynthesis, most plants get extra nutrients through their root systems. Plants in places such as bogs that don't have many nutrients catch and digest animals instead. The Venus flytrap is one of these carnivorous plants. When insects land on the red inner surface of its leaves, they touch small hairs that trigger the trap to shut.

1 If an insect lands on or crawls across the leaf and touches a trigger hair twice within 20 seconds, the trap snaps shut

2 When the struggling prey touches the hairs five more times, the trap tightens, and digestive juices start to flow

3 After ten days, the prey is digested, leaving only an empty exoskeleton. The trap opens. The husk blows away, and the trap is reset

Red alert

Unable to make their own food, fungi feed on decaying plants or animals. Some, like the bright red and poisonous fly agaric, grow near tree roots. They help the tree gather nutrients through a network of threadlike pipes called mycelium. In return, the tree supplies the fungi with sugars. Like many other fungi, the fly agaric multiplies by shedding spores—tiny reproductive cells.

NOTE from the expert!

MATTHEW P. NELSEN
Research scientist

Matthew P. Nelsen is fascinated by fungi and how they interact with other organisms. He describes fungi as beautiful, complex, and bizarre and wants to know how their evolution influenced the world.

" There are a lot of species out there that have never been seen or described. There are more species of lichen-forming fungi than there are birds and mammals combined. "

ANIMALS

Animalia (animals) forms one of the five kingdoms of living things. Unlike plants, animals cannot manufacture food themselves, so they need to eat other animals or plants. Animals that eat plants are called herbivores, and meat-eaters are called carnivores. Animals, such as bears, that eat plants and meat are called omnivores. Most animals are mobile, although some species, such as corals, are mobile when young but anchored to a spot as adults.

Life span

Scientists think the Greenland shark can live in the Arctic Ocean for more than 500 years. It is the longest-living vertebrate. Females of the species don't even reproduce until they are about 150 years old. Elephants, which often live into their sixties, and killer whales, which can reach 100 years of age, are among the longest-living mammals. In these species, old grandmothers, which have the most experience, often lead their families.

Does it have a backbone?

Animals are often divided into two groups—invertebrates, without a backbone, and vertebrates, with a backbone. A backbone protects the spinal chord, which carries messages between the brain and the body. Instead of a brain, most invertebrates have nerve cells called ganglia.

SELECTED INVERTEBRATES

Arthropods
These include insects, spiders, crustaceans (such as lobsters, crabs, and shrimps), and millipedes.

Platyhelminthes
This group includes flatworms and tapeworms. They absorb oxygen through their skin.

Mollusks
Often found in rivers, streams, ponds and oceans, mollusks include snails, clams, and squid.

Annelids
There are around 9,000 species of annelids—segmented worms. They include the earthworm.

Porifera
Scientists thought porifera (sponges) were plants until they noticed them eating food and moving.

Echinoderms
These have tough spiny skin. They include starfish and sea urchins, which look like pin cushions.

VERTEBRATES

Mammals
These breathe air and grow hair. Most female mammals give birth to live young, and all produce milk.

Birds
All birds have feathers and wings, though not all can fly. They lay eggs instead of giving birth to live young.

Fish
Most fish have scales and breathe through gills. Their temperature changes with their environment.

Reptiles
These breathe air and have dry skin covered in scales. Apart from snakes, they generally have four legs.

Amphibians
Frogs, toads, and salamanders can live on land and in water. They often breathe in more than one way.

EXPERT CONSULTANT: Karen McComb **SEE ALSO:** Classifying Life, p.152–53; Plants & Fungi, p.156–57; The Rain Forest, p.164–65; The Taiga & Temperate Forests, p.166–67; Grasslands, p.168–69; Deserts, p.172–73; Life in Freshwater, p.174–75; The Seashore, p.176–77; The Open Ocean, p.180–81

An animal cell

All animal cells are roughly the same size. About 10,000 human cells can fit on the head of a pin. Animal cells are similar to plant cells, but with a cell membrane rather than a thick cell wall. This allows useful substances to enter the cell while keeping harmful ones out. Organelles perform the vital functions of the cell, such as converting food particles into energy and producing proteins.

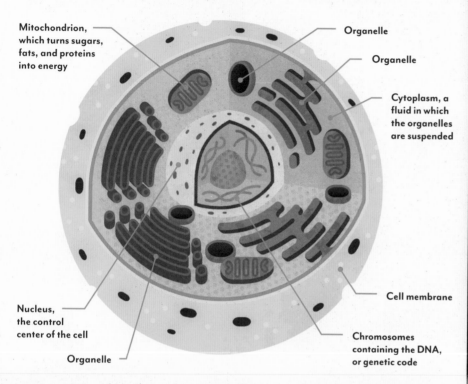

Mitochondrion, which turns sugars, fats, and proteins into energy

Organelle

Organelle

Cytoplasm, a fluid in which the organelles are suspended

Nucleus, the control center of the cell

Organelle

Cell membrane

Chromosomes containing the DNA, or genetic code

Tool-using animals

In Australia, three species of birds use fire to catch prey. They drop burning twigs onto dry vegetation to flush out small creatures such as rodents, small mammals, lizards, insects, and other birds. This is the only known example of animals other than humans using fire, but many animals use other tools. For example, crows dig out grubs with twigs, elephants use branches to scratch themselves, and orangutans shelter under leaf umbrellas.

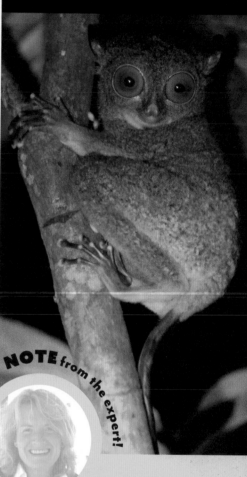

NOTE *from the expert!*

KAREN McCOMB
Zoologist

Professor Karen McComb likes to get inside animal minds by playing back recordings of their calls or showing them photographs. She has done this with many different species, including African lions, elephants, and horses. She has been amazed at how good these animals are at skills that are important to them.

❝ *I want to find out what it is really like to see the world as an animal sees it, to live inside their skin.* ❞

A whopping 80 percent of all known species on Earth are insects. They include butterflies, ants, flies, bees, wasps, and grasshoppers, as well as many other creatures. Beetles form the largest insect group, with about 360,000 known species, and probably more than a million that we haven't yet discovered. One beetle expert once found 1,200 species of beetle in a single rain forest tree!

Long-horned beetle

Most numerous in the tropics, long-horned beetles can be up to 6½ inches (17 cm) long, excluding their antennae. They are members of the Cerambycidae family, which has about 25,000 species. Adults feed on flowers and leaves, while the larvae eat the bark of trees.

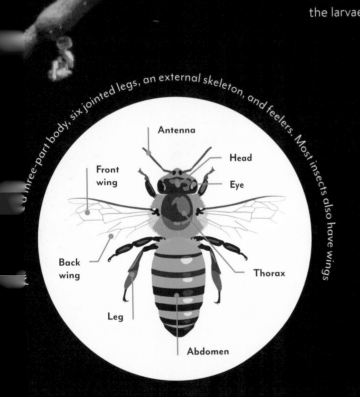

a three-part body, six jointed legs, an external skeleton, and feelers. Most insects also have wings

- Antenna
- Head
- Eye
- Front wing
- Back wing
- Thorax
- Leg
- Abdomen

Design of a honeybee

The honeybee has two pairs of wings that are joined by tiny hooks. Honeybees beat their wings more than 200 times a second and not only use them for flying but also as fans to cool down their hive and to dry their honey. They also flex their flight muscles to warm up when the weather is cold.

EXPERT CONSULTANT: Dino J. Martins SEE ALSO: Classifying Life, p.152–53; Plants & Fungi, p.156–57; Animals, p.158–59; The Rain Forest, p.164–65;

The antennae, sometimes called feelers, are often longer than the body. They use them to detect the chemical smells (pheromones) of potential mates

Working like a bank of TV cameras, compound eyes allow the beetle to see a mosaic of images. Each eye is made up of tiny ommatidia (simple eyes), which send messages to the brain

A beetle's front wings are not used for flying. They have become hard wing cases, or elytra. They protect the beetle's delicate back wings that are tucked underneath when the beetle is not in flight

Mandibles are hard, jawlike mouthparts that are used for chewing. The female beetle also uses them to create a place in the bark of trees where she can lay her eggs

Like other arthropods, beetles have jointed legs. The tarsi at the end have special claws for gripping

ECOLOGY

Living things cannot live in isolation. They interact with other living organisms and with the nonliving parts of the world, such as water, soil, and weather. Generally, an organism lives in a particular place within a community of plants, animals, and other forms of life. This community, together with its environment, is known as an ecosystem. The relationships between organisms and their environment is called ecology.

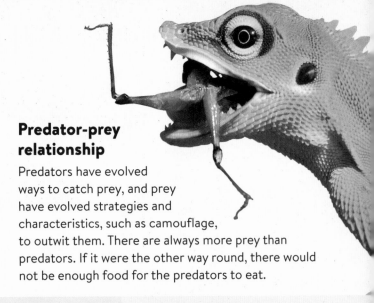

Predator-prey relationship

Predators have evolved ways to catch prey, and prey have evolved strategies and characteristics, such as camouflage, to outwit them. There are always more prey than predators. If it were the other way round, there would not be enough food for the predators to eat.

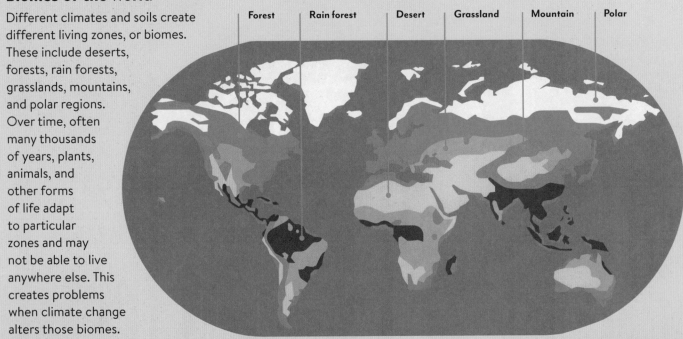

Sunlight

One-celled life (magnified)

Krill (magnified)

Small fish

Mackerel

Tuna

Great White Shark

Good to eat

All living things depend on energy, which they get from food. Food chains show how energy flows through an ecosystem—who eats whom. At the top of the marine food chain, predators like sharks consume large fish, which eat smaller fish. These small fish eat shrimplike creatures called krill, which feed on phytoplankton, a tiny algae that makes its own food using energy from sunlight. Phytoplankton forms the base of the marine food chain.

Biomes of the world

Different climates and soils create different living zones, or biomes. These include deserts, forests, rain forests, grasslands, mountains, and polar regions. Over time, often many thousands of years, plants, animals, and other forms of life adapt to particular zones and may not be able to live anywhere else. This creates problems when climate change alters those biomes.

Forest   Rain forest   Desert   Grassland   Mountain   Polar

EXPERT CONSULTANT: Tal Avgar **SEE ALSO:** Climate, p.92–93; The Rain Forest, p.164–65; The Taiga & Temperate Forests, p.166–67; Grasslands, p.168–69; Mount Everest, p.170–71; Deserts, p.172–73; The Seashore p.176–77; Ends of the Earth, p.184–85; Shrinking Ice, p.186–87

Keystone species

Ecosystems often have a keystone species—one on which other species in the system depend. The beaver is a keystone species. It builds dams that create ponds and wetlands where other species, such as frogs, ducks, and aquatic plants live. If the beaver disappears, other living organisms in the ecosystem decline.

Uniquely placed

Giant pandas live in bamboo forests in China. Wild pandas cannot live anywhere else. They have what is known as a unique ecological niche—they thrive in the bamboo forests because bamboo, their food source, is plentiful, they have no competitors, and there are few predators.

Bamboo is low in protein but plentiful. Pandas eat shoots in spring and leaves and stems at other times

Giant pandas eat about 28 lb (12 kg) of bamboo per day and spend up to 14 hours a day eating

FACTastic!

In Queensland, Australia, it is against the law to own a pet rabbit. This is because it might escape from its cage and mate with other rabbits. In Australia, rabbits are an invasive species—a non-native species whose rapid population growth has caused native species to decline.

163

THE RAIN FOREST

Rain forests grow in parts of the world that are very wet. They are important because they absorb carbon dioxide from the atmosphere and produce oxygen, helping to stabilize the climate. Tropical rain forests such as the Amazon rain forest are hot and humid, while temperate rain forests are cooler and often near the coast. More than half of the world's plants and animal species live in rain forests, where food is plentiful.

Layered habitats

Tropical rain forests have distinct layers that are determined by the amount of light and moisture available. The tallest trees can achieve heights over 200 feet (60 meters). They emerge from the dense canopy layer, where the leaves of the trees have "drip tips" to drain away water. This helps stop algae from forming. In the dark understory below, the plants have large leaves to capture the little light that gets through the canopy.

The tallest trees are called emergents

The thick forest canopy blocks out sunlight

Strangler figs climb the tree and compete for resources

The understory has small trees and bushes

Only about 1 percent of light reaches the ground, so there are few plants here

Buttress roots help support the tree

Lowland gorilla

The western lowland gorilla lives in the Congo rain forest, the second largest rain forest on Earth. It lives in small family groups led by a male, the silverback, and eats mostly plants. Even though the gorilla is large and heavy, it is a good tree climber. The loss of its forest habitat and poaching are threatening its existence.

EXPERT CONSULTANT: Gregory Nowacki **SEE ALSO:** Plants & Fungi, p.156–57; Bugs, p.160–61; Ecology, p.162–63; The Taiga & Temperate Forests, p.166–67; The Effects of Climate Change, p.372–73; Stopping Climate Change, p.374–75

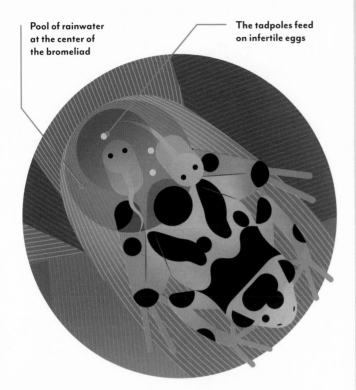

Pool of rainwater at the center of the bromeliad

The tadpoles feed on infertile eggs

Poison frogs

South American poison frogs live mostly on the forest floor and in the understory plants of the Amazon rain forest. Their bright colors warn birds and monkeys that they are highly poisonous. They are good parents. The female lays her eggs on land. When the tadpoles hatch, the male carries them on his back up to the high forest canopy. There he puts them in tiny pools that form on plants called bromeliads and protects them as they grow.

FACTastic!

The golden poison frog, only about 2 inches (5 cm) long, is one of the most poisonous animals on Earth. The skin secretions from a single frog could kill 10 people. Frogs reared in captivity tend not to be poisonous. Scientists believe this is because the frog does not make its own poison but acquires the chemicals from its natural food—tiny beetles and ants.

High and mighty

The biggest trees in the world are the redwoods and giant sequoias that live in rain forests along the West Coast of the US. They are the tallest trees, and their trunks have some of the largest diameters. The tallest living tree is currently a redwood called Hyperion—the "High One"—in Redwood National Park that is 380 feet (116 meters) tall.

HYPERION
380 feet (116 m)

The lower trunk has no branches. Branches drop off because of the lack of light

A giraffe is 17 feet (5.2 meters) tall on average, so Hyperion is as tall as 22 giraffes

Tail
A side-to-side movement or sudden flicks of the tail indicate aggression

Back legs
Long back legs act as a springboard. They help the tiger jump

Eyes
The eyes have a shiny layer that reflects light onto the retina (light-sensitive cells at the back of the eye), so the tiger's night vision is six times better than our own

Whiskers
These help tigers navigate, especially in the dark, by detecting changes in the air

Stripes
These are like fingerprints, as no two tigers have the same stripe pattern

Fur
Two layers of fur provide warmth

Tiger in the Taiga

The largest predator in the taiga is the Siberian tiger. It was once the biggest of the big cats, but a reduction in prey such as boars, caused by human hunting, means it is now a similar size to other kinds of tiger populations. There are now only around 500 animals in the wild, but conservationists are hopeful that the Siberian tiger population will increase.

THE TAIGA & TEMPERATE FORESTS

The taiga is a band of forest that stretches across the northern lands of Eurasia and North America. Also called boreal forest, it mainly has conifer trees with tough needlelike leaves that do not drop in fall. Temperate forests are found in slightly warmer climates and have many broad-leaved trees. These trees lose their leaves in fall in order to reduce water loss and save energy in winter. New leaves then grow in spring.

Winter slowdown

In winter, some woodland animals, like this dormouse, hibernate—a state that is close to death. They use very little energy and their body temperature and heart rate fall. In Alaska, the wood frog appears to freeze solid in winter. In fact, the frog produces an antifreeze inside its cells that prevents it from dying. When the weather warms up, the frog thaws out.

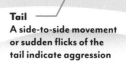

EXPERT CONSULTANT: Matthew P. Nelsen **SEE ALSO:** Climates, p.92–93; Natural Climate Change, p.94–95; Evolution in Action, p.150–51; Plants & Fungi, p.156–57; Animals, p.158–59; The Rain Forest, p.164–65; The Senses, p.206–07; Extinction Event, p.368–69; The Effects of Climate Change, p.372–73

Masters of disguise

The wings of an adult brimstone butterfly mimic an alder leaf, the plant on which its caterpillars, also green, feed. Like many other woodland creatures, it uses camouflage to hide from predators. In the taiga, snowshoe hares, which are red-brown in summer, grow white fur in winter so that they blend in with the snow.

The toughest trees

Conifer trees such as fir and spruce are designed to survive extreme cold. Their needlelike leaves store water and the drooping branches help the trees shed snow. The sap, which carries water and nutrients through the tree, undergoes a chemical change that stops it from freezing. Tough scales packed into tight cones protect the seeds.

Needles Tough and thin, conifer leaves are called needles

Closed cone The closed scales of a pine cone enclose seeds

Open cone When the seeds are mature, the cone opens and releases its seeds

What can tree rings show us?

A tree's trunk expands from the center, laying down a new "ring" each year. In good years, when there is plenty of rain and sunshine, the rings are thick; in very dry years, they are thin. By counting the number of rings, we can find out the age of a tree that has died or been chopped down.

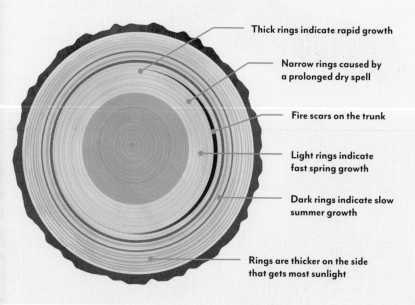

Thick rings indicate rapid growth

Narrow rings caused by a prolonged dry spell

Fire scars on the trunk

Light rings indicate fast spring growth

Dark rings indicate slow summer growth

Rings are thicker on the side that gets most sunlight

FACTastic!

The Great Basin bristlecone pines in the Rocky Mountains are the oldest living thing on Earth. Around 5,000 years old, they were alive at the same time as the last woolly mammoths.

Talking trees

Scientists have discovered that trees can communicate. If a tree is attacked by insects, its leaves produce a scent that tells neighboring trees to produce more anti-insect chemicals such as tannins. Networks of fungi growing among tree roots also pass on chemical alarm signals.

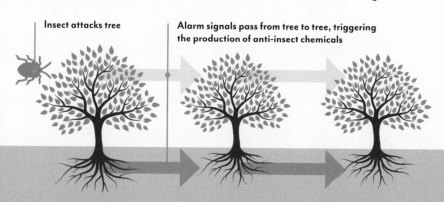

Insect attacks tree

Alarm signals pass from tree to tree, triggering the production of anti-insect chemicals

GRASSLANDS

Grasslands cover a large part of Earth's land surface. They have different names in different parts of the world. They are called prairies in North America, the steppe in Eurasia, the pampas in South America, and the savannah in Africa. Grass is very strong. It grows from the base rather than the top, so it can be cropped close to the ground by grass-eating animals. It can even survive being trampled.

Herd animals

Grassland animals often live in herds and sometimes in mixed groups, such as these wildebeest, zebra, and gazelle on the African savannah. There is safety in numbers, as predators cannot eat the whole herd. Newborn young are especially vulnerable, but luckily they can run within minutes of being born.

East-west highway

The Eurasian steppe is a corridor of grassland between East Asia and Europe. In past centuries, humans used it as a trade route and to mount military invasions. It was easier to ride horses across rolling grasslands than to climb over mountains.

FACTastic!

In the South American pampas, the giant anteater can scoop up more than 30,000 termites and ants a day. It digs into their mounds using its pointed nose, then licks up the ants with its 24-inch (61-cm) tongue. Its sticky saliva and tongue bumps help it grip the insects.

A marabou stork looks out for insects disturbed by the herd

The safest place for an individual is at the center of the herd

EXPERT CONSULTANT: Tal Avgar **SEE ALSO:** Classifying Life, p.152–53; Plants & Fungi, p.156–57; Animals, p.158–59; Ecology, p.162–63; Harnessing Nature, p.190–91; Environmental Challenges, p.366–67

Early warning system

North American prairie dogs build networks of tunnels and burrows that also provide shelter for other animals, such as owls, toads, and ferrets. The World Wildlife Fund for Nature (WWF) thinks the prairie dog's activities—digging, tunneling, and calling to warn of predators—help 136 other species.

Prairie dogs build a mound of earth at the entrances to burrows

Prairie dogs stand on their hind legs to spot danger. They use different alarm calls for different kinds of predators

Coyotes prey on prairie dogs and the other animals that use the burrows and tunnels

Burrowing owls sometimes make their nests in prairie dog tunnels

The burrows have separate areas for sleeping, rearing newborn prairie dogs, and going to the bathroom

Wildebeest often graze with zebra. Large mixed herds mean more eyes to look out for predators, such as lions and spotted hyenas

Zebra and gazelle are good at sharing the same habitat. Zebra prefer grasses that are long and coarse, while gazelle like short, tender grasses

NOTE from the expert!

TAL AVGAR
Ecologist

Dr. Tal Avgar believes that studying animal movements and their use of the landscape will help us predict where species will be and move in the future, when the environment will be very different. He thinks small biting insects may play an important part in driving movements, particularly of large herbivores.

"My job is like being a detective in the best amusement park in the world—nature!"

UNT EVEREST

At 29,035 feet (8,850 meters) above sea level, Mount Everest is the world's highest peak. It lies in the Himalayas, on the border between Nepal and Tibet. Lots of plants and animals live on Everest and the surrounding slopes. Only a few species can survive near the top of the mountain, which is rocky and icy year-round. In winter, winds at the top of Everest can reach 174 mph (280 km/h), stronger than a category 5 hurricane.

Mount Everest grows about 0.2 inches (5 mm) every year due to movements in the underlying rock

The area above 26,000 feet (7,925 meters) is known by climbers as the death zone. It has a third of the oxygen found at sea level

High flyer

On migration between north and south Asia, bar-headed geese fly across the Himalayas in seven hours, at a record-breaking maximum altitude of 23,000 feet (7,000 meters). They have large lungs and a fast-pumping heart to help move oxygen around their body.

Jumping spider

The Himalayan jumping spider has been found at 22,000 feet (6,700 meters), making it the world's highest permanent resident. The spider eats tiny insects blown up from below by the wind.

NIVAL ZONE

Above about 18,000 feet (5,480 meters) lies the nival zone. Plants here are hardy. They include low-growing members of the thistle, daisy, and mustard families that move in when glaciers melt. No plants grow above about 22,000 feet (6,700 meters), and very few animals can survive here, as the air has little oxygen.

Agile climber

The Himalayan tahr eats grasses and woody plants. It lives at altitudes of about 16,400 feet (5,000 meters) in summer, but moves to lower ground in winter. Its hooves have a rubbery sole, so that they can grip rock.

ALPINE ZONE

Between about 12,400 feet (3,780 meters) and 18,000 feet (5,480 meters), you'll find grasses and plants, such as cushion plants that can store water and withstand the dry winds. There are no trees above about 13,000 feet (4,000 meters). This point is called the tree line.

SUBALPINE ZONE

At about 9,800–12,400 feet (3,000–3,780 meters), trees such as blue pine, East Himalayan fir, and drooping juniper grow in mountain valleys. In summer, Himalayan black bears and wolves can be seen in this zone, but they migrate to lower slopes in winter.

FORESTED TEMPERATE ZONE

Plants growing between about 3,000 feet (900 meters) and 9,800 feet (3,000 meters) include the silver birch, tree-sized rhododendrons, and bamboo. Hiding among them are red pandas, mountain monkeys, and musk deer. Yellow-throated martens, the largest of the Asian martens (weasel-like mammals), hunt the deer.

12,400 ft (3,780 m)

9,800 ft (3,000 m)

3,000 ft (900 m)

Top cat

Snow leopards are the top predator in the alpine and subalpine zones. Tahr and sheep are its main prey, but it also ambushes wild goats and small prey, such as pikas and voles.

Upland pheasant

In winter, the Himalayan monal digs through snow for roots and insects. In summer, it eats larvae such as grubs and caterpillars, wild strawberries, and mushrooms.

Mountain monkey

The Nepal gray langur mainly eats buds, fruit, and leaves. It is usually found in temperate or sub-tropical forests, but it has been spotted as high as about 13,100 feet (4,000 meters).

Red panda

The red panda forages at night. Like the giant panda, its distant relative, it eats bamboo, but red pandas also catch small mammals and birds and gather flowers and fruits.

FACTastic!

Limestone rocks near the top of Mount Everest contain fossilized seashells. This is proof that the Himalayas once formed part of the seafloor and that this part of the world was once a sea separating two continents.

EXPERT CONSULTANT: Tai Avgar **SEE ALSO:** Mountains, p.68–69; Animals, p.158–59; Ecology, p.162–63; The Taiga & Temperate Forests, p.166–67

DESERTS

Deserts are the driest places on Earth. They can be hot, like the Sahara in North Africa, or cold, like the Gobi Desert in Central Asia. Not all deserts have sand dunes. Many are stony, and sometimes the Arctic and Antarctica are classified as deserts, even though they are covered in ice. Despite the lack of liquid, some plants and animals thrive in the desert, thanks to their ability to find and store the little water there is.

Each of the white, waxy flowers has hundreds of stamen producing pollen

Elf owls take over nest holes made by other birds

Finches, woodpeckers, and doves eat the fruit

Gila woodpeckers hack out nest holes half way up the stem

Saguaro cactus

The saguaro cactus in the Sonoran Desert in the US and Mexico looks like a giant candle holder. It grows slowly but steadily, taking up water and nutrients through its wide root system. It begins blooming at between 30 and 65 years old and takes 200 years to reach its full height. It can be extremely tall. One record-breaking cactus measured 78 feet (24 meters).

More than 40 arms can grow on one plant

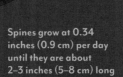

Spines grow at 0.34 inches (0.9 cm) per day until they are about 2–3 inches (5–8 cm) long

The thick stem stores water

The saguaro's wide root system can spread 50–100 feet (15–30 meters). The central taproot can be about 3 feet (1 meter) deep

Chief pollinator

Unlike many plants, saguaro cacti open some of their flowers at night. They do this from about late April to early June, and bats come to lap up their nectar. When the lesser long-nosed bat pushes its snout into the flowers, it picks up pollen, which it transfers to other saguaro flowers.

EXPERT CONSULTANT: Tal Avgar **SEE ALSO:** Water World, p.82–83; Evolution in Action, p.150–51; Plants & Fungi, p.156–57; Ecology, p.162–63; Ends of the Earth, p.184–85

Head-stander beetle

In Africa's Namib Desert, the head-stander beetle stands on the top of dunes with its head down and abdomen up, waiting for the morning fog. When the fog rolls in, droplets of water collect on the beetle's body and then run down its back and legs to its mouth. In this way, the beetle can survive in the very dry environment.

1 Fog forms out at sea and drifts into the desert

2 Fog condenses on the beetle's back and runs down its body

3 The beetle drinks the water droplets

Arabian oryx

Known as the Arabian unicorn, the Arabian oryx is perfectly adapted to its hot habitat. It has a light coat that reflects sunlight, and it can go without water for months. The brain is the organ in an animal that is most sensitive to heat, so a special blood system in the oryx's nose cools the blood going to the brain. Conservation projects have rescued the Arabian oryx from extinction in the wild.

FACTastic!

The Saharan silver ant runs 34 inches (86 cm) per second, the equivalent of a human sprinting 200 meters in a second. The ant dashes over the sand at midday, when predators are scarce, to scavenge for insects that have died in the heat. It would also die if it didn't get back to its nest quickly.

KNOWN UNKNOWN

Why do scorpions glow in moonlight?

Nobody knows for certain, but there is a theory that chemicals in the scorpion's skin convert faint ultraviolet light from the stars into blue-green light. It could be that the entire body is a light collector that confuses predators. When an object such as a rock casts shade over the scorpion's skin, the glow reduces. This may indicate that it sees the rock as a safe hiding place from predators.

NOTE from the expert!

KRISTIN H. BERRY
Ecologist

Kristin H. Berry grew up in the Mojave Desert in California. When she was eight or nine years old, she began hunting for lizards. She became a herpetologist (a person who studies reptiles and amphibians) and a population ecologist. She is currently studying desert tortoises.

66 Reptiles became a passion that has continued throughout my life. 99

LIFE IN FRESHWATER

Most of the world's water is saltwater, held in oceans, seas, and salt lakes. Only a tiny fraction is freshwater, yet humans and most animals depend on freshwater to survive. Freshwater habitats—streams, rivers, ponds, lakes, and wetlands—are also rich ecosystems full of animal and plant life. Special adaptations enable creatures to live in water, and some species have evolved to use the boundary between water and air to their advantage.

The four-eyed fish

Found in South America and Mexico, the four-eyed fish actually has two eyes, but each eye is divided into two parts. The top half looks above the surface of the water, and the bottom half looks below. The fish can catch insects flying down to the water while also looking out for creatures that already live there.

Take aim, fire

In Asia and Australia, the banded archerfish knocks insects off overhanging branches by spitting water at them. The fish achieves this by pressing its tongue against a groove in its mouth to create a channel and then closing its gills, forcing water out through its mouth like a water pistol. Its aim is extremely accurate, even when the prey is 6 feet (2 meters) away.

Walking on water

The raft spider sits at the edge of a pond, its front legs resting on the water to detect the vibrations of approaching prey. Using the surface tension of the water to support its weight, the spider then races across to catch the insect or tiny fish that has disturbed the water.

EXPERT CONSULTANT: Alexander D. Huryn **SEE ALSO:** Water World, p.82–83; Evolution in Action, p.150–51; Classifying Life, p.152–53; Animals, p.158–59; Bugs, p.160–61; The Seashore, p.176–77; The Open Ocean, p.180–81; The Deep Sea, p.182–83

Opportunists

The piraputanga, a troutlike fish from South America, has learned to shadow capuchin monkeys as they forage for fruit in overhead trees. The monkeys are messy eaters and drop scraps, which the fish gobble up. When the monkeys move on, the fish leap up and grab any low-growing fruit themselves.

Piraputanga weigh about 8 pounds (3.5 kg). A large part of their diet is fruit

The water must be clear so that the piraputanga can see the monkeys and the fruit

FACTastic!

Relative to its body size—less than $^1/_{10}$ inch (2.5 mm)—the male water boatman *Micronecta scholtzi* is the world's loudest animal. When it wants to attract a mate, it rubs a body part the width of a hair against ridges on its abdomen. The sound is loud enough for a person walking along the riverbank to hear.

Skillful fishers

In summer in Alaska, brown bears catch migrating salmon as they make their way to breeding sites upstream. The salmon come close to the surface when swimming over rapids and waterfalls. Plunging into the water, the hungry bears catch the fish with their mouths. Competition is fierce, and large male bears battle each other for the best fishing spots.

THE SEASHORE

The seashore, where the land meets the sea, includes sandy, rocky, and muddy shores, as well as estuaries, salt marshes, and mangroves. It is a dynamic world that changes with the tides, which rise and fall, pulled by the gravity of the Moon and Sun. Wildlife on seashores has adapted to contrasting conditions—hot and cold, saltwater and freshwater, wet and dry, as well as battering by the waves.

FACTastic!

A starfish pulls apart the shells of mussels and clams by using its tube feet as tiny suction cups. It then squeezes its stomach through the gap it has made and digests the soft parts of the shellfish inside the shell. If attacked, some species of starfish can lose an arm and grow a new one. A few can regrow four new arms from a single arm!

Seagull

Gulls are the garbage collectors of the beach. They scan the seashore from above, swooping down to eat anything that's edible. Sometimes they might try to take the ice cream out of your hand!

Oystercatcher

You hear the long peeping call of oystercatchers before you see them. They eat clams and mussels, prying them open with a strong, flattened bill.

ON THE BEACH

Sandy beaches are formed when loose sand particles are deposited on the beach by the action of waves and currents. The particles can come from the land, such as eroded volcanic rocks, or from the sea, such as ground-up corals and seashells. The sand, water, and air on a sandy beach are constantly in motion.

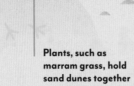

Plants, such as marram grass, hold sand dunes together

Ghost crab

This crab lives in burrows in the intertidal zone—the shore between the high- and low-tide marks. Ghost crabs are both scavengers and predators.

Razor clam

Hard shells protect many creatures from danger. The razor clam also has a powerful "foot," which it uses to burrow into the sand to escape predators.

EXPERT CONSULTANT: Gil Rilov **SEE ALSO:** Moons, p.32–33; Earth in Space, p.54–55; Plate Tectonics, p.62–63; Mountains, p.68–69; Water World, p.82–83; Gravity, p.134–35; Life in Freshwater, p.174–75; Coral Reef Crisis, p.178–79; The Open Ocean, p.180–81

KNOWN UNKNOWN

What will happen to sea turtles as the climate warms?

Sea turtles bury their eggs in the sand. If the temperature of the sand is above 87.8°F (31°C), the hatchlings will be female; if it is below 81.86°F (27.7°C), they will be male. It is not known why this happens or how global warming will affect turtle populations in the future.

Rocky shore

Plants and animals of the rocky shore spend half the day in the open air and the other in seawater. They have adaptations to stop them drying out. Seaweed, for example, has a slippery jellylike coating. Many animals live in rock pools. They emerge from hiding places when the tide is out but scuttle for cover when the tide comes in.

Creatures of the mangroves

Mudskippers live among the tangled roots of mangroves—the only trees that live in seawater. The fish spend up to 90 percent of their time on mud, using eyes that see better in air than in water. They obtain oxygen through the skin and lining of their mouth rather than using gills the way most fish do.

Heron

With long legs, the heron can wade into the water and grab fish or shellfish with a quick dart of its head and long, pointed bill.

Sea grass is a flowering plant that lives in warm, shallow waters. It is a food source and a hiding place for many marine creatures

NOTE from the expert!

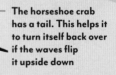

GIL RILOV
Marine biologist

Dr. Gil Rilov investigates how climate change is affecting the habitats of coastal species. He lives on the shore of the Mediterranean Sea, where many native species are disappearing and new ones are moving in. This disrupts the ecological balance.

❝ *We live in a fast-changing world, and I am worried that some parts of nature will not keep up.* ❞

Horseshoe crab

During spring tides, millions of horseshoe crabs come ashore to lay their eggs. Migrating shorebirds arrive at the same time so they can eat the buried eggs.

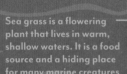

The horseshoe crab has a tail. This helps it to turn itself back over if the waves flip it upside down

CORAL REEF CRISIS

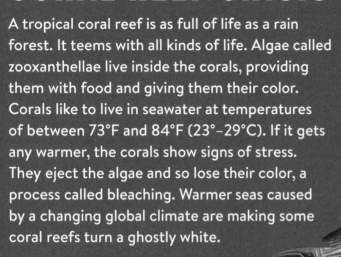

A tropical coral reef is as full of life as a rain forest. It teems with all kinds of life. Algae called zooxanthellae live inside the corals, providing them with food and giving them their color. Corals like to live in seawater at temperatures of between 73°F and 84°F (23°–29°C). If it gets any warmer, the corals show signs of stress. They eject the algae and so lose their color, a process called bleaching. Warmer seas caused by a changing global climate are making some coral reefs turn a ghostly white.

This zebra surgeonfish depends on the algae found in a healthy coral reef for food, as do lots of other fish, turtles, snails, shellfish, and sponges

This coral has lost its algae and all we see is its white skeleton. Coral bleaching events happen more often than in the past. Scientists fear temperatures are rising faster than the coral can adapt to warmer waters

EXPERT CONSULTANT: Janice Lough

Feed me!

Corals are animals, not plants. They feed at night, using their tentacles to capture tiny animals called zooplankton, which drift in the water. They sting their prey using special cells called nematocysts. The plantlike algae, which live in the coral, add to the coral's diet by using energy from the Sun to make food, a process called photosynthesis. In return, the coral provides shelter for the algae.

The relationship between corals and the zooxanthellae is called a mutualism—they benefit by depending on each other

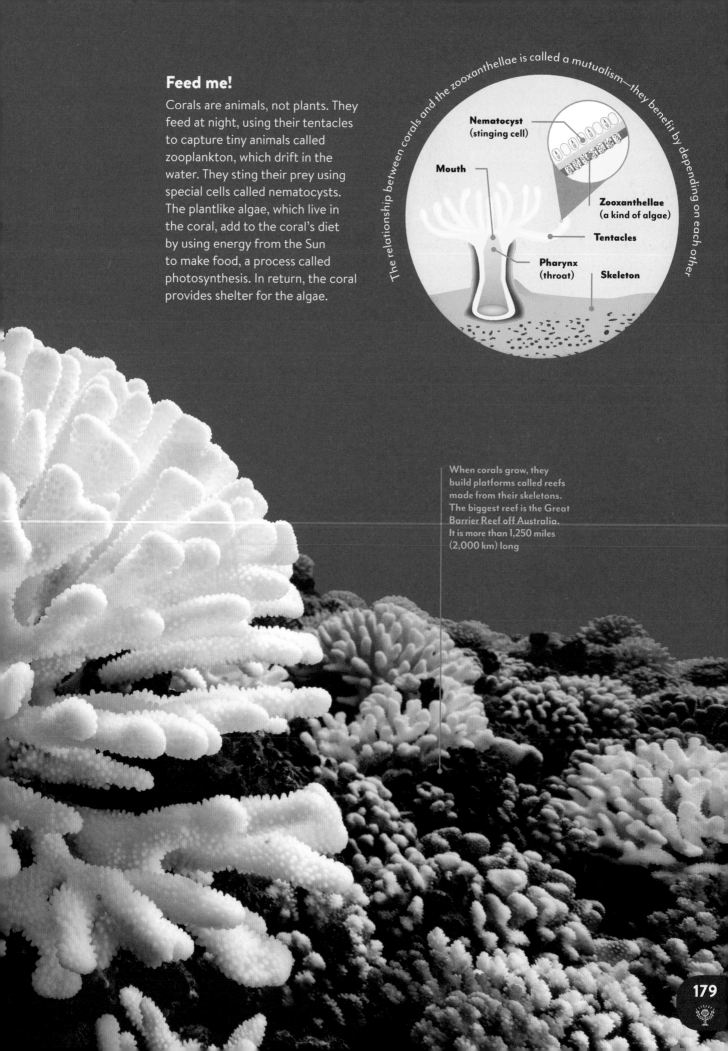

Nematocyst (stinging cell)

Mouth

Zooxanthellae (a kind of algae)

Tentacles

Pharynx (throat)

Skeleton

When corals grow, they build platforms called reefs made from their skeletons. The biggest reef is the Great Barrier Reef off Australia. It is more than 1,250 miles (2,000 km) long

THE OPEN OCEAN

The area from the surface of the ocean to a depth of about 656 feet (200 meters) is known as the sunlight, or epipelagic, zone. This means it gets enough sunlight for microscopic creatures called phytoplankton to photosynthesize—use the energy in sunlight to convert water and carbon dioxide from the air into food. As producers of food, phytoplankton form the base of the oceans' food chain, allowing a huge variety of fish and marine mammals to thrive.

Bill
The sailfish uses its bill like a sword rather than a spear, swiping it from side to side

Dorsal fin
This large fin can be raised to offset the sideways movement of the bill when the sailfish is attacking prey. At other times, the fish keeps it close to its body

Prey
Sardines live in vast shoals that can be up to 4 miles (7 km) long, 1 mile (1.6 km) wide and 66 feet (20 meters), or more deep

Gills
Fish use gills to take oxygen from the water

Skin
Patterns on the skin darken and become more prominent when the sailfish attacks

Tail fin
Strong tail muscles help fish to swim

Scales
Overlapping scales help fish glide smoothly through the water

Atlantic sailfish

The Atlantic sailfish, which can grow up to 10 feet long (3 meters), mainly swims near the surface of the ocean, but it sometimes dives 320 feet (100 meters) to find food. It is one of the world's fastest fish. When feeding, it powers along at 22 mph (36 km/h). Many open ocean fish are fast swimmers, as there is nowhere in the open ocean to hide from predators.

EXPERT CONSULTANT: Linda J. Walters **SEE ALSO:** The Earth, p.60–61; Climate, p.92–93; The Origin of Life, p.148–49; Animals, p.158–59; Ecology, p.162–63; Life in Freshwater, p.174–75; Coral Reef Crisis, p.178–79; The Deep Sea, p.182–83; Environmental Challenges, p.366–67; Endangered, p.370–71

Blue whale

The biggest animal that has ever lived, the blue whale can grow up to 100 feet (30 meters) long, the same length as a basketball court. It feeds on krill, each just 2½ inches (6 cm) long. Whaling had drastically reduced the number of blue whales by the 20th century, but numbers are now increasing.

Following the drift

The body of the lion's mane jellyfish can be 6½ feet (2 meters) across, and the tentacles 100 feet (30 meters) long, the same length as a blue whale. Like sea turtles, jellyfish travel on ocean currents. These are like giant rivers in the sea. By moving warm water north and south from the equator, currents transfer heat across the planet, helping to even out our climate.

FACTastic!

The Great White Shark never stops swimming. It must keep moving so that oxygen-rich water continually enters its mouth and passes over its gills. If the shark stopped swimming, it would drown.

Polluting plastic

Plastic pollution of the oceans is a huge problem. In addition to the damage done by pieces of plastic, wastewater from washing machines contains microscopic plastic fibers found in some clothes. When these reach the ocean, tiny organisms eat them and the plastic fibers are passed up the food chain.

Ocean currents called gyres round up the plastics, creating vast garbage patches. The worst of these are two that make up the Great Pacific Garbage Patch, which is twice the size of Texas

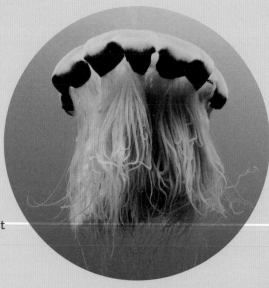

Western Great Pacific Garbage Patch

Eastern Great Pacific Garbage Patch

Texas

ASIA

NORTH AMERICA

PACIFIC OCEAN

THE DEEP SEA

The ocean is the planet's largest habitat, most of which is deep sea, yet scientists have explored only a fraction of the deep sea floor. In fact, we know more about the surface of the Moon than we do about the deepest ocean. The invention of new underwater vehicles called submersibles is changing all that, revealing many kinds of strange and fascinating creatures.

LAYERS OF THE SEA

Scientists divide the ocean into layers according to depth, pressure, and the amount of sunlight they receive. In the deepest zone, the pressure is so great it's as if an elephant is standing on each square inch of the ocean floor.

Sunlight zone (epipelagic), 0–650 ft (0–200 m)
Pressure 0 to 20 times that at the surface

Twilight zone (mesopelagic) 650–3,300 ft (200–1,000 m)
Pressure 20–100 times that at the surface

Midnight zone (bathypelagic) 3,300–13,100 ft (1,000–4,000 m)
Pressure 100–400 times that at the surface

Dumbo octopus

This species reaches the greatest depth of any known octopus. It is 8–12 inches (20–30 cm) high and gets its name from its flaplike fins, which resemble the ears of Disney's Dumbo.

Abyssal zone (abyssopelagic) 13,100–19,700 ft (4,000–6,000 m)
Pressure 400–600 times that at the surface

Tripod fish

The tripod fish is 12–15 inches (30–40 cm) long and stands on stilts formed by its pelvic and tail fins. It is then at the right height to catch passing prey swimming in the current.

Hadal zone (hadalpelagic) 19,700–33,000 ft (6,000–10,000 m)
Pressure 600–1,100 times that at the surface

Snailfish

The snailfish is 6–12 inches (15–30 cm) long. In 2017, Japanese scientists filmed a snailfish 26,831 feet (8,178 meters) deep in the Pacific Ocean's Mariana Trench—the deepest place on Earth.

EXPERT CONSULTANT: Monika Bright **SEE ALSO:** Inside Earth, p.58–59; Plate Tectonics, p.62–63; Earthquakes & Tsunamis, p.66–67; Pressure, p.136–37; The Open Ocean, p.180–81

Glow-in-the-dark

Many animals in the deep sea are bioluminescent—they light up in the dark. They can do this because of a chemical reaction in their bodies or in bacteria that they host. Female deep sea angler fish, which live in the twilight and midnight zones, have a bioluminescent bacteria-filled lure on the end of a long fin like a fishing rod. The light attracts prey toward its tooth-filled mouth.

Only female angler fish have a light-producing lure

The large mouth has long, sharp teeth, giving the angler fish a fierce reputation. They eat other deep-sea fish and shrimps

Angler fish can inflate their stomachs to incredible sizes. This allows them to consume prey far bigger than themselves

Angler fish look fierce, but female angler fish are only 7 inches (18 cm) long and males are just 1 inch (2.5 cm) long

Like many deep-sea fish, the angler has a soft body. In some species, the male anglerfish latches onto the body of the female with its teeth, and the two stay connected for the rest of their lives

NOTE from the expert!

Deep-sea exploration

Underwater vehicles called submersibles are specially strengthened to resist high pressures at great depths. They enable scientists to observe deep-sea animals. Scientists sometimes bring creatures to the surface in cooled and pressurized tanks so that they can study them in the laboratory.

These scientists sit in a spherical capsule with views all around

MONIKA BRIGHT

Marine biologist

Monika Bright's first encounters with the ocean were during vacations to the Mediterranean Sea as a child. Fascinated by the diversity of animals in the sea, she went on to study zoology and marine biology.

66 *Only when you go down to the bottom of the ocean in a submersible do you start to understand how huge this habitat is.* 99

ENDS OF THE EARTH

The polar regions are icy. In the North, the Arctic Ocean is frozen for nine months of the year and surrounded by icy tundra where little can grow. In the South, Antarctica's mountainous landscape is covered by an ice cap over a mile (1.9 km) thick. Satellites have recorded winter temperatures as low as -144.4°F (-98°C) on the Eastern Antarctic Plateau, the coldest place on Earth.

Arctic terns weigh about 3.5 oz (100 g)—the weight of a medium-sized apple—and have long, narrow wings that are ideal for gliding and soaring

Terns nest on the ground in Greenland. Chicks are fed small fish called capelin, which are plentiful

On the journey south, terns stop for nearly a month to feed in the middle of the North Atlantic

Off northwest Africa, about half the birds cross the Atlantic to fly south along the South American coast

GREENLAND

ARCTIC

ATLANTIC OCEAN

AFRICA

SOUTH AMERICA

ATLANTIC OCEAN

During the southern summer birds feed in Antarctica's Weddell Sea, which is rich in small fish

ANTARCTICA

On the return journey, the birds fly 320 miles (520 km) a day, taking about 40 days to reach Greenland. They are helped by winds and feed and sleep while flying

Long-haul flight

Each year the Arctic tern flies between the Arctic and Antarctica to take advantage of the long summer days at both ends of the world. The round trip is about 44,050 miles (70,900 km). During a 30-year life span, a tern travels almost as far as three times to the Moon and back.

EXPERT CONSULTANTS: Tal Avgar, John P. Rafferty **SEE ALSO:** Climate, p.92–93; Evolution in Action, p.150–51; Classifying Life, p.152–53; Animals, p.158–59; Ecology, p.162–63; Mount Everest, p.170–71; Shrinking Ice, p.186–87; The Effects of Climate Change, p.372–73

Coming up for air

How do sea mammals, which need air, breathe when the sea has iced over? Weddell seals, which live in the Antarctic, use their teeth to open holes in the ice. In the Arctic, belugas, narwhals, and bowhead whales seek out leads—channels of water caused by fractures in the ice.

KNOWN UNKNOWN

Why are sea spiders so big?

Sea spiders as large as dinner plates thrive under Antarctica's sea ice. Scientists are puzzled by their size, but think the highly oxygenated cold water and the spiders' slow metabolism have something to do with it.

Struggle for survival

In Antarctica, male emperor penguins help rear the chicks. Once the female has laid an egg, the male takes over. Balancing the egg and later the hatchling on his feet, he stays on the ice while the female marches up to 70 miles (112 km) to the sea to feed. She dives as deep as 1,755 ft (535 meters) to catch fish and squid. On her return, she regurgitates food for the chick.

A snug brood pouch below the male's belly protects the chick

NOTE from the expert!

The penguins huddle together to protect themselves from the cold blast of 89 mph (144 km/h) winds

JOHN P. RAFFERTY
Earth and Life Sciences editor

John Rafferty is Britannica's expert on Earth and Earth processes. He is amazed by how Earth and its living things continually affect and change one another.

" Earth is the only planet we've discovered with life, but that life exists in areas of extreme heat, extreme cold, extreme pressure, and everywhere in between. "

Built for the climate

Musk ox survive the Arctic winters because of their layered coats and the thick hollow hairs around their feet. Without this hair, their feet could freeze to the ground. Like polar bears, they also have large bodies and small legs. This means that they lose less heat from their bodies than smaller animals do.

SHRINKING ICE

Because the climate is warming, each year there is less ice in the Arctic Ocean. This affects polar bears, which travel over the ice in search of ringed seals. Faced with going hungry, most polar bears head for land and survive on birds' eggs, berries, and seaweed, but bears in Hudson Bay, Canada, have learned to stand on rocks and catch belugas as they swim in on the tide.

The polar bear is one of the largest of the bears. It is classified as a marine mammal, as it spends most of its life on the sea ice or swimming in the sea

Like dolphins, belugas belong to a group of aquatic mammals called toothed whales. Unlike the dolphin, it has no dorsal (top) fin, as this could get trapped under the ice

EXPERT CONSULTANT: John P. Rafferty **SEE ALSO:** Ice, p.84–85; Climate Change, p.94–95; Evolution in Action, p.150–51; Ecology, p.162–63; The Open Ocean, p.180–81; Ends of the Earth, p.184–85; The Effects of Climate Change, p.372–73; Stopping Climate Change, p.374–75

Polar bear cubs

Female polar bears give birth in snow caves in winter. They usually have between one and three cubs. The cubs are born blind and weighing less than a bag of sugar, but they quickly put on weight, fed by their mother's rich milk. The cubs emerge from the den in spring when they are between three and four months old.

Cubs stay with their mother for about three years, learning to swim, hunt seals, and survive in the harsh environment

Baby belugas stay close to their mothers. Belugas communicate by calling to each other like birds, so are sometimes known as "sea canaries"

Summer visitors

Each summer, belugas visit the Seal River estuary in Hudson Bay in Canada, where they molt (shed their outer layer of skin) and give birth. The water here is warmer than in the bay, so it makes a good nursery for the newborn belugas.

Daytime in the city

Seagulls and birds of prey nest on building ledges because they are similar to rocky cliffs, their natural nesting sites. Gulls visit dumps for food, while peregrine falcons hunt in the canyons between high-rise buildings, preying on city pigeons.

Peregrine falcons have been deliberately introduced to cities to catch pigeons, which are often seen as pests.

Nesting sites on city buildings are often safer than those in the wild. Predators like foxes can't access such spots.

Squirrels are usually daytime animals, but in the warmth and light of cities, they forage at night, too.

URBAN WILDLIFE

Wild animals patrol our cities day and night, often looking for food. People are wasteful, and wild animals are happy to steal food from trash cans or bird feeders. Raccoons and coyotes visit North American backyards, and foxes and badgers do the same in Europe. In other parts of the world, urban wildlife ranges from monkeys and marsupials to reptiles.

Nature's sopranos

Songbirds in the cities sing shorter, faster, and higher-pitched songs than birds in the country. The pitch change is so great that country birds don't recognize the city birds' songs.

City slickers

In the Caribbean region, city anole lizards have evolved longer legs and stickier feet to help them climb glass and concrete. With these adaptations, they can take advantage of the urban environment and are not restricted to patches of forest.

The lizard makes the loose skin on its throat look bigger, perhaps to warn others against coming into its territory

EXPERT CONSULTANT: Michael D. Bay **SEE ALSO:** Evolution in Action, p.150–51; Classifying Life, p.152–53; Animals, p.158–59; Ecology, p.162–63; Harnessing Nature, p.190–91

Nighttime in the city

When humans living in cities go to sleep, the night shift takes over. It includes white-footed mice and meadow voles, some of which have bigger brains than those of their country cousins. Scientists are investigating whether this could be because of the complexity of city life.

Barred owls thrive in cities. They live in parks and yards, where they catch mice, rats, and squirrels.

Cockroaches live inside buildings. They take advantage of the warm, protected environment, where food is plentiful.

Metropolitan monkey business

In southern Asia, some types of monkeys thrive in cities. They steal food, bite anybody who frightens them, and clamber about on buildings and power lines, just as they would in trees in the wild. Some people want their numbers controlled, but Hindus revere the monkeys as living representations of the god Hanuman. Traditionally, Hindus give the monkeys food on Tuesdays and Saturdays.

FACTastic!

A mountain lion has been spotted in the hills around Los Angeles. In 2012, the lion, known as P-22, was caught on camera living in Griffith Park, a tiny island of wilderness surrounded by freeways in the Hollywood Hills. Scientists have tracked the lion, but few of the area's celebrities, or the park's 10 million visitors a year, have ever seen it.

Raccoons raid garbage cans and will even use cat doors to enter houses in search of food. They've become known as trash pandas.

HARNESSING NATURE

About 15,000 years ago, some of our ancestors began to live in villages instead of moving from place to place to hunt and forage. To make sure they still had reliable supplies of food, they took animals and plants from the wild and allowed only those animals and plants that had certain qualities to reproduce. They did the same with the next generation, and the ones after that. Eventually, every specimen had the qualities that humans wanted. This process is called domestication.

Wild origins

Before humans domesticated horses, they hunted wild horses like these, painted on the walls of Chauvet Cave in France more than 30,000 years ago. They hunted wild horses for meat, along with bison, deer, and aurochs (a type of wild ox).

Selective breeding

Humans domesticated horses around 6,000 years ago, first for riding and warfare and then for specific tasks, such as pulling heavy loads, and more recently for racing. While farmers select animals that are very strong, racehorse owners breed horses with long and powerful legs so they can run fast.

Draft horses had to have a calm temperament as well as strength

Farm horses were bred to be tall and powerful in order to pull plows, carts, and logs

Many from one

These plants are all the same species, *Brassica rapa*, even though they look and taste different. They all come from the wild mustard plant, which grows wild from Southern Europe to Central Asia. By choosing specimens with large flower buds over many generations, farmers produced broccoli and cauliflower. By selecting ones with large roots, they produced turnips, and by choosing specimens with lots of leaves, they eventually created kale.

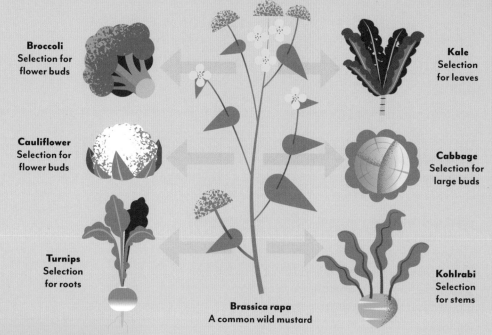

Broccoli
Selection for flower buds

Kale
Selection for leaves

Cauliflower
Selection for flower buds

Cabbage
Selection for large buds

Turnips
Selection for roots

Kohlrabi
Selection for stems

Brassica rapa
A common wild mustard

Arctic herders

The Sami people of northern Scandinavia and Russia care for reindeer herds. The reindeer are classified as semidomesticated. They provide the Sami with meat, hides, milk, and transportation.

Getting bigger

There are more than 20 billion chickens on the planet, more than any other type of bird. A combination of selective breeding and intensive farming methods, such as boosting feed with additives, make chickens grow faster, often creating health and welfare problems. Chickens today are four times bigger than they were 60 years ago.

FACTastic!

Hundreds of dog breeds have evolved from one ancient species of wolf. This is because humans have selectively bred them for different purposes, such as hunting, herding, and cuteness. The latest "designer dogs" are cross-breeds such as the cockapoo, a cross between a cocker spaniel and a poodle.

Chihuahua · Dachshund · Border terrier · French bulldog · Cavalier King Charles Spaniel · Miniature pincher · English bulldog · Border collie · Labrador · Vizsla · German shepherd · Bernese Mountain Dog · Wolf

ASK THE EXPERTS!

KEVIN FOSTER
Evolutionary biologist

What questions do you want to find the answers to?
Our bodies are home to lots of microbes, particularly bacteria, that live in dense and diverse communities. They affect almost every aspect of our lives but we understand very little about them. How do they evolve? Why do they sometimes harm our health?

What is surprising about your field?
Bacteria like to fight! They carry a vast array of armaments that they use to attack other strains and species of bacteria. They also release toxins into the environment and use a range of draconian machines, including poisoned molecular spearguns that fire into competing cells and kill them.

What do you enjoy about your research?
I find it amazing that each of us carries hundreds of species of microbes that live, like tiny rain forests, on and inside us. Understanding these miniature worlds is vital for our well-being, as they are often the difference between health and disease.

JANICE LOUGH
Climate scientist

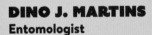

What do you enjoy about your research?
Being a scientist is fun! Asking questions about the world around us is fascinating. One of the things I do is take cores from large corals. When we X-ray slices from these cores, we see annual growth bands, similar to tree rings. Some corals tell us what the environment was like long ago and how fast they grew. Coral skeletons are natural reef history books!

Can you tell us a surprising fact?
Corals are animals! What makes tropical coral reefs special is the relationship between the host coral animal and tiny plants (algae) that live in the coral's tissue. This special relationship benefits both the coral and the plant: the coral gets energy that allows it to form its calcium carbonate skeleton, and the algae gets a protected shelter from the coral.

DINO J. MARTINS
Entomologist

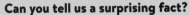

What do you enjoy about your research?
My research looks at how insects and plants work together and keep the planet running. I love watching them interact with each other and figuring out some of the many puzzles and mysteries that are part of their complex lives. It is a great honor and joy to share in their world and make discoveries.

Can you tell us a surprising fact?
One in three bites of food is thanks to a pollinator.

What do you want to discover most?
We face many challenges in our world today. Understanding the connections between ourselves and the many other creatures we share our planet with will help us figure out how to solve problems without creating new ones.

Life
THE QUIZ

1) During the first two billion years of Earth's history our planet had very little:
   a. Water
   b. Oxygen
   c. Land
   d. Life

2) What is the scientific term for classifying, or categorizing, living things?
   a. Taxonomy
   b. Taxidermy
   c. Taxology
   d. Taxation

3) The process of using the Sun's energy to turn water and carbon dioxide into food and oxygen is known as:
   a. Fermentation
   b. Combustion
   c. Photosynthesis
   d. Respiration

4) About how many human cells could fit on the head of a pin?
   a. 10
   b. 100
   c. 1,000
   d. 10,000

5) The tallest living tree in the world is a redwood tree called Hyperion. How tall is it?
   a. 250 feet (76 meters)
   b. 300 feet (91 meters)
   c. 380 feet (116 meters)
   d. 500 feet (152 meters)

6) Where is the Nival Zone located?
   a. Deep under the oceans
   b. High up on mountains
   c. In the hottest parts of deserts
   d. On ice caps

7) Limestone rocks near the top of Mount Everest contain:
   a. Gold
   b. Seashells
   c. Pumice
   d. Weevils

8) The desert-dwelling handstander beetle gets its water by:
   a. Digging underground
   b. Finding an oasis
   c. Drinking camels' urine
   d. Collecting droplets of water from fog

9) The banded archerfish knocks its insect prey off of hanging branches by:
   a. Throwing twigs
   b. Singing songs
   c. Spitting water
   d. Leaping through the air

10) What makes the raft spider special?
   a. It can weave webs of gold
   b. It can jump extremely high
   c. It can kill rats
   d. It can walk on water

11) Mudskippers are fish that:
   a. Get oxygen through their skin
   b. Sleep on the seafloor
   c. Dig tunnels underground
   d. Hop on one fin

12) The Great Pacific Garbage Patch in the Pacific Ocean is thought to be how large?
   a. The size of Texas
   b. Twice the size of Texas
   c. Three times the size of Texas
   d. Ten times the size of Texas

13) Some female anglerfish can:
   a. Produce their own light
   b. Walk on the bottom of the ocean
   c. Breathe on land
   d. Grow their own food

14) An aurochs was a type of wild:
   a. Pig
   b. Horse
   c. Ox
   d. Ostrich

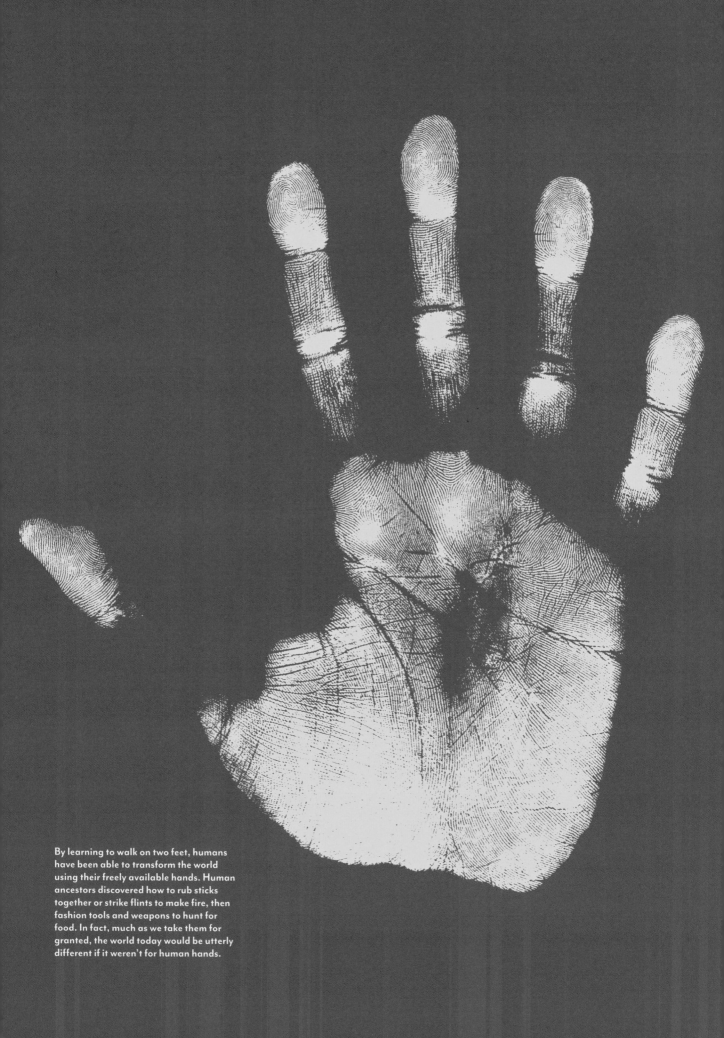

By learning to walk on two feet, humans have been able to transform the world using their freely available hands. Human ancestors discovered how to rub sticks together or strike flints to make fire, then fashion tools and weapons to hunt for food. In fact, much as we take them for granted, the world today would be utterly different if it weren't for human hands.

CHAPTER 5
HUMANS

What does it mean to be human? The human story begins a few million years ago when our distant ancestors begin to walk on two feet. These creatures, members of the genus *Homo*, are adaptable. They use their hands to light fires, craft weapons, and design tools. By 10,000 years ago, the only surviving species of *Homo* on planet Earth, *Homo sapiens*, is bargaining grain for jewelry, wool for pots, and leather for carts with wheels. And it isn't long before money makes all that easier.

Humans develop a distinctive culture that gradually shapes and reshapes the world. We share ideas through writing, art, music, dance, video, and the Internet. We kill each other in war but also interact peacefully through sports and games, through invention and exploration, through dress. We create governments to regulate our behavior and festivals to celebrate our joys. We mourn our dead in many different ways. Even more than upright walking, it is this complex culture that sets humans apart.

BECOMING HUMAN

Human beings did not always look the way they do today. The modern human evolved over millions of years, and in the past, several species of human existed. Most of the members of this group are called *Homo*. Over time, human bodies adapted and changed to suit different environments. The human brain grew to be three times larger than that of our earliest humanlike ancestors.

FACTastic!

Goose bumps helped our human ancestors stay warm. When it is cold, the skin responds by raising the hairs. This traps air to keep the skin warm. This does not work for humans today because we have lost most of our body hair. But our ancestors were a lot hairier than we are!

HUMAN RELATIVES

Today only one species of genus *Homo* exists—modern humans, known as *Homo sapiens*. Scientists do not always agree about which species are the direct ancestors of other species. But all members of the genus *Homo* are closely related. Some are shown here, right to left, in the order that they are thought to have emerged.

Homo neanderthalensis was shorter than a modern human, but its brain was just as large

Uniquely, modern humans have a flat, high forehead

Homo erectus means upright man. This species lived in Africa and Asia

Homo neanderthalensis

Emerging 200,000 years ago, *Homo neanderthalensis* are human beings' closest, extinct relatives. They made clothing and used tools.

Homo sapiens

All humans belong to the *Homo sapiens* species, which originated in Africa as much as 315,000 years ago. *Homo sapiens* means wise human.

Homo erectus

This species emerged about 1.9 million years ago. *Homo erectus* may have been the first of our near relatives to make and control fire at will.

Homo habilis

This species lived in Africa about 2.4 to 1.5 million years ago. It had humanlike hands and feet and may have lived at the same time as other types of early humans.

Australopithecus afarensis

More than 400 fossils of *Australopithecus afarensis* have been found, mostly in Ethiopia. They date to between 3.8 and 2.9 million years ago.

EXPERT CONSULTANT: John P. Rafferty **SEE ALSO:** Fossils, p.76–77; Combustion, p.108–09; The Origin of Life, p.148–49; Evolution in Action, p.150–51; Classifying Life, p.152–53; The Human Body, p.198–99; The Brain, p.202–03; Endangered, p.370–71

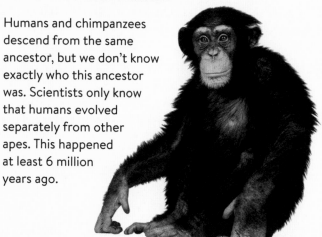

Walking on two feet

We are the only primates that walk or run on two feet all the time. The name for this is bipedalism. Scientists don't know for sure why members of the human lineage evolved to walk on two legs. Even Usain Bolt, who ran the 100-meter dash in a record-beating 9.58 seconds in 2009, is not as fast as some four-legged animals (quadrupeds).

How old are humans?

Earth is 4.6 billion years old. *Homo sapiens* probably originated in Africa as many as 315,000 years ago, although our bipedal ancestors emerged at some time in the last 6 million years. Complex language, art, and technology developed only in the last 100,000 years.

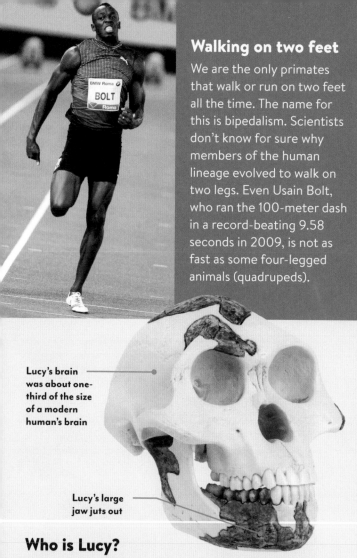

Lucy's brain was about one-third of the size of a modern human's brain

Lucy's large jaw juts out

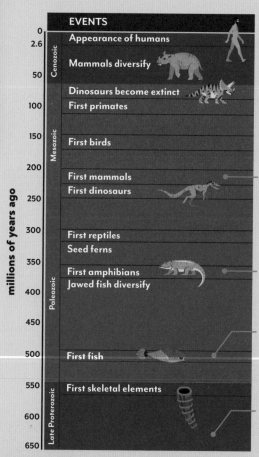

millions of years ago		EVENTS	
0	Cenozoic	Appearance of humans	
2.6			
50		Mammals diversify	
100	Mesozoic	Dinosaurs become extinct	
		First primates	
150		First birds	
200			
250		First mammals	Mammals evolved from mammal-like reptiles
		First dinosaurs	
300		First reptiles	
350	Paleozoic	Seed ferns	
		First amphibians	Amphibians developed from fish
400		Jawed fish diversify	
450			The earliest fish were small and jawless
500		First fish	
550		First skeletal elements	
600	Late Proterozoic		First multi-celled living things emerged
650			

Who is Lucy?

Lucy is the name given to a 3.2-million-year-old skeleton found in Ethiopia in 1974. Lucy belonged to the species *Australopithecus afarensis*, a group of early human ancestors. Like apes, Lucy had long arms and short legs, but she also had a pelvis like that of a human. Lucy walked on two legs, like modern humans.

KNOWN UNKNOWN

Who is our common ancestor?

Humans and chimpanzees descend from the same ancestor, but we don't know exactly who this ancestor was. Scientists only know that humans evolved separately from other apes. This happened at least 6 million years ago.

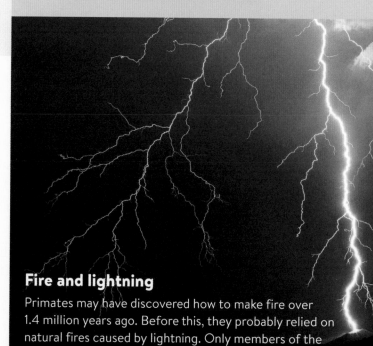

Fire and lightning

Primates may have discovered how to make fire over 1.4 million years ago. Before this, they probably relied on natural fires caused by lightning. Only members of the genus *Homo* have learned to make and control fire. This skill led to cooking and other major advances.

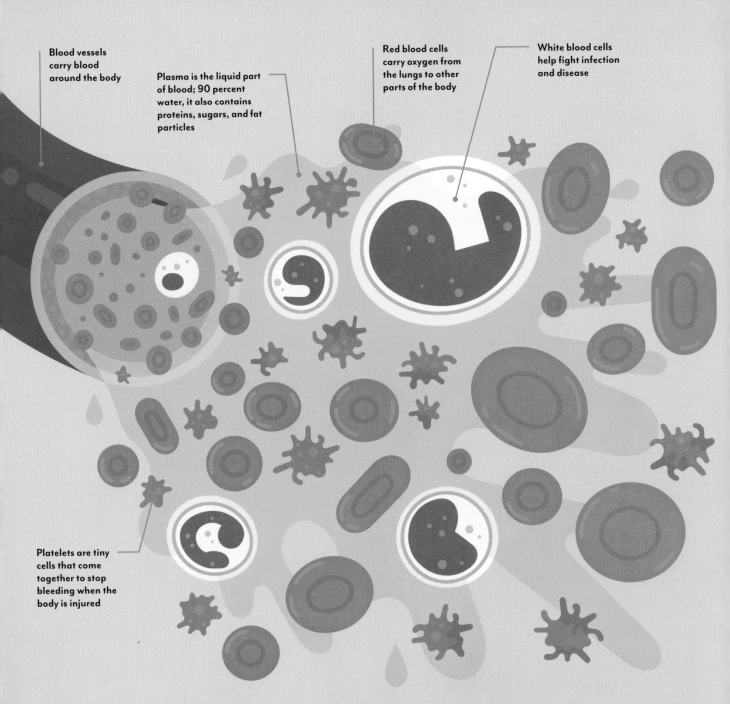

Blood vessels carry blood around the body

Plasma is the liquid part of blood; 90 percent water, it also contains proteins, sugars, and fat particles

Red blood cells carry oxygen from the lungs to other parts of the body

White blood cells help fight infection and disease

Platelets are tiny cells that come together to stop bleeding when the body is injured

HUMAN BODY

The human body is an amazing organism made up of more than 30 trillion cells. It is about 60 percent water, but also contains proteins, carbohydrates, and other organic chemical compounds. Cells make up the body's four major types of tissues, including the muscle tissues that are used for moving. The body's many organs are made of tissues. The organs work together in large systems that enable humans to think, move, digest food, and more.

Blood and cells

Cells make up all living things. They grow and divide and come in different shapes and sizes. Each type of cell has a purpose. Blood cells come from bone marrow, the tissue inside most bones. Bone marrow produces red and white blood cells and platelets. The body relies on blood to carry oxygen, proteins, and nutrients to its cells. Blood also takes away waste products, such as carbon dioxide.

EXPERT CONSULTANT: Kara Rogers **SEE ALSO:** DNA & Genetics, p.200–01; The Brain, p.202–03; The Senses, p.206–07; Medical Milestones, p.312–13

Human Body Systems
LISTIFIED.

The human body has a number of systems, or groups of organs, that work together to do certain jobs.

1. Skeletal Bones and cartilage provide structure for the body. They aid movement and protect vital organs. Bones contain marrow, which produces blood cells.

2. Muscular Muscles attached to bones and organs support the body and allow movement. Muscles also help the body to maintain a healthy temperature.

3. Respiratory When we breathe, the nose and mouth take in air to the lungs. The blood takes in oxygen from the lungs and delivers it to all the cells in the body. The lungs, nose, and mouth exhale, or breathe out, carbon dioxide as a waste product.

4. Circulatory The blood is in constant motion around the body. The heart beats around 72 times per minute, pumping blood through arteries, veins, and capillaries.

5. Digestive The intestines and stomach break down food into nutrients that the body uses to stay healthy.

6. Nervous The brain, spinal cord, nerves, and sensory organs transmit signals around the body.

KNOWN UNKNOWN

How many bones do you have?

Although the average adult has 206 bones, not all people have the same number of bones. An average baby has 270 bones because the bones have not joined together. However, these numbers do not include tiny bones called sesamoids that can vary in size and number from person to person.

GAME CHANGER

TROTA OF SALERNO
Physician, lived 12th century
Italy

Trota wrote about medicine and treatments for women. She became famous in France and England. One of her books became part of the Trotula—three texts on women's medicine that originated in Salerno, Italy. Until the late 19th and early 20th centuries, people assumed that men had written all three texts, but then historians identified part of the Trotula as being derived from a book Trota had written.

Getting around

The human skeleton is made up of bones that support the body and protect its organs. It also works with muscles to allow the body to move. Bones consist of minerals, water, and fibers of protein. Joints are the places where two or more nearby parts of the skeletal system meet. There are five main kinds of joints in the human body.

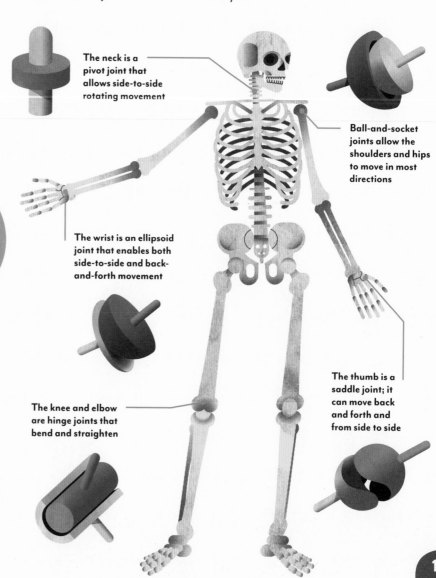

The neck is a pivot joint that allows side-to-side rotating movement

Ball-and-socket joints allow the shoulders and hips to move in most directions

The wrist is an ellipsoid joint that enables both side-to-side and back-and-forth movement

The thumb is a saddle joint; it can move back and forth and from side to side

The knee and elbow are hinge joints that bend and straighten

DNA & GENETICS

What makes humans different from one another? What makes family members look alike? It is all in the genes. Genes are a set of instructions carried on strands of a chemical called DNA, or deoxyribonucleic acid. DNA contains all the information that determines what people look like and how their bodies work. The way DNA is coded, or ordered, is slightly different for every human. Genetics is the study of genes: how they are passed from one generation to another and how they work together to make you you.

The shape of DNA is called a double helix

DNA has two strands connected by "rungs"

The rungs between the strands of DNA are made up of chemical building blocks called bases. There are four altogether, known as A, T, C, G

The bases fit together in pairs, like pieces of a puzzle. So A and T always fit together, and C and G always fit together

A strand of human DNA

Inside each cell of the human body is a sacklike structure called the nucleus. It holds tiny threadlike structures called chromosomes. Each cell normally contains 23 pairs of chromosomes, one set from your father and one from your mother. Each chromosome is made up of a single gigantic strand of a chemical called DNA. Each chromosome is very long, but the strand is so thin it is microscopic. DNA is made up of genes—the information the body needs to make proteins, the body's building blocks. There are 20,000–25,000 genes in the human body.

EXPERT CONSULTANT: Abigail H. Feresten **SEE ALSO:** Becoming Human, p.196–97; The Human Body, p.198–99; Crime & Law, p.228–29; Medical Milestones, p.312–13; Med Tech, p.362–63; Future Humans, p.382–83

Family traits

Where did you get your nose, curly hair, or dark brown eyes? Children inherit traits from their parents, but that does not mean they look exactly the same. It all depends on how the genes behave in the body and the kind of trait. The shape of the nose, or at least the tip and the area just below it, is more likely to be handed down than other features of the face.

Mutations and eye color

All human DNA is 99.9 percent identical. Yet everyone is different. Most of these differences come from tiny changes, called mutations, in important parts of genes. New mutations result in a new version of a gene called an allele. You get about half of your alleles from your mother and half from your father. Your unique combination of alleles determines how you look. Eye color comes from two genes—one that makes eyes more yellow and one that makes them more red. If you don't have a strong allele for either color, you will have blue eyes. Strong alleles for both mean brown eyes. A strong red gene but a weak yellow one makes hazel eyes.

Crime solving

Fingerprints are very useful in identifying criminals because every fingerprint is unique. A criminal might also leave behind "touch DNA" in the form of skin cells. Forensic scientists can recover this from a crime scene. Using a technique that makes copies of the genes, they can create a full genetic picture of a criminal from one fingerprint and then compare it to DNA from suspects.

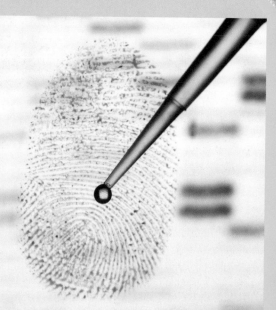

FACTastic!

Scientists found 5,700-year-old DNA in a piece of gum. They analyzed the DNA and then asked an artist to produce a picture of the person who chewed the gum (below), based on their findings. They called her Lola, for Lolland, in Denmark, where the gum was found. The gum DNA was the first complete extract of DNA from something other than bones or teeth.

NOTE *from the expert!*

ABIGAIL H. FERESTEN
Geneticist

Abigail H. Feresten studies brain development in microscopic worms. The genes that control their brain development also do so in humans! The more we understand about brain development in all species, the more we'll be able to treat human brain disorders.

66 *Our genetic code is what makes each of us unique, and also what makes us all human.* 99

THE BRAIN

The brain is the body's control center. It receives and sends messages, enabling people to breathe, move, talk, and learn. It weighs about 3 lbs (1.5 kg) and has two sides, called hemispheres. The right hemisphere of the brain controls muscles on the left side of the body; the left hemisphere of the brain controls muscles on the right side of the body. But people use all parts of their brains all of the time, even when they are sleeping.

Neurons

Neurons are brain cells with long wirelike extensions. They send electrical currents down these wires to where they meet other neurons. When an electrical current gets to the end of a wire, it releases a signal, like a light going on. It's the light that the other neuron responds to, not the current. Neurons transmit information within the brain and between the brain and the rest of the body.

The frontal lobe controls movement, memory, behavior, and intelligence

The parietal lobe registers temperature and other sensations such as touch and taste

The occipital lobe is responsible for vision

CEREBRUM

CEREBELLUM

The cerebellum handles balance, movement, and how our muscles work together

BRAIN STEM

The temporal lobe controls memory, behavior, and emotions. It enables people to understand language

The brain stem controls automatic functions such as breathing

The vertebrae protect the spinal cord

The major areas of the brain

The brain has three major areas—the cerebrum, cerebellum, and brain stem. The cerebrum contains four lobes: the frontal, temporal, parietal, and occipital, each of which is responsible for different functions in the body. Neurons in the brain—cells that send and receive messages—communicate with our sense organs and other parts of the body. They travel along the spinal cord—a long bundle of nerves inside the spine.

EXPERT CONSULTANT: Abigail H. Feresten **SEE ALSO:** Becoming Human, p.196–97; The Human Body, p.198–99; Emotions, p.204–05; The Senses, p.206–07; Smart Tech & AI, p.364–65; Future Humans, p.382–83

Brain Waves
LISTIFIED.

Brain waves are detected with very sensitive instruments that pick up how regularly neurons flash. This is an indication of how active the cells are. Brain wave patterns change, depending on what people are doing and feeling.

1. Delta The slowest brain waves occur when a person is asleep.

2. Theta These very slow brain waves happen when the brain is extremely relaxed, such as when going to sleep.

3. Alpha The brain produces these large, slow brain waves when a person is relaxed and calm.

4. Beta These small, faster brain waves occur when the brain is alert and active, such as when talking.

5. Gamma The brain produces the fastest waves when it is actively thinking, such as working out difficult problems.

Reflexes

A reflex action is when your body does something without your having to think about it. Reflexes protect your body from harm—for example, automatically moving your hand away from a hot flame. Reflex action pulls your hand away from the heat before the signal that is sent from your hand to your spinal cord arrives in your brain to let it know you are in pain.

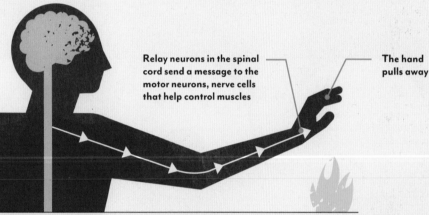

Sensory neurons send a message to the spinal cord that the flame is hot

The spinal cord runs from the brain stem and along the back

Hot flame

Relay neurons in the spinal cord send a message to the motor neurons, nerve cells that help control muscles

The hand pulls away

Tricking the brain

Magicians trick people's brains by creating illusions for the senses. Sight, smell, touch, and hearing all play a part. For example, they make the brain focus on seeing one thing and not another, so the object—like the rabbit here—seems to disappear. Or the brain may continue to see something, even if it is not there. Tricks like these can help neuroscientists figure out how the brain works.

KNOWN UNKNOWN

Why do people dream?

Scientists are still trying to figure out why people dream. To do this, they use a machine to study electrical activity in the brain during sleep and dreaming. They know that the brain's limbic system, which lies under the cerebrum and deals with emotions, is very active during dreams. Parts of the outer layer of the cerebrum determine what people dream about.

EMOTIONS

Joy, sadness, fear. These are emotions—and we experience a huge range of them. Emotions are the way we react to the world around us. Inside your brain, there's an emotion control center called the limbic system. It's made up of different parts. One part, the hippocampus, helps you remember and learn things. The amygdala is almond shaped and helps regulate emotions such as anger. The tiny hypothalamus controls how you react to an emotion, like giving you goose bumps if you're afraid.

Mind and body

Emotions can make your body act in different ways. If you feel excited or scared, your heart may beat faster. You might cry when you feel sad, angry, or even happy. Facial expressions can also show your emotions. Scientists have identified seven emotions that we all share and that produce similar expressions across all cultures. They are happiness, sadness, disgust, anger, fear, surprise, and contempt.

EXPERT CONSULTANT: Kara Rogers **SEE ALSO:** The Human Body, p.198–99; The Brain, p.202–03; The Senses, p.206–07

Fight or flight

Your brain has an automatic safety system. If you're afraid, the amygdala sends an alarm signal to the hypothalamus. The hypothalamus alerts the adrenal glands, just above your kidneys, to release a natural substance called adrenaline. Adrenaline makes your heart beat faster and your lungs fill with oxygen. This is the "fight or flight" response. You're now ready to stay and deal with something scary or run away from it.

Chemicals at work

Humans often feel better when they exercise or spend time with family and friends. This is because when you do these activities, the brain sends out chemical messengers called neurotransmitters that produce certain emotions and behaviors. Serotonin, for example, helps you feel happy. Dopamine tells your brain when something good happens, like eating tasty food. Norepinephrine helps us deal with stress.

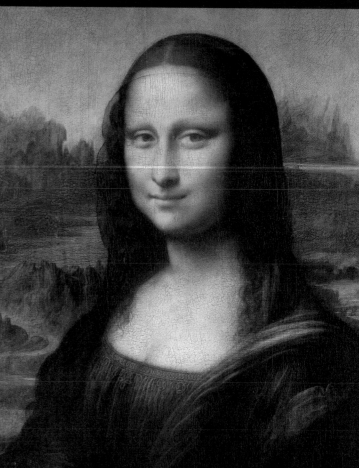

FACTastic!

A human being can make more than 10,000 different faces! Many of these are reactions to various emotions, such as smiling when you're happy, or wrinkling your nose at something disgusting. Many facial expressions are such tiny movements they last less than a second. Researchers found that we use 43 different face muscles to make facial expressions.

When is a smile not a smile?

Is the woman in the *Mona Lisa* painting by Leonardo da Vinci smiling? People have argued about this for centuries. There are about 18 different kinds of smile, but only one shows real joy. A genuine, or real, smile is called a Duchenne smile. It uses more face muscles than a fake smile and wrinkles the outer corner of each eye. You can only do this if you are really smiling.

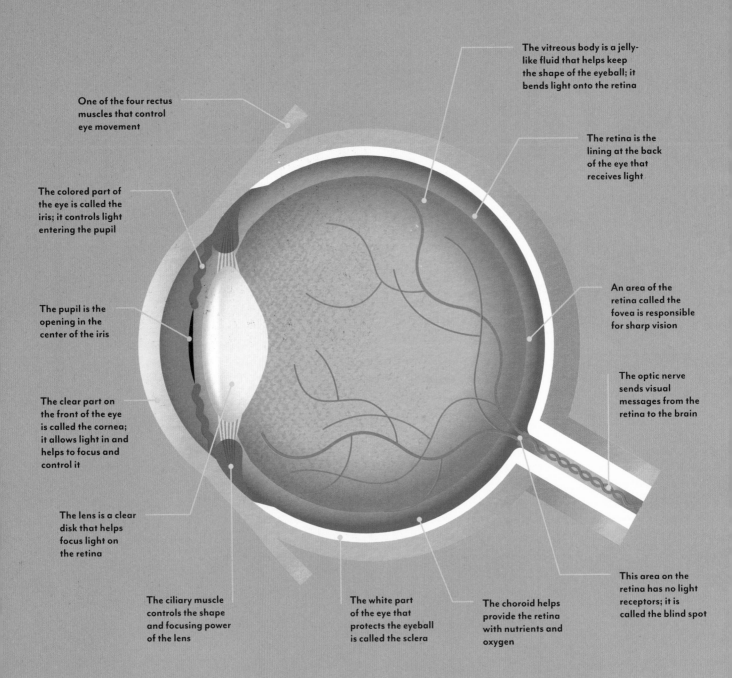

One of the four rectus muscles that control eye movement

The vitreous body is a jelly-like fluid that helps keep the shape of the eyeball; it bends light onto the retina

The retina is the lining at the back of the eye that receives light

The colored part of the eye is called the iris; it controls light entering the pupil

The pupil is the opening in the center of the iris

An area of the retina called the fovea is responsible for sharp vision

The optic nerve sends visual messages from the retina to the brain

The clear part on the front of the eye is called the cornea; it allows light in and helps to focus and control it

The lens is a clear disk that helps focus light on the retina

This area on the retina has no light receptors; it is called the blind spot

The ciliary muscle controls the shape and focusing power of the lens

The white part of the eye that protects the eyeball is called the sclera

The choroid helps provide the retina with nutrients and oxygen

THE SENSES

Sight, taste, hearing, touch, and smell are the senses that help humans understand and interact with the world and other people. Organs in your body, such as the eyes, ears, and skin, have sense receptor cells that pick up signals. These cells relay information to your brain. Your brain decodes the information so that you know what you are seeing, hearing, feeling, and experiencing. In addition to the five basic senses, nearly all animals sense motion, heat, cold, pressure, pain, and balance.

The eye

Human eyes are powerful organs that can detect objects and see up to 10 million colors. When you look at an object, light reflects off it and enters your eyes. The light travels to the retina at the back of each eye. Millions of nerve cells, called rods and cones, convert the light into electrical signals. These signals travel to the brain, which processes an image of whatever it is you are looking at.

EXPERT CONSULTANT: Kara Rogers **SEE ALSO:** Sound, p.124–25; Light, p.128–29; The Human Body, p.198–99; DNA & Genetics, p.200–01; The Brain, p.202–03; Emotions, p.204–05; Future Humans, p.382–83

The tongue and taste

You have between 2,000 and 8,000 taste buds on your tongue, and each taste bud contains 50 to 75 taste receptor cells. The cells pick up sweet, salty, sour, bitter, and umami, or savory, tastes and send this information to your brain. Your nose picks up smells at the same time, adding to the sensation. This is why food may not taste the same if your nose is blocked with a cold.

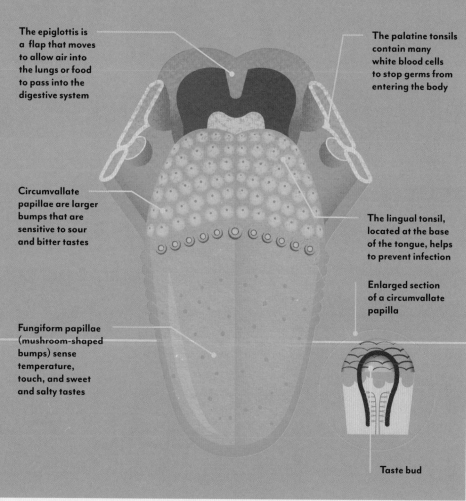

The epiglottis is a flap that moves to allow air into the lungs or food to pass into the digestive system

The palatine tonsils contain many white blood cells to stop germs from entering the body

Circumvallate papillae are larger bumps that are sensitive to sour and bitter tastes

The lingual tonsil, located at the base of the tongue, helps to prevent infection

Enlarged section of a circumvallate papilla

Fungiform papillae (mushroom-shaped bumps) sense temperature, touch, and sweet and salty tastes

Taste bud

Hearing

The ear picks up vibrations in the air, sending them into the middle and then the inner ear. In the inner ear, the cochlea organ picks up the signal. The hearing nerve sends the information from here to your brain. Sound is measured in decibels (db). Listening to sounds over 120 db can damage the ears.

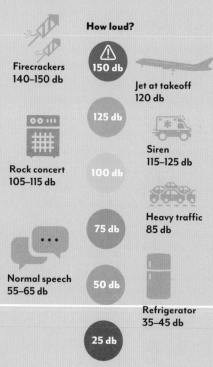

How loud?

Firecrackers 140–150 db

150 db

Jet at takeoff 120 db

125 db

Rock concert 105–115 db

100 db

Siren 115–125 db

75 db

Heavy traffic 85 db

Normal speech 55–65 db

50 db

Refrigerator 35–45 db

25 db

The most sensitive touch

The ridges of your fingertips contain thousands of touch receptor cells just beneath the surface of the skin. These ridges make your fingertips able to sense the tiniest differences in textures and temperatures. Like other sense receptors, touch receptor cells alert your brain. Your brain immediately decides how something feels, and identifies it as smooth, rough, hot, cold, wet, dry, and more.

FACTastic!

The human nose can detect at least one trillion distinct odors. Your nose takes in air that contains odorants, or odor molecules. High up inside your nose, around 400 different types of odor receptors pick up these odorants. The receptors send the information to the olfactory bulb in your brain. The human nose can smell a skunk (right), which emits a smell like rotten eggs, from half a mile (1 km) away.

207

Food and geography

What people eat depends on when and where they live. Traditionally, people ate what lived or grew nearby. The Inuit people in the Arctic depended on fish and other seafood. The Inca, in Peru, grew potatoes. Early Mexicans planted and ate tomatoes. European explorers brought these foods back to Europe. Today, countries import foods from all over the world, but different cultures have their own ways of cooking them.

In the Arctic, the Inuit use all parts of the animals they hunt. Coats made of caribou hide keep them warm

Inuit hunters use harpoons (long spears) to hunt seals for food

Hunters capture the seals when they come up for air through holes in the ice

FOOD & COOKING

All animals, including humans, need food to live and grow. It is how we get the energy our bodies require to function. The first people hunted wild animals and gathered wild plants to eat. Farming changed the way people ate, since communities began relying on the crops they grew. Early farmers in North America depended on beans, corn, and squash. Over time, cultures around the world developed their own combinations of foods and flavors.

FACTastic!

The shiny coating on jelly beans comes from an insect. The covering is shellac, produced by the female Indian lac insect that lives on trees in India and Thailand. When heated and filtered, the substance turns into flakes, which are then dissolved in a chemical called ethanol. This produces a glaze that hardens when it cools.

EXPERT CONSULTANT: Chef Suzi Gerber **SEE ALSO:** Combustion, p.108–09; Becoming Human, p.196–97; The Human Body, p.198–99; Anything, Anywhere, p.342–43; Feeding the World, p.346–47; Cities, p.354–55; Environmental Challenges, p.366–67; Cities of Tomorrow, p.380–81

KNOWN UNKNOWN

When did people start cooking food?

No one knows exactly when humans began cooking. All other animals eat their food raw. Cooking makes food easier to chew and digest. An early species of human, *Homo erectus*, learned to control fire but left no evidence of cooked food. However, both Neanderthals and early *Homo sapiens* left behind burnt animal bones, suggesting that these human ancestors did cook.

What food does the body need?

This plate shows the proportions of fruit, vegetables, whole grains, and protein we need in order to eat a balanced, nutritious diet. Humans can eat both meat and plants. Some people, known as vegans, choose to eat only plants. We should all eat fiber, such as whole grains, to stay healthy.

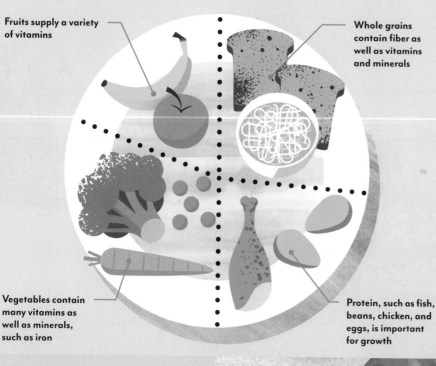

Fruits supply a variety of vitamins

Whole grains contain fiber as well as vitamins and minerals

Vegetables contain many vitamins as well as minerals, such as iron

Protein, such as fish, beans, chicken, and eggs, is important for growth

Food waste

Farmers sometimes throw away misshapen vegetables because no one will buy them. Around the world, people waste about one-third of all the food produced. Meanwhile, more than 820 million people go hungry. One way to help stop food waste is to buy food that is not perfect.

Staple foods

Foods that people rely on and eat regularly are called staples. They include corn, rice, and wheat. These three cereals make up more than half the world's food energy, even though there are some 50,000 different plants that are edible. More than 3.5 billion people around the world depend on rice as their main food source. In parts of Africa and Asia, beans, lentils, and chickpeas are also staple foods. Potatoes are staples, too.

DRESS & DECORATION

Humans have always clothed and decorated their bodies. We know that prehistoric people wore jewelry, applied body paint, and tattooed their skin. Dress and adornment can be symbols of beauty, wealth, status, or religion, or show that someone belongs to a certain group. Often, people simply want to follow the latest fashions or express their own personal style.

FACTastic!

In Ancient Rome, a purple dye made from sea snails and urine cost almost as much as pearls! Only royals and other important people could afford clothes dyed with Tyrian purple. To produce just one ounce of the dye, mucus squeezed from 250,000 sea snails was soaked in urine for 10 days.

Look at me!

People often dress to impress others. The American rapper Cardi B wore a huge red dress to the Met Gala in New York in 2019 (below). Events like the Met Gala give celebrities a chance to show how glamorous they are. Parties and weddings are opportunities for anyone to do the same.

EXPERT CONSULTANT: Pravina Shukla **SEE ALSO:** Earth's Riches, p.74–75; The Brain, p.202–03; Emotions, p.204–05; Performing Arts, p.222–23; Festivals, p.236–37

Crowning glory

People have worn wigs from the earliest recorded times. For example, the ancient Egyptians shaved their heads and wore wigs. From the 1500s to the 1700s, wealthy European men wore elaborate and expensive wigs. This cartoon makes fun of the fashion. The man's wig is so high, his servant has to adjust it with a pole.

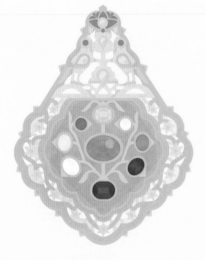

Precious stones

In India, the *navaratna*, a Sanskrit word that can mean "nine gems," has special significance. Wearing the nine gems is thought to bring luck and health. The gems are arranged in a particular way. In the center is a ruby, which represents the Sun. It is surrounded by a diamond, a pearl, an orange coral, a garnet, a blue sapphire, a cat's eye, a yellow sapphire or topaz, and an emerald.

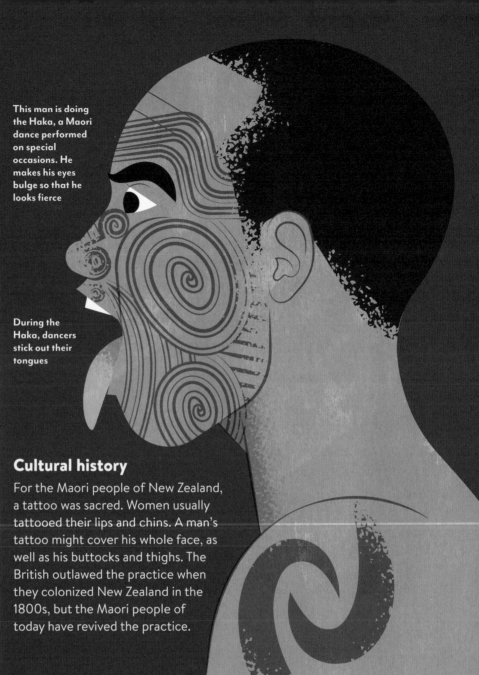

This man is doing the Haka, a Maori dance performed on special occasions. He makes his eyes bulge so that he looks fierce

During the Haka, dancers stick out their tongues

Cultural history

For the Maori people of New Zealand, a tattoo was sacred. Women usually tattooed their lips and chins. A man's tattoo might cover his whole face, as well as his buttocks and thighs. The British outlawed the practice when they colonized New Zealand in the 1800s, but the Maori people of today have revived the practice.

Earth, air, and water

The colorful fabrics and jewelry worn by the Maasai of Kenya and Tanzania are more than just decorative. Each color has a meaning. The *shuka*, a traditional robe, is often red: the color of blood, it represents courage. Bracelets, collars, and earrings indicate the wearer's status and clan. At one time the Maasai used materials such as iron and bone, but today they use glass beads and cloth.

Blue represents the sky, which provides rain—important for cattle and crops

In Maasai culture, red is for bravery, and some say it scares off lions

RELIGIOUS BELIEF

What do people believe in? Statistics show that with 4.4 billion followers between them, Christianity and Islam are the world's two largest religions. Each has many branches. For example, Catholicism is a branch of Christianity, and Sunni is a branch of Islam. Some religions are a mix of different beliefs and practices. There are also millions of people who have no religious beliefs.

CHRISTIANITY
2.5 billion

A religion started in the 1st century CE, based on the teachings of Christ, or Jesus of Nazareth, who Christians believe to be the son of God. Followers believe in one God. The Bible is the religious book of Christianity.

ISLAM
1.9 billion

The prophet Muhammad founded Islam in Arabia in the 7th century CE. The word Islam means "to surrender." Muslims surrender to one God, Allah. The sacred book is the Qur'an, written in Arabic.

HINDUISM
1 billion

Hinduism began in India more than 3,000 years ago. Hindus believe in many gods and consider Brahma the creator of the universe. The Vedas, written in Sanskrit, are the oldest sacred texts of Hinduism.

BUDDHISM
550 million

Buddhism is based on the teachings of Siddhartha Gautama, or the Buddha, in India, about 500 BCE. The focus is on a way of living to reach nirvana, a state of perfect understanding and peace.

SIKHISM
28 million

Followers of the Indian spiritual teacher Nanak (late 1400s), Sikhs believe in one God. The sacred work *Guru Granth Sahib* contains Nanak's teachings.

JUDAISM
15 million

The Jewish religion began at least 3,000 years ago in what is now Israel. Jews believe in one God and follow teachings written in the Tanakh (Hebrew Bible), Midrash, and Talmud.

24.3%

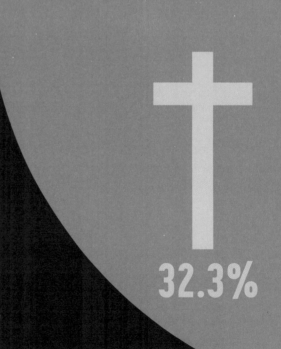

32.3%

EXPERT CONSULTANT: Gina A. Zurlo **SEE ALSO:** The First Chinese Dynasties, p.252–53; Ancient Gods, p.256–57; The Byzantine World, p.278–79; Tang China, p.282–83; The Golden Age of Islam, p.284–85; Medieval Europe, p.286–87; African Empires, p.292–93; The Mughal Empire, p.300–01

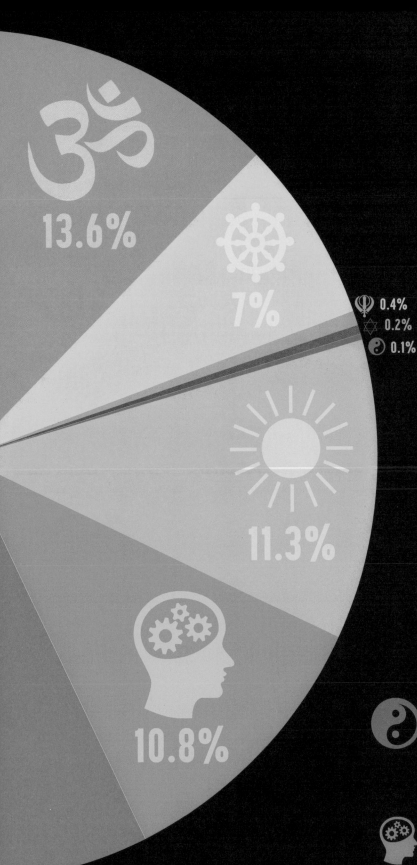

13.6%

7%

℗ 0.4%
✡ 0.2%
☯ 0.1%

11.3%

10.8%

⚛ OTHER RELIGIONS
850 million, including:

1. **Falun Gong** (10 million): Combines meditation techniques and ritual exercises. Founded in China, 1992.
2. **Cao Dai** (8 million): Takes ideas from Daoism, Buddhism, Confucianism, and Roman Catholicism. Founded in Vietnam, 1926.
3. **Baha'i faith** (5–7 million): Belief that all people belong to one religion with one God. Founded in Iran, 1863.
4. **Confucianism** (5–6 million): An ancient religion that follows the teachings of the great Chinese thinker Confucius.
5. **Jainism** (4 million): Faith with belief in the eternal human soul. Has roots in India in the 6th century BCE.
6. **Shinto** (3–4 million): Followers believe in "kami" (spirits) and visit shrines. Founded in ancient Japan.
7. **Wicca** (1–3 million): Centers on witchcraft, with a focus on nature. Spread from England in the 1950s.
8. **Rastafari** (1 million): A religion and political movement that began in Jamaica in the 1930s.
9. **Tenrikyo** (1 million): Shinto-based religion whose followers believe in one god called Tenri-O-no-Mikoto. Started in Japan in the 1800s.
10. **Zoroastrianism** (1 million): Worship the supreme god Ahura Mazda. Began in Iran in the 6th century BCE.

DAOISM
9 million

This Chinese religion began over 2,000 years ago. Followers believe in acting in harmony with the Dao ("the way") and strive not to disrupt the natural course of things.

NONRELIGIOUS
880 million

Nonreligious people include atheists, agnostics, or those without any religious affiliation. Many do not believe in any god or higher being but do participate in some spiritual practices, including prayer and meditation.

CONFLICT & WAR

There are many theories about why people fight or go to war with one another. Warfare may arise from fear of attack or a struggle over money, religion, food sources, or territory. Civil wars—wars between opposing groups within a country—are often about who will run the country. Some scientists argue that conflict is part of human nature. Others disagree. Today, there are many ongoing conflicts, but much of the world is peaceful.

The Battle of Little Bighorn

Oglala Lakota artist Amos Bad Heart Buffalo depicted the Battle of Little Bighorn (above). On June 25, 1876, Lakota and Cheyenne warriors beat the US army. The war ended with the army driving Plains tribes off their land to make room for white settlers.

Peaceful protest

Not all conflicts are violent. Peaceful protests can lead to political change, too. Starting in late 2018, people in Sudan, in Africa, demonstrated against the harsh rule in the country. The president was tried and put in prison. A new government is in power, but the country still faces problems.

EXPERT CONSULTANT: Michael Ray **SEE ALSO:** DNA & Genetics, p.200–01; Religious Belief, p.212–13; Crime & Law, p.228–229; Age of Revolutions, p.310–311; World War I, p.316–17; World War II, p.324–25; The Cold War, p.326–27; Decolonization, p.328–29; Modern Warfare, p.350–51

United Nations

When World War II ended in 1945, 51 countries came together as the United Nations (UN). Their mission was to maintain peace across the world and to oversee issues such as human rights. Today, the UN has 193 member states.

Identifying the dead

Millions of soldiers and civilians have died in the world's wars. Many were buried quickly, and without any record of their identity. Since the 1990s, DNA testing can match human remains, such as bones, to information on missing persons. Sometimes knowing who the victims were can help bring their killers to justice.

The effects of war

War destroys schools, hospitals, and whole areas of cities. People face the deaths of loved ones and sometimes go hungry. Many are forced to move, becoming refugees. Parts of Syria, including eastern Aleppo (below), were destroyed in the Syrian Civil War, which started in 2011. Millions of people fled their homes to seek safety—5.6 million Syrian refugees now live outside Syria. Millions more are displaced within Syria.

Killing machines

Having better weapons can help people win a war. The first successful machine gun was the Gatling gun, invented in 1862 during the American Civil War. The gun changed the way armies fought wars. Unlike a rifle, it could fire repeated shots without the need for reloading. The Maxim gun (pictured) was invented in about 1884. It was the first fully automatic machine gun and was used in battles against colonial peoples and in World War I.

NOTE *from the expert!*

MICHAEL RAY

European History and Military Affairs editor

Michael Ray writes about history and conflict for Encyclopaedia Britannica. He thinks that learning about the wars of the past can help us avoid them in the future.

66 *If history does repeat itself, we should try not to repeat the fighting.* 99

LANGUAGE & STORYTELLING

Language is a system we use to communicate with each other. Through language, we can express thoughts, feelings, and ideas, and talk about the past and the future. Language can be spoken or signed, which means expressed by hand, face, and body gestures. It becomes an art form through storytelling, and it is always changing.

Storytelling

Humans passed history and knowledge from one generation to the next long before they developed writing. They used words to tell stories and sing songs. This tradition features in cultures all over the world. It ranges from traditional storytelling in Morocco to modern rap lyrics.

Learning to talk

From birth, a baby's brain is wired to learn language. The baby does this by observing and interacting with the people around them. Early babbling, whether spoken or signed, turns into words, which turn into whole sentences. By the age of five, most children are fluent speakers of their language.

EXPERT CONSULTANT: Laura Kalin **SEE ALSO:** The Brain, p.202–03; Reading & Writing, p.218–19; Creating Art, p.220–21; Education, p.230–31; Ancient Egypt, p.254–5; The Internet, p.356–57; The Media, p.358–59.

Sign language

Sometimes people produce language with their hands—that's sign language. It is not the same thing as when speaking people use their hands—that's gesture. (People who sign use gesture, too.) Sign languages are just like spoken languages in many ways. There are hundreds of sign languages in use worldwide. They include American Sign Language (ASL) in the US.

World languages

This chart shows the ten languages most commonly spoken as a first or second language. Mandarin Chinese has the most native speakers, and English is the most widely spoken second language. People speak more than 6,000 languages today. However, 40 percent of world languages are endangered (at risk of no longer being spoken), and many others are extinct already. On average, a language becomes extinct every 90 days.

Chart data (speakers):

- English (1.3 billion speakers)
- Mandarin Chinese (1.1 billion speakers)
- Hindi (637 million speakers)
- Spanish (537 million speakers)
- French (280 million speakers)
- Arabic (274 million speakers)
- Bengali (265 million speakers)
- Russian (258 million speakers)
- Portuguese (252 million speakers)
- Indonesian (199 million speakers)

Y-axis: 0, 100 million, 200, 300, 400, 500, 600, 700, 800, 900, 1 billion, 1.1, 1.2, 1.3

FACTastic!

Around 840 different languages are spoken in Papua New Guinea.

This small Pacific country has about seven million people. With so many languages, most are spoken by fewer than 3,000 people. English and Tok Pisin are the common languages that allow different groups to communicate. Tok Pisin is a Creole language, which means it developed from a Pidgin language. Pidgins are simple communication systems that arise when speakers of multiple languages need to talk to each other.

NOTE from the expert!

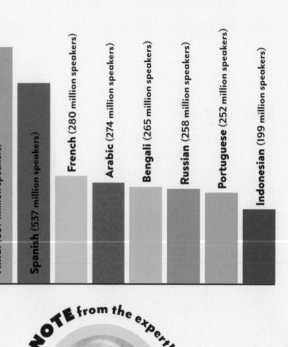

LAURA KALIN
Linguist

Even languages that seem wildly different from each other have many of the same properties, from Senaya in Iran to Malagasy in Madagascar, to Hixkaryana in Brazil. Professor Kalin is trying to find out what these properties are, and why they exist.

66 *Everywhere there are humans, there is language.* 99

READING & WRITING

How is writing different from language? We speak using language, but writing allows us to express our ideas at greater length, with more permanence. Although early humans did not have a writing system, they made markings on stone and created pictures. Writing evolved from this into a way for people to keep records and, later, stories. Then it was used to put down thoughts into a code, which others can read and understand. Like speech, we communicate with one another and pass down knowledge through reading and writing.

KNOWN UNKNOWN

What came first—numbers or writing?

Long before there were symbols for numbers, people counted on their fingers. Then they made scratches in stone or clay. Over 5,400 years ago, Egyptians made straight marks for small numbers and a symbol for 10. Did those symbols lead to writing? No one knows for sure.

Making marks

The Sumerians invented the first true writing system, called cuneiform, over 5,000 years ago. The ancient Mayans used hieroglyphs—signs that represent words, objects, or sounds. They wrote on stones like this one, but also created books written on the bark of fig trees.

Alphabets

The Phoenicians invented an alphabet around 1500 BCE that the Greeks adopted and added to. The Latin alphabet we know today came from it, through other alphabets, including this Etruscan one (left). English and most European languages still use the Latin alphabet.

Breaking the code

Reading ancient writing is like breaking a code. After people stop using a writing system, the next generations do not know what the symbols mean. The Rosetta Stone was crucial for the deciphering of Egyptian hieroglyphics. The message on the stone appears three times in different types of writing. All three inscriptions celebrate the anniversary of the ruler, Ptolemy V.

Hieroglyphs feature a cartouche symbol for the name Ptolemy

Demotic script developed from hieroglyphs. It was used into the Roman period

Scholars knew Ancient Greek and used it to decode the other writing

EXPERT CONSULTANT: Paul Dilley **SEE ALSO:** The Brain, p.202–03; Ancient Mesopotamia, p.248–49; The First Chinese Dynasties, p.252–53; Ancient Egypt, p.254–55; The Golden Age of Islam, p.284–85; Aztecs & Incas, p.296–97; The Media, p.358–59; Smart Tech & AI, p.364–65

The printing press

The first books were handwritten. They cost a lot and took a long time to make. Around 1450, the German Johannes Gutenberg developed the first printing press in Europe. It could produce many books in a short time. For the first time, people other than the rich could afford to buy books.

The lever turned a wooden screw that pushed the platen, or flat plate, down

Lowering the platen pressed the paper onto the inked type (letters) held in the form

Gutenberg printed many copies of the Bible

The printer pulled on a lever

The press could print about 250 sheets an hour—much faster than copying by hand!

Paper was placed on inked metal type held in a wooden form (frame)

The form was movable and went back and forth

GAME CHANGER

MURASAKI SHIKIBU

Writer, lived about 978–1014
Kyōto, Japan

Murasaki Shikibu wrote the world's first novel, *The Tale of Genji*, over 1,000 years ago. Shikibu was a lady-in-waiting in the Japanese royal court. In English, the novel is 54 chapters and 1,300 pages long. Shikibu's handwritten manuscript was lost, but the poet Teika made a copy of the book in the 1200s. Just five of the copied chapters have been found. The fifth chapter was discovered in Tokyo in 2019.

Chinese script

The Chinese invented their writing system about 4,000 years ago. It uses characters, rather than an alphabet. Some of these were pictographs, so the character for "man" looked like a standing person. With a few changes over time, the system is still used today. An educated Chinese person knows between 3,000 and 8,000 characters.

CREATING ART

Some of the earliest known artworks are cave paintings made more than 40,000 years ago. Early people rarely painted human figures. Instead, they usually carved and painted animals. Scholars do not know the purpose of these artworks. Early people may have created this art for religious or spiritual reasons or to teach others. Some ancient examples are found in caves in Indonesia, France, and Bulgaria.

The paintings of bison in the Covaciella Cave look three-dimensional due to the dark shading

Animal art

Pictures of bison, horses, and deer decorate a few caves in northern Spain. Some may date back 36,000 years. For thousands of years, the caves were sealed, which helped protect them from light and air. Now, because moisture from people's breath damages cave paintings, the caves are closed, and replicas have been built for visitors. The paintings in Spain's Covaciella Cave were created about 14,000 years ago—this picture was taken in the replica cave.

Stencils in the Cave of the Hands, in Argentina, were made between 13,000 and 9,500 years ago

Making handprints

Handprints and stencils can be found on the walls of caves and rock shelters all over the world, including in the Cave of the Hands, in Argentina. To make a handprint, artists put one hand on the cave wall, then blew color over the hand using their mouths or a blow pipe.

EXPERT CONSULTANT: Mark Sapwell **SEE ALSO:** Rocks & Minerals, p.70–71; Earth's Riches, p.74–75; Language & Storytelling, p.216–17; The First Australians, p.244–45; The Minoans, Mycenaeans & Phoenicians, p.262–63

Cave painters sometimes engraved the outlines of animals, then drew over them, usually with charcoal or soot

Artists often used natural bumps in the cave wall to suggest an animal's hump

Artists used red ocher, a reddish clay, to paint things red

221

PERFORMING ARTS

Actors, dancers, and musicians often perform for an audience. They use their bodies, voices, and instruments to express themselves, sometimes working in much-loved traditions, sometimes experimenting with new sounds and forms. Theater, dance, and music all have different genres. Pop is a music genre, while tango is a dance genre. Some of the most exciting works mix styles and genres. A dance, for example, might include jazz, ballet, and hip-hop.

The entertainers

Performance is partly about entertaining and thrilling audiences. The Cirque du Soleil (right) showcases the amazing feats of the human body. Acrobats, dancers, and contortionists bend and twist their bodies in extraordinary ways. The first circuses, in Roman times, involved animal fights, gladiator contests, and chariot races.

The play begins

The word theater comes from the ancient Greek word *theasthai*, meaning "to see." The ancient Athenians hosted a festival for Dionysus, the god of theater and wine, in the Theater of Dionysus (left). Greeks watched comedy, tragedy, and satire performed in outdoor theaters.

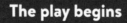

EXPERT CONSULTANT: Abigail H. Feresten, Alicja Zelazko **SEE ALSO:** The Brain, p.202–03; Emotions, p.204–05; The Senses, p.206–07; Language &

Peking opera

In the late 1700s, a genre of musical drama called Peking opera, *Jingxi*, arose in China. There are now more than 1,000 different operas based on well-known Chinese legends. The operas often feature acrobatics and sword fights and have colorful costumes and sets. The makeup of some characters symbolizes particular traits, such as red for bravery and white for treachery. Until the late 20th century, all the characters were played by men.

WILLIAM SHAKESPEARE

Playwright, lived 1564–1616
England

The world's most famous playwright is William Shakespeare, who lived more than 400 years ago. Shakespeare's plays were enjoyed by all members of society, from royalty to the working class. Everyone identified with his themes, which ranged from revenge, as in *Hamlet*, to tragic love, as in *Romeo and Juliet*. Shakespeare wrote some 37 plays. They have been translated into more than 100 languages.

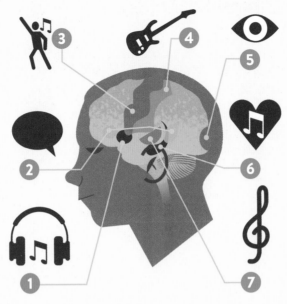

1. **Nucleus accumbens**
The hormone dopamine increases in this area when you listen to music, making you feel excited.

2. **Broca's area and Wernicke's area**
Used to understand the written and spoken word. Serves a role in speech production.

3. **Motor cortex**
Activated when you play an instrument, dance, or move to music.

4. **Sensory cortex**
Triggered when you touch an instrument, dance, or tap a foot.

5. **Visual cortex**
Used to read music, follow dance moves, and watch videos.

6. **Hippocampus**
Where music stirs memories and emotions.

7. **Auditory cortex**
This part of the brain processes sound, including music.

Stimulating the brain

Scientists have discovered that many areas of the brain switch on when the ear hears music. Different types of music affect the brain's chemistry in different ways. If you listen to calming music, for example, it will lower your levels of cortisol, the hormone that causes stress. Caregivers often use music therapy to help engage people who suffer from dementia.

FACTastic!

In 2013, astronaut Chris Hadfield recorded an album in space. At the time, he was working at the International Space Station. He called the album *Space Sessions: Songs from a Tin Can* and released it in 2015. There are 12 songs on the album, including a cover version of David Bowie's song "Space Oddity."

Street dance

Some of the most exciting and creative performance art springs up in local youth groups. The first break dancers performed in New York in the late 1960s and early 1970s using martial arts moves developed by street gangs. As hip-hop music developed, break dancing became part of the culture. In California, Sam Solomon introduced the boogaloo and popping moves.

CALENDARS

Ancient people marked the passing of time by watching the position of the Sun, the stars, and the Moon in the sky. Early calendars were based on these observations. A day is the time it takes Earth to revolve on its axis. A lunar month roughly corresponds to the 29.5 days it takes the Moon to go through its phases, from full moon to full moon. It takes about 365.25 days for Earth to orbit the Sun. We call that time period a solar year. Because they are based on different phenomena, days, months, and years don't easily fit together. Different cultures created calendars that solved this problem in different ways.

2600 BCE
The Babylonian calendar has 12 lunar months of 29 or 30 days. Each day is divided into 12 equal parts

1400 BCE
The lunar Chinese calendar has 12 months of 29 or 30 days. A leap month is added every two or three years. The calendar has a 12-year cycle of years named for animals

543 BCE
The Buddhist calendar follows the Moon and Sun and has 12 months, which alternate between 29 and 30 days. This adds up to 354 days, so a leap month is added about every three years

57 BCE
Nepal and parts of India use the Vikram Samvat calendar, which has lunar months and the sidereal year. New Year is after Diwali, a festival in October or November

78 CE
Some people in Bali and parts of India use the Saka lunar calendar. An extra month is added every 30 months so that the calendar stays in line with the solar year

2500 BCE

350 BCE

100 CE

2500 BCE
The Egyptian calendar has 365 days of 24 hours each and three seasons—planting, growing, and harvesting. In 238 BCE, it adds a leap day every four years: the first to have a 365.25-day year

600 BCE
The Jewish year has 354 days divided into 12 months. A leap year occurs seven times during a 19-year cycle. During a leap year a 13th month is added called Adar Sheni

500 BCE
The Maya have a complex system called the Calendar Round. It has three calendars with different numbers of days. The calendars match every 52 solar years

46 BCE
The Julian calendar, named after Julius Caesar, has a leap year every fourth year. The month of July is named in Caesar's honor. In 8 CE, Augustus also named a month after himself (August)

79 CE
In India, the Shaka Samvat calendar follows the sidereal year, which is the time it takes Earth to orbit the Sun and return to exactly the same position in relation to the stars

EXPERT CONSULTANT: Daryn Lehoux **SEE ALSO:** Earth in Space, p.54–55; Climate, p.92–93; Reading & Writing, p.218–19; Festivals, p.236–37; Ancient Greece, p.268–69

The coming of spring

Many cultures celebrate spring with festivals to mark the sowing of crops. This close-up of the painting *Primavera* (The Allegory of Spring), by Renaissance Italian artist Sandro Botticelli, shows Flora, goddess of spring and flowers. It was inspired by a tale from Roman mythology which said that a nymph called Chloris was turned into Flora when Zephyrus, the West Wind, kissed her.

350 CE
The Ethiopian calendar includes 12 months of 30 days and one month of five days. Every four years, the last month has six days. The calendar is linked to Christian feast days and saints' days

1079
In Persia, a group of astronomers—scientists who study the stars and planets—create the Jalali calendar, based on the old Persian solar calendar but including leap years

1300
The Incas in South America study the Sun, Moon, and stars to calculate their calendar. The Incas have 12 lunar months that link to important times for planting and harvesting

1400
The Aztecs make changes to the Mayan calendar system and include a year of 365 days. Like the Maya, the Aztecs believe the five days at the end of the year are unlucky

1000

1500

622 CE
The Muslim lunar calendar has 12 months of 29 or 30 days and no leap years. Dates of festivals move 10 to 11 days earlier each year when compared to the Gregorian calendar

1084
The ancient Armenian solar calendar is adjusted by the Armenian scientist Hovhannes Sarkavag who adds a leap day every four years

1350
In Bali, the Pawukon calendar sets the times of most festivals and holidays. The calendar year has 210 days. There are six months of 35 days

1582
The Gregorian calendar corrects the Julian one, whose year was 11 minutes too long. By 1923, it becomes the official calendar of all countries except some Muslim ones, Ethiopia, and Nepal

MONEY

People have used money to pay for things for more than 4,000 years. Ancient Egyptians made gold bars, the value of which depended on their weight. The Chinese invented paper money in about 806 CE. Most countries have their own money, like the dollar in the US, or share a currency, such as the euro in parts of Europe. Today, the US Bureau of Engraving and Printing prints 26 million bills a day, about $974 million.

How money developed

The earliest forms of money were things found in nature, such as shells. The first coins were made of copper, silver, or gold. Now people can use banking apps to pay for things.

Barter was the system of trading, or exchanging goods like grain, livestock, and pots.

Metal money represented the value of goods. Precious metals had a greater value.

Paper money was like a promise by a government. It could be exchanged for gold.

Money like credit cards, checks, and electronic transfers are linked to money held in banks.

Virtual money such as Bitcoin is not backed up by a bank or a government.

Square coins

The earliest coins were square, not round. This gold coin from ancient China is called Ying Yuan. It is stamped with its value or weight. Metal money in the form of coins was first regularly used in about 600 BCE in what is now Turkey. These coins were bean-shaped and made from electrum, a mixture of gold and silver.

Money Materials
LISTIFIED.

Buying and selling goods became easier with money. It had an agreed value and could be carried easily.

1. Metals such as gold and silver have been used for thousands of years. Australia's Kangaroo One Tonne Gold Coin is the world's most valuable coin. It is worth over $60 million Australian dollars (US $40 million).

2. Paper money was first used more than 1,000 years ago in China. Today, most paper money is made of cellulose or polymer, a plastic.

3. Stone is used as money on the Pacific island of Yap. Large, round limestone pieces can weigh up to 8,800 pounds (3,992 kg).

4. Shells are the oldest form of money. Africans used cowrie shells from 1200 BCE. Some indigenous Americans traded shell beads.

EXPERT CONSULTANT: Silvana Tenreyro **SEE ALSO:** Earth's Riches, p.74–75; Dress & Decoration, p.210–11; Work, p.232–33; Boom & Bust, p.322–23; The Mega Rich, p.352–53

Cryptocurrency

Unlike other forms of money, cryptocurrencies such as Bitcoin and Ether have nothing to do with governments or banks. They have value because people have agreed to treat them as valuable. There are already more than 2,000 cryptocurrencies, and more are being invented all the time.

What is interest?

Money deposited in a bank account can earn more money. This is called interest. It is paid as a percentage of the amount deposited. Banks pay interest in return for using the money. They might loan it to a person or business who would have to pay it back with interest. Compound interest (shown below) is paid on the first deposit plus any interest earned over time.

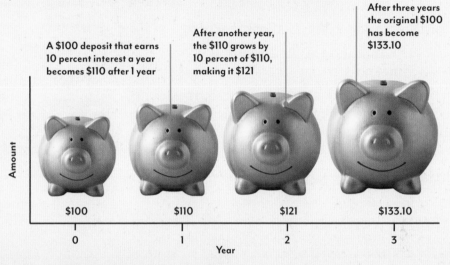

A $100 deposit that earns 10 percent interest a year becomes $110 after 1 year

After another year, the $110 grows by 10 percent of $110, making it $121

After three years the original $100 has become $133.10

Amount

$100 $110 $121 $133.10

0   1   2   3

Year

Stocks and shares

People can buy shares, or stocks, in a company. These make them a part owner of the company, so they get a share in any money the company makes. People can also loan companies money in the form of bonds, which companies promise to pay back with interest. Shares are bought and sold on stock markets. The New York Stock Exchange (left) is the world's biggest stock market. It began in 1792 when 24 dealers met under a tree on what is now Wall Street.

FACTastic!

The Zimbabwean 100 trillion-dollar bill, produced in 2009, has the most zeros of any banknote in history. Zimbabwe had to print this money because of terrible inflation. Prices rose so quickly that the money they had before was worthless. A $10 bill is useless if a roll of toilet paper costs $145,000.

CRIME & LAW

Governments have laws, or sets of rules, to help people get along. Crimes are acts that go against these laws. Different countries have their own laws, so crimes are not always the same. Most nations recognize felonies, or serious crimes, such as murder. Misdemeanors are lesser crimes, such as stealing something that is not worth much. Organized crime involves a network of criminals who work together.

Early laws and lawmakers

The Byzantine emperor Justinian I, depicted on this gold coin, created a system of laws in the 6th century CE. It became the basis for the legal code still used in continental Europe and South America, as well as parts of Asia and Africa. Common Law is the other major system of law. It developed in British courts in the Middle Ages and spread to the US and other former British colonies.

Magna Carta is born

English-speaking countries follow a system of common law rooted in Magna Carta, or "The Great Charter." Magna Carta established the principle that everyone is subject to the law, even the king. It was the first document to lay down the idea of rights for free people, including the right to a trial by jury, a panel of fellow citizens.

In 1215, England's nobles and bishops forced King John to put his seal on Magna Carta

Magna Carta was written on parchment—stretched and dried sheepskin

EXPERT CONSULTANT: Jack Snyder **SEE ALSO:** Ancient Mesopotamia, p.248–49; Ancient Rome, p.276–77; Medieval Europe, p.286–87; British & French Colonies in North America, p.306–07; Slavery in the Americas, p.308–09; Age of Revolutions, p.310–11; Civil Rights, p.330–31; Votes for Women, p.318–19

Witch trials

From the 1300s to the late 1700s, European courts executed 40,000 to 60,000 people for witchcraft. Courts accused suspects, most often women, of acting on behalf of the devil. Witch trials in Salem, Massachusetts, in 1692, sent many to prison and 19 to their deaths. Trials like this could not happen today.

Suspects put in a dunking chair often confessed, even though they were not guilty

FACTastic!

Chickens may not cross the road! A law in the US town of Quitman, Georgia, bans chickens, ducks, and geese from town streets. Chickens appear in other laws, too. Drivers must not drive from Minnesota to Wisconsin with chickens on their heads. In New Zealand, it used to be illegal to fly with a rooster in a hot-air balloon.

Going to court

Courts make decisions about laws. There are many types of courts, including criminal courts that deal with crimes such as theft or murder, and civil courts that deal with disputes between people or businesses. The International Criminal Court deals with offenses such as war crimes. All courts have at least one judge. Some use a jury, often 12 people, to make decisions, or verdicts.

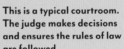

This is a typical courtroom. The judge makes decisions and ensures the rules of law are followed

Witnesses give accounts of the crime or provide expert opinions

Attorneys, or lawyers, represent people in court— they defend or prosecute

A jury listens to the arguments of both sides and decides the outcome

Crime & Punishment
LISTIFIED.

What purpose does punishment serve? There are basically five theories behind the reasons for punishing criminals.

1. Deterrence Punishment makes a criminal less likely to commit other crimes. Also, it makes an example of the criminal, so that others don't commit the same crime.

2. Protection It removes the criminal from society. Imprisoning criminals protects the public from becoming victims of the criminal.

3. Retribution It gives criminals the punishment they deserve. This aims to make the penalty fit, or be equal to, the crime committed.

4. Reparation It aims to make criminals repay, or give something back, to the victims or society. A fine can be a reparation.

5. Reform It aims to educate criminals and make them law-abiding citizens.

NOTE from the expert!

JACK SNYDER
Political scientist

Professor Snyder studies the International Criminal Court, which can put people, including country leaders, on trial for crimes against humanity. In many places in the world, laws are unfair or weakly enforced, so he believes that communities must work together to improve the law, police, and courts.

❝ *Good laws, enforced in a fair way, are needed to help people cooperate.* ❞

229

EDUCATION

Ancient Egypt had some of the world's first schools. Students, mostly boys, learned reading, math, science, and other subjects. Education has continued to be a key part of every civilization. It is the way that people gain knowledge and understanding about the world. Education is so important that it is part of the Universal Declaration of Human Rights, drawn up in 1948. The declaration states that everyone has the right to an education, beginning with free elementary schooling.

Higher education

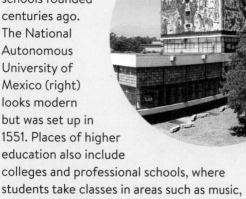

Today's universities developed from schools founded centuries ago. The National Autonomous University of Mexico (right) looks modern but was set up in 1551. Places of higher education also include colleges and professional schools, where students take classes in areas such as music, business, education, medicine, and law.

Equal education

Around the world, about 130 million girls between the ages of 6 and 17 are not in school, even though boys in the same places are. Some girls leave school to help their families at home. Others never attend classes at all and cannot read and write. Organizations around the world are fighting to change this. If girls are allowed to stay in school, they lead healthier lives, get more highly skilled jobs, and contribute more to their community and society.

The Power of Education
LISTIFIED.

Education has many benefits for individuals and society. Here are just a few of them.

1. Reduces poverty Research shows that having even basic reading and writing skills can lift millions of people out of poverty. They can get better paid jobs, and will then pay taxes to the government. The government can use tax money to benefit society as a whole.

2. Boosts the economy
Education leads to innovations, entrepreneurship, and training that provide new or better jobs.

3. Increases social skills Children learn to work with others and see other points of view. They become more involved in society.

4. Encourages self-discipline In higher education especially, people learn how to manage their time and be responsible for themselves. This means they can be more successful in their communities and society.

5. Advances social equality
Education allows people from all backgrounds, rich or poor, to have opportunities to achieve their goals.

6. Broadens horizons Education teaches people more about the world, giving them different perspectives and helping them understand others better.

7. Empowers people Education encourages people to think, ask questions, and take action. It provides people with choices and control over their lives.

EXPERT CONSULTANT: Miranda Lin **SEE ALSO:** The Brain, p.202–03; Language & Storytelling, p.216–17; Reading & Writing, p.218–19; Work, 232–33; Ancient Egypt, p.254–55; The Golden Age of Islam, p.284–85; The Renaissance, p.294–95; New Tensions, New Hopes, p.332–33; Inequality, p.344–45

Floating schools

In Bangladesh, flooding during the monsoon season means children cannot get to school. To solve this problem, an architect named Mohammed Rezwan created an innovative solution: schools on boats! These floating schools (one of which is shown here) pick the children up every morning and drop them off at home at the end of each day.

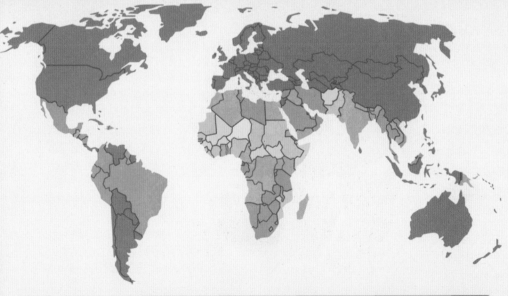

World literacy

Being literate means being able to read and write, which largely depends on having access to education. This map shows the percentage of literate people in different countries.

| No data | 0% | 20% | 40% | 60% | 80% | 95% | 100% |

Changing job markets

Welding requires skill, but it is also dirty and very noisy. Perhaps because of this, fewer people have wanted to train to be welders in recent years. This creates a skills shortage. Pay and conditions are just two of many factors that influence the kinds of jobs that people want to do.

WORK

People work to earn money to pay for food, shelter, and other necessities. But we also work to do something that we love. Some people build and make things, from computers to skyscrapers; others provide services, such as medical care; others cook, clean, or work in stores. Scientists invent things and help us to understand the world; artists produce work that makes life more enjoyable.

Child labor

More than 150 million children around the world work in order to add to their family's income. Many work in dangerous jobs in factories and mines. They usually can't go to school. Some richer countries have made child labor illegal. International organizations such as UNICEF are trying to end child labor around the world.

EXPERT CONSULTANT: Silvana Tenreyro **SEE ALSO:** Earth's Riches, p.74–75; Money, p.226–27; Education, p.230–31; Slavery in the Americas, p.308–09; The Industrial Revolution, p.314–15; Anything, Anywhere, p.342–43; Inequality, p.344–45; Future Humans, p.382–83

Working without pay

Sometimes people do unpaid jobs. Unpaid work is called volunteering. It often involves helping others, such as coaching local sports teams or working for good causes, like this woman helping out at an animal shelter in the Democratic Republic of the Congo. Volunteering connects people within communities and lets them share their skills. Sometimes people volunteer in order to gain experience in a job they want to do for a living.

KNOWN UNKNOWN

What will be the jobs of the future?

Some work can now be done entirely by machines, such as loading boxes in a factory. Throughout history, new technology has created a demand for new jobs and skills and made old ones unnecessary. Artificial intelligence (AI) may make even very skilled jobs unnecessary in the future. Robots are already helping surgeons perform some types of surgery.

The robot arm picks up the packages and loads them onto the palette

Computers scan bar codes, and measure, count, and weigh packages

Robots can do the same job over and over again without getting tired

Learning on the job

Becoming good enough to do a job well requires on-the-job training. People who want to be chefs often study at a culinary school. They might then become an apprentice to a more experienced chef. An apprentice learns how to do a skilled job or craft by working with an expert.

Be a dog food taster!

Pet owners expect the best food for their animals. That's why many pet food companies use human testers to make sure their products are tasty and nutritious. Most testers, however, spit out the food instead of swallowing it. Experienced taste testers can earn more money by helping to create new pet food recipes.

233

GAMES & SPORTS

Our love of games and sports goes back at least 5,000 years. They were used to help train hunters and warriors before turning into special events for others to watch. Sports and games fulfill many human needs. They are a way for people to interact and have fun, they test and stretch our physical and mental skills, and they are a nonviolent way in which we can compete against each other, either as individuals or in groups.

FACTastic!

World Cup soccer players run as many as 9.5 miles (15 km) in one game. This is the same as running around an Olympic-sized track almost 38 times. On average, soccer players run 7 miles (11 km) per game. This is more than athletes in any other sport.

Soccer firsts

A game similar to soccer was played over 2,000 years ago in China. The game was known as *cuju*, pronounced tsoo-joo, which means "kick ball." It had two teams, and both men and women played. To score, players kicked a ball through a goal. The Chinese military used *cuju* to train soldiers to be physically fit. It was very popular. The modern game of soccer was created separately in Europe in the 1300s.

Early balls were stuffed with fur or feathers and covered in leather

Players and team captains elected a referee who made sure the game was fair

EXPERT CONSULTANT: Martin Polley **SEE ALSO:** Energy, p.122–23; Becoming Human, p.196–97; The Human Body, p.198–99; The Brain, p.202–03; Food & Cooking, p.208–09; Ancient Egypt, p.254–55; The Olmecs & the Maya, p.264–65

Game of kings

The ancient Egyptian game Senet is over 5,000 years old. King Tutankhamun and other pharaohs enjoyed it. They played with five to seven tokens that they moved around squares on a small board. As the game developed, the squares included instructions in hieroglyphs—writing using pictures and symbols. Egyptians believed in life after death, and some of the squares offered players advice about the afterlife. King Tutankhamun had at least five Senet boxes buried with him in his tomb. Senet is an ancestor of another popular board game—backgammon.

Wrestling

These ancient Greeks are wrestling. Like all Greek athletes, they were naked. Wrestling is one of the world's oldest and most common sports. It became part of the Olympic Games in 708 BCE. Greco-Roman wrestling, freestyle, and Sumo wrestling are popular today.

Blades, prosthetics, and bionics

Inventions such as running blades allow athletes with disabilities to compete at a high level. The blades, first developed in the 1970s, are made of about 80 layers of strong, but lightweight, carbon fibers. Some of these are thinner than a human hair. Other athletes wear prosthetic, or artificial, limbs, for swimming, climbing, and other sports. In the future, athletes may be able to use bionic limbs in competitions. These work electronically using brain signals.

Blades attach to the prosthetic. The J-shaped blades allow better sprinting, like running on the front part of the feet

Blades are like springs—they take the runner's weight and then release this energy when lifted from the ground

Young Olympians
LISTIFIED.
....

Young Olympians compete against adults, winning medals and breaking records. Here are some of the youngest Olympic medal winners.

1. Dimitrios Loundras, age 10
The Greek gymnast competed in 1896, winning the bronze medal with his team in parallel bars.

2. Inge Sørensen, age 12
Sørenson, from Denmark, won the bronze medal for 200 meter breaststroke in 1936.

3. Kim Yun-Mi, age 13
In 1994, Kim Yun-Mi from South Korea speed-skated her way to an Olympic gold medal.

4. Marjorie Gestring, age 13
American Marjorie Gestring won gold in the 3-meter springboard diving event in 1936.

5. Nadia Comăneci, age 14
In 1976, the Romanian gymnast scored a perfect 10—the first for an Olympian. She won three gold medals, a bronze, and a silver.

Chinese New Year

A 15-day festival launches the Chinese New Year with firecrackers, glowing lanterns, and processions. A huge dragon, a symbol of good fortune, is carried through the middle of the procession, held up by sticks. The festival starts with the new moon, between January 21 and February 20, and lasts until the full moon.

The dragon has horns and claws, too, as it is made up of various animal parts

A Chinese dragon may be up to 330 feet (100 meters) long!

EXPERT CONSULTANT: Michelle Duffy **SEE ALSO:** Moons, p.32–33; Rockets, p.38–39; Combustion, p.108–09; Calendars, p.224–25; Ancient Mesopotamia, p.248–49; The First Chinese Dynasties, p.252–53; Ancient Egypt, p.254–55; The Persian Empire, p.266–67

FESTIVALS

Dancing, music, and feasting mark many festivals around the world. People come together in families, communities, and even larger groups to celebrate their culture and customs, or to mark important religious days or celebrate the seasons. Some festivals may follow or come before a time of prayer and fasting, but most are simply a celebration of life. Thousands of people take part in the largest events, such as the Mardi Gras festival in New Orleans.

New Year Festivals
LISTIFIED.

For many people, New Year marks a fresh start. Different calendars start at different times of the year—not all new years start on January 1.

1. **Diwali** marks the Hindu New Year with a five-day festival of lights in late October or November.
2. **Rosh Hashanah** starts the Jewish New Year with a solemn holiday at the start of the Hebrew month Tishri between September 5 and October 5.
3. **Muharram**, a holy time for Muslims, is the Islamic New Year. It falls on the first day of the first month of the Islamic year. In Islam, the year moves around the seasons.
4. **Songkran**, Thailand's Buddhist New Year holiday, is celebrated on April 13 with a water festival.
5. **Shogatsu** on January 1 marks a joyful start to the New Year in Japan. Celebrations can last for a week!
6. **Hogmanay** in Scotland sees the New Year in with three-day festivities, starting on December 30.
7. **Nowruz**, the Persian New Year on March 21, is celebrated in Iran, India, and other countries.
8. **Enkutatash**, the Ethiopian New Year, celebrated with hymns, prayers, and colorful processions, comes at the end of the rainy season in September.
9. **Ghaaji**, which means end of the growing season, is the Navajo New Year. It is in October. Like many other indigenous American nations, the Navajo mark New Year by the seasons.
10. **Seollal**, the traditional Korean New Year's festival, is celebrated—like the Chinese New Year—in January or February.

Red, the color of this dragon's beard, is said to be lucky and to ward off evil

Remembering the dead

People in Mexico celebrate the Day of the Dead on November 1 and 2. Families remember dead loved ones with feasts and parades, and everyone welcomes the spirits of the dead with food and skeleton-shaped toys.

DEATH RITUALS

Cultures around the world have special ways to honor the end of life. Death rituals, such as funerals, are a chance both to mourn and to celebrate the dead. Most rituals come from religious or spiritual traditions. Hindus cremate (burn) the dead in order to release the spirit to be born again. Jewish families sit shiva—seven days of mourning, prayer, and remembrance.

Ancient burial sites

Rock tombs called dolmens, like this one in the UK, date from early neolithic times, almost 6,000 years ago. They are found all over the world but especially in Europe. A rocky shelter in Qafzeh, Israel, which dates back more than 90,000 years, may be the world's oldest known burial place.

EXPERT CONSULTANT: Nicola Laneri **SEE ALSO:** The Origin of Life, p.148–49; Religious Belief, p.212–13; Ancient Egypt, p.254–55; Ancient Monuments, p.246–47; Ancient Gods, p.256–57; Ancient African Kingdoms, p.280–81; Medieval Europe, p.286–87; Aztecs & Incas, p.296–97; New Empires, p.304–05

The cobra and vulture represent goddesses to protect Tutankhamun

The crook symbolizes Tutankhamun's right to rule, like a shepherd leading a flock of sheep

The flail—always held with the crook in the crossed hands—represents the king's power. Both are symbols of the god Osiris

The king's body lay inside a nest of coffins. This richly decorated middle coffin has hieroglyphs, a kind of writing

FACTastic!

There is a "merry" cemetery in Romania. It has more than 800 colorfully painted wooden crosses. Villager Stan Pătras started carving the crosses in the village of Săpânta when he was 14. Each cross has pictures and humorous poems about the life of the person buried there.

Gifts for the dead

In some cultures, feasts and gifts are taken to graves to honor the dead. In China, some people burn flowers and fake paper money (known as ghost money) for the dead to use in the afterlife. People in Nepal offer candles, rice, and flowers for the spirit of the person who has died.

The afterlife

Tutankhamun, an Ancient Egyptian pharaoh, had three coffins, one inside the other. Each was covered in symbols that were meant to protect him in the afterlife, where it was believed he would live forever. Many religions throughout history have included a belief that some aspect of a person—a spirit or soul—lives on forever. It might exist in a separate place, such as the Ancient Egyptian afterlife or the heaven found in some forms of Christianity, or be reincarnated in a new body on Earth, as in Hinduism.

Humans
ASK THE EXPERTS!

PRAVINA SHUKLA
Folklorist

What do you want to discover most?
I want to know what people find beautiful, what kinds of artistic activities they engage in on a daily basis. We all add pleasure to our lives, but that pleasure may be gardening, or cooking, or sewing; it may be woodwork, or singing, or telling jokes. Everyone has an artistic talent as long as we expand our notion of what art is.

What do you enjoy about your research?
Most people around the world don't leave written documents behind, but all people have a sense of their history and can talk about it well. In describing everyday things such as family, worship, and work, we get a sense of the history of people and the places they come from.

GINA A. ZURLO
Historian

What do you study?
I study religion around the world. I think it's super interesting to think about why people believe what they believe. I love to see the differences in people by what holidays they celebrate, what special rituals they perform, and how they serve their communities through religion.

Can you tell us a surprising fact about your field?
A lot of people don't realize that the world is becoming more religious every day. Islam, Buddhism, Baha'i, Christianity, and Hinduism are all growing, not shrinking. For most people around the world, their lives are organized around religious holidays, rituals, beliefs, and practices. That is what makes my work worth doing.

MARTIN POLLEY
Sports historian

What sparked your interest in sports history?
I grew up loving sports and have always been fascinated about its past. I love how so many sports have long traditions, like club nicknames and colors. Becoming a sports history professor has allowed me to dig deeper and find out more about how sports in the past were linked to where and when they were played and to the communities and people who played them.

What is an unsolved problem in your field?
People always want to know exactly how a sport was invented, but in most cases there was no magic moment. Sports tend to evolve gradually over time. The origin of different sports and games is a big theme that lots of sports historians are researching.

Can you tell us a surprising fact about your field?
I love details about the challenges early athletes set for themselves. In 1809, Captain Barclay, a British solider, walked 1,000 miles (1,609 km) in 1,000 hours. He was on the move for 41 days! There were lots of stunts like this back then.

THE QUIZ

1) **What is the name given to the 3.2-million-year-old skeleton found in Ethiopia in 1974?**
   a. Lucy
   b. Lucky
   c. Lula
   d. Ludo

2) **Which of the following was NOT a human species?**
   a. *Homo neanderthalensis*
   b. *Homo habilis*
   c. *Homo bono*
   d. *Homo erectus*

3) **Which of the following is NOT a part of the brain's emotional control center?**
   a. Hippocampus
   b. Amygdala
   c. Hypothalamus
   d. Thyroid

4) **Approximately how many different facial expressions can a human being make?**
   a. 10
   b. 1,000
   c. 10,000
   d. 100,000

5) **The shiny coating on jelly beans comes from:**
   a. A fish
   b. An insect
   c. A snake
   d. Slime

6) **Approximately how much of the world's food production is wasted?**
   a. One-eighth
   b. One-fifth
   c. One-quarter
   d. One-third

7) **An expensive purple dye called Tyrian, once produced in ancient Rome, was made from:**
   a. Sea snails and urine
   b. Pigeon droppings and ladybugs
   c. Seashells and chocolate
   d. Monarch butterflies and butter

8) **How many countries are members of the United Nations?**
   a. 185
   b. 193
   c. 198
   d. 210

9) **Red ocher, a type of reddish clay, was used thousands of years ago for what purpose?**
   a. Making pottery
   b. Creating cave paintings
   c. Cooking
   d. Building houses

10) **In 2009, the African country of Zimbabwe printed a bill worth how many Zimbabwe dollars?**
   a. 1 million
   b. 1 billion
   c. 1 trillion
   d. 100 trillion

11) **Which Byzantine emperor created a new system of laws in the sixth century?**
   a. Augustus Caesar
   b. Justinian I
   c. Constantine the Great
   d. Nero

12) **A game similar to modern-day soccer was played in which country more than 2,000 years ago?**
   a. England
   b. Germany
   c. China
   d. Italy

13) **Senet, a board game played in ancient Egypt, was similar to what popular modern-day game?**
   a. Backgammon
   b. Monopoly
   c. Chess
   d. Tiddlywinks

14) **Rosh Hashanah, Songkran, and Seollal are all what kind of holiday?**
   a. New Year's celebrations
   b. Birthdays of famous people
   c. Anniversaries of historical events
   d. Harvest festivals

These giant stone statues, called Moai, were carved from about 700 CE by people living on the remote Easter Island in the Pacific Ocean. Then, from about 1050–1680, they were deliberately destroyed—but no one really knows why. It's just another example of history's many Known Unknowns.

CHAPTER 6
ANCIENT & MEDIEVAL TIMES

Ancient history is full of firsts. It's at this time we see the world's first towns and cities. New technologies, such as the wheel, are developed, and the first carts and chariots revolutionize trade, transport, and war. The invention of writing allows merchants to keep records of how much they have bought and sold.

This is when the world's first kings and queens, emperors and pharaohs rise to power. One Chinese emperor tries to defy death by building himself a mighty 8,000-soldier army of clay. But empires, like the Sun, rise and fall. Around the Mediterranean, the Syrians are defeated by Persians, the Persians by Greeks, and the Greeks by Romans. In the Americas, the Maya Empire rises and falls, too. Plague and disease strike Medieval Europe. Artists flourish in kingly courts, celebrating new beliefs that rise up to make sense of the fast-changing world. Judaism, Christianity, Islam, and Zoroastrianism come from the Middle East, Buddhism and Hinduism from Asia. See how their competing world views converge and collide, leading to profit and loss, war and peace.

THE FIRST AUSTRALIANS

Aboriginal Australians belong to a culture that dates back thousands of years. Australia is thought to have been first settled over 50,000 years ago, when people came to the northern part of the continent, probably from Southeast Asia. By 35,000 years ago, they had settled all over Australia. Along with another group, Torres Strait Islander peoples, they were the continent's first known inhabitants.

Sacred places

According to Aboriginal beliefs, mythic beings created all places, animals, and people during a period known as Dreamtime. For this reason, Aboriginals consider many places to be sacred. Kata Tjuta (below) is the sacred resting place of the spirits of the Anangu group of Aboriginal people.

Ancient evidence

Stone and bone tools and fossils found in Lake Mungo, New South Wales, which is now completely dried up, are some of the oldest evidence of human habitation in Australia. The fossilized remains of a man and woman date back 42,000 years.

Sixteen miles (26 km) to the east is Uluru, a huge oval rock that rises 1,142 feet (348 meters) above the surrounding desert. It is famous for its red color

Kata Tjuta (meaning "many heads"), also called the Olgas, has 36 domes. It covers more than 8 square miles (20 sq. km)

Swing and flick

The first Australians are known for creating the boomerang, a curved, wooden throwing stick. They used it for hunting, warfare, and ceremonies. There are two main types of boomerangs. The non-returning version was longer, straighter, and heavier, but they also invented a boomerang that was more curved. If thrown correctly, this stick can fly in a circle and come back to the thrower.

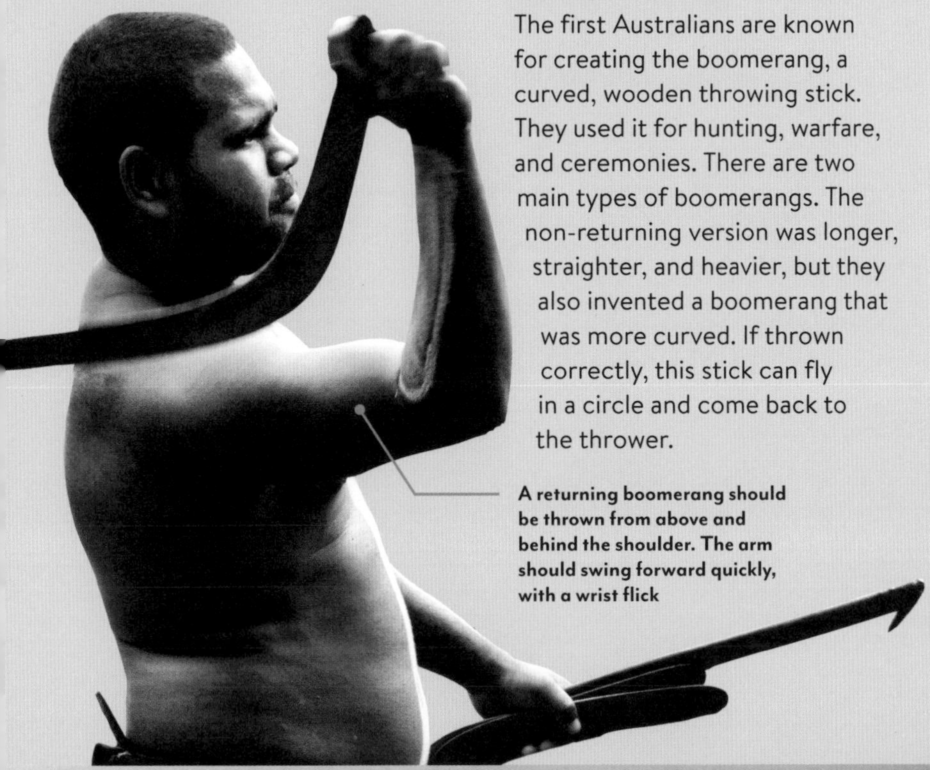

A returning boomerang should be thrown from above and behind the shoulder. The arm should swing forward quickly, with a wrist flick

Aboriginal art

Surviving artworks from the first Aboriginal people show that they had many artistic styles. Some groups created sacred objects by marking patterns into stones or wood that were probably then used in religious ceremonies or as memorials. Others painted on bark with ocher (a colored clay) or made paintings or engravings on rocks, like this one in Kakadu National Park, Northern Territory.

NOTE *from the expert!*

DAVE ELLA
Cultural educator

Dave Ella improves educational chances for Aboriginal children and teaches all children about Aboriginal culture, including dot painting, traditional weapons, foods, and medicinal plants. He shows students how to shape timber into tools such as spears, hunting clubs, and boomerangs.

66 *I have a great job. I want to help students go on to further education or employment.* 99

245

THE FERTILE CRESCENT

Humans began to practice agriculture around 10,000 years ago in a region of the Middle East known as the Fertile Crescent. This meant that people no longer had to travel to find food. This way of life brought new challenges. Some communities overcame them with new inventions, such as writing and the wheel.

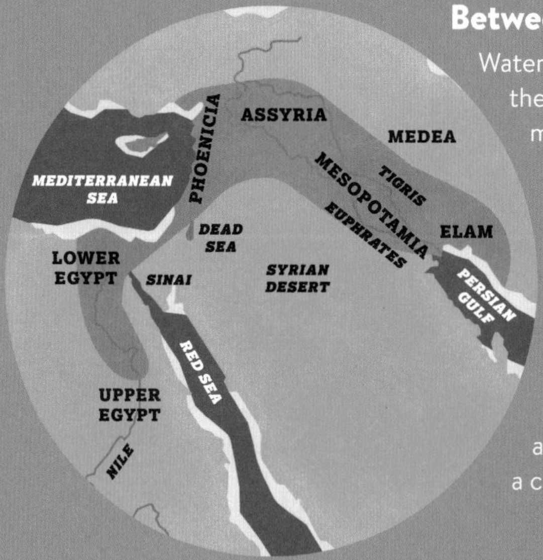

Between two rivers

Water from the Tigris and the Euphrates rivers made the land between them—Mesopotamia—particularly suitable for farming. By about 5000 BCE, people also farmed along the Nile River in Egypt. The whole fertile area formed a curved shape called a crescent.

Map labels: MEDITERRANEAN SEA, PHOENICIA, ASSYRIA, MEDEA, TIGRIS, MESOPOTAMIA, EUPHRATES, ELAM, PERSIAN GULF, DEAD SEA, LOWER EGYPT, SINAI, SYRIAN DESERT, UPPER EGYPT, RED SEA, NILE

Early farming

Farmers in the Fertile Crescent used canals to reroute water from nearby rivers for their crops. They also bred local animals for food and farm work. They used aurochs, an ancestor of oxen, to drag their plows. The plow is a simple tool with a blade that loosens the soil so seeds can grow in it.

The two most important grains were barley and emmer wheat

By 4500–4200 BCE, farmers were probably not only producing food for themselves but for elite people

EXPERT CONSULTANT: Mark Sapwell **SEE ALSO:** Harnessing Nature, p.180–81; DNA & Genetics, p.202–03; Food & Cooking, p.208–09; Reading & Writing, p.218–19; Ancient Mesopotamia, p.250–51; Ancient Egypt, p.254–55

The wheel revolution

By 4500 BCE, people in Mesopotamia had developed the wheel—but not for transport. Wheels were used to turn and shape clay for making pots. The Sumerians in southern Mesopotamia, perhaps inspired by the use of logs to roll heavy loads, made early wheeled vehicles around 3500 BCE. The first were simple sleds with solid wheels added. Within 500 years, they were making wagons and chariots. Lighter-spoked wheels appeared in the Middle East about 2000 BCE.

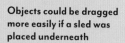
Objects could be moved by placing rollers underneath

Objects could be dragged more easily if a sled was placed underneath

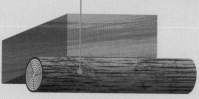

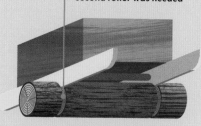
The roller and the sled were combined

Grooves allowed the sled to go farther before a second roller was needed

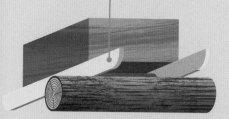

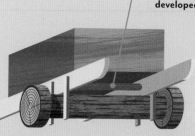
Wheels and an axle (central shaft) were developed as one piece

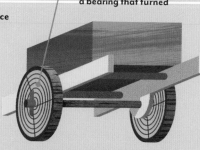
The axle was fixed into a bearing that turned

Domesticating Wild Plants
LISTIFIED.

Fertile Crescent farmers were some of the first to grow wild plants and breed them to create useful varieties. The most important were these:

1. Barley was ground into flour for bread, cooked to create a type of porridge, and used as a base for beer.

2. Emmer wheat was the most common grain for making bread. It was also used as a form of payment.

3. Flax produced seeds that people could eat, but its main use was to make linen, a type of material.

4. Dates are the fruit of a type of palm tree and were highly valued for their natural sweetness.

5. Plums, apples, and grapes were among the other fruits that Fertile Crescent farmers domesticated and grew in orchards and vineyards.

6. Legumes, such as chickpeas, peas, and lentils, were important because they were nutritious and could be easily dried and stored.

Breeders are bringing the ancestor of all cattle back to life. The aurochs, the original wild ox, was hunted to extinction in 1627 CE. As strands of its DNA—its genetic footprint—live on in other ancient cattle strains, the Tauros Programme seeks to breed the aurochs from its closest relatives.

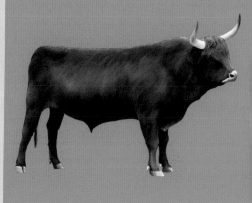

First script

The earliest evidence of writing comes from Mesopotamia. From around 3300 BCE, the Sumerians, who lived in southern Mesopotamia, began to use a system of symbols called cuneiform to record things like the amount of crops grown or taxes paid. This involved developing a system of written numbers as well as words. They used reeds to make marks on wet clay, which was then baked hard, to make a permanent record.

ANCIENT MESOPOTAMIA

Mesopotamia, between the Tigris and Euphrates rivers in the Middle East, was home to one of history's earliest cities. The first to be built was Uruk in around 3300 BCE in the region of Mesopotamia known as Sumer. Some of the earliest empires were also based in Mesopotamia. The Akkadians came to power there in around 2334 BCE, followed by the Babylonians and Assyrians, who battled for dominance.

Goddess Inana

The Mesopotamians worshiped many gods. Inana was the goddess of war and fertility, shown here with eyes made of rubies. An Akkadian priestess wrote poems and hymns to her. Inana later merged with the Semitic goddess Ishtar.

Set in stone

This is a fragment of the Stele of the Vultures. A stele is a stone carved as a monument. It was made some time between 2600 BCE and 2350 BCE. It records the conflict between two Sumerian cities and the victory of King Eannatum of Lagash over his rival King Enakalle of Umma.

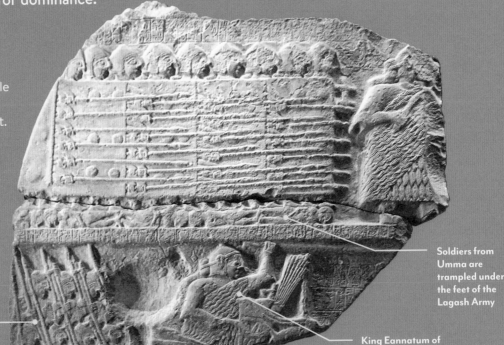

Soldiers from Umma are trampled under the feet of the Lagash Army

Lagash soldiers march behind their king, carrying spears

King Eannatum of Lagash leads his soldiers from a chariot

Ziggurats

The Mesopotamians built temples called ziggurats with ramps to allow priests to perform ceremonies on top. They had to be rebuilt every 100 years because they were made mostly of mud, which crumbled.

Shifting Power
TIMELINE

Around 3300–1900 BCE The first Sumerian cities developed. At first they were ruled by groups of powerful men but from 3000 BCE they were mainly ruled by kings. The cities often battled for power.

Around 2334–2154 BCE Sargon the Great conquered other cities in Mesopotamia to create the Akkadian Empire. It fell apart in 2154 BCE, and Mesopotamia once more was made up of many different powerful city-states.

Around 1850–1595 BCE Babylon was a city on the Euphrates River. Under King Hammurabi, Babylon began to conquer surrounding areas. Babylon controlled most of Mesopotamia by around 1595 BCE.

Around 1900–612 BCE At first, the Assyrians controlled just a small part of northern Mesopotamia. Their strength peaked around 900 BCE. They were finally defeated by the Babylonians and others in 612 BCE.

EXPERT CONSULTANT: Mark Sapwell **SEE ALSO:** Festivals, p.236–37; The Fertile Crescent, p.246–47; Ancient Egypt, p.254–55; Ancient Gods, p.256–57; The Persian Empire, p.266–67; The Golden Age of Islam, p.284–85

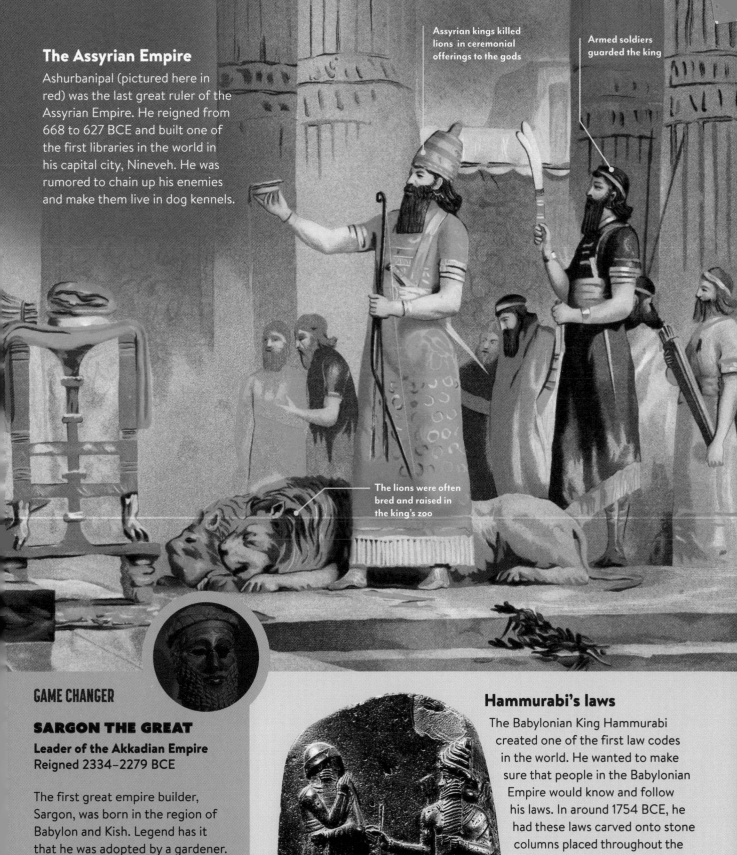

The Assyrian Empire

Ashurbanipal (pictured here in red) was the last great ruler of the Assyrian Empire. He reigned from 668 to 627 BCE and built one of the first libraries in the world in his capital city, Nineveh. He was rumored to chain up his enemies and make them live in dog kennels.

Assyrian kings killed lions in ceremonial offerings to the gods

Armed soldiers guarded the king

The lions were often bred and raised in the king's zoo

GAME CHANGER

SARGON THE GREAT

Leader of the Akkadian Empire
Reigned 2334–2279 BCE

The first great empire builder, Sargon, was born in the region of Babylon and Kish. Legend has it that he was adopted by a gardener. Sargon worked as a servant to the king of Kish, but overthrew him and seized power himself. From around 2334 BCE, he started to conquer Mesopotamia and built a new city called Akkad, which became the capital of the Akkadian Empire. We don't know when he died.

Hammurabi's laws

The Babylonian King Hammurabi created one of the first law codes in the world. He wanted to make sure that people in the Babylonian Empire would know and follow his laws. In around 1754 BCE, he had these laws carved onto stone columns placed throughout the empire. The columns recorded 282 laws on topics ranging from trade to marriage. Each column was topped with a relief carving of Hammurabi, seated on his throne, receiving the laws from Shamash, the sun god.

STONEHENGE

The prehistoric people of Britain and Ireland built stone circles. Stonehenge is the most famous of these. It is visited by more than a million people each year. It was built in five stages from 3000 to 1600 BCE on a chalky plain near Salisbury, England. Its huge, heavy stones were brought (probably on wooden sleds) from sites 15 miles (24 km) away. Two circles of smaller bluestones came from even farther—up to 150 miles (240 km) away.

Why was Stonehenge built?

No one knows the true purpose of Stonehenge. People used to think it was an ancient temple or was used to predict the movement of the Sun and Moon. More recently, experts have argued that it was a seasonal gathering place for many tribes and a monument to the ancestors.

The top stones (lintels) weigh about 7 tons (6,350 kg)

Most of the large upright stones, called sarsens, weigh about 25 tons (22,679 kg)

EXPERT CONSULTANT: Mike Parker Pearson **SEE ALSO:** Rocks & Minerals, p.70–71; Religious Beliefs, p.212–13; Death Rituals, p.238–39; Ancient Egypt, p.254–55; The Olmecs & the Maya, p.264–65; Ancient Greece, p.268–69

Earth's Ancient Monuments
TIMELINE

Thousands of years ago, civilizations built huge monuments. The ones in this timeline are still standing.

3200 BCE Newgrange, Ireland Ancient people build this elaborate burial chamber within a 40-foot- (12-meter-) high earth mound. It is reached by a stone passage and enclosed by a wall.

3000–1600 BCE Stonehenge, UK Ancient Britons erect this circle of massive stones surrounded by a large earthen bank and ditch.

2500 BCE The Great Sphinx of Giza, Egypt Ancient Egyptians carve this huge sculpture of a lion with a human head. The statue is 240 feet (73 meters) long.

515 BCE Temple Mount, Israel Jewish kings finish the Second Temple to house the Ark of the Covenant—a chest containing stones inscribed with the Ten Commandments that are believed to come from God.

432 BCE The Parthenon, Greece This huge temple dedicated to the goddess Athena is completed. It forms part of the Acropolis, a hilltop complex of buildings overlooking Athens.

600 BCE–900 CE Tikal, Guatemala This ancient Mayan center develops into a great city with 3,000 structures. These include palaces and temples in the shape of pyramids.

1st century BCE The Treasury, Petra, Jordan This temple or burial place is built by the Nabateans. It has a decorated facade around 130 feet (40 meters) high and three chambers. Its Arabic name is Al-Khazneh.

Each upright stone had a carved stone "tenon" (peg) that fit into a "mortise" (hole) in the lintel

Many of Stonehenge's stones were removed in more recent times, leaving gaps in its outer circle

The smaller bluestones weigh up to 4 tons (3,628 kg) and came from South Wales in the west of the UK

THE FIRST CHINESE DYNASTIES

Ancient China was ruled by a series of families, which we call dynasties. The first dynasty may have been the Xia, from 2070–1600 BCE, but we don't know for certain as the Xia kings feature only in legends. Under the Shang and Zhou dynasties, arts and crafts, such as pottery and bronzes, flourished, and the earliest known Chinese writing emerged under the Shang.

KNOWN UNKNOWN

Did China's great flood really happen?

One early Chinese civilization lived by the Yellow River. According to legends, the river once had a great flood, but Yu the Great was able to control it. The people made him king, leading to the founding of the Xia dynasty. Recent research provides evidence that a huge freshwater flood occurred in about 1920 BCE.

The Shang dynasty

The first Chinese dynasty to leave us written records was the Shang, who ruled for more than 500 years. The Shang started out as a small local state, but in around 1600 BCE, the Shang king is said to have overthrown the Xia Dynasty to rule China. At the time, China covered a much smaller area than the modern nation. In around 1300 BCE, the Shang built a new capital city, Yin, where many important Shang tombs have been found. The most intact one belongs to Fu Hao, a female military general who was married to King Wu Ding.

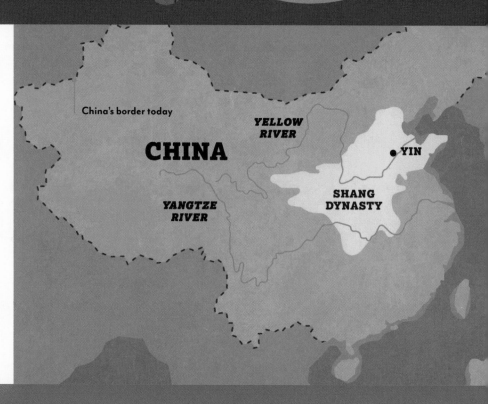

China's border today

YELLOW RIVER

CHINA

YIN

YANGTZE RIVER

SHANG DYNASTY

Ancient Chinese Kings
LISTIFIED.

Many ancient Chinese kings were said to be beloved for their great deeds. Others were hated for being cruel and harsh rulers.

1. King Jie of Xia The final ruler of the Xia Dynasty is said to have built a special lake that he then filled with wine.

2. King Tang of Shang Said to be a kind and good king, Tang of Shang reduced taxes and worked to improve the lives of his people.

3. King Wu Ding of Shang Wu Ding became king in 1250 BCE. As a prince, he lived with common people and learned about their lives.

4. King Di Xin of Shang Defeated in 1046 BCE, Di Xin was said to be a cruel ruler who raised taxes.

5. King Wu of Zhou Wu defeated Di Xin with an army said to have 45,000 soldiers and 300 chariots. He started the Zhou Dynasty.

6. King Cheng of Zhou Ruling from about 1042 to 1006 BCE, he was the second king in the Zhou dynasty.

7. King You of Zhou The rule of the last Western Zhou king was marked by earthquakes, eclipses, and drought, all viewed as bad omens.

EXPERT CONSULTANT: Man Xu **SEE ALSO:** Reading & Writing, p.218–19; Performing Arts, p.222–23; Festivals, p.236–37; Tang China, p.282–83; The Rise of Communism, p.320–21

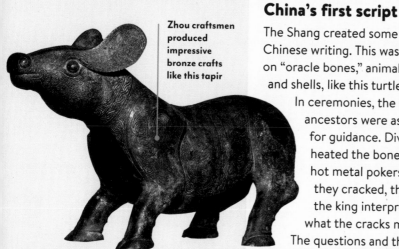
Zhou craftsmen produced impressive bronze crafts like this tapir

China's first script

The Shang created some of the first Chinese writing. This was carved on "oracle bones," animal bones and shells, like this turtle shell. In ceremonies, the kings' ancestors were asked for guidance. Diviners heated the bones with hot metal pokers until they cracked, then the king interpreted what the cracks meant. The questions and their interpretations would then be recorded onto the bones.

The Zhou dynasty

The Zhou defeated the Shang dynasty in 1046 BCE. Historians divide the Zhou into two periods. The first is the "Western Zhou." In 770 BCE, after a rebellion by a local lord, the Zhou king moved his capital east to Luoyang. The dynasty then became known as the "Eastern Zhou" and ruled until 256 BCE. The Zhou era was a time of technological progress. Craftsmen made detailed objects out of bronze. From around 600 BCE, tools and weapons made out of iron became common.

The Chinese calendar

Although China now uses the Western calendar, its traditional calendar, created between 770 and 476 BCE, has a cycle of 12 years. Each year in the cycle is named after one of 12 animals, each of which is said to determine the personalities of people born in that year. So people born in the year of the tiger (such as 2010) are believed to be brave and confident. Those born in the year of the rat (such as 2008) are thought to be hardworking and sociable.

Rat: 2008, 2020

Ox: 2009, 2021

Tiger: 2010, 2022

Hare: 2011, 2023

Dragon: 2000, 2012

Snake: 2001, 2013

Horse: 2002, 2014

Sheep: 2003, 2015

Monkey: 2004, 2016

Rooster: 2005, 2017

Dog: 2006, 2018

Pig: 2007, 2019

GAME CHANGER

CONFUCIUS

Philosopher, lived 551–479 BCE
China

Confucius came from a small state in eastern China called Lu. After working for his local ruler, he started to teach followers about his philosophies of life and how society should be organized, based on respect for elders, scholarship, and rituals. Confucius's ideas were rarely appreciated while he was alive. After his death, his ideas became very important in China and across Asia.

ANCIENT EGYPT

By 3530 BCE, farming had developed along the Nile River, allowing civilization to flourish. According to legend, in about 2925 BCE, a ruler called Menes united Upper (southern) and Lower (northern) Egypt and became the first king. Later called pharaohs, the kings were thought to be godlike. After death, they were mummified and placed in pyramids or tombs with their possessions.

Giza's Great Pyramid

The largest pyramid ever built was for King Khufu in Giza in about 2550 BCE. Originally measuring 481 feet (146.6 meters) high and made from 2.3 million limestone blocks, it took approximately 20 years to build. It includes several chambers and passages. Archaeologists recently located a hidden void within the pyramid— they are using scanning equipment to determine its size and purpose.

River of life

The Nile was the main source of water, and mud from its banks was used to make bricks. In July, the river would flood, leaving a layer of black mud that made the land fertile. The Nile was also a highway: the current took sailboats down the river, and winds brought them back.

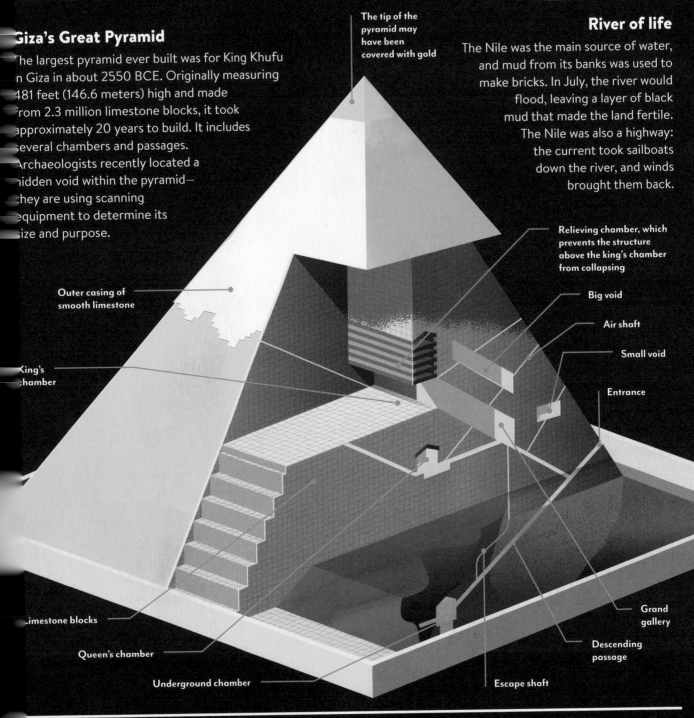

The tip of the pyramid may have been covered with gold

Relieving chamber, which prevents the structure above the king's chamber from collapsing

Big void

Air shaft

Small void

Entrance

Outer casing of smooth limestone

King's chamber

Grand gallery

Descending passage

Limestone blocks

Queen's chamber

Underground chamber

Escape shaft

EXPERT CONSULTANT: Salima Ikram SEE ALSO: Reading & Writing, p.218–19; Death Rituals, p.238–39; The Fertile Crescent, p.246–47;

Mummification

Ancient Egyptians preserved the bodies of the dead, believing their spirits would then live forever. The process is called mummification. In the time of King Tut, it took 70 days from start to finish. Priests removed all the internal organs except the heart, which was thought to be the source of intelligence. Ancient Egyptians believed Anubis, the god of embalming, watched over the process.

Anubis, god of embalming

1

Remove the organs
The intestines were put in a falcon-headed jar, the liver in one with a human head, the lungs in a baboon-headed jar, and the stomach in a jar with the head of a jackal

2

Cover the body in salt
The body and the cavity where the organs had been were covered in a special salt called natron, which soaked up moisture. After about 40 days, the body was completely dry

3

Wrap the body in bandages
Finally, the body was filled with linen, painted with resins, and wrapped in linen. It was then put in a coffin and placed in a tomb, along with the jars and items such as furniture that were needed in the afterlife

Hieroglyphs

From around 3200 BCE, ancient Egyptians used the hieroglyphic writing system. More than 700 symbols represented different words and sounds. Hieroglyphs were carved into stone or written on fabric made from the papyrus plant—from which we get the word "paper."

A	A	B	C/K
D	F/V	G	H
Ḥ	I/Y/E	J	L
M	M	N	P
Q	R	S	SH
T	TH	U/W/O	
Y/E/I	Z		

GAME CHANGER

QUEEN HATSHEPSUT

Pharaoh, reigned 1473–58 BCE
Egypt

Queen Hatshepsut reigned over Egypt for 15 years from around 1473 BCE. Hatshepsut's reign was essentially a peaceful one, based on trade, not war. She built a great temple and sent a sea-trading mission to Punt on the Red Sea. Statues usually depict her as a male pharaoh with a false beard, a symbol of royalty. Hatshepsut died in 1458 BCE and was buried in the Valley of the Kings near Luxor.

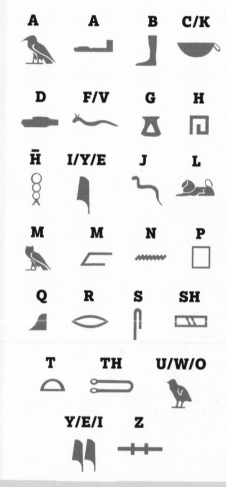

FACTastic!

During mummification the brain was removed through the nose. It was once thought this was done by poking the brain with a stick and then hooking it out through the nostrils. Most scientists now think it was done by stirring the brain with a stick through a hole in the skull. The brain, which is squishy, would then turn to liquid and drip out through the nose.

The liquefied brain came out through the nose

ANCIENT GODS

Ancient cultures had many higher powers that they believed were involved in the world and its creation. Most cultures worshiped several gods; a few had one principal god. Gods were often thought to control natural phenomena such as weather and the night sky, and also to determine the outcome of warfare, disease, and agriculture. The vast number of ancient gods were shown in art and writing in many different forms, both human and nonhuman.

Egypt's gods

Ancient Egypt had more than 2,000 gods. The ancient Egyptians believed the gods could help them in their life and after death, so they performed rituals in their honor, as shown in this scroll. The pharaohs (kings) were in charge of the temples where religious ceremonies took place. The pharaohs also claimed to be the successors of the gods and their representatives on Earth.

1 Priests
Temple rituals were performed by priests (shown here) and priestesses.

2 Pharaoh
The pharaoh also held the title of "High Priest of Every Temple."

3 Ptah
A creator god, Ptah was also the patron of craftspeople and architects.

4 Sekhmet
The goddess of war, healing, and medicine, Sekhmet took the form of a lioness.

5 Seth
A trickster, Seth was the god of chaos, storms, and fire.

6 Hathor
The goddess of sky, women, and fertility was sometimes depicted with a cow's ears.

7 Isis
This goddess could help cure the sick and bring the dead to life.

8 Osiris
The god of resurrection and the dead was also the god of fertility and farming.

EXPERT CONSULTANT: Paul Dilley **SEE ALSO:** Religious Belief, p.212–13; The First Australians, p.244–45; Ancient Mesopotamia, p.248–49; Stonehenge, p.250–51; Ancient Egypt, p.254–55; Andean Civilizations, p.258–59; The Olmecs & the Maya, p.264–65; The Mauryan Empire, p.272–73; Ancient Rome, p.276–77

Ancient Gods
LISTIFIED.

The ancient world had thousands of gods. Here are 10 notable ones; some are still worshiped today.

1. Horus The son of Isis and Osiris, Horus was the national god of ancient Egypt. He takes the form of a falcon or a falcon-headed man.

2. Janus The Roman god of time and transitions, Janus is often shown with two faces. The gates of his temple were opened during war and closed in times of peace.

3. Marduk The most important Babylonian god, Marduk was also known as Bel, which means "Lord."

4. Mithra A god of covenants (treaties or pacts) who originated in Iran, Mithra was worshiped across a wide area, from Britain to India.

5. Quetzalcóatl A Mesoamerican god of the morning and evening star, Quetzalcóatl takes the form of a feathered serpent.

6. Thor Armed with a hammer and associated with thunder, Thor was worshiped by Germanic peoples, including the Vikings.

7. Three Pure Ones The highest gods in the Taoist religion are credited with creating the Universe.

8. Trimurti This is a group of three supreme deities in Hinduism—Brahma, Vishnu, and Shiva.

9. Zeus The ancient Greek god of sky and thunder ruled over all of the other Greek gods.

10. Yahweh This is the personal name given to the one God in the Hebrew Bible. Originally the god of the Israelites, the one God is now worshiped in Judaism, Christianity, and Islam.

ANDEAN CIVILIZATIONS

The western coast of South America was home to many peoples of the Andes mountains. They included the Norte Chico (3000–1800 BCE), Chavín (900–200 BCE), and Nasca (200 BCE–600 CE). These peoples built ceremonial buildings such as temples and irrigation systems to water the land. They domesticated crops and bred animals for their wool to make fabrics. They traded these goods, as well as metals and precious seashells.

FACTastic!

Studying poop helps scientists know more about the Norte Chico. Fossilized poop shows that the Norte Chico ate corn and seafood such as anchovies. Potatoes, sweet potatoes, and guava fruit were important, too. Tools with pollen from corn plants still on them indicate that the Norte Chico farmed corn. They also grew cotton.

Sacred city

Caral in northern Peru was one of the first cities in South America. The Norte Chico people built it between 3000 and 1800 BCE. Caral is one of more than 30 ancient settlements archaeologists have found in the area. In the main part of Caral, there are more than 32 buildings including ceremonial centers, sunken plazas, and houses. This sacred city was an important center for religious ceremonies.

The remains of the amphitheater in Caral

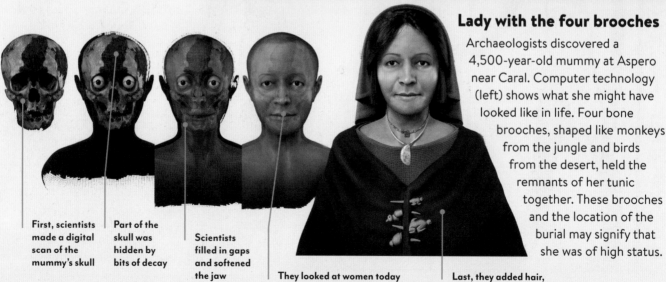

First, scientists made a digital scan of the mummy's skull

Part of the skull was hidden by bits of decay

Scientists filled in gaps and softened the jaw

They looked at women today to help add more details

Last, they added hair, clothing, and a headdress

Lady with the four brooches

Archaeologists discovered a 4,500-year-old mummy at Aspero near Caral. Computer technology (left) shows what she might have looked like in life. Four bone brooches, shaped like monkeys from the jungle and birds from the desert, held the remnants of her tunic together. These brooches and the location of the burial may signify that she was of high status.

EXPERT CONSULTANT: Alicia Boswell **SEE ALSO:** Dress & Decoration, p.210–11; Ancient Gods, p.256–57; The Olmecs & the Maya, p.264–65; Aztecs & Incas, p.296–97; New Empires, p.304–05; Slavery in the Americas, p.308–09; World Map, p.334–35

Supreme being

The Staff God is a key deity in Andean culture. He is a powerful figure who people believe created the world. Pictures show him as half-human, often with fangs. His name comes from the two staffs, or long sticks, he holds. They can be shaped like snakes. The oldest image that has been found of this supreme being dates back to about 2250 BCE.

Chavín culture

The ruined city of Chavín de Huántar in northern Peru was a major political and religious center. Its temples were richly decorated with carvings and sculptures. The religion of the people who lived there was very important to peoples across the Central Andes. Some made pilgrimages to Chavín, and artists created religious art for the city. Chavín stone carvings show fantastical humans and animals.

The Nasca Lines

The Nasca Lines in Peru were made starting over 2,000 years ago, probably by the Nasca or the Paracas, an earlier people. The drawings were made by removing surface rocks to reveal lighter ground beneath. Some are lines that run for miles. Others form pictures of animals and humanlike figures. The giant shapes are only visible from the air. The people who made them would never see the complete shapes, yet they are perfectly drawn. Scholars think the lines had a ritual purpose.

NOTE from the expert!

ALICIA BOSWELL
Archaeologist

Most societies left written records that tell their stories. In the ancient Andes, they did not use a written script. Instead they used knots and cords to set down information. If scholars could decipher this system, they would be able to understand a lot more about Andean societies.

66 *Trash is an archaeologist's treasure trove! We can learn so much about people by what they throw away.* 99

SETTLING THE PACIFIC

The indigenous peoples of the Pacific Ocean were great navigators. Ancestors of the people who live in what is now New Guinea settled western Melanesia around 40,000 years ago. The islands of Micronesia and Polynesia were settled by Austronesian speakers, perhaps from Taiwan. They explored and settled the Pacific's many islands by carrying out daring long-distance voyages. Starting in 1500 BCE and continuing for 1500 years, they peopled Oceania.

Voyagers' canoe

The Polynesians used big wooden canoes on their voyages of discovery. Some were a type called outriggers, meaning they had floats attached to one side. Others, like this one, had two hulls. The Polynesians used their knowledge of the stars and seas to find their way. In the 1970s, the Polynesian Voyaging Society built a traditional Polynesian canoe and sailed it across thousands of miles of ocean. This proved that the Polynesians would have been capable of long-distance voyages.

Triangular sails allowed the canoes to travel far longer distances than if they had only been powered by paddles

The wooden parts of the canoes were often bound together with coconut fibers

When traveling long distances, canoes were often equipped with shelter for their passengers and cargo

The two wooden hulls made the Polynesian canoes stable even on rough seas. They were large enough to carry all the plants and animals needed to colonize an island

EXPERT CONSULTANT: Patrick V. Kirch **SEE ALSO:** Constellations, p.14–15; Dress & Decoration, p.210–11; Language & Storytelling, p.216–17; The First Australians, p.244–45; Ancient Gods, p.256–57; Age of Exploration, p.298–9; New Empires, p.304–05; World Political Map, p.334–35

Exploring Oceania

The Austronesians explored and settled far away islands throughout Melanesia, Micronesia, and Polynesia. Population growth may have caused some of these voyages. Other journeys may have been accidents, when weather blew canoes far off course. But most often, the Polynesians went as explorers, searching for new lands to settle and developing sophisticated new ways to sail in the process.

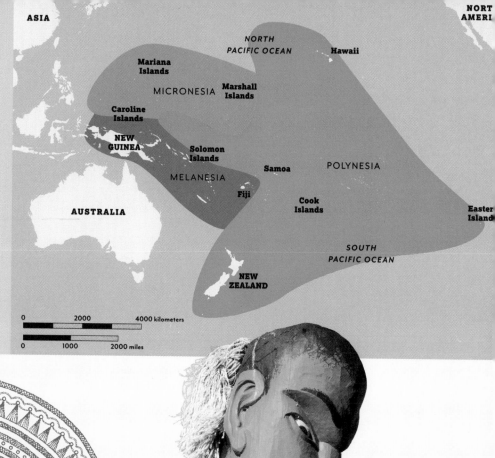

ASIA

NORTH AMERI

NORTH PACIFIC OCEAN

Hawaii

Mariana Islands

MICRONESIA

Marshall Islands

Caroline Islands

NEW GUINEA

Solomon Islands

Samoa

POLYNESIA

MELANESIA

Fiji

Cook Islands

Easter Island

AUSTRALIA

SOUTH PACIFIC OCEAN

NEW ZEALAND

0   2000   4000 kilometers

0   1000   2000 miles

Lapita culture

The Lapita people from East Asia colonized islands in Melanesia and western Polynesia from 1300 to 800 BCE. They decorated their clay pottery with intricate designs (above). Lapita pottery has been found between New Guinea in the east and Samoa in the west. The Lapita people were the first major Pacific culture.

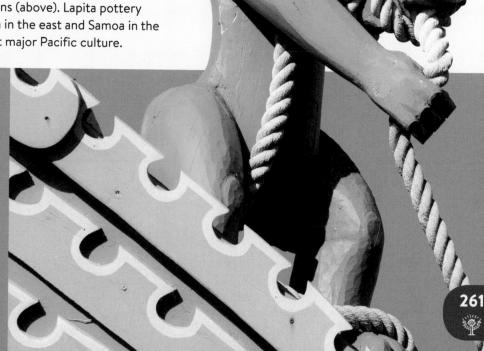

A carved post in New Zealand shows Maui pulling up the giant fish that became the North Island of New Zealand in Polynesian myth

Amazing Maui

The trickster hero Maui plays a role in the stories of many different Polynesian societies. These stories were passed on orally—by being spoken out loud—and are still told today. In these stories, Maui is often associated with amazing feats. He was said to have stolen fire from the underworld to give to humans and to have pulled up the islands from the seabed with his fishing hook.

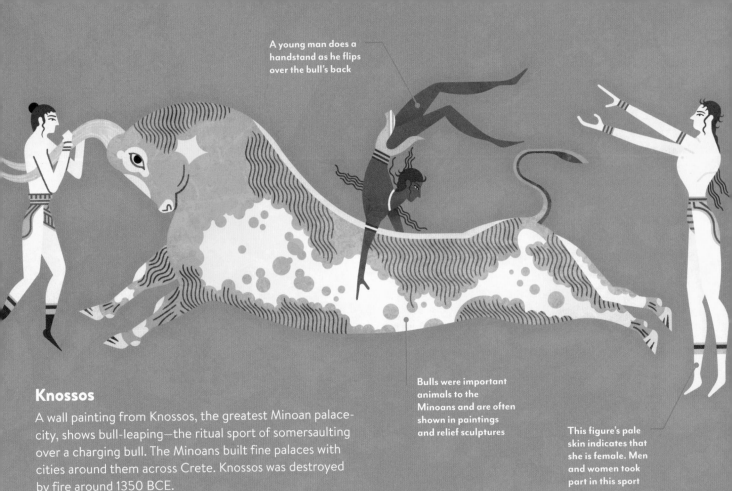

A young man does a handstand as he flips over the bull's back

Bulls were important animals to the Minoans and are often shown in paintings and relief sculptures

This figure's pale skin indicates that she is female. Men and women took part in this sport

Knossos

A wall painting from Knossos, the greatest Minoan palace-city, shows bull-leaping—the ritual sport of somersaulting over a charging bull. The Minoans built fine palaces with cities around them across Crete. Knossos was destroyed by fire around 1350 BCE.

THE MINOANS, MYCENAEANS & PHOENICIANS

Two of Europe's earliest civilizations developed between 3000 and 1000 BCE in and around the Aegean Sea. The Minoans were named after Minos, their mythical first king. They lived on the island of Crete, whose capital was Knossos. The later Mycenaean culture dominated Greece from 1500 to 1200 BCE. The Mycenaeans conquered Crete around 1400 BCE, but their civilization collapsed mysteriously around 1200 BCE. Meanwhile, the Phoenicians, in the eastern Mediterranean, had established a string of trading ports along the Mediterranean coast.

TROY

AEGEAN SEA

THEBES

MYCENAE
ARGOS
ATHENS
MEDEA
TIRYNS

PYLOS

KNOSSOS
CRETE

Aegean Sea

The Aegean Sea is an arm of the eastern Mediterranean Sea. To its west is Greece, home to the Mycenaeans. Crete, where the Minoans lived, lies to the south. To the east is present-day Turkey. The Hittites created an empire there from 1700 to 1200 BCE.

EXPERT CONSULTANT: John Bennet **SEE ALSO:** Conflict & War, p.214–15; Reading & Writing, p.218–19; Death Rituals, p.238–39; Ancient Greece, p.268–69; Alexander the Great, p.270–71

The Minotaur

According to a Greek myth, King Minos of Crete kept the Minotaur—a beast with a man's body and a bull's head—in a maze called the Labyrinth. When people from Athens killed one of his sons, Minos forced the Greek city to send seven young men and seven young girls every nine years to be sacrificed to the Minotaur. The Athenian hero Theseus finally killed the beast and escaped the maze with the help of Minos's daughter Ariadne, who had fallen in love with him.

The Minotaur was, according to myth, the son of Minos's wife and a white bull

The hero Theseus thrusts his sword into the Minotaur and kills him

Mycenaean cities

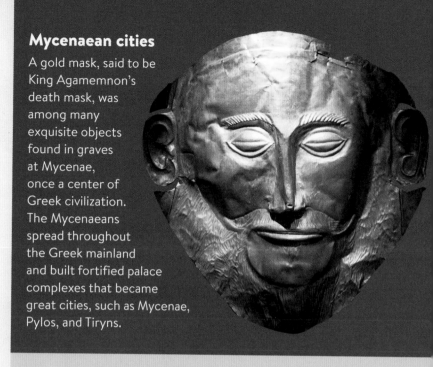

A gold mask, said to be King Agamemnon's death mask, was among many exquisite objects found in graves at Mycenae, once a center of Greek civilization. The Mycenaeans spread throughout the Greek mainland and built fortified palace complexes that became great cities, such as Mycenae, Pylos, and Tiryns.

The Phoenicians

In the second and first millennia BCE, the Phoenicians, whose homeland is in modern Lebanon on the eastern shores of the Mediterranean, built a trading empire that extended to Spain in the West. Merchants and colonizers, they were skilled shipbuilders.

The real life Trojan War

According to legend, a raiding party of Greeks hid in a wooden horse in order to launch an attack on their enemies in Troy. The Trojans wheeled the horse into the city and, after dark, the Greeks attacked. Two truths lie behind this myth—wet horse hides covered siege engines (machines that hurled missiles) to protect them from fire, and the Mycenaeans waged war near Troy in about 1200 BCE.

KNOWN UNKNOWN

Will the Minoan writing systems ever be deciphered?

The Minoans had two writing systems. One, known as Linear A, used symbols to represent sounds and some objects such as cows, pigs, and grain. Scholars can't fully translate Linear A, but they can read Linear B, the Mycenaean writing system. Linear B was an adaptation of the Minoan Linear A. It was used to set down the Greek language.

The script on this tablet, discovered at Mycenae, is from the Linear B system

THE OLMECS & THE MAYA

Two great civilizations developed in the tropical forests of Mesoamerica, an area stretching from Mexico to Central America. By 1500 BCE, the Olmecs were farming and living in villages and towns, some of which would become urban centers. Olmec culture influenced the Maya of southeastern Mexico, Guatemala, and Belize, whose civilization dates back to about 1200 BCE.

Olmec players of the Mesoamerican ballgame wore helmets like this

Colossal heads

The Olmecs sculpted huge stone heads out of boulders. The helmeted heads were 5 feet to 11 feet (1.5 meters to 3.4 meters) high and weighed several tons. To date, 17 heads have been found—the largest bigger than an elephant. They may be images of Olmec rulers or ballgame players.

Olmec craftsmen used stone tools to chip away at the stone and sculpt the facial features

The giant boulders are basalt, a pitted, volcanic rock

Trade and culture

Olmec craftsmen used materials from far away to carve decorative items such as this statue. The Olmecs controlled a trading network that spread across Mesoamerica. They exchanged gemstones and seashells for materials such as feathers, colored stones, and obsidian, a kind of volcanic glass, from which they made blades and dart points.

Maya Achievements
LISTIFIED.
....

Maya civilization was highly developed, with an excellent understanding of mathematics and astronomy.

1. Mathematics The Mayan number system used only three symbols for numerals. A bar equalled five, a dot equalled one, and a shell shape, zero. With those three symbols, they could write any number.

2. Calendar By observing the movements of the planets, stars, Sun and Moon, the Maya developed accurate time-keeping. They had a monthly calendar, and a week of 20 named days.

3. Architecture The Maya built great cities from around 600 BCE. High, terraced platforms supported temples, palaces, and civic buildings that were arranged around plazas.

4. Art The Maya decorated buildings with colorful friezes, relief carvings, and wall paintings, often showing mythological scenes.

5. Writing Maya writing had over 800 characters known as glyphs. Although the glyphs look like pictures, they represent sounds and can stand for whole words. The Maya made paper from tree bark.

EXPERT CONSULTANT: Elizabeth Graham **SEE ALSO:** Conflict & War, p.214–15; Games & Sport, p.234–35; Stonehenge, p.250–51; Ancient Gods, p.256–57; Andean Civilizations, p.258–59; Aztecs & Incas, p.296–97; Environmental Challenges, p.366–67; Cities of Tomorrow, p.380–81

The Mesoamerican ballgame

The Olmecs and Maya, like all Mesoamerican people, played a game with a rubber ball. The game was a little like a combination of volleyball and squash, and was often played on a court. There were two teams, or even just two individuals. Players had to get the ball over the center line to their opponents, who had to keep the ball in play or lose the point. Elbows, a knee, or the hips kept the ball in play.

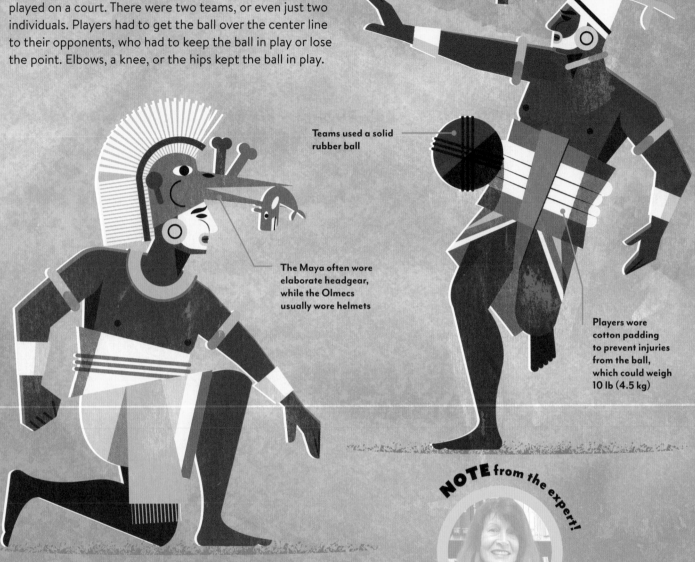

Teams used a solid rubber ball

The Maya often wore elaborate headgear, while the Olmecs usually wore helmets

Players wore cotton padding to prevent injuries from the ball, which could weigh 10 lb (4.5 kg)

NOTE from the expert!

KNOWN UNKNOWN

Why did some Maya cities collapse?

From about 800 to 950 CE, Maya cities experienced decline. Some cities in parts of Guatemala and Mexico were abandoned. Other cities and towns in Yucatán and coastal Belize thrived. After the collapse, trade, especially by sea, became very important. Scholars are still not sure what caused this collapse and change. Some point to drought or land erosion; others think warfare was responsible. The mystery remains unsolved.

ELIZABETH GRAHAM
Archaeologist

The Maya built great cities and fed thousands of people without ever raising cattle or sheep. They ate a largely plant-based diet, although they also ate turkeys, ducks, fish, and turtles, and hunted deer. Their cities were green cities with lots of trees, plants, and gardens.

66 By copying Maya cities, modern cities could become sustainable. 99

THE PERSIAN EMPIRE

The Medes and Persians emerged from Iranian tribes who had spread west from Central Asia. In 550 BCE, Cyrus the Great, founder of the Persian Empire, seized the kingdom of the Medes and later conquered the Babylonians. Conquests under Darius the Great extended the empire. His son Xerxes failed to conquer Greece, but Persia remained a great power for the next 150 years. It finally fell to Alexander the Great in 330 BCE.

Gold

Important men and women wore gold jewelry studded with lapus lazuli, turquoise, and other stones. This intricate gold earring depicts Bes, an Egyptian god whose worship spread across the Persian empire. The Persians and the other ethnic groups they ruled often exchanged cultural and religious ideas.

Persian warriors

The figure (left), depicted on a wall of Darius the Great's palace at Shush (ancient Susa) in Iran, shows the dress of Persian warriors and their weapons—spears and bows. The Persian army included foot soldiers and cavalry—fighters on horseback. Some soldiers were permanently stationed at palaces and fortresses, and others were hired or drafted for temporary service.

EXPERT CONSULTANT: John O. Hyland **SEE ALSO:** Dress & Decoration, p.210–11; Conflict & War, p.214–15; Money, p.226–27; Ancient Mesopotamia, p.248–49; Ancient Greece, p268–69; Alexander the Great, p.270–71

Persian Achievements
LISTIFIED.

Under its great rulers, the Persian Empire (also called the Achaemenid Empire, after the family dynasty of its kings) became highly developed.

1. The Cyrus Cylinder A declaration by Cyrus the Great, inscribed on a clay cylinder around 539 BCE, celebrates the takeover of Babylon and claims that Babylon's chief god invited Cyrus to rule there and save its people.

2. Government The empire was divided into 20 satrapies (or provinces), each ruled by a satrap (governor), who had to keep order, raise armies, and collect taxes.

3. Postal service The Persian kings set up an early postal service. Messengers on horseback took decrees around the empire using a relay system.

4. Money Under Darius the Great, gold and silver coins began to be used, making trade more flexible than in a system based on barter only.

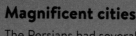

GAME CHANGER

DARIUS THE GREAT
King, reigned 522–486 BCE
Persia

In 522 BCE, Darius I seized the Persian throne. Thanks to conquests in India and Thrace (in modern-day Bulgaria), the empire reached its greatest size, stretching over 3,000 miles (5,000 km) from the Balkans to the Indus Valley. The Persepolis Fortification Tablets record the skills of Darius's officials at organizing workers and managing taxation at the empire's center.

One road was 1,500 miles (2,400 km) long

The Persian Empire under Darius the Great

EUROPE
BLACK SEA
CASPIAN SEA
SARDIS
ASIA
MEDITERRANEAN SEA
BABYLON
SUSA
AFRICA
PARSA

The royal road
To link their empire together and allow rapid travel by armies and messengers, the Persian kings built a complex highway system called the Royal Road. Its branches connected the Persian capitals at Susa and Parsa to other cities including Sardis (in modern Turkey) and Babylon (in modern Iraq).

Queen Atossa
Persian queens owned large estates and workforces, gifts from the king. They sometimes traveled the empire separately from their husbands. One famous queen was Atossa, the daughter of Cyrus the Great, and one of the six wives of Darius the Great. Atossa helped make sure that their son Xerxes succeeded Darius in 486 BCE.

Magnificent cities
The Persians had several great imperial cities, including Babylon and Memphis, but Susa and Parsa (known by the Greeks as Persepolis) held the most important royal palaces. Both were built by Darius the Great in southern Iran, starting around 520 BCE. Parsa housed many official buildings, including the Apadana, a royal audience hall that could hold 10,000 people.

ANCIENT GREECE

In ancient times, Greece was not a nation ruled by a single leader. It was made up of city-states—independent cities and the areas around them. Each of the more than 1,000 city-states had its own armed forces, marketplace, customs, and laws. Rival city-states often fought each other for territory and influence. Some also set up overseas colonies across the Mediterranean and beyond, spreading their culture. The richest city-state was Athens, which had a powerful navy.

Spartan women

The city-state of Sparta, which was famous for its warriors, trained women to be athletes. This statuette of a Spartan girl dates from the 6th century BCE. Although women could not perform as athletes in the Olympic Games, a Spartan princess and expert rider called Cynisca became the first female Olympic champion when a chariot team she trained won an event in 396 BCE.

Spartan women participated in sports, such as running, wrestling, and javelin throwing

Center of trade and learning

This drinking cup depicts a school. The cup was made in Athens, a major center of learning that was home to great philosophers such as Plato, Socrates, and Aristotle. Such scenes were popular motifs on Greek drinking cups, amphorae (jars for storing olive oil and wine), and vases, all of which were traded across the Mediterranean.

The teacher holds a stylus, a type of pen, and a wax-covered tablet to write on

Pupils learned music, reading, poetry, and how to argue persuasively

Teachers were tough and expected pupils to memorize long poems

This scene of pupils and masters was painted on a drinking cup around 500 BCE

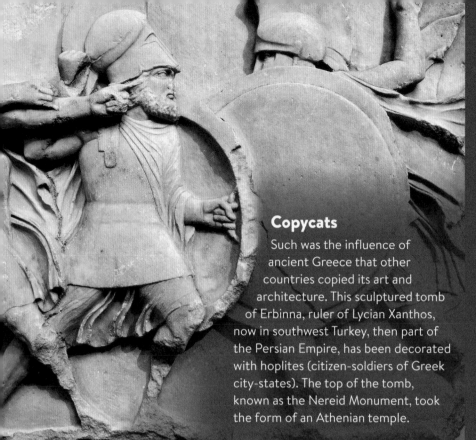

Copycats

Such was the influence of ancient Greece that other countries copied its art and architecture. This sculptured tomb of Erbinna, ruler of Lycian Xanthos, now in southwest Turkey, then part of the Persian Empire, has been decorated with hoplites (citizen-soldiers of Greek city-states). The top of the tomb, known as the Nereid Monument, took the form of an Athenian temple.

Zeus
The king
of the gods

Hermes
Messenger
of the gods

Poseidon
Sea god

Aphrodite
Goddess of
love

Apollo
Sun god

Hera
Goddess of
marriage

Artemis
Goddess of
the hunt

Athena
Goddess of
wisdom

Demeter
Goddess of
the harvest

Dionysus
God of wine

Hephaestus
God of fire

Ares
God of war

Gods and goddesses

The ancient Greeks worshiped lots of gods, who all had different powers and personalities. Each of the 12 major gods, known as the Olympians because they were believed to live on Mount Olympus in northern Greece, looked after a different part of life. The king of the gods was Zeus, and the queen was Hera, the goddess of marriage.

Greek Government
LISTIFIED.

The Greek city-states had four main types of government.

1. Monarchy Before around the 9th century BCE, a king ruled each city-state and passed on the title to a member of his family (usually a son). Sparta had two kings with equal power who ruled together.

2. Oligarchy This means "rule by the few," where a small group of citizens (usually from wealthy or noble families) ruled the city together.

3. Tyranny In ancient Greece, a "tyrant" was not necessarily bad. He was simply someone who had seized power (rather than inheriting it like a monarch) and ruled by himself.

4. Democracy By 400 BCE, some city-states were democracies, which means "rule by the people." Adult male citizens (but not women and slaves) could vote for public officials.

NOTE *from the expert!*

BILL PARKINSON
Archaeologist

Archaeologists try to understand how human cultures changed over time. For example, they want to know why people started living together in big farming villages that gave rise to cities. Archaeology, which goes back much further than written history, can provide evidence about the past.

❝ We study people. We can get a ton of information from ancient poop!❞

269

ALEXANDER THE GREAT

One of the mightiest rulers and generals the world has ever seen, Alexander III is known in history books as Alexander the Great. In 334 BCE, he began a long series of conquests in Asia and North Africa that created a huge empire, stretching from his homeland of Macedonia to Egypt in the south and India in the east. In a decade spent traveling and fighting, he and his fearsome army were undefeated in battle. He died of unknown causes at the age of 32 in 323 BCE.

5 At the battle of Issus (now in southern Turkey) in 333 BCE, Alexander played a central role. He fought on foot and horseback to defeat the army of Darius III, king of Persia, who fled.

BLACK SEA

ALEXANDER III

THRACE

1 Alexander was born in 356 BCE in Pella, capital of Macedonia.

PELLA

GRANICUS

TROY

MACEDONIA

3 In 338 BCE, Alexander fought in the Battle of Chaeronea in Greece. His victory brought all of the Greek city-states except Sparta under his father Philip II's rule. Four years later, Alexander succeeded his father as king.

CHAERONEA

ATHENS

GORDIUM

ISSUS

TIGRIS RIVER

GAUGAMELA

ARBELA

AEGEAN SEA

PHILIP II

MEDITERRANEAN SEA

4 In 334 BCE, Alexander sailed across the Hellespont (now Dardanelles, the narrow stretch of water between Europe and Asia). Leading an army of 30,000 foot soldiers and 5,000 soldiers on horseback, his aim was to conquer the mighty Persian Empire.

MESOPOTAMIA

ASSYRIA

BABYLON

BABYLONIA

TYRE

EUPHRATES RIVER

2 In 343 or 342 BCE, Alexander's father, Philip II, the king of Macedonia, hired the great philosopher Aristotle to be his son's tutor.

ALEXANDRIA

GAZA

7 In 331 BCE, Alexander's great victory in the Battle of Gaugamela brought down the Persian Empire, vastly increasing the land Alexander held.

MEMPHIS

AMMON

EGYPT

NILE RIVER

ARABIA

RED SEA

6 In 332 BCE, Alexander conquered Egypt and founded the city of Alexandria. The city's huge lighthouse, shown here on an ancient coin, would become one of the Seven Wonders of the Ancient World.

LIGHTHOUSE OF ALEXANDRIA

EXPERT CONSULTANT: Duncan Keenan-Jones **SEE ALSO:** Conflict & War, p.214–15; Ancient Mesopotamia, p.248–49; Ancient Egypt, p.254–55; The Persian Empire, p.266–67; Ancient Greece, p.268–69; The Mauryan Empire, p.272–73

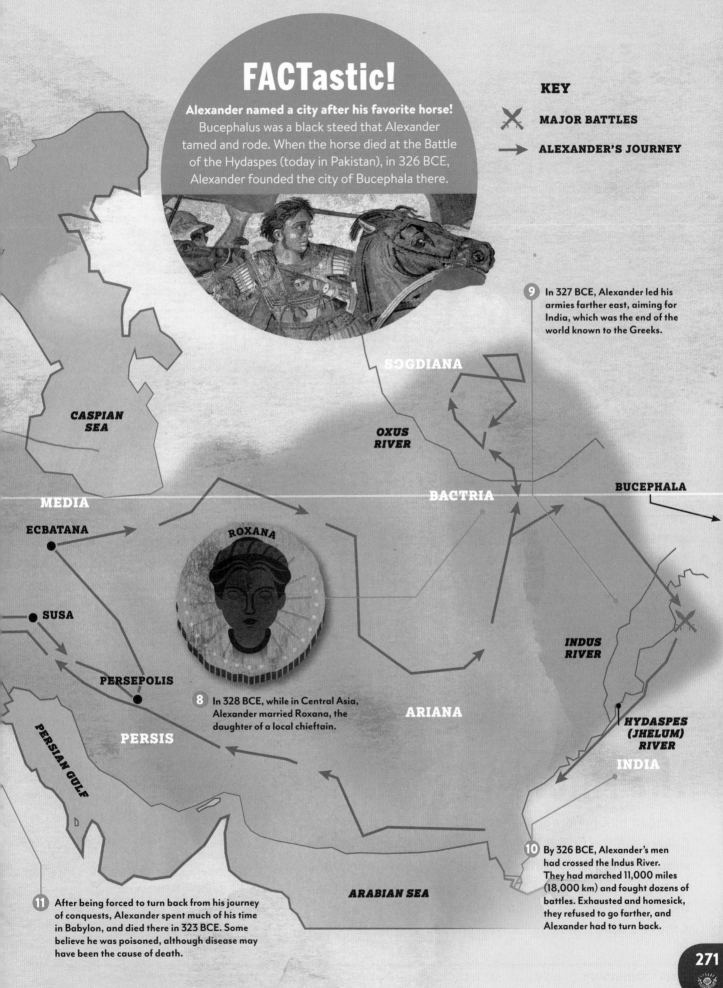

FACTastic!

Alexander named a city after his favorite horse!
Bucephalus was a black steed that Alexander tamed and rode. When the horse died at the Battle of the Hydaspes (today in Pakistan), in 326 BCE, Alexander founded the city of Bucephala there.

KEY

✗ MAJOR BATTLES

→ ALEXANDER'S JOURNEY

9 In 327 BCE, Alexander led his armies farther east, aiming for India, which was the end of the world known to the Greeks.

SOGDIANA

CASPIAN SEA

OXUS RIVER

BACTRIA

BUCEPHALA

MEDIA

ECBATANA

ROXANA

INDUS RIVER

SUSA

PERSEPOLIS

8 In 328 BCE, while in Central Asia, Alexander married Roxana, the daughter of a local chieftain.

ARIANA

PERSIS

HYDASPES (JHELUM) RIVER

INDIA

PERSIAN GULF

ARABIAN SEA

10 By 326 BCE, Alexander's men had crossed the Indus River. They had marched 11,000 miles (18,000 km) and fought dozens of battles. Exhausted and homesick, they refused to go farther, and Alexander had to turn back.

11 After being forced to turn back from his journey of conquests, Alexander spent much of his time in Babylon, and died there in 323 BCE. Some believe he was poisoned, although disease may have been the cause of death.

The carvings on the gate show events in the Buddha's life but do not show the Buddha himself

The dome is said to represent heaven enclosing Earth. Its diameter is 120 feet (36.6 meters)

THE MAURYAN EMPIRE

Founded by Chandragupta Maurya in 321 BCE, the Mauryan Empire was the first and largest ever to exist on the Indian subcontinent. Under Chandragupta's grandson Ashoka, who ruled from 273–232 BCE and helped make Buddhism its main religion, the empire spanned 2 million square miles (5 million sq. km). After Ashoka's death, the empire weakened and fell in 185 BCE.

Sacred Buddhist shrine

The gateway to the Great Stupa, a domed shrine at Sanchi in central India, is decorated with elaborate sculptures of symbols and scenes relating to the Buddha. Built by Ashoka in the third century BCE, the shrine is believed to house ashes of the Buddha. It was originally a simple structure but was greatly enlarged in the second century BCE.

EXPERT CONSULTANT: Dominik Wujastyk **SEE ALSO:** Religious Belief, p.212–13; Conflict & War, p.214–15; Stonehenge, p.250–51; Alexander the Great, p.270–71; The Mughal Empire, p.300–01

Mauryan Empire
TIMELINE

321 BCE Chandragupta, ruler of the Kingdom of Magadha in northern India, founds the Mauryan Empire.

305 BCE Chandragupta defeats Seleucus Nicator, a former general of Alexander the Great, stopping Seleucid expansion into India.

297 BCE Chandragupta dies and is succeeded as emperor by his son Bindusara.

c. 273 BCE At Bindusara's death, Ashoka claims the throne. Legend has it that he was challenged by his many brothers. He does not fully secure his position as emperor until around 268 BCE.

261 BCE The ten-year Kalinga War ends in victory for Ashoka.

249 BCE Ashoka makes a pilgrimage to Lumbini in Nepal, the birthplace of the Buddha, where he constructs a sandstone pillar, inscribed with a sacred text.

185 BCE Brihadratha, the last Mauryan emperor, is killed by his military commander Pushyamitra, whose Shunga dynasty rules central India for about a century.

100 BCE–100 CE The *Artha-shastra* ("The Science of Material Gain"), a work on the art of political thought and how to be an effective ruler, is composed by Kautilya.

320 CE Chandra Gupta I founds the Gupta Empire, the next power to dominate the Indian subcontinent. The empire remains a major power until the mid-6th century CE.

GAME CHANGER

ASHOKA THE GREAT
Emperor, reigned c. 268–232 BCE
India

Ashoka is remembered as a thoughtful, kind, and enlightened ruler. In 261 BCE, he finally ended a long, bloody war against Kalinga, an eastern coastal state, conquering it. Sickened by all the bloodshed, Ashoka vowed to rule peacefully and later converted to Buddhism. At his death, his empire stretched across most of the Indian subcontinent.

FACTastic!

Chandragupta slept in a different bed each night. According to legend, the founder of the Mauryan Empire was afraid his enemies might break in and kill him as he slept. His servants tasted his food before he ate it in case it was poisoned, and he had spies to warn him of plots.

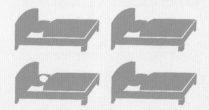

Buddhism

After Ashoka became a follower of the Buddha, shown here meditating, he encouraged his subjects to follow Buddhism. Ashoka used his wealth to help his people. He became a vegetarian and went on pilgrimages, built shrines, and sent monks out across Asia to spread the Buddha's teachings.

The rock edicts of Ashoka

A lion sits atop one of many pillars of highly polished sandstone that Ashoka erected across his empire. Skilled craftsmen inscribed them with Buddhist symbols, animals, and teachings; details of Ashoka's life; and his religious and political ideas. These inscriptions are known as Ashoka's rock edicts. More than 30 survive. Most are on boulders, but some are carved on cave walls.

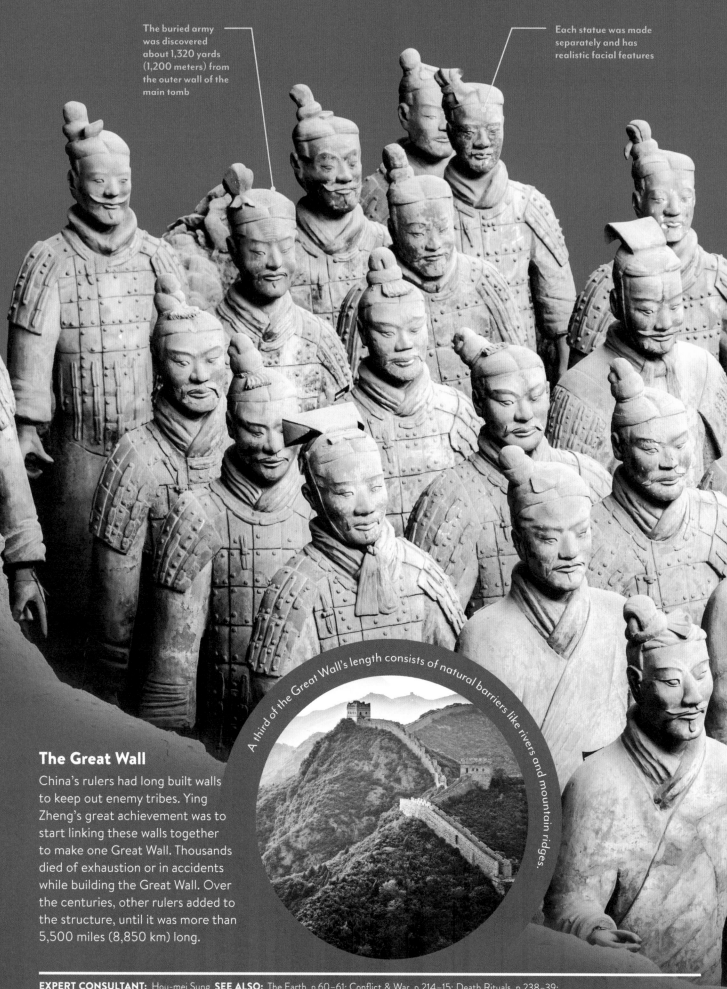

The buried army was discovered about 1,320 yards (1,200 meters) from the outer wall of the main tomb

Each statue was made separately and has realistic facial features

A third of the Great Wall's length consists of natural barriers like rivers and mountain ridges.

The Great Wall

China's rulers had long built walls to keep out enemy tribes. Ying Zheng's great achievement was to start linking these walls together to make one Great Wall. Thousands died of exhaustion or in accidents while building the Great Wall. Over the centuries, other rulers added to the structure, until it was more than 5,500 miles (8,850 km) long.

EXPERT CONSULTANT: Hou-mei Sung **SEE ALSO:** The Earth, p.60–61; Conflict & War, p.214–15; Death Rituals, p.238–39; The First Chinese Dynasties, p.252–53; Ancient Egypt, p.254–55; Tang China, p.282–83

THE TERRA-COTTA ARMY

In the 1970s, archaeologists discovered around 8,000 life-size terra-cotta (clay) figures buried outside the tomb of a mighty ruler of ancient China called Ying Zheng. Ying Zheng had united China under his rule in 221 BCE and called himself Qin Shi Huang ("First Sovereign Emperor"). The figures were his terra-cotta army, designed to guard him in the afterlife.

On parade

Ying Zheng ordered his enormous tomb to be built before he died. It covers around 20 sq. miles (50 sq. km). The army was found in multiple pits deep underground, together with pottery horses and bronze chariots. It faces east, ready to battle the emperor's old enemies.

The discovery of at least 10 different face shapes suggests that at least 10 basic molds were used

The figures were modeled by hand and painted in different colors . Most figures have now lost their colors

ANCIENT ROME

Ancient Rome started out as a city in what is now Italy and grew into a vast empire that stretched from Britain to North Africa and the Middle East. The empire lasted 1,000 years, from about 500 BCE to around 476 CE, when it was defeated by invading peoples from the north. The Romans saw themselves as the inheritors of the traditions of ancient Greece. They merged Roman gods with Greek ones and experimented with Greek-style democracy.

Romulus and Remus

According to legend, Rome was founded by Romulus, the son of a princess. Romulus and his twin brother, Remus, were raised by a woodpecker, a she-wolf, and a shepherd, after their uncle tried to drown them. As adults, the twins built a city together but then quarreled. Romulus killed Remus, named the city Rome, and became its first king.

The Punic Wars

Hannibal was a mighty general from Carthage, in North Africa, who fought against Rome. He is famous for using elephants in war the way some armies used horses. In the 3rd and 2nd centuries BCE, Rome fought three Punic (Carthaginian) Wars. The wars ended when the Roman army destroyed Carthage in 146 BCE.

Julius Caesar

After conquering Gaul, a large area of Europe north of Italy, Roman general Julius Caesar returned to Rome in 49 BCE and made himself dictator. Five years of civil war followed. Caesar's followers were victorious, but some senators feared he wanted to be king. Sixty stabbed him to death in 44 BCE on March 15 (the "Ides of March" in the Roman calendar).

EXPERT CONSULTANT: Duncan Keenan-Jones **SEE ALSO:** Volcanoes, p.64–65; Conflict & War, p.214–15; Language & Storytelling, p.216–17; Crime & Law, p.228–29; The Minoans, Mycenaeans & Phoenicians, p.262–63; Ancient Greece, p.268–69; The Byzantine World, p.278–79

The Roman Empire

From the 5th century BCE, Rome greatly expanded its empire. Its armies conquered what is now Italy, then defeated Carthage, adding land in North Africa and Hispania. They took Greece, Syria, and Asia Minor, conquered Gaul, and invaded Britain. At its height, under Emperor Trajan (98–117 CE), the empire stretched 2,300 miles (3,700 km) from north to south and over 2,500 miles (4,000 km) east to west.

In 220 BCE, Rome began invading Hispania (what is now Spain and Portugal)

Romans occupied Britain (part of what is now the UK), the northern limit of the empire, from 43–410 CE

In 146 BCE, Rome conquered Greece

Syria fell to Rome in 64 BCE

Julius Caesar brought all of Gaul under Roman rule by 50 BCE

Carthage, capital of the Carthaginian Empire, fell to Rome in 146 BCE

Egypt became a Roman province in 31 BCE, when the future emperor Augustus defeated its queen, Cleopatra

Art and the Romans

Colorful wall paintings (called frescoes), such as this one of a woman playing a *kithara*, a Greek stringed instrument, show how important the arts were to the Romans. This fresco came from Pompeii, a city in southern Italy that was buried and preserved under volcanic ash when the volcano Mount Vesuvius erupted in 79 CE. Excavations at Pompeii uncovered jewelry, paintings, sculptures, and many details about daily Roman life.

GAME CHANGER

AUGUSTUS
Emperor, reigned 27 BCE–14 CE
Rome

Augustus, Caesar's heir, pretended not to want to be king, but carefully tightened his grip on power, to become Rome's first emperor. After Caesar's death, he ruled with Mark Antony, but eventually they turned on each other. Augustus defeated Antony and Cleopatra, the Egyptian queen, in 31 BCE. Augustus encouraged the arts, founded cities, and built roads. The Empire flourished and enjoyed peace and prosperity.

Rome's Legacy
LISTIFIED.

The Romans influenced the languages, literature, laws, government, roads, and buildings of all the places they ruled.

1. Politics Between 509 BCE and 27 BCE, a period called the Roman Republic, the Romans replaced their monarchy with a democracy, though only free men could vote.

2. Language The modern languages French, Spanish, Portuguese, Italian, and Romanian have their roots in Latin, the language of the ancient Romans.

3. Architecture The Romans designed and constructed great buildings. Some, such as Rome's Colosseum, still survive.

4. Engineering The Romans took on huge engineering projects. They built hundreds of miles of roads that connected their empire and aqueducts to carry fresh water to their cities.

5. Warfare Rome's army was so effective because it was highly trained and organized. It influenced later warfare.

6. Literature Rome produced great poets, such as Virgil, Horace, and Ovid, whose works influenced many later writers, including Shakespeare.

THE BYZANTINE WORLD

A great new power rose up when the Roman Empire split into two parts in 395 CE. Rome and the western Roman Empire fell to the Huns and tribes of Germanic peoples—around 476 CE. The eastern part of the Roman Empire, known as the Byzantine Empire, flourished, living on for nearly a thousand years, until 1453, when the Ottoman Turks stormed its capital, Constantinople.

The early Christians

Christianity, a religion stemming from the life and teachings of Jesus Christ, became the official religion of the Roman empire in 380 CE. As more people converted to the new religion, pagan temples were demolished and churches were built, some of them richly decorated with mosaics and icons (pictures of holy figures). A series of meetings attended by senior Christians resulted in statements of faith, setting down which beliefs about Christ should be taught.

The Hagia Sophia

Built by Justinian I in 537 CE, the Hagia Sophia in Constantinople was the world's largest cathedral for a thousand years. The church, whose name means holy wisdom, became a mosque in 1453 when Sultan Mehmed II conquered the city. Today Constantinople is known as Istanbul and the building is a mosque.

The cathedral is more than 180 feet (56 meters) tall

Its huge dome was rebuilt as it partly collapsed after an earthquake in 558

The line of arched windows just below the dome fill the building with light

EXPERT CONSULTANT: Eugenia Russell **SEE ALSO:** Religious Belief, p.212–13; Conflict & War, p.214–15; Ancient Rome, p.276–77; The Golden Age of Islam, p.284–85; Medieval Europe, p.286–87; Crime & Law, p.228–29

A Golden Age

The Empire reached its greatest extent under Justinian I (the Great), lawgiver and patron of the arts. Basil II (976–1025) led its armies to keep it the most important power in southeastern Europe and the Middle East. Its capital, Constantinople, was the largest and wealthiest city in Europe, the center of trade, architecture, art, manuscript production, and Orthodox Christianity. Wall paintings, mosaics, and domed buildings from this time still survive. This picture shows a widow asking for help from the emperor Theophilus (829–42).

The Byzantine World
TIMELINE

395 The Roman Empire splits. The eastern half becomes the Byzantine Empire; Constantinople is its capital.

441–52 Attila the Hun invades the Byzantine Empire, and later Gaul (an area of western Europe) and Italy. He dies in 453.

527–65 Emperor Justinian I wins territory in Persia, North Africa, and Europe and makes Constantinople one of the world's greatest cities. By the end of his reign, the Byzantine Empire stretches from the Middle East to Spain.

963 The Great Lavra monastery is built on Mount Athos, Greece. Mount Athos becomes an important center of Byzantine Christianity.

1054 The Great Schism divides Christianity into eastern and western sections, later called Eastern Orthodoxy and Roman Catholicism. Eastern Orthodoxy becomes the official religion of the Byzantine Empire.

1071 The Byzantine Empire loses most of Anatolia (Turkey) to the Seljuk Turks.

1204 The Crusaders (Christian warriors) seize Constantinople. Michael VIII retakes the city for the Byzantium Empire in 1261.

1453 After a 55-day siege, the Ottoman Turks take Constantinople, and the Byzantine Empire collapses.

GAME CHANGER

THEODORA

Empress, reigned 527–565 CE
Byzantine Empire

The most powerful woman in Byzantine history began life as the daughter of a bear trainer. After her marriage to Emperor Justinian, she became his most trusted adviser. She used her influence to promote religious and social policies and was one of the first rulers to recognize the rights of women. She helped pass laws to protect young girls and to give divorced women more rights.

FACTastic!

The Byzantines threw fire at their enemies. Under constant attack, the Byzantines had a secret weapon—Greek fire, a petroleum-based mixture that couldn't be put out by water. The Byzantines squirted it through tubes or put it in pots and threw it. They used it to destroy an invading Arab fleet in 673.

ANCIENT AFRICAN KINGDOMS

Before about 1000 CE, powerful empires ruled large areas of the huge and diverse continent of Africa. Some of them, like the Ghana Empire, became very rich by controlling the trade routes that crossed Africa, particularly those that went across the Sahara desert.

Kingdoms and empires

The ancient African powers spanned the continent from Carthage on the Mediterranean Sea to the Ghana Empire, south of the Sahara. Farther south, the Kingdom of Aksum was in present-day Ethiopia and Eritrea. Many different kings and rulers built powerful states that were sometimes larger than countries today.

CARTHAGE

EGYPT

SAHARA

GHANA EMPIRE

KUSH

AKSUM

AFRICA

ATLANTIC OCEAN

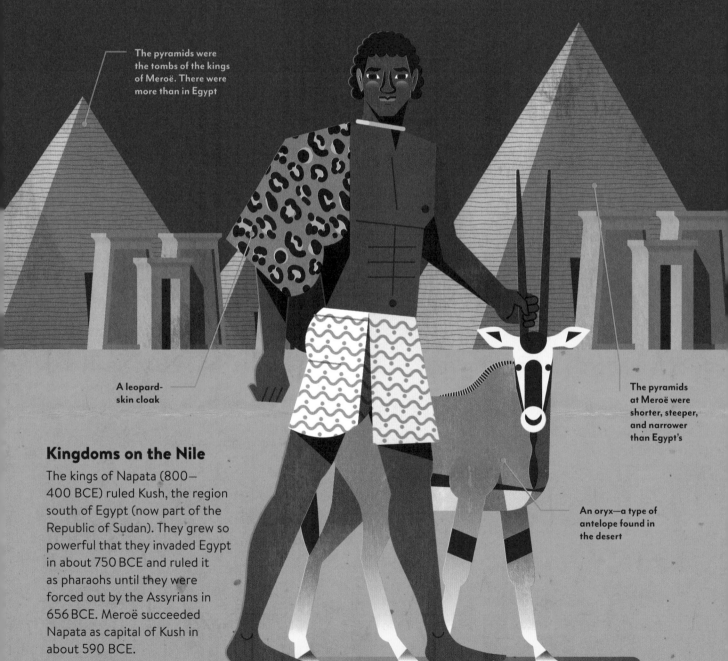

The pyramids were the tombs of the kings of Meroë. There were more than in Egypt

A leopard-skin cloak

The pyramids at Meroë were shorter, steeper, and narrower than Egypt's

An oryx—a type of antelope found in the desert

Kingdoms on the Nile

The kings of Napata (800–400 BCE) ruled Kush, the region south of Egypt (now part of the Republic of Sudan). They grew so powerful that they invaded Egypt in about 750 BCE and ruled it as pharaohs until they were forced out by the Assyrians in 656 BCE. Meroë succeeded Napata as capital of Kush in about 590 BCE.

EXPERT CONSULTANT: Ghislaine Lydon **SEE ALSO:** Deserts, p.172–73; The Fertile Crescent, p.246–47; Ancient Egypt, p.254–55; The Minoans, Mycenaeans & Phoenicians, p.262–63; Ancient Rome, p.276–77

Mighty Carthage

Carthage, in modern-day Tunisia, in North Africa, was the center of the great Carthaginian Empire. Founded by Phoenicians as a trading port in the 9th century BCE, the city eventually controlled much of the North African coast, southern Spain, and islands in the Mediterranean. From 264 BCE, Carthage clashed with Rome in a series of conflicts called the Punic Wars. Rome eventually conquered Carthage in 146 BCE.

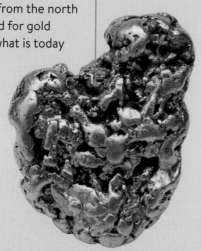

This is a statuette of the goddess Tanit, who was worshiped by the Carthaginians along with her partner Baal Hammon

Aksum monuments

The powerful kingdom of Aksum in northern Ethiopia sprang from a trading center in the 1st century CE. To mark the burial sites of important people, the Aksumites often built decorated columns called obelisks. The largest, at about 108 feet (33 meters) tall, is no longer standing. This one commemorates King Ezana, who ruled from about 330–356 CE. Aksum's power declined from the 6th century. It was replaced by an Agau dynasty in the 10th century CE.

The obelisks were built of huge blocks of a stone called nepheline syenite

The surface is carved with shapes representing doors and windows

FACTastic!

Salt was worth nearly as much as gold! Used to preserve food, salt was brought mainly from the north on camels and traded for gold from gold mines in what is today Senegal, Western Mali, and Guinea. The Ghana Empire, which flourished from the 600s–1200s CE, also grew rich by collecting taxes on trade goods carried through its territory.

Gold made the Ghana Empire wealthy

TANG CHINA

The Tang period is often considered a golden age of Chinese history. Emperor Gaozu founded the Tang dynasty in 618, and early rulers expanded their empire to the west. The Tang empire was powerful and prosperous. The dynasty was weakened by rebellions in the 8th century, and the empire eventually split into separate kingdoms in 907.

Central Asian men are shown to be foreign by their full, curly beards; the Chinese had thin, straight beards

Musicians came to China from central Asia, traveling on the Silk Road

Tang figurine

Tang craftsmen produced figurines (small statues) out of clay. They put them inside the tombs of important people to protect them in the afterlife. Horses, warriors, and traders on camels were common themes.

Tradespeople often used camels to carry goods on the Silk Road

Some Tang ceramics use *sancai* (three-color) glaze

Merchant nation

Ancient Chinese coins had a hole in the middle so that people could string them together. This coin was produced under the Tang emperor Gaozong.

EXPERT CONSULTANT: Man Xu **SEE ALSO:** Religious Belief, p.212–13; The First Chinese Dynasties, p.252–53; The Terra-Cotta Army, p.274–75; Age of Exploration, p.298–99; The Rise of Communism, p.320–21; The Cold War, p.326–27; New Tensions, New Hopes, p.332–33

The Silk Road

The expansion of the Tang empire opened it up to an important trading route now known as the Silk Road. This linked China to Central and South Asia and brought caravans of foreigners into the city of Chang'an (now X'ian)—China's capital at the time. They came to trade goods and share their diverse cultures.

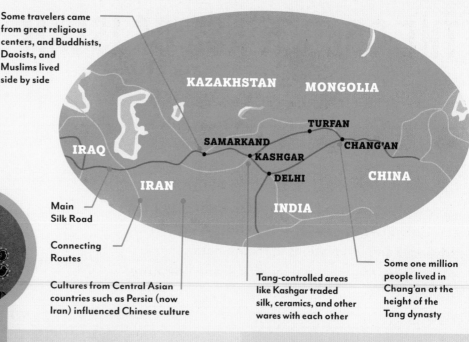

Some travelers came from great religious centers, and Buddhists, Daoists, and Muslims lived side by side

KAZAKHSTAN

MONGOLIA

TURFAN

SAMARKAND

CHANG'AN

IRAQ

KASHGAR

IRAN

DELHI

CHINA

INDIA

Main Silk Road

Connecting Routes

Cultures from Central Asian countries such as Persia (now Iran) influenced Chinese culture

Tang-controlled areas like Kashgar traded silk, ceramics, and other wares with each other

Some one million people lived in Chang'an at the height of the Tang dynasty

GAME CHANGER

WU ZETIAN

Empress, reigned 690–705
China

Wu Zetian was the only Chinese empress to rule in her own right. She took power from her husband when he fell ill and for the last 23 years of his life was the real ruler of China. After his death, she ruled through her sons but took power from them in 690. She declared herself emperor and founded her own short-lived Zhou dynasty.

FACTastic!

Tang emperors introduced a law to stop people from wearing yellow clothes. The Tang emperors wore yellow robes, as yellow represented good fortune. Emperors of the Sui dynasty (589–618) had also worn yellow robes. But Tang laws prohibited officials and commoners from wearing the color.

Tang Arts

LISTIFIED.

The Tang period is known for a flourishing of art and culture.

1. Music There was a resurgence of orchestras accompanied by large bands of courtly dancers.

2. Poetry Nearly 50,000 works survive; this era is considered the Golden Age of Chinese poetry.

3. Painting The use of rich colors in depicting court life—especially images of court ladies—developed.

4. Pottery Tang potters created white porcelain, three-color pottery, and clay figurines.

Spread of Buddhism

Buddhism spread under the Tang, in part thanks to pilgrims such as Monk Xuanzang, who brought Buddhist texts back from India. People from all walks of life, including the imperial family, aristocrats, and commoners, were active in sponsoring Buddhist projects. It was during this time that the tallest Buddha in the world was built, at Leshan.

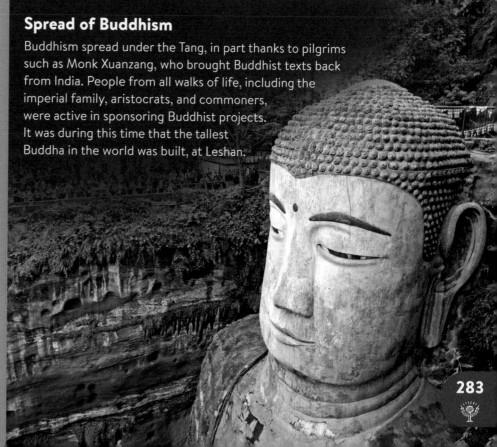

283

THE GOLDEN AGE OF ISLAM

Shortly after 600, the Prophet Muhammad preached a new faith, Islam, in Arabia. After Muhammad's death in 632, Islam spread both west and east, from Spain to India, with Muslims growing massively in numbers. The most important Muslim dynasty was the Abbasid dynasty, lasting from 750 to 1258. Known as the Golden Age of Islam, this period saw major advances and innovations in mathematics, philosophy, the sciences, medicine, and literature.

The world of Islam

In 750, the Islamic world stretched from Spain to Persia. The Abbasids' capital, the great new city of Baghdad, became a center of learning. People of all faiths, languages, and backgrounds went there and fashioned a new culture. Baghdad was the cultural center of Islam until its destruction by the Mongols in 1258.

Mechanical mastery

The Muslim inventor al-Jazari wrote his *Book of Ingenious Devices* in the 1200s. He is known for creating fantastical machines. One of the most detailed was an elephant clock. A mahout (keeper) rides an elephant that supports a tower containing a scribe, dragons, and a falconer. Every half hour a mechanism inside the elephant—driven by water—sets different parts in motion.

A bird at the top of the tower spins around

The falconer drops a ball into a dragon's mouth

The mahout strikes the elephant with a mallet or an ax

The dragon drops the ball into an urn

The scribe rotates; his pen points to the number of minutes that have passed

EXPERT CONSULTANT: David J. Wasserstein **SEE ALSO:** Religious Belief, p.212–13; The Fertile Crescent, p.248–49; The Persian Empire, p.266–67; The Renaissance, p.292–93

Islamic books

The Qur'an is the sacred text of Islam. Above are two pages from a Qur'an from the 800s. During this period, Abbasid patronage of the "House of Wisdom" in Baghdad brought many Greek, Persian, and other texts into Arabic and led to the development of sciences under Islam. Arabic became the main language from Spain eastward to Iraq.

Beautiful patterns

Islamic art is not allowed to show the faces of living beings. Islam avoids representations of the human form. Because of this, buildings such as mosques are decorated with intricate patterns. They reflect plants and flowers, or have geometric designs inspired by the mathematical discoveries of the Golden Age.

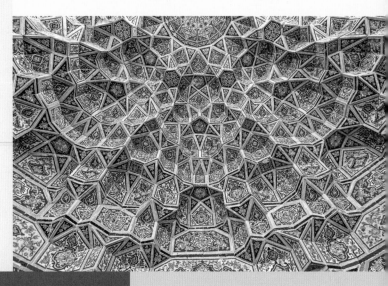

Innovators of the Muslim Golden Age

LISTIFIED.

Many of the greatest scholars of the Islamic Golden Age are now considered founding fathers of entire fields of study.

1. Jabir ibn Hayyan (about 721–815)
Many scientific works, especially in chemistry, are attached to this figure.

2. Al-Khwarizmi (about 780–850)
This astrologer and mathematician from Baghdad invented algebra. The English word algebra comes from his name.

3. Al-Kindi (about 800–870)
Hailed as the "philosopher of the Arabs," he wrote around 250 works. He also helped introduce Indian numerals to the Middle East, from where they spread to Europe.

4. Al-Sufi (903–986)
Al-Sufi recorded the first sighting of the Andromeda Galaxy. In about 964 CE, he published a key book on astronomy called *The Book of Fixed Stars*.

5. Ibn al-Haytham (about 965–1040)
Known in the West as Alhazen, he wrote more than 100 works on science, mathematics, and philosophy. His *Book of Optics* explained how we see things using light.

6. Ibn Sina (about 980–1037) Known in the West as Avicenna, he was the most influential Islamic scientist-philosopher. He wrote a medical textbook that was translated into Latin and studied for centuries.

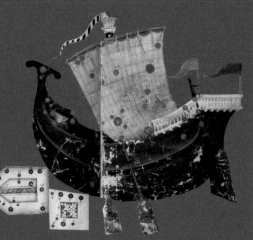

Illustration from al-Sufi's *The Book of Fixed Stars* showing Argo Navis, a constellation shown as a ship

Al-Andalus

From 711 until the 1200s, much of Spain was under Islamic rule. In 756, the Muslim ruler Abd al-Rahman made Córdoba his capital. As the center of a powerful state, it became well known for its trade and culture. Its Great Mosque was one of the world's biggest Islamic buildings. It was later converted to a Christian cathedral. Today, the minaret (tower from which Muslims are called to prayer) serves as a belltower (pictured).

285

MEDIEVAL EUROPE

The word medieval comes from the Latin *medium aevum* (middle of the ages) and is used to describe a period from around 500–1500 CE. This was a time of great of change in Europe. The warrior king Charlemagne unified many kingdoms into one empire. Christianity spread across the continent and to the British Isles, and fatal disease ravaged populations across the continent.

The medieval castle

Medieval rulers kept control over their kingdoms through feudalism—a system in which kings gave lords land in exchange for loyalty and military service. Lords in turn gave pieces of land to peasants. In exchange, peasants worked their lord's land as well as their own. Both kings and nobles built castles to defend themselves from enemies.

Thick stone walls protected the castle and its inhabitants against attacks from enemy forces

People lived in a tower called a keep; it was always the best fortified (defended) part of a castle

In Britain, a lord needed a license from the king to build crenellations—walls with gaps for shooting arrows through

Vegetable gardens and livestock provided food for the kitchen

Cooks, gardeners, cleaners, craftspeople, and many others lived and worked within the castle walls

Castles often had a moat (a ring of water); inhabitants lowered a drawbridge across the moat to allow people to enter

Lords or kings dined, entertained guests, and conducted official business in the castle's great hall

Castles were the private homes of noble or royal families; they employed knights to defend them

EXPERT: Michael Ray **SEE ALSO:** Natural Climate Change, p.94–95; Religious Belief, p.212–13; Conflict & War, p.214–15; The Golden Age of Islam, p.284–85; The Effects of Climate Change, p.372–73

The Vikings

Viking is an old word for "pirate." It refers to Scandinavian seafaring warriors from the 9th to the 11th centuries. These warriors traded and raided along the coast of Europe. They also invaded. In France, they settled in with the locals and became the Normans. In Russia, they did the same and were known as the Rus for their red hair (*rus* means red). Russia is named after them.

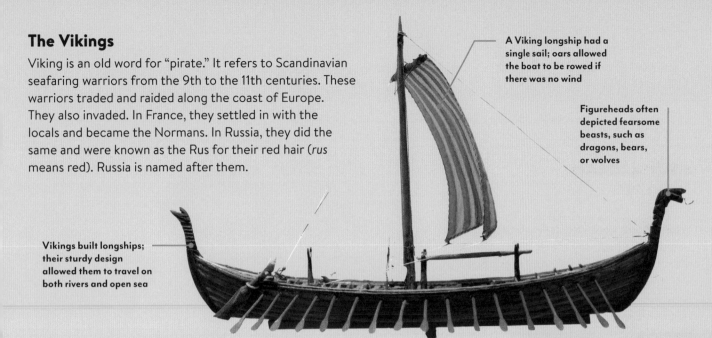

A Viking longship had a single sail; oars allowed the boat to be rowed if there was no wind

Figureheads often depicted fearsome beasts, such as dragons, bears, or wolves

Vikings built longships; their sturdy design allowed them to travel on both rivers and open sea

KNOWN UNKNOWN

How many people died of the Black Death?

The Black Death was a plague that spread across Europe from 1347 to 1351. It was originally carried by infected fleas that jumped from rats to humans. Historians are divided on how many people died from this plague. Some say 25 million—around one-third of Europe's population. Others think the death toll was as high as 50 million.

Medieval Warm Period

Between 900 and 1300 CE, parts of Europe benefited from the climate becoming a little warmer. This led to agricultural changes in northern Europe, in particular. Grain crops flourished in Norway, and wine grapes were grown as far north as England. It was during this time that the Vikings settled in Greenland, where warmer temperatures partially freed the Arctic Ocean of ice.

The Crusades

Many Europeans were united by their Christian beliefs. From 1095, Western European armies fought in the Crusades. These were a series of military campaigns to recapture formerly Christian territories that Muslims had conquered and to take control of non-Christian lands. The first three Crusades had some success, and Christian states were founded in the Middle East. But later Crusades in that region were pushed back and the Europeans failed to hold onto the land.

ASK THE EXPERTS!

SALIMA IKRAM
Archaeologist

What do you want to discover most?
I want to find out why the ancient Egyptians mummified two kinds of crocodiles: the Nile crocodile and the West African crocodile. I would also like to know where they got the West African crocodiles from, as they are not usually found in the Egyptian Nile River. I love crocodiles, and I want to know how and why the more calm West African species came to be buried in Egypt.

What is an unsolved problem in your field?
Many of us are working on finding out the steps for mummification. So many millions of ancient Egyptians were mummified, and we still don't know all the details about this process.

Can you tell us a surprising fact?
The word for cat in ancient Egypt was *miaw*!

JOHN O. HYLAND
Historian

What do you want to discover most?
I'm interested in how Persia and other ancient empires expanded and maintained control over enormous territories. Persia ruled a territory comparable in size to the continental US. It waged wars 2,000 miles (3,219 km) away from the empire's center—how did this work so long ago?

What is a challenge in your field?
The ancient Persians did not leave behind narrative histories that described their empire in their own words. So historians continue to debate how to understand Persia's wars and diplomacy with Greece, when we have only Greek sources. On the positive side, we have a great number of primary documents and remains from archaeological sites that tell us a lot about how the empire worked.

PATRICK V. KIRCH
Archaeologist

What do you want to discover most?
I want to find out how people living on the remote islands of the Pacific Ocean adapted to their island world. Many of these islanders developed sustainable ways of living. Perhaps we can learn from their traditional cultures in ways that will help us adapt to global change.

What do you enjoy about your research?
Archaeology is a rewarding field—you are always making unexpected discoveries. Once, I uncovered the "god of the Lapita people," a small bone carving on an ancient site in the Mussau Islands, which are located in the western South Pacific Ocean. The carving dated back to about 3,000 years ago. It was made from the bone of a porpoise and may have represented a mythical god of the sea.

Ancient & Medieval Times
THE QUIZ

1) The region of the Middle East where humans first started to practice agriculture is known as the:
   a. Fertile Zone
   b. Fertile Crescent
   c. Fertile Plains
   d. Fertile Farms

2) The Akkadian Empire was founded by which ruler?
   a. Sargon the Great
   b. Cyrus the Great
   c. Hammurabi
   d. Cleopatra

3) Stonehenge is the world's most famous prehistoric stone circle structure. It is located near which English city?
   a. Shaftesbury
   b. Sittingbourne
   c. Salisbury
   d. Sandwich

4) Which of the following animals is NOT part of the Chinese 12-year calendar cycle?
   a. Snake
   b. Hare
   c. Hedgehog
   d. Rooster

5) The Norte Chico people were part of an ancient civilization located on which continent?
   a. South America
   b. North America
   c. Africa
   d. Asia

6) The Polynesian god Maui is said to have created the North Island of New Zealand after:
   a. Pulling down clouds from the sky
   b. Pulling up a giant fish from the ocean
   c. Catching a meteorite before it hit the ground
   d. Stirring up a giant volcano

7) Which body part was NOT used in the ball game developed by the Olmec and Maya civilizations of Central and South America?
   a. Elbow
   b. Hip
   c. Knees
   d. Feet

8) In Greek mythology, Zeus was the king of the gods. Who was the queen?
   a. Athena
   b. Hera
   c. Dionysus
   d. Daphne

9) Where was the Mauryan Empire located?
   a. India
   b. Indonesia
   c. Malaysia
   d. Philippines

10) According to legend, the founders of Rome, Romulus and Remus, were raised by a she-wolf, a shepherd, and what other creature?
   a. Elephant
   b. Hyena
   c. Tortoise
   d. Woodpecker

11) The Roman Empire was at its height under the rule of which emperor?
   a. Hadrian
   b. Trajan
   c. Titus
   d. Caesar Augustus

12) In the 1970s, archaeologists discovered how many life-sized pottery figures buried outside a tomb in China?
   a. 2,000
   b. 5,000
   c. 8,000
   d. 10,000

13) Which of the following poets was NOT Roman?
   a. Virgil
   b. Homer
   c. Ovid
   d. Horace

14) The Hagia Sophia in Constantinople (now Istanbul, Turkey) was originally built as a:
   a. Church
   b. Mosque
   c. Museum
   d. Market

289

When inventor Richard Trevithick created his primitive high-pressure steam engine, little did he know what revolutions would stem from his zealous curiosity! From 1830 onward, high-pressure steam power revolutionized the world, allowing humans to travel great distances, like on this steam train. Even today's nuclear power stations work by heating up water into pressurized steam, which in turn drives the turbines to generate electric power.

CHAPTER 7
MODERN TIMES

Modern is a funny word. Sometimes we use it to talk about things that are happening right now. Other times, as in this chapter, it means everything after the Middle Ages—that's more than 500 years ago! During this time, exploration to new lands leads to an era of rapidly expanding empires. Colonialism alters or even destroys the lives of countless native peoples.

Victory for some and misfortune for others spiral through revolutions, world wars, and 21st-century terrorism. But it's not all conquest and misery. In modern times we see great leaps in art, medicine, and technology. Witness the skill of the painters of Renaissance Italy. Discover how advances in medical science make surgery painless. New machines disrupt the age of individual craftspeople but provide ordinary folks with warmth, food, and electricity. Humans blast themselves off the planet in a race into space. And bit by bit, groups who have been discriminated against and treated as inferior begin to win rights that were denied to them. It's a bumpy ride, so fasten your seat belt.

AFRICAN EMPIRES

Africa has been home to many empires and kingdoms. Among them, the Mali Empire stretched from the Atlantic coast of West Africa east into the Sahara desert. The Ethiopian Empire occupied modern-day Ethiopia and Eritrea. Spanning seven centuries, it was one of the longest empires in world history. The Ashanti Kingdom occupied what is now southern Ghana, on the West African coast.

Mansa Musa of Mali

One of the wealthiest men ever to have lived, Mansa Musa was an emperor of the Mali Empire. He came to the throne around 1307. Trading and gold mining made the Mali Empire very rich. Although nobody knows the details of Musa's fortune, historians believe the wealth he created from trading in gold and salt was worth $400 billion in today's money.

Muslim learning

The trading cities of Gao and Timbuktu were part of the Mali Empire. In Timbuktu, Musa ordered many buildings to be constructed, including three mosques, Muslim places of worship. Built in 1327, the Djinguereber Mosque (pictured), became a learning center.

In 1324, Musa made a great journey, or pilgrimage, to the holy Muslim city of Mecca in what is now Saudi Arabia

Musa gave pieces of gold to people as he rode by

As well as 60,000 people, Musa's retinue included 80 camels, each carrying 300 lb (135 kg) of gold

EXPERT CONSULTANT: Etana H. Dinka **SEE ALSO:** Earth's Riches, p.74–75; Metals, p.114–15; Religious Belief, p.212–13; Medieval Europe, p.286–87; Slavery in the Americas, p.308–09; World Political Map, p.334–35

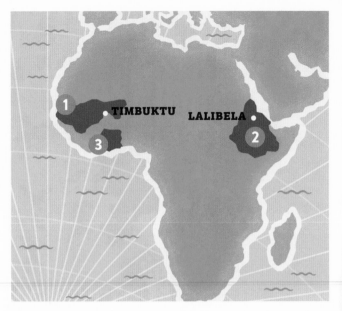

1. **Mali Empire**
The Mali Empire was prominent in West Africa from the 1200s to the 1500s

2. **Ethiopian Empire**
The Ethiopian empire reached its peak under the Solomonic kings, who reigned from 1270

3. **Ashanti Kingdom**
This West African kingdom existed in Ghana from the late 1600s to the late 1900s

Imperial territories

The Mali and Ethiopian empires aren't the same as the modern countries that share their names. Ethiopia is in about the same spot as the Ethiopian Empire, but the Mali Empire is in a different place from modern Mali. Ashanti is not a country today. The Ashanti people live in three African countries, Ghana, Togo, and Ivory Coast.

KNOWN UNKNOWN

Who built the rock churches of Lalibela?

Ethiopia has been Christian since around 330 CE. Its kings traced their families back to the biblical King Solomon. At the city of Lalibela, there are 11 churches carved from rock. Most of them were built sometime in the 12th–13th centuries, during the reign of King Lalibela, but nobody knows who built them. Locals believe that angels carved the rock churches.

Kente cloth

Vibrant woven cloth originated with the Ashanti people of Ghana. The cloth was usually made from cotton, which was grown locally. Weavers wove colorful threads into 4-inch (10-cm) strips of cloth with complex designs. Then they sewed the strips together to make clothing. The style is known as kente cloth. Kente cloth and prints that imitate it are still worn in the area and all around the world. Gold is a dominant color in many designs. It stands for royalty, wealth, high status, glory, and spiritual purity.

West African gold

Gold was mined in several African regions, including West Africa, part of which was named the Gold Coast for a time. The Fulani and Ashanti peoples of West Africa, southern Africans, and the ancient Egyptians all made beautiful artifacts from gold. The lion pictured is an Ashanti ornament. For the Ashanti people, gold symbolized the soul and wealth of the nation.

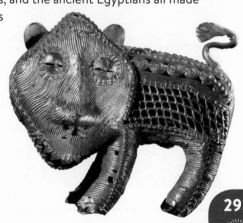

293

EXPERT CONSULTANT: Jane Long **SEE ALSO:** Creating Art, p.220–21; Ancient Greece, p.268–69; Ancient Rome, p.276–77; The Golden Age of Islam, p.284–85; Age of Exploration, p.298–99

THE RENAISSANCE

With roots in 14th-century Italy, the Renaissance, meaning "rebirth," revived European interest in the cultures of ancient Greece and Rome. Knowledge was a key theme, with an emphasis on understanding the natural world and creating realistic art. Renaissance ideas spread across Europe, thanks in part to the invention of the printing press in 1439. It led to some magnificent works of art, literature, and scholarship.

The School of Athens (1509–11)

Italian Renaissance artist Raphael painted this fresco for the library of Pope Julius II, inside the Vatican in Rome. It features key cultural and artistic ideas that emerged during the Renaissance. It depicts men sharing their knowledge of the natural world. There are no women in this painting, as few women were allowed access to knowledge in Renaissance Italy.

1 Renaissance architects admired the symmetry and grand scale of ancient Roman buildings.

2 Each arch is smaller than the one "in front" of it. This creates the illusion of depth (called perspective) on the flat surface of the wall.

3 The figures look and behave like real people. They all have individual faces, bodies, and clothing, and act naturally.

4 Plato and Aristotle, the two most famous ancient Greek philosophers, are central to the work.

5 Raphael hints at the influence of Islam's Golden Age by including the Muslim philosopher Averroës in the work.

6 The central figure of this group is Pythagoras, an important ancient Greek thinker and mathematician.

7 Renaissance artists sought to represent human anatomy and posture accurately in their works.

8 Highlights on skin and clothing show how Raphael creates the impression of natural sunlight coming in from the right.

9 Globes refer to the study of the stars and the Earth—scientists made great advances in astronomy during this period.

10 To show his pride in understanding the natural world, Raphael includes a portrait of himself (dressed in black).

11 Mathematical instruments suggest the huge interest in the sciences that characterized knowledgeable men of the period.

12 The doorway that leads into the pope's library, above which the fresco was painted.

AZTECS & INCAS

Among the major civilizations of the Americas were the Aztecs, in what is now Mexico, and the Incas, whose territories lined the Pacific coast of South America. Both cultures had rulers who claimed to be chosen by their gods. They also had large cities and established vast trade networks.

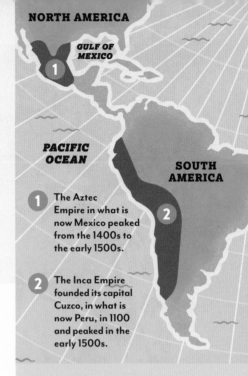

NORTH AMERICA

GULF OF MEXICO

PACIFIC OCEAN

SOUTH AMERICA

1 The Aztec Empire in what is now Mexico peaked from the 1400s to the early 1500s.

2 The Inca Empire founded its capital Cuzco, in what is now Peru, in 1100 and peaked in the early 1500s.

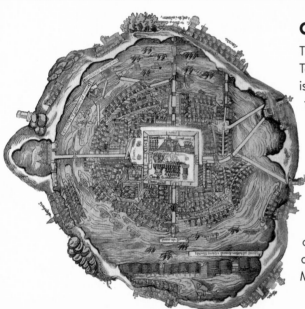

City in a lake

The Aztec capital Tenochtitlán was in what is now Mexico City. It was founded on a mostly artificial island in Lake Texcoco. Around 300,000 people lived there in the early 1500s. At its heart lay an impressive ceremonial precinct surrounded by the palaces of nobles, including that of the Aztec emperor Moctezuma II.

Imperial spread

The Inca Empire stretched from what is now Ecuador and Colombia to 50 miles (80 km) south of Santiago, Chile. It had a population of around 12 million people. The Aztec Empire reached from the Pacific Ocean to the Gulf Coast and from what is now central Mexico to what is now Guatemala. It had a population of 5–6 million.

Inca quipus

The Incas made quipus to record important information and historical events. They attached strings of dyed llama fibers to a thick cord and tied knots in them. They read these quipus by feeling the knots. The sequence of strings along the main cord, the numbers and types of knots, and the distances between them coded large amounts of data.

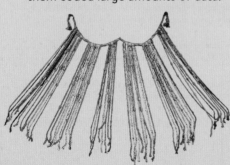

Skilled engineers

The Incas were brilliant engineers. One of their biggest achievements was to build 24,000 miles (38,500 km) of transportation routes. In mountainous terrains they suspended rope bridges across deep gorges. The Incas used llamas, rather than wheeled vehicles, to transport goods and merchandise.

High walkways
Rope bridges stretched across canyons, gorges, and rivers

Woven grass
The Incas wove bridges from ichu grass, which was very strong in bundles

Cables
These needed replacing each year to keep a bridge strong

EXPERT CONSULTANT: Javier Urcid **SEE ALSO:** Stretching & Squashing, p.140–41; Language & Storytelling, p.216–7; Calendars, p.224–25; The Olmecs & the Maya, p.264–65; Age of Exploration, p.298–99; New Empires, p.304–05; Age of Revolutions, p.310–11; World Political Map, p.334–35

Solid stone
The stone is around 3 feet (91 cm) thick and measures almost 12 feet (3.65 meters) across

High god
The sun god Tonatiuh, lord of heaven, sits in the center

Sun gods
Four rectangle-framed figures surround Tonatiuh; they represent four previous ages ("suns") of the world

Heavens
The border symbols seem to relate the night sky to the underworld

Cycles
The inner circle shows 20 named days; both calendar systems worked on cycles of these 20 days

Opposites
Xiuhtecuhtli, god of fire (left) and Tonatiuh, god of wind (right); their personification represents the desperate struggle between night and day

Fire
This ring depicts the mythical fire serpents (*xiuhcocoah*) and their intense flames

Aztec calendar stone

Archaeologists discovered this "sun stone" in 1790. The Aztecs used it as a kind of calendar. It is very complex and features two systems—an agricultural system of 365 days and a ritual system of 260 days. Originally, the stone was painted in bright colors.

AGE OF EXPLORATION

The years 1400 to 1700 are often described as the Age of Exploration. Of course, the desire to explore was not new—people had traveled great distances in search of new worlds for centuries beforehand. But it was during this time that some of the most notable explorations took place. This fascination with far-flung places continued, with expeditions being made well into the 18th and 19th centuries.

The magnetic compass

As early as 1100, Chinese explorers were using magnetic compasses. These devices contained magnetized needles that responded to Earth's own magnetic field, so they always pointed north. The magnetic compass became a useful tool for early explorers, who also navigated by studying the stars and guiding winds.

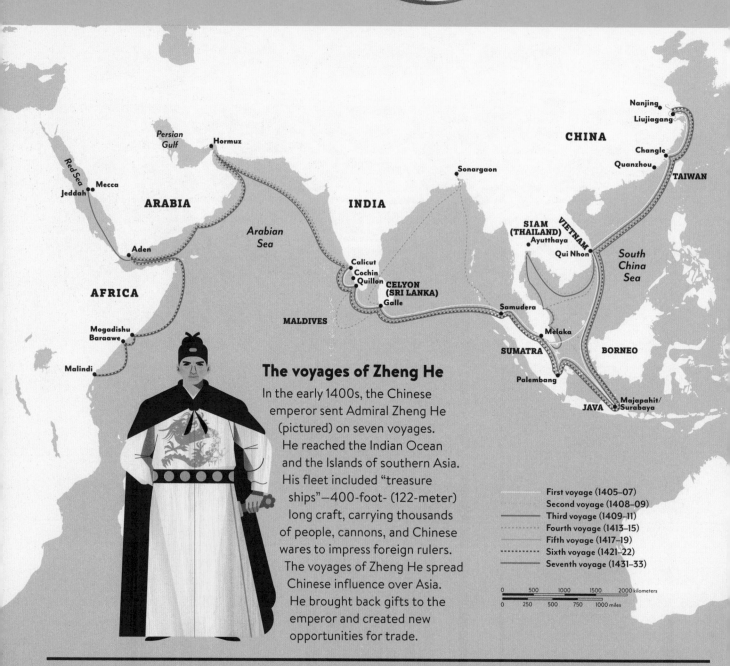

The voyages of Zheng He

In the early 1400s, the Chinese emperor sent Admiral Zheng He (pictured) on seven voyages. He reached the Indian Ocean and the Islands of southern Asia. His fleet included "treasure ships"—400-foot- (122-meter) long craft, carrying thousands of people, cannons, and Chinese wares to impress foreign rulers. The voyages of Zheng He spread Chinese influence over Asia. He brought back gifts to the emperor and created new opportunities for trade.

First voyage (1405–07)
Second voyage (1408–09)
Third voyage (1409–11)
Fourth voyage (1413–15)
Fifth voyage (1417–19)
Sixth voyage (1421–22)
Seventh voyage (1431–33)

0   500   1000   1500   2000 kilometers
0   250   500   750   1000 miles

EXPERT CONSULTANT: Lorenzo Veracini **SEE ALSO:** Inside Earth, p.58–59; Aztecs & Incas, p.296–97; New Empires, p.304–05; British & French Colonies in North America, p.306–08; Slavery in the Americas, p.308–09; Age of Revolutions, p.310–11; Decolonization, p.328–29

FACTastic!

Of about 250 people who departed Spain with Ferdinand Magellan's round-the-world expedition in 1519, only 18 returned. The rest died along the way. The Portuguese explorer departed from Spain in 1520. Just one of five ships returned to Europe in 1522, but Magellan was not onboard. He died fighting indigenous islanders in the Philippines in 1521.

KNOWN UNKNOWN

Was the Franklin expedition doomed by its own supplies?

On May 19, 1845, a British expedition led by Captain Sir John Franklin departed England to explore the Arctic. It sailed with two ships, the HMS *Erebus* and HMS *Terror*, carrying 128 officers and men. It was last seen north of Baffin Island, in what is today the Canadian territory of Nunavut, in late July 1845. Both ships then disappeared and lay undiscovered for more than 150 years. Research suggests the men may have suffered from lead poisoning from metal in their food cans. No one can know for sure, but this may have contributed to the failure of the men to survive once their ships became trapped in the ice.

Age of Exploration
TIMELINE

1417–1419 Chinese admiral Zheng He reaches East Africa.

1492 Italian admiral Christopher Columbus lands in the Caribbean.

1497 Italian explorer and navigator John Cabot lands on the east coast of North America.

1498 Portuguese explorer Vasco da Gama becomes the first European to reach India by sea.

1500 Portuguese commander Pedro Álvares Cabral sails from Europe to Brazil.

1519 Spanish explorer Hernán Cortés arrives in Mexico.

1606 Dutch navigator Willem Janszoon becomes the first European to land in Australia.

1642 Dutch merchant Abel Tasman is the first European to reach New Zealand.

NOTE *from the expert!*

LORENZO VERACINI
Historian

Dr. Veracini studies the history of many different colonies. He thinks it is important to examine the way in which the world has been explored: for trade, diplomacy, settlement, prestige, and wealth.

❝ *I love to discover how the present is shaped by the past.* ❞

THE MUGHAL EMPIRE

Emperor Babur founded the Indian Mughal Empire in 1526. By the 17th century, it had become one of the most powerful states in the world. The Muslim Mughal rulers were skilled at uniting Hindu and Muslim cultures, and ruled effectively for around two centuries. Their reputation for wealth and splendor spread far and wide. The empire flourished until the British colonized India in the mid-18th century.

Koh-i-Noor

The Koh-i-Noor is a famous diamond. It was first known as an adornment on the gem-encrusted Peacock Throne of Mughal emperor Shah Jahan. During the years of British colonization, the diamond became a possession of Queen Victoria, and it remains in the UK today.

Taj Mahal

Sitting on the banks of the Yamuna River in Agra, the Taj Mahal is one of the crowning glories of the Mughal Empire. Emperor Shah Jahan ordered the building of this mausoleum, or tomb, after the death of his favorite wife, Mumtaz Mahal, in 1631. He is buried there with her. Perfectly symmetrical in its design, the Taj Mahal took more than 15 years to build.

Above the dome, a bronze spire is tipped with a crescent moon, a symbol of world dominance

Minarets (slender towers) surround the Taj Mahal; they are modeled on Turkish mosque architecture

Muslim designs are often based on natural themes; flowers represent the heavenly garden of paradise

The architecture uses a mathematical formula associated with perfection and harmony

The fine white marble that covers the Taj Mahal symbolizes purity

The water in the charbagh (a four-part garden) comes directly from the Yamuna River

FACTastic!

Akbar the Great, who ruled from 1556 to 1605, owned 101 elephants. Many of them probably formed part of his army—Mughals rode into battle on armored elephants. The huge animals charged at enemy soldiers, who risked being trampled underfoot if they attempted to get close enough to fight.

Mughal women

Women accompanied armies on expeditions, were active in building beautiful monuments, and contributed to trade and charitable projects. Many were also interested in the arts. Emperor Babur's daughter Gulbadan Begun wrote one of the earliest histories of the empire. Emperor Aurangzeb's daughter Zeb-un-Nisa was a poet. Nur Jahan (pictured) built a white marble tomb for her father, a nobleman called Itimaduddaulah.

GAME CHANGER

AKBAR THE GREAT

Emperor, reigned 1556—1605
Sindh (present-day Pakistan)

Akbar the Great was the third Mughal emperor. He extended his power over most of the Indian subcontinent. Akbar built an empire in which diverse groups of people were able to hold positions of power. He was particularly known for his interest in the arts.

66 *A monarch should be ever intent on conquest; otherwise, his neighbors rise in arms against him.* 99

Emperor Babur sits talking with Akbar (wearing orange) in the palace grounds

Many miniatures were featured as illustrations in books

Painters used fine brushwork to create intricate patterns on the small canvases

Nature and animals were common features of Mughal art

Mughal miniatures

Mughal painting often took the form of miniatures, illustrating court scenes, history, and literature. Each work might involve a team of artists, each responsible for a different stage—right down to the detail artist, who added the portraits. This style of painting is a feature of the personal journal of Emperor Babur.

JAPAN'S GREAT PEACE

From 1603 to 1867, a series of warrior leaders called shoguns ruled Japan. Edo (now Tokyo) was its capital. Despite their warlike name, these rulers focused on developing a peaceful nation. Following what is known as a seclusion policy, they had limited foreign relations and traded only with China, Holland, Korea, and the Ryukyu Kingdom (now Okinawa). This period is referred to as the Edo era. Besides Edo, the merchant city of Osaka and the ancient city of Kyoto both grew during this time.

Shogunate social hierarchy

Japan had a strict social hierarchy, or status system, beneath its emperor. The shogun, a warrior leader, held the real power. Beneath him were five classes: lords (*daimyo*), warriors (*samurai*), peasants, artisans, and merchants. People could not move between these classes.

Way of tea

The Japanese tea ceremony, *sadō*, dates from the pre-Edo period, but then became popular among ordinary people in Edo Japan. Drinking green tea was a formal event that could take up to four hours and had specific rituals and tools. This was a time for people to escape the fast pace of daily life in the company of friends and family.

Shogun
The supreme military leader, and actual ruler making all the decisions

Emperor
Figurehead, but without any real power himself

Daimyo
A lord who looked over and governed certain land areas

Samurai
The country's warriors, who also worked as government officials

Peasants
The farmers that supplied a stable economy for the empire

Artisans
People who made weapons and supplies for the samurai

Merchants
Some of the wealthiest people in society, but considered low class

EXPERT CONSULTANT: Katsuya Hirano **SEE ALSO:** Performing Arts, p.222–23; World War II, p.324–25; World Political Map, p.334–35

"Window to the West"

Japan's national seclusion policy prevented Japanese people from leaving the country. They could also not reenter Japan if they had been living elsewhere before this time. Japan closed itself to trade with all Europeans except the Dutch in 1639. They traded goods such as spices, textiles, silk, and porcelain (left). In 1641, the Dutch established a trading post in Nagasaki. It was the only port allowed to continue to trade with the West until 1854. For this reason, people referred to Nagasaki as the window to the West.

FACTastic!

As many as 7 percent of the population were samurai. As well as being warriors samurai studied math and calligraphy, and wrote poetry. Some were women. *Onna-bugeisha*, female samurai, received the same martial instruction as male samurai, but were specifically trained in the *naginata*, a long weapon designed with women's balance in mind.

Theater icons

Kabuki is a traditional Japanese form of musical theater, in which actors wore thick, colorful makeup to express their characters. Portraits of celebrated kabuki actors became popular during the Edo period, often shown in woodblock prints known as *ukiyo-e*. These actors became style icons—thanks, in part, to these inexpensive *ukiyo-e* that were produced in the thousands.

NOTE from the expert!

KATSUYA HIRANO
Historian

Katsuya Hirano loves finding out about life in Edo-era Japan, a time when there was a strong belief in ghosts. Because people didn't have electricity and candles were very expensive, when night fell, darkness triggered their imaginations.

66 *People believed they were most likely to encounter ghosts and spirits around 2:00–2:30 am!* 99

NEW EMPIRES

In 1494, the Spanish Empire signed the Treaty of Tordesillas with the Portuguese Empire. This agreement between the two powers divided the world between them. The colonizers overran many civilizations that had long been established in the Americas. They wanted to gain wealth from the Americas, as the land was rich in silver, gold, and indigenous people they could force to work for them. They also believed they had the responsibility to convert the locals to their religion, Catholicism.

Conquistadors

The leaders of the Spanish conquest in the Americas were known as conquistadors, or conquerors. They sought to return to Europe with valuable resources, which would bring them great wealth. The Spanish also forced the indigenous populations to convert to Christianity and destroyed many of their religious symbols (pictured).

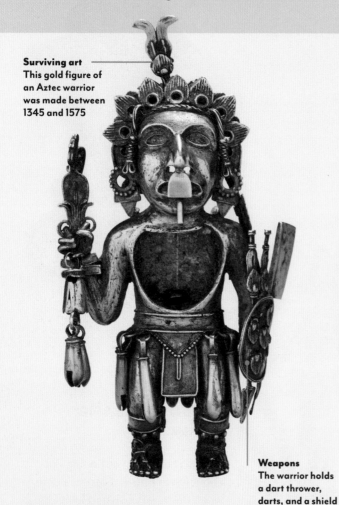

Surviving art
This gold figure of an Aztec warrior was made between 1345 and 1575

Weapons
The warrior holds a dart thrower, darts, and a shield

FACTastic!

The Spanish *peso de ocho* reales, or "piece of eight," was the world's first global currency. The Spanish produced huge numbers of these coins from silver mined in their South American colonies, especially from El Potosí, now in Bolivia. Within 25 years of its first minting in 1497, the coin was in use across Asia, Europe, Africa, and the Americas. It remained the currency of trade for 300 years.

Driven by gold

The lust for gold drove European exploration in the Americas during the early years. The Aztec king Montezuma II sent representatives to the conquistador Hernán Cortés with extravagant gifts of gold and silver. He hoped to prevent the Spanish from taking his city. Instead, Cortés entered the Aztec capital and imprisoned the king. Montezuma was killed in captivity soon after.

Deadly diseases

The Spanish conquistadors introduced European diseases that were previously unknown in the Americas. These included smallpox and measles. Indigenous people were vulnerable to such diseases, and many died. Historians estimate that at least one-third of the indigenous population died of smallpox alone.

EXPERT CONSULTANT: Ivonne Del Valle **SEE ALSO:** Religious Belief p.212–13; Money, p.226–27; Aztecs & Incas, p.296–97; Age of Exploration, p.298–99; Decolonization, p.328–29

The Spanish mission

Spanish and Portuguese explorers claimed that they colonized the New World to spread the Catholic faith. Both built cathedrals and churches for this purpose. Eventually, the Spanish began to build missions—whole communities in which they forced indigenous populations to adjust to Spanish culture. They established 21 missions in what is now California and connected them to one another by building a 600-mile- (965-km) long road known as El Camino Real (the royal road).

This illustration is modeled on the San Juan Capistrano mission in California that Spanish Franciscan missionaries founded in 1776

Miles of surrounding countryside contained the orchards, gardens, fields, and livestock that fed and clothed inhabitants

Indigenous people were forced to convert to Christianity and to participate in Catholic mass in church

A typical mission site featured a rectangular enclosure

A sacred cemetery offered a final resting place for the indigenous people who lived on the mission

Made from adobe bricks and plaster, mission buildings often needed thick walls to support their roofs

Regular mission features included a convent, dormitories, workshops, and storerooms

GAME CHANGER

AMERIGO VESPUCCI

**Explorer, lived 1454–1512
Portugal**

It was Portuguese explorer Amerigo Vespucci who first said that the Americas were not part of Asia, as Europeans had thought, but a totally different landmass. Rather than adopting its native names, Europeans named this New World America, after Vespucci.

❝ *Those new regions . . . we may rightly call a new world.* ❞

305

BRITISH & FRENCH COLONIES IN NORTH AMERICA

In the early 1600s, Europeans began to cross the Atlantic to start new lives in North America. The main settlers were English and French. Some wanted new opportunities. Others fled their countries because their rulers would not allow them to follow their religion of choice. The English first settled in Virginia, then in Massachusetts. The French initially made settlements in Acadia, on the present border of the US and Canada.

Early settlers

The *Mayflower*, a replica of which is pictured, left England in September 1620 and, after 66 days at sea, eventually landed in Plymouth, Massachusetts. Its passengers included a group of people seeking religious freedom. They became known as the Pilgrims.

Crow's nest
Served as a high lookout point

Clash of cultures

Europeans settled on land belonging to indigenous peoples. Some welcomed the newcomers as possible allies in their struggles with other groups. Others were less trusting. Eventually, conflict over land led to violence in most places.

Upper deck
Where seamen worked and attended to the ship

Main deck
Historians believe that many of the passengers slept on this deck

Cargo hold
A storage space for food, tools, and supplies. Some passengers may have slept in the cargo hold, too

EXPERT CONSULTANT: Jeff Wallenfeldt **SEE ALSO:** Religious Belief, p.212–13; Age of Exploration, p.298–99; New Empires, p.304–05;

The real Pocahontas

Pocahontas, whose birth name was Matoaka, was the daughter of a powerful indigenous chieftain in what is now Virginia. English colonists captured her, as a teenager, in 1613, and she soon converted to Christianity and was married to English tobacco farmer John Rolfe. Pocahontas was held for ransom, and many historians believe she converted against her will.

The growth of trade

Europeans and indigenous nations fought over land and its resources, but they also traded. In Canada, for example, the Huron-Wendat, Algonquin, and other indigenous peoples traded furs with the French in exchange for metal goods and cloth that they could use for their traditional gift-giving ceremonies. Europeans also traded for local craft goods, such as the box embroidered with porcupine quills below.

Territorial warfare

While Britain and France fought each other in the Seven Years War in Europe, British and French troops and settlers also fought in North America. The conflicts in the colonies were known as the French and Indian War (1754–1763). Both sides recruited indigenous nations as allies by promising to preserve their land rights. The settlers later broke these promises. The war ended with France giving Canada and other territories to the British.

FACTastic!

According to legend, the fearsome pirate Blackbeard wore lighted matches in his hair. The slow-burning matches (used to light ships' cannons) were said to have surrounded his face with fire and smoke! Blackbeard was one of several pirates who terrorized settlers in Virginia, North Carolina, and the Caribbean. Ruthless villains, they often attacked English and French ships headed back to Europe and stole the trade goods onboard.

SLAVERY IN THE AMERICAS

Slavery was not new in the 16th century, but this is when Europeans started buying large numbers of West Africans and shipping them to the Americas for enslavement. The enslaved Africans became central to a complex trade across the Atlantic Ocean. The products they raised, mined, and processed were sold in Europe and the American colonies. The result was an Atlantic world of exploitation in which those who worked the hardest were treated the worst.

Why it happened

The idea was to replace indigenous workers, who were dying in large numbers from forced labor and European diseases. Traders shipped 12.5 million Africans across the Atlantic Ocean. The African workers were treated as property. They had no rights. They could be bought and sold, beaten, and even worked to death.

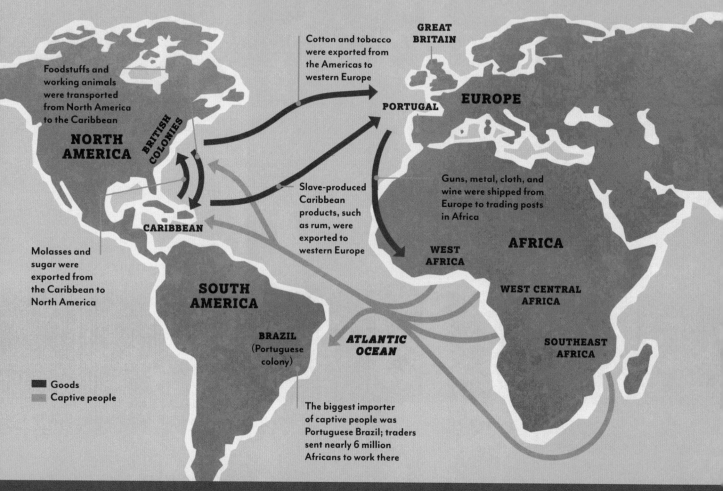

GREAT BRITAIN

Cotton and tobacco were exported from the Americas to western Europe

Foodstuffs and working animals were transported from North America to the Caribbean

PORTUGAL

EUROPE

NORTH AMERICA

BRITISH COLONIES

Slave-produced Caribbean products, such as rum, were exported to western Europe

Guns, metal, cloth, and wine were shipped from Europe to trading posts in Africa

CARIBBEAN

Molasses and sugar were exported from the Caribbean to North America

AFRICA

WEST AFRICA

WEST CENTRAL AFRICA

SOUTH AMERICA

BRAZIL (Portuguese colony)

ATLANTIC OCEAN

SOUTHEAST AFRICA

■ Goods
■ Captive people

The biggest importer of captive people was Portuguese Brazil; traders sent nearly 6 million Africans to work there

The Middle Passage

The journey captive people made across the Atlantic was known as the Middle Passage and lasted for up to 90 days. As many as 1.5 million died on the voyage due to food shortages and sickness. Life on the plantations was little better. People worked in the fields from sunup to sundown six days a week. The food they had to eat was neither plentiful nor nutritious.

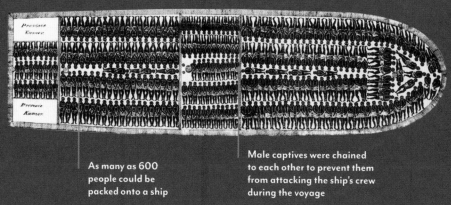

As many as 600 people could be packed onto a ship

Male captives were chained to each other to prevent them from attacking the ship's crew during the voyage

EXPERT CONSULTANT: Joseph E. Inikori **SEE ALSO:** Crime & Law, p.228-29 ; Age of Exploration, p.298-99; New Empires, p.304-05; British & French Colonies in North America, p.306-07; Age of Revolutions, p.310-11; Decolonization, p. 328-29; Civil Rights, p.330-31

FACTastic!

Henry Brown shipped himself out of slavery in a box. He escaped to Pennsylvania inside a 3 x 2 x 2.5-foot (90 x 60 x 76-cm) box. Members of the Underground Railroad aided his escape. This organization of free blacks and white people operated a network of secret routes and safe houses. Besides Henry "Box" Brown, it helped between 30,000 and 100,000 enslaved people escape into free states and Canada.

Abolition and civil war

People trying to end—or abolish—slavery are known as abolitionists. In the 1st century of US history, a powerful abolitionist movement developed in the North, which was less dependent on enslaved labor than the South. Eventually, the South tried to leave the US and create a new country where slavery would stay legal. The North went to war to keep the South part of the US and won. Though slavery was abolished, the work of making sure people of all races are treated equally was not finished and continues even today.

Atlantic Slave Trade
TIMELINE

1502 Spanish merchant Juan de Córdoba sends the first captive Africans to the Americas.

1619 First captive Africans in British America arrive in Jamestown, Virginia.

1804 Haitian Revolution ends French colonial rule and slavery on the island.

1807 The British Parliament passes the Abolition of the Slave Trade Act, making it illegal to trade in slaves on British territory.

1808 Importation of captive Africans is abolished in the US, though slavery continues.

1863 President Abraham Lincoln's Emancipation Proclamation marks the first step toward the abolition of slavery in the US.

1888 Slavery is abolished in Brazil.

NOTE *from the expert!*

JOSEPH E. INIKORI
Historian

The contributions of slavery to the modern world as it exists today are considerable—especially when considering the enslavement of Africans in the Americas. Everyone agrees slavery in any society is evil.

❝ *Historians try hard to ensure their personal considerations do not influence their study of historical issues.* ❞

AGE OF REVOLUTIONS

In the late 18th century, ideas of liberty and freedom encouraged people to rebel against their rulers. The spirit of these uprisings spread around the world. In Europe, so many rebellions took place in 1848 that it has been called the year of revolutions.

The American Revolution

In the late 18th century, people living in 13 of Britain's North American colonies protested British taxes that were imposed to pay for an earlier war and for the defense of the colonies. Representatives from the colonies gathered to decide how to respond. After months of discussion, they opted to declare the 13 colonies an independent country. Not all citizens agreed this was the right choice. War broke out, with some colonial forces (Loyalists) joining the British side. Pictured is one of many conflicts, the Battle of Princeton. When the revolutionary forces (Patriots) won the war, the 13 colonies became the United States of America.

The Boston Tea Party

Before war broke out, the British taxed tea to reassert their right to tax the colonies. On December 16, 1773, colonists in Boston, Massachusetts, protested the tax. Some were dressed as indigenous people. They boarded three British ships in the harbor and dumped 342 chests of tea overboard. The British imposed punishments, turning even more colonists against them.

George Washington, a revolutionary general, became the first president of the new United States

Soldiers used muskets, slow and unwieldy guns, with bayonets (knifelike attachments)

Flags of the British troops often featured the Union Jack

British troops became known as redcoats because of the red jackets they wore

Soldiers used drums to give signals or to call for urgent medical assistance in battle

Ideals of the Enlightenment

A movement known as the Enlightenment inspired many of the revolutions that swept through Europe and the Americas during the late 18th and 19th centuries. The movement encouraged people to question whether it was right for a ruler to have control over everyone in a country without having to obey the law him- or herself.

Individualism
The belief that every person is unique and in charge of him- or herself

Rationalism
The idea that reason and logic, rather than belief or feeling, are the best sources of knowledge

Egalitarianism
The belief that all people are equal and should have the same rights

Secularism
The idea that humans can think for themselves instead of believing what the Church tells them

Democracy
The idea that all members of a population should have a say in the ways in which their country is governed

The French Revolution

In 1787, the French began to challenge the absolute rule of their monarchy. The new wealthy class wanted power. French thinkers sought equal rights. Farmworkers were angry at unfair taxes. The people staged a revolution that ended monarchical rule temporarily. A republic was created, but a "Reign of Terror" followed. Those who took power killed many who failed to support their version of the revolution—often beheading them using a guillotine (below).

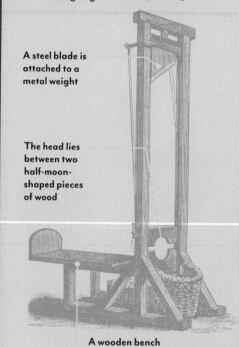

A steel blade is attached to a metal weight

The head lies between two half-moon-shaped pieces of wood

A wooden bench supports the body

GAME CHANGER

SIMÓN BOLÍVAR

South American revolutionary, lived 1783–1830
Venezuela

Simón Bolívar was a pioneer of South American independence. A military and political leader, he helped liberate various territories from Spanish colonial rule. This resulted in the creation of Colombia, Bolivia, Ecuador, Panama, Peru, and Venezuela. Bolivia is named for him.

" A people that loves freedom will in the end be free. "

Revolution in Haiti

The Haitian revolution (1791–1804) took place in the French colony of Saint-Domingue (Haiti). More than 500,000 people of African descent lived there. The great majority of them were slaves. From 1791, they fought for their independence. Their leader was Toussaint Louverture (right), a former slave turned soldier and politician. He died while imprisoned by the French in 1803. When forces led by Jean-Jacques Dessalines, one of Toussaint's lieutenants, defeated the French in 1804, Haiti became the world's first independent black republic.

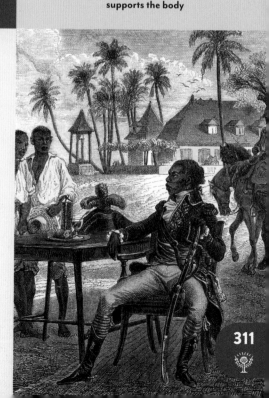

311

MEDICAL MILESTONES

Since the medieval period, discoveries about the human body have allowed doctors and surgeons to improve the treatment of patients. Major medical milestones have led to a greater understanding of anatomy (the parts of the body) and the reasons people get ill. New inventions and medical procedures have helped more people to live longer. Medical technology has advanced rapidly since the 1800s, but there are still many mysteries to solve.

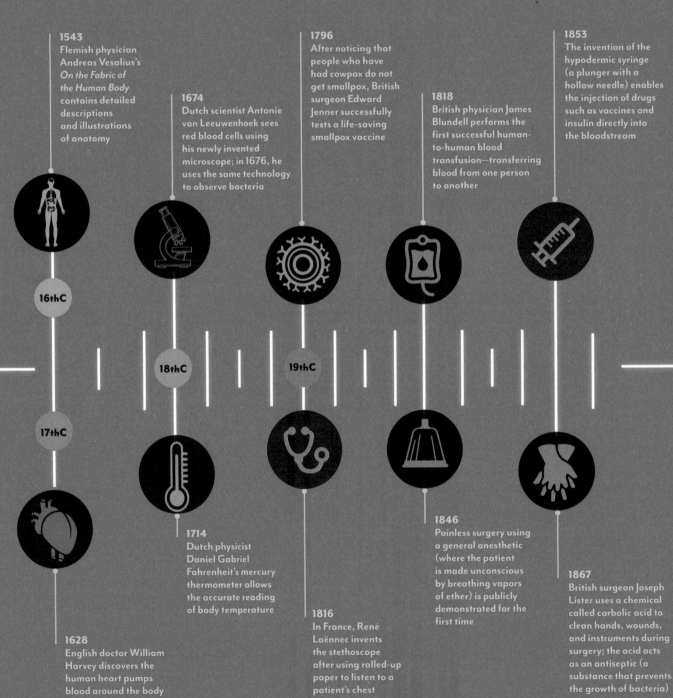

1543
Flemish physician Andreas Vesalius's *On the Fabric of the Human Body* contains detailed descriptions and illustrations of anatomy

1674
Dutch scientist Antonie van Leeuwenhoek sees red blood cells using his newly invented microscope; in 1676, he uses the same technology to observe bacteria

1796
After noticing that people who have had cowpox do not get smallpox, British surgeon Edward Jenner successfully tests a life-saving smallpox vaccine

1818
British physician James Blundell performs the first successful human-to-human blood transfusion—transferring blood from one person to another

1853
The invention of the hypodermic syringe (a plunger with a hollow needle) enables the injection of drugs such as vaccines and insulin directly into the bloodstream

16thC

18thC

19thC

17thC

1714
Dutch physicist Daniel Gabriel Fahrenheit's mercury thermometer allows the accurate reading of body temperature

1816
In France, René Laënnec invents the stethoscope after using rolled-up paper to listen to a patient's chest

1846
Painless surgery using a general anesthetic (where the patient is made unconscious by breathing vapors of ether) is publicly demonstrated for the first time

1628
English doctor William Harvey discovers the human heart pumps blood around the body

1867
British surgeon Joseph Lister uses a chemical called carbolic acid to clean hands, wounds, and instruments during surgery; the acid acts as an antiseptic (a substance that prevents the growth of bacteria)

EXPERT CONSULTANT: Mike Jay **SEE ALSO:** Chemistry of Life, p.120–21; The Human Body, p.198–99; DNA & Genetics, p.200–01; Med Tech, p.362–63; Future Humans, p.382–83

3D medical aid

In 2018, 3D printing technology aided physicians in the removal of a tumor from a human kidney. Doctors at Belfast City Hospital, Northern Ireland, were treating a young mother with fatal kidney failure. Her father donated a kidney, but it was found to have a cyst (abnormal growth). A medical printing company created an exact model of the father's kidney. Doctors then studied the model to plan how to remove the cyst cleanly. The transplant went ahead successfully.

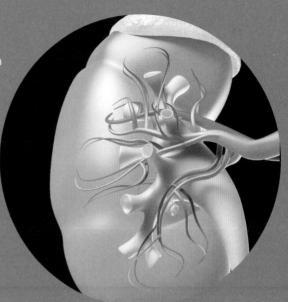

1870s and 1880s
German Robert Koch and Frenchman Louis Pasteur prove germ theory, which explains how people catch and pass on diseases via pathogens, or germs

1952
US physician Virginia Apgar develops the "Apgar score" to assess whether or not newborn babies need urgent medical attention

1964
Scottish-born June Almeida, a pioneer of virus imaging, discovers the first human coronavirus

1983
Scientists discover that HIV (human immunodeficiency virus) causes AIDS (Acquired Immune Deficiency Syndrome), which allowed the development of treatments

20thC

21stC

1895
German physicist Wilhelm Conrad Röntgen creates the X-ray machine, enabling doctors to see into the body without surgery

1928
Scottish scientist Alexander Fleming discovers penicillin, the first naturally occurring antibiotic found

1952
English physical chemist Rosalind Franklin takes X-ray photographs that reveal the structure of DNA to be shaped like a double helix

1978
Louise Brown, the first "test-tube" baby, is born in the UK; the fertilization of her mother's egg happened in a laboratory

2006
The HPV vaccine, the first vaccine to target a cause of cancer, is approved for use; HPV (human papillomavirus) is a cause of cancer in the female reproductive system

The industrial landscape

Industrialization transformed the face of the countries it came to. Factories, coal mines, textile mills, and ironworks were built across the land, and many people left farming behind to work in them. City populations grew quickly, and some developers built new infrastructure around their emerging industries—from houses and stores to canals and railroads.

Hoping to secure workers' loyalty, some employers provided churches, infirmaries, and schools in their factory villages

Industrialization started to spread across the open countryside

Houses for workers were built close by

Tall chimneys spewed smoke from the coal fires that were used to produce steam to drive the machines

Large and sturdy, factory buildings had to accommodate heavy machinery

Flowing rivers provided power for mills

New road and railroad networks connected one city to another

THE INDUSTRIAL REVOLUTION

The Industrial Revolution began in Great Britain toward the end of the 18th century. It then spread to mainland Europe, the US, and Japan during the 19th century. Rather than making goods by hand in small workshops, laborers mass-produced them in large factories. Steam- and water-driven machines allowed people to work faster and more efficiently. Cities grew larger as people moved away from their agricultural lives to find jobs in these new urban centers.

Child labor

Many families living in poverty sent their children to work in factories. In the US, the census of 1870 counted more than 750,000 workers under the age of 15. Children undertook hard manual work in filthy conditions, for shifts of 12 hours (or more) at a time.

EXPERT CONSULTANT: Brian Duignan **SEE ALSO:** Metals, p.114–15; Energy, p.122–23; Electricity, p.126–27; Simple Machines, p.142–43; Education, p.230–31; Work, p.232–33; Slavery in the Americas, p.308–09; Anytime, Anywhere, p.342–43; Smart Tech & AI, p.364–65; Mega Rich, p.352–53

Division of labor

Workers often concentrated on a specific task, such as operating spinning machines or attaching heels to shoes. Each person performed a task over and over, repeating the same motions as one small part of the larger manufacturing process. This eventually led to the moving assembly line, where a mechanized system moved a product from one work station to the next with workers performing their individual tasks as it progressed.

Low wages, especially for women

Thanks to mass production, the cost of many goods fell, and more people were able to save money for the first time. However, factory hands and other laborers worked long and exhausting hours for little pay. In England, women's wages accounted for between one-third and two-thirds of men's. Historians debate whether this was due to gender discrimination or a result of them doing different tasks with lower skill levels.

  British men, 10–15 shillings per week

 British women, 5 shillings per week

British children, 1 shilling per week

FACTastic!

Andrew Carnegie gave away his massive $350 million fortune. Born in poverty in Scotland, Carnegie became a pioneer of the steel industry in the US. When he retired, in 1901, he vowed to give his money away ($4.8 billion in today's money). Ten years later, he had donated 90 percent of his fortune, mainly to schools and libraries.

Innovations of the industrial age

Industrialization led to the development of groundbreaking machinery and modes of transportation. Some of the major inventions are listed below. These new technologies often relied on fossil fuels such as coal and gas for energy. These fuels gave rise to pollution and, eventually, global warming—we live with the consequences of this today.

Spinning machines
The spinning jenny (1764) and spinning mule (1779) could mass-produce quality textiles.

 C 18th

Steam engine (c. 1765)
James Watt's steam engine powered trains and industrial machines.

Electric generator and motor (1831)
Michael Faraday's inventions laid the foundations for all future uses of electricity.

 C 19th

Telegraph (1837)
Samuel Morse's telegraph allowed people to send messages across long distances more swiftly.

Telephone (1876)
Alexander Graham Bell invented the telephone, revolutionizing human communication.

Incandescent bulb (1878–79)
Chemist Joseph Swan made the first filament light bulb.

Internal combustion engine (c. 1859)
Karl Benz created the first gasoline-fueled car with an internal combustion engine (1885).

First airplane (1905)
Aviation pioneers Wilbur and Orville Wright built the world's first successful motorized airplane.

 C 20th

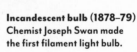

WORLD WAR I

Also known as the Great War, World War I pitched some of the world's most powerful countries against each other. Germany, Austria-Hungary, the Ottoman Empire, and Bulgaria (Central Powers) fought on one side. Great Britain, France, Russia, the United States, and their allies (Allied Powers) fought on the other. This was the first truly global war, with conflict in Europe, the Middle East, Africa, Asia, and the Pacific.

Trench warfare

Soldiers dug networks of channels, or trenches, in the ground. Aboveground, the area between the trenches of opposing forces was called no-man's-land. To advance forward, soldiers had to come up from the trenches and enter no-man's-land. This exposed them to enemy fire and bombs. Life in the trenches was a little safer—though soldiers often waded through filthy mud, and disease spread fast.

Gas attacks

German forces released chlorine gas at the Second Battle of Ypres (1915). Wind carried the gas into Allied trenches and thousands died. Both sides raced to develop more effective chemical weapons. They included phosgene, which caused the lungs to fill with fluid, and mustard gas, a blistering agent. Some 91,000 soldiers were killed by gas during WWI.

The front of the trench, facing the enemy, was called the parapet

A periscope allowed soldiers to look out at the enemy from below the parapet

Men stood watch around the clock to see if enemy soldiers entered no-man's-land

Soldiers rested and sheltered from the weather in holes dug into the trench wall

Sandbags provided cover—from both the enemy and from the weather

Boards embedded in the trench wall provided a fire step for soldiers to stand on when firing out into no-man's-land

Wooden duckboards provided a more stable trench floor

EXPERT CONSULTANT: Lora Vogt

Big Bertha

One of the largest cannons used in the war was a German gun nicknamed Big Bertha. Big Bertha was a howitzer—an artillery piece with a short barrel that was designed to fire missiles high into the air. The Germans made 12 Big Berthas during the war, and used them to attack French and Belgian forts.

The gun fired projectiles weighing up to 1,785 lbs (810 kg)

Missiles penetrated up to 40 feet (12 meters) of concrete and earth

Weighing around 47 tons, Big Bertha had to be dismantled for transportation

Teams of 240 men operated and serviced each howitzer

Some missiles had delayed-action fuses that exploded after their initial impact

WWI was a conflict of many firsts, with the following among them.

1. Steel helmet The French were first to use a steel helmet in battle.

2. Military use of X-rays Mobile units allowed the taking of X-rays of the wounded on French frontlines.

3. Submarines The Germans used "U-boats." The "U" stands for *untersee*—German for "undersea."

4. Tank battles British forces were the first to use tanks effectively, at the Battle of Cambrai in 1917.

5. Aerial warfare Both sides developed aircraft with machine guns for shooting enemy planes.

6. Aircraft carrier British HMS *Argus* was the first aircraft carrier.

7. Wireless communications WWI was the first conflict to see widespread use of this technology.

FACTastic!

On Christmas Day, in 1914, some German and British units put down their weapons and walked out to meet the enemy. Soldiers shared their holiday parcels, sang songs, and some even played soccer with a makeshift ball and goals. Others took advantage of the temporary peace to repair their trenches and bury their dead.

Carrier pigeons

Carrier pigeons delivered messages during the war—placed in canisters attached to their legs. The birds flew over battlefields and were especially useful to those at sea. One pigeon flew 22 miles (35 km) in 22 minutes to deliver a message that saved two stranded seaplane pilots. Cher Ami, a US Army pigeon, was even awarded the Croix de Guerre, one of France's highest military medals.

The cost of war

World War I affected all members of society, not only combatants. Five million people died fighting for the Allied forces and 3.5 million fighting for the Central Powers. The conflict also took the lives of 13 million civilians, many of whom were forced to flee their homes to escape the fighting.

VOTES FOR WOMEN

The women's suffrage movement was a worldwide fight for women's right to vote. In the early years, groups in the UK and the US drove the movement. The first victory for women's suffrage, however, was in New Zealand, where women gained the right to vote in 1893. In many countries, the right to vote was given to recognize women's work in wartime.

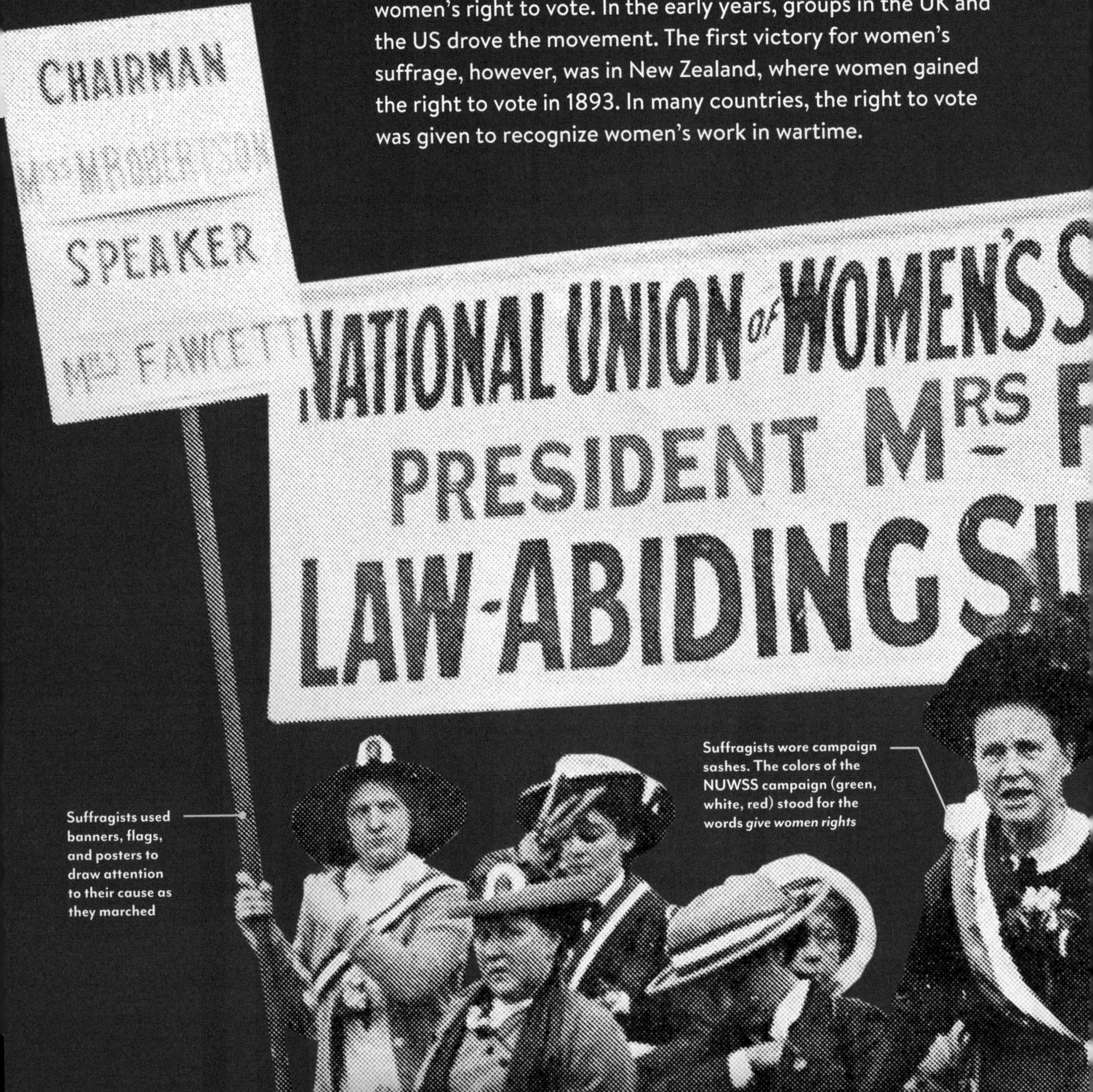

CHAIRMAN

SPEAKER

Mrs FAWCETT

NATIONAL UNION of WOMEN'S S

PRESIDENT Mrs F

LAW-ABIDING SU

Suffragists wore campaign sashes. The colors of the NUWSS campaign (green, white, red) stood for the words *give women rights*

Suffragists used banners, flags, and posters to draw attention to their cause as they marched

EXPERT CONSULTANT: Lori Ann Terjesen **SEE ALSO:** Education, p.230–31; The Industrial Revolution, p.314–15; World War I, p.316–17; Boom & Bust, p.322–23; Civil Rights, p.330–31

The British NUWSS was just one of several suffragist groups. Women in the US supported the National American Woman Suffrage Association (NAWSA)

SUFFRAGE SOC
AWCETT
FRAGI

When Women Got the Vote
TIMELINE

1893 New Zealand	**1944** Jamaica
1902 Australia	**1945** Italy
1906 Finland	**1946** Vietnam
1913 Norway	**1947** Argentina
1915 Denmark	**1947** Japan
1917 Russia	**1947** Mexico
1918 Canada	**1947** Pakistan
1918 Germany	**1949** China
1918 UK	**1949** India
1919 The Netherlands	**1955** Ethiopia
1920 US	**1957** Zimbabwe
1930 South Africa	**1963** Morocco
1931 Spain	**1967** Ecuador
1931 Portugal	**1971** Switzerland
1931 Sri Lanka	**1972** Bangladesh
1932 Thailand	**1999** Qatar
1932 Uruguay	**2002** Bahrain
1934 Turkey	**2005** Kuwait
1935 Myanmar	**2006** United Arab Emirates
1944 France	**2011** Saudi Arabia

Suffragist meeting

In this photograph, the English suffragist and educational reformer Dame Millicent Fawcett addresses a meeting in Hyde Park, London. Fawcett was the president of the National Union of Women's Suffrage Societies (NUWSS) from 1897 to 1919.

While some men protested against women's suffrage, the suffragists did have male support—even from members of Parliament in the United Kingdom

THE RISE OF COMMUNISM

By the 19th century, many people worked in factories. The factory owners were wealthy, but the workers were poor. Because there were more workers than owners, many workers supported socialist ideas that said the wealth produced in the factories should benefit everyone. In 1848, Karl Marx published the *Communist Manifesto*, proposing that workers should take ownership away from the capitalists (factory owners) and put it in the hands of a new government, controlled by the workers.

Revolution! "Workers of the world unite! You have nothing to lose but your chains."

Socialism: People's well-being should be more important than profit.

Communism: The workers should take control of the government and use it to benefit the working class.

DAS KAPITAL

Marx's *Das Kapital* explained why he thought capitalism did not work

Karl Marx

Karl Marx was a political economist and philosopher. His work influenced the communist governments of the 20th century. Marx believed that society advanced through "class struggles." He introduced the main communist belief that unhappy workers needed to rise up and revolt against the industry-owning capitalists.

Soviet symbolism

The first communist nations focused on people working together for the state. The hammer and sickle symbol represented the union of industrial workers (the hammer) and farmworkers (the sickle). Today's communist countries mix communism with elements of capitalism. Working for personal gain is encouraged, meaning some people are far richer than others.

Communist Countries
LISTIFIED.

Today, five countries remain communist, although each embraces aspects of capitalism. They represent 20 percent of the world's population.

1. China The Chinese Communist Party was founded in 1921. It established the People's Republic of China under leader Mao Zedong in 1949. Population: 1,397,364,000

2. Vietnam Ho Chi Minh declared Vietnam a communist state in 1945, gaining control of the north only. The whole country was communist by 1976. Population: 96,479,000

3. North Korea North Korea fell under Soviet control after World War II. It went on to become a communist state in 1948. Population: 25,727,000

4. Cuba In 1958, Fidel Castro led the overthrow of Cuba's military dictator. Castro then ruled himself, as dictator of an independent, communist Cuba. Population: 11,194,000

5. Laos Communist revolutionaries seized power in Laos in 1975. Population: 7,271,000

VLADIMIR ILYICH ULYANOV (LENIN)

Soviet leader, lived 1870–1924
Simbirsk, Russia

Vladimir Lenin led the Bolshevik Party—the first Marxist political party to take power in a country. He and his allies seized power in the Russian capital of Petrograd in October 1917. Lenin then emerged victorious from the Russian Civil War (1918–1921). He was the first head of what became the Soviet Union in 1922.

The Cuban Revolution

The Cuban Revolution was a movement to return control of Cuba to the Cuban people. It began in 1953 and ended with the overthrow of dictator Fulgencio Batista on December 31, 1958. Batista's unpopularity, along with the promise to take land from foreign owners and use Cuba's wealth to provide public education and healthcare, brought leader Fidel Castro's (seated, right) movement widespread support from the Cuban population.

The people in this poster hold Mao Zedong's *Little Red Book*, which contained 267 sayings from the Chinese leader

毛泽东选集

Mao's China

Mao Zedong, leader of the Communist Party of China (CPC), spent years building support for communist ideas in the Chinese countryside. He was a hero to many citizens who believed that their country was not being run in the people's best interests. Mao led his followers in a revolution against the government. The communists won the war, and Mao became the leader of China in 1949. After Mao's death in 1976, Deng Xiaoping, who had fought alongside Mao in the Chinese Revolution, became China's new leader.

321

BOOM & BUST

After World War I, many nations in the West experienced a "boom" period. People were generally more wealthy, so factories mass-produced goods in larger numbers. This generated more wealth. But the boom was short-lived. A huge stock market crash occurred in the US in 1929. This "bust" made existing weaknesses in the economy worse. It marked the start of the Great Depression—ten years of global economic downturn.

The Roaring Twenties

The decade that followed World War I was a time of rapid change in the West. Many people experienced wealth on a scale that they had never seen before. New social and cultural trends emerged, including the rise of the modern woman, or "flapper."

Prohibition and the jazz age

During the boom years, people sometimes went to clubs to drink alcohol and dance to jazz music. Such entertainments were not welcomed by all. In 1919, the US government passed Prohibition laws forbidding people to buy and sell alcohol. Criminal organizations operated bars called speakeasies, which sold alcohol illegally.

Western women gained greater independence after having taken on men's roles during World War I

Manufacturers placed advertisements for their goods in newspapers and magazines; this ad is for Renault cars

Many industries experienced a boom, as more people spent money on their goods

Manufacturing things such as automobiles in larger numbers made them cheaper to buy

EXPERT CONSULTANT: Margaret C. Rung **SEE ALSO:** The Industrial Revolution, p.314–15; World War I, p.316–17; Votes for Women, p.318–19; World War II, p.324–25; New Tensions, New Hopes, p.332–33; The Media, p.358–59

FACTastic!

When Charles Lindbergh made the world's first solo flight across the Atlantic Ocean, he could barely see where he was going!
He needed extra fuel to make the 3,600-mile (5,800-km) journey, and gas tanks were placed in the wings and over his front field of vision. It meant he had to use a periscope to see where he was going. Any extras (including radio and parachute) were dumped to allow for the extra weight of the fuel.

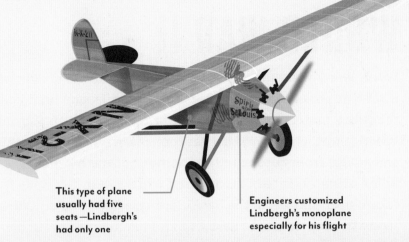

This type of plane usually had five seats—Lindbergh's had only one

Engineers customized Lindbergh's monoplane especially for his flight

Golden Age of Hollywood

The 1920s were considered a "Golden Age" in Hollywood, as movies became a popular way for people to spend their leisure time. The silent-movie era produced many famous stars, including Laurel and Hardy (pictured). The first feature-length "talkie," a film with sound, was *The Jazz Singer*, which came out in 1927. Disney's Mickey Mouse first appeared in 1928, in the movie *Steamboat Willie*.

Rise of fascism

The Great Depression helped fascist leaders rise to power in the 1930s. Fascism is a style of government that focuses on the strength of a nation rather than the welfare of its individuals. In Germany, Adolf Hitler's Nazi Party promised to improve the economy and restore pride after the country's loss in World War I. National pride, or nationalism, also brought Benito Mussolini to power in Italy. Hitler's policies were among the causes of World War II.

The Great Depression

The Great Depression was the longest and most serious downturn ever experienced by the world economy. It began in the US in 1929 and spread rapidly throughout the world. The US experienced the biggest drop in economic growth and income in the first few years of the depression. Unemployment rates rose across the globe, leaving people impoverished and starving.

Production
Between 1929 and 1933, production in US factories, mines, and utilities fell by almost half

Spending power
The average American's spending money dropped by 50%

Market value
US stock prices collapsed to about one-seventh of their precrash value

Jobs
The number of unemployed Americans rose from 1.4 million in 1929 to 10.6 million in 1933

Poverty
Soup kitchens opened around the country to provide free bread and soup to starving people

323

WORLD WAR II

World War II was the biggest and bloodiest war in human history. It saw the Axis powers—Germany, Italy, and Japan—fight against the Allied powers of France, Great Britain, the US, the Soviet Union, and China. Fierce battles took place on land, in the air, and at sea, from Europe to the Pacific and North Africa. The Allied powers wanted to stop Adolf Hitler's Nazi Germany from taking over Europe. In the Pacific arena, after invading China, Japan tried to take over East Asia and the Southwest Pacific.

The Holocaust

In Nazi-occupied territories, the secret police rounded up Jewish citizens. They forced them to wear badges identifying themselves and and sent them to labor camps and death camps. The Nazis killed at least six million Jews as well as huge numbers of Roma, disabled people, LGBT people, Eastern Europeans, and others they considered inferior.

Evacuated to safety

Bombs posed a threat to children, especially in cities such as London (pictured below) that were easy targets. Across Europe, children moved to the countryside for safety. Finland fought against the neighboring Soviet Union from 1939 until 1944. At risk from Soviet invasion during this time, 80,000 Finnish children evacuated to Sweden and Denmark. The war made 21 million people homeless—mostly through bombing and enemy occupation of their land.

The war in China

Japan went to war with China in 1937, invading large parts of the country. They continued to fight until 1945. In China, patriotic films and posters boosted people's spirits and encouraged resistance.

Shock tactics

The countries at war developed new fighting methods. German forces adopted Blitzkrieg tactics. This "lightning warfare" combined attacks from bombers in the air with rapidly advancing tanks over land. Japanese kamikaze pilots deliberately crashed their airplanes into Allied ships to cause massive destruction, killing themselves in the process. Another surprise tactic was to fire torpedos from submarines (pictured here).

EXPERT CONSULTANT: Keith Huxen **SEE ALSO:** Conflict & War, p.214–15; The Industrial Revolution, p.314–15; World War I, p.316–17; The Rise of Communism, p.320–21; Boom & Bust, p.322–23; The Cold War, p.326–27

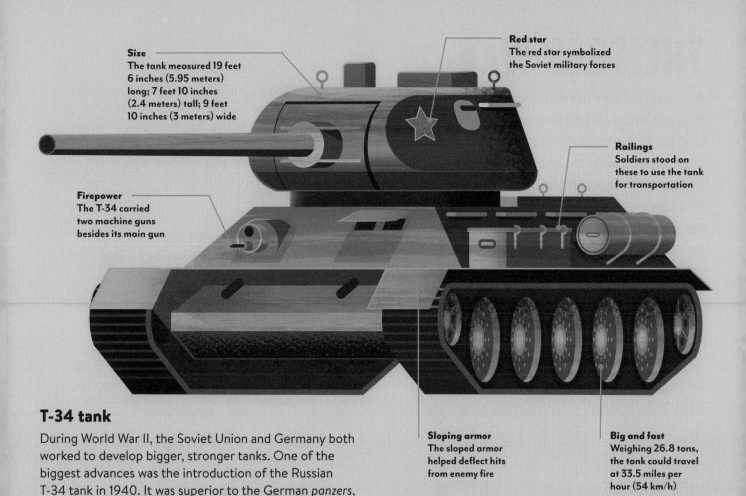

Size
The tank measured 19 feet 6 inches (5.95 meters) long; 7 feet 10 inches (2.4 meters) tall; 9 feet 10 inches (3 meters) wide

Red star
The red star symbolized the Soviet military forces

Railings
Soldiers stood on these to use the tank for transportation

Firepower
The T-34 carried two machine guns besides its main gun

Sloping armor
The sloped armor helped deflect hits from enemy fire

Big and fast
Weighing 26.8 tons, the tank could travel at 33.5 miles per hour (54 km/h)

T-34 tank

During World War II, the Soviet Union and Germany both worked to develop bigger, stronger tanks. One of the biggest advances was the introduction of the Russian T-34 tank in 1940. It was superior to the German *panzers*, and one German field marshal even declared it to be the "finest tank in the world." Produced on a massive scale—40,000–60,000 tanks—the T-34 helped to slow, and finally stop, the German invasion of the Soviet Union.

The atom bomb

The most lethal weapon of the war was the atom bomb. Japan had entered the war hoping to expand its empire. In 1941, the Japanese attacked a US base at Pearl Harbor, Hawaii. This drew the US into the conflict. In 1945, to force a Japanese surrender, US aircraft dropped atomic bombs on the cities of Hiroshima and Nagasaki. More than 200,000 people died.

Casualties of World War II

Death tolls can only be estimates, and total figures vary from 50 million to 80 million—two-thirds of them civilians. Many got caught up in land battles and aerial bombardments. Others suffered political and racial executions, war-induced disease and famine, and the sinking of ships.

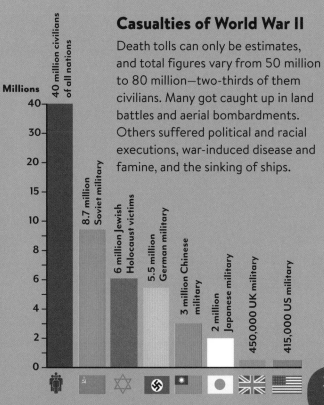

Millions

40 million civilians of all nations

8.7 million Soviet military

6 million Jewish Holocaust victims

5.5 million German military

3 million Chinese military

2 million Japanese military

450,000 UK military

415,000 US military

THE COLD WAR

After World War II, the US and Western Europe feared the spread of communist ideas from the Soviet Union (USSR) and China. Both sides produced nuclear weapons, and this increased the tension. The conflict became a "cold" war, because neither side launched any weapons. The threat of mutually assured destruction prevented this—if one nation attacked, the other would counterattack, and all would be destroyed.

Nuclear bunker

For some time after a nuclear explosion, the air aboveground is full of harmful radioactive dust. Companies advertised underground bunkers for shelter. We now know that they couldn't protect inhabitants from nuclear contamination.

Nuclear football

The US president has an emergency briefcase. Dating back to the Cold War, it is dubbed the nuclear football. It contains all that's needed to authorize a nuclear attack when away from a command center. Should an enemy launch nuclear weapons against the US, the president can strike back without delay.

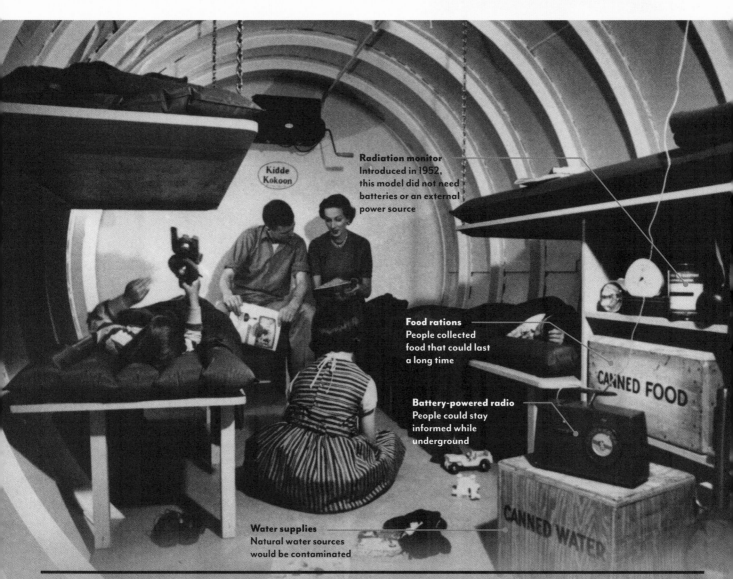

Kidde Kokoon

Radiation monitor
Introduced in 1952, this model did not need batteries or an external power source

Food rations
People collected food that could last a long time

CANNED FOOD

Battery-powered radio
People could stay informed while underground

Water supplies
Natural water sources would be contaminated

CANNED WATER

EXPERT CONSULTANT: Henry R. Maar III **SEE ALSO:** Moons, p.32–3; Rockets, p.38–9; Radioactivity, p.104–05; Conflict & War, p.214–15; The Rise of Communism, p.320–21; World War II, p.324–25

Hot Wars
LISTIFIED.

A series of armed conflicts occurred around the world as a result of Cold War tensions.

1. Korean War (1950–53) Around 2.5 million people died in a war between Soviet-backed communist North Korea and capitalist South Korea, which had US support.

2. Vietnam War (1954–75) Communist North Vietnam (supported mainly by the USSR and China) fought for control of capitalist South Vietnam (supported mainly by the US).

3. Hungarian Uprising (1956) Hungarians rebelled against Soviet influence. They tried to leave the Warsaw Pact, an organization that allied them with the USSR. The Soviets sent in troops to stop the rebels.

4. Invasion of Czechoslovakia (1968) Members of the Warsaw Pact sent in 200,000 men to take control of the former Czechoslovakia. Its government had been trying to introduce reforms to give its people greater freedom.

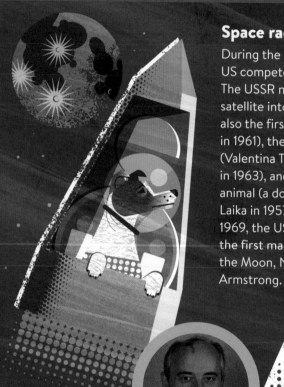

Space race

During the Cold War, the USSR and the US competed over space exploration. The USSR not only sent the first satellite into space in 1957, but also the first man (Yuri Gagarin in 1961), the first woman (Valentina Tereshkova in 1963), and the first animal (a dog named Laika in 1957). In 1969, the US put the first man on the Moon, Neil Armstrong.

FACTastic!

China uses pandas to seal alliances, and has done so for centuries. In the 1950s, China sent pandas as gifts to its communist allies in the USSR and North Korea. But relations between China and the USSR broke down during the Cold War. In 1972, two pandas arrived in the US, symbolizing that China had accepted the West and capitalism.

GAME CHANGER

MIKHAIL GORBACHEV

Soviet leader, born 1931
Privolye, Russia

Mikhail Gorbachev was the last leader of the Soviet Union (USSR) that had formed under Vladimir Lenin in 1922. He introduced policies of *glasnost* (transparency) and *perestroika* (restructuring) that helped bring about the end of communism in the Soviet Union. His negotiations with the United States ended the Cold War.

Germany reunited

Divided into communist East and capitalist West after World War II, Germany was a site of Cold War tensions. In Berlin, a huge wall separated communist and capitalist zones. When the USSR began to collapse in 1989, Germany tore down the wall and reunited a year later.

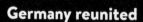

DECOLONIZATION

After World War II, many countries under colonial rule across the world demanded self-determination. This meant they wanted independence from the empires that governed them and to rule their countries for themselves. The colonial empires included the UK, France, and the Netherlands. From 1945–1970, newly independent regions of the world included South Asia, most of Africa, Southeast Asia, and the Caribbean. Independence movements in these regions achieved success at varying rates. Some were peaceful, while others involved revolution and warfare.

Issued in 1946, this banknote features the first Indonesian president, Sukarno

New currencies

Newly independent countries set out to establish their national identities. One way to do this was to develop currencies of their own. Indonesia, for example, was previously under Dutch rule and had used the old Dutch East Indies guilder as money. In 1949, Indonesia fully replaced the guilder with the Indonesian rupiah.

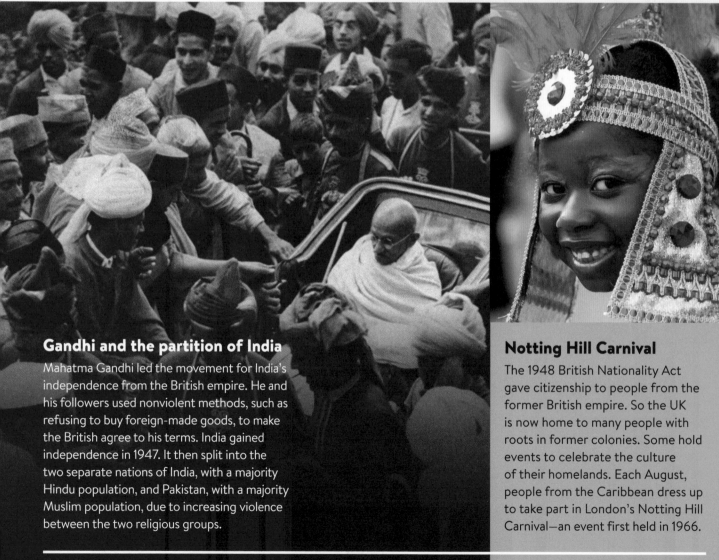

Gandhi and the partition of India

Mahatma Gandhi led the movement for India's independence from the British empire. He and his followers used nonviolent methods, such as refusing to buy foreign-made goods, to make the British agree to his terms. India gained independence in 1947. It then split into the two separate nations of India, with a majority Hindu population, and Pakistan, with a majority Muslim population, due to increasing violence between the two religious groups.

Notting Hill Carnival

The 1948 British Nationality Act gave citizenship to people from the former British empire. So the UK is now home to many people with roots in former colonies. Some hold events to celebrate the culture of their homelands. Each August, people from the Caribbean dress up to take part in London's Notting Hill Carnival—an event first held in 1966.

EXPERT CONSULTANT: Robtel Neajai Pailey **SEE ALSO:** African Empires, p.292–93; The Mughal Empire, p.300–01; New Empires, p.304–05; World War I, p.316–17; The Rise of Communism, p.320–21; World War II, p.324–25; The Cold War, p.326–27; Civil Rights, p.330–31; World Political Map, p.334–35

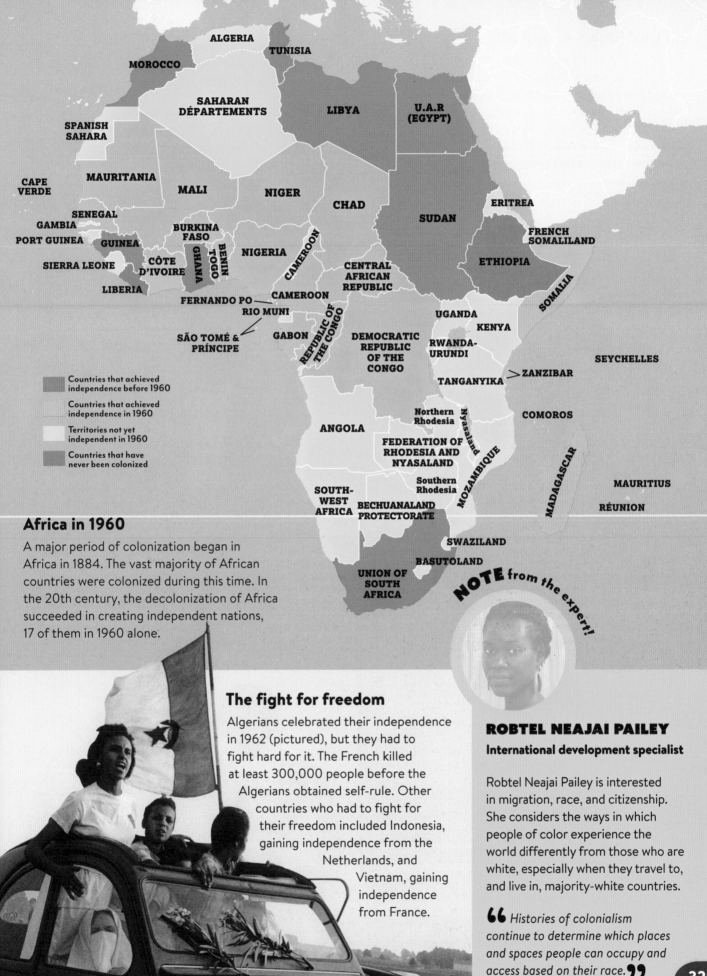

MOROCCO
ALGERIA
TUNISIA
SPANISH SAHARA
SAHARAN DÉPARTEMENTS
LIBYA
U.A.R (EGYPT)
CAPE VERDE
MAURITANIA
MALI
NIGER
CHAD
SUDAN
ERITREA
FRENCH SOMALILAND
SENEGAL
GAMBIA
PORT GUINEA
GUINEA
SIERRA LEONE
BURKINA FASO
CÔTE D'IVOIRE
GHANA
TOGO
BENIN
NIGERIA
CAMEROON
CENTRAL AFRICAN REPUBLIC
ETHIOPIA
SOMALIA
LIBERIA
FERNANDO PO
RIO MUNI
CAMEROON
SÃO TOMÉ & PRÍNCIPE
GABON
REPUBLIC OF THE CONGO
DEMOCRATIC REPUBLIC OF THE CONGO
UGANDA
KENYA
RWANDA-URUNDI
TANGANYIKA
ZANZIBAR
SEYCHELLES
ANGOLA
Northern Rhodesia
Nyasaland
FEDERATION OF RHODESIA AND NYASALAND
COMOROS
MOZAMBIQUE
MADAGASCAR
SOUTH-WEST AFRICA
Southern Rhodesia
BECHUANALAND PROTECTORATE
MAURITIUS
RÉUNION
SWAZILAND
BASUTOLAND
UNION OF SOUTH AFRICA

Countries that achieved independence before 1960

Countries that achieved independence in 1960

Territories not yet independent in 1960

Countries that have never been colonized

Africa in 1960

A major period of colonization began in Africa in 1884. The vast majority of African countries were colonized during this time. In the 20th century, the decolonization of Africa succeeded in creating independent nations, 17 of them in 1960 alone.

The fight for freedom

Algerians celebrated their independence in 1962 (pictured), but they had to fight hard for it. The French killed at least 300,000 people before the Algerians obtained self-rule. Other countries who had to fight for their freedom included Indonesia, gaining independence from the Netherlands, and Vietnam, gaining independence from France.

NOTE from the expert!

ROBTEL NEAJAI PAILEY
International development specialist

Robtel Neajai Pailey is interested in migration, race, and citizenship. She considers the ways in which people of color experience the world differently from those who are white, especially when they travel to, and live in, majority-white countries.

❝ Histories of colonialism continue to determine which places and spaces people can occupy and access based on their race. ❞

US Civil Rights Movement

The US Civil War ended slavery, but it didn't provide African Americans with rights and opportunities equal to those of whites. In the South, legal segregation kept black citizens from living, working, playing, shopping, or going to school alongside whites. State and local laws made it difficult for African Americans to vote. Even in the North, African Americans were seldom given the same opportunities whites had.

From the 1950s, African Americans organized the Civil Rights movement to demand that they be treated equally. African Americans and their white allies staged peaceful protests around the country (including the 1963 March on Washington shown here). They fought for their rights in court and won important changes. Although the US Supreme Court declared segregation illegal, and Congress passed a series of laws protecting voting rights, African Americans continue to face challenges in the US today.

A life of leadership
John Lewis was a seasoned protest leader and chair of the Student Nonviolent Coordinating Committee at the time of the march. He went on to spend his whole adult life advocating for equality, including as a congressman from Georgia.

King's dream
The Reverend Dr. Martin Luther King, Jr., led the 1963 March on Washington, where he gave his famous "I Have a Dream" speech. In it, he said that he dreamed his children would live to see a world where people were not "judged by the color of their skin but by the content of their character."

Support from clergy
Many religious groups joined in the Civil Rights movement. Eugene Carson Blake was the executive director of the United Presbyterian Church in the US. Joachim Prinz (wearing sunglasses two people to the right of Blake) was president of the American Jewish Congress.

CIVIL RIGHTS

Civil rights include political rights, such as the right to vote, as well as social freedoms and equality. In many societies, various groups are discriminated against, meaning they do not have the same rights and privileges as others. This could be because of gender, race, religion, or other factors. In recent decades, groups have taken part in movements to demand civil rights that have been—and in some cases continue to be—denied to them.

Take a knee
Since August 2016, some US athletes have protested racism and police violence by kneeling during the national anthem before a game. It is traditional to stand for the anthem, so kneeling draws attention to their message. Football star Colin Kaepernick (pictured) was the first to use this form of nonviolent protest.

EXPERT CONSULTANT: Jeff Wallenfeldt **SEE ALSO:** Religious Belief, p.212–14; Education, p.230–31; The First Australians, p.244–45; Slavery in the Americas, p.308–09; Votes for Women, p.318–19; World War II, p.324–25

Keep us flying!

Indigenous rights

Indigenous peoples in the Americas, Australia, Africa, Asia, and Europe have long struggled for equal treatment in their ancestral homes and respect for their sacred places. The Australian Anangu people won a major victory in 2019, when the government agreed to allow them to keep tourists off Uluru (Ayer's Rock), a sacred rock formation.

FACTastic!

WWII fueled the American Civil Rights movement. Some 1.2 million African Americans served in segregated units during the war—many with distinction. The Tuskegee Airmen flew 1,578 missions, destroyed 261 enemy aircraft, and won more than 850 medals. Having fought to end Nazi racism, African Americans felt it was crueler than ever before to subject citizens to racism at home.

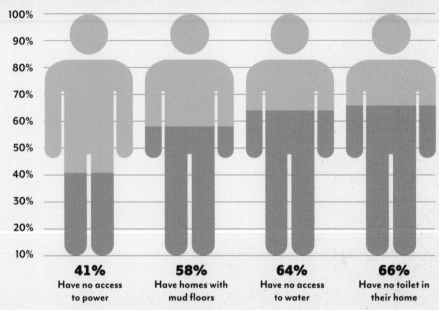

41%	58%	64%	66%
Have no access to power	Have homes with mud floors	Have no access to water	Have no toilet in their home

India's Scheduled Caste

India's Hindu caste system splits society into five groups. Members of the lowest-ranking group, the Scheduled Caste, are known widely as Dalits. Dalits have historically been treated as inferior and have been allowed to work in only the least desirable jobs. Discrimination was made illegal in 1949, but continues. According to the 2011 census, more than 200 million Dalits live in India, many in poverty.

GAME CHANGER

NELSON MANDELA
President, served 1994–99
Mvezo, Cape Province, South Africa

Nelson Mandela joined the movement to end apartheid, a system that discriminated against black South Africans. Imprisoned for his protests, he became a symbol of the struggle. When apartheid laws fell, he was released from prison and became the first black president of South Africa.

" *If needs be, it is an ideal for which I am prepared to die.* "

LGBTQ+ rights

The mass movement for LGBTQ+ rights emerged in the 1970s. There has been progress over the years, particularly in the West. Victories include legalization of the right to love and marry, and to adopt children. In many cities, an annual Pride event celebrates LGBTQ+ freedoms and renews demands for the rights for which the community is still fighting.

9/11 and the rise of terrorism

On September 11, 2001, four attacks on the US killed 2,977 people. Terrorists associated with the Islamic extremist group Al-Qaeda launched the attacks. Two of these attacks happened in New York City, where terrorists crashed airplanes into the towers of the World Trade Center. US president George W. Bush called for a global "War on Terror." The 21st century has seen more such attacks, although not on this scale.

NEW TENSIONS, NEW HOPES

The last millennium ended with humanity being better connected globally than ever before. Yet many people also remained divided, fighting over territory and resources because of differences in ethnicity and religion. At the dawn of the 21st century, people faced fears arising from struggling economies and increased threats to the environment. Despite these challenges, new pioneers have emerged to give us new hope for the future.

Tech giant Apple Inc.

In 2018, Apple became the world's first public company (one in which the public owns shares) to be worth $1 trillion. Amazon.com, Microsoft, and Alphabet (parent company of Google) all followed. This milestone marked the growing influence of a small number of big companies, some of which are now richer and more powerful than several countries. Because of this, activists (people who seek social or political change) are calling for these companies to address problems such as human rights and privacy.

Speaking out

In Pakistan, the extremist Taliban movement prevented young girls from going to school. Malala Yousafzai, an 11-year-old girl from Swat, in northern Pakistan, blogged about life under the Taliban. When she was 15, a Taliban gunman shot Malala in the head in an attempt to silence her. She survived and is now an activist for female education. In 2014, Malala was awarded a Nobel Peace Prize for her work.

FACTastic!

By 2050, more than two-thirds of the world's population will be living in cities. By 2030, more than 40 cities are projected to have become "megacities," with populations exceeding 10 million. The biggest megacity today, Tokyo, has about 37 million residents—roughly the same number of people living in all of Canada. Cities have many advantages. Basic services—water and electricity supply, schooling, and transportation—are more efficient when people live close together. However, rapid growth can lead to overcrowding and risk of pandemics.

Growing greener

The destruction of forests (deforestation) threatens animal habitats and is a major cause of global warming. In the 21st century, many countries have started to counter the effects of this through reforestation—planting new trees to rebuild forest land. For example, in July 2019, Ethiopians planted 350 million trees across the country over the course of only 12 hours.

WORLD POLITICAL MAP

Today's world is made up of 193 countries that are recognized by the United Nations (UN). This number could change in the future, as some states seek independence, just as others have done in the past. Becoming a recognized country is fairly complex. Not all countries agree on names and boundaries for themselves or others. Founded in 1945, the UN works toward global peace, security, and human rights.

Arctic Ocean

GREENLAND (DENMARK)

Greenland Sea

Chukchi Sea

Beaufort Sea

Baffin Bay

ICELAND

ALASKA (U.S.A.)

Bering Sea

Gulf of Alaska

Hudson Bay

Labrador Sea

CANADA

North America
There are 23 independent nations in North America, from the large country of Canada to the tiny St. Kitts and Nevis in the Caribbean

UNITED STATES OF AMERICA

Atlantic Ocean

HAWAII (U.S.A.)

Gulf of Mexico

MEXICO

THE BAHAMAS

CUBA
HAITI
DOMINICAN REPUBLIC

BELIZE
GUATEMALA
HONDURAS
EL SALVADOR
NICARAGUA
COSTA RICA
PANAMA

JAMAICA
PUERTO RICO

Caribbean Sea

TRINIDAD & TOBAGO

VENEZUELA
GUYANA
SURINAME
FRENCH GUIANA

COLOMBIA

GALÁPAGOS ISLANDS (ECUADOR)

ECUADOR

PERU

BRAZIL

BOLIVIA

PARAGUAY

Pacific Ocean

Atlantic Ocean

THE BAHAMAS

CUBA
HAITI
DOMINICAN REPUBLIC

ST. KITTS & NEVIS
ANTIGUA & BARBUDA

BELIZE
JAMAICA
HONDURAS
NICARAGUA
OR
COSTA RICA
PANAMA

PUERTO RICO
DOMINICA
ST. LUCIA
GRENADA

Caribbean Sea

BARBADOS
ST. VINCENT & THE GRENADINES
TRINIDAD & TOBAGO

VENEZUELA

GUYANA
SURINAME
FRENCH GUIANA

COLOMBIA

ECUADOR

PERU

BRAZIL

PITCAIRN IS. (UNITED KINGDOM)

Caribbean
Part of North America, the Caribbean includes thousands of islands and has 13 independent states. The United Nations classes another 12 territories as dependent, which means they are still under the control or administration of other nations.

CHILE
ARGENTINA
URUGUAY

South America
There are 12 independent nations in South America. Nearly half of the population of the continent lives in Brazil

FALKLAND ISLANDS (UNITED KINGDOM)

EXPERT CONSULTANT: Jeremy Crampton **SEE ALSO:** Age of Exploration, p.298–99; New Empires, p.304–05; Age of Revolutions, p.310–11; World War II, p.324–25; Decolonization, p.328–29

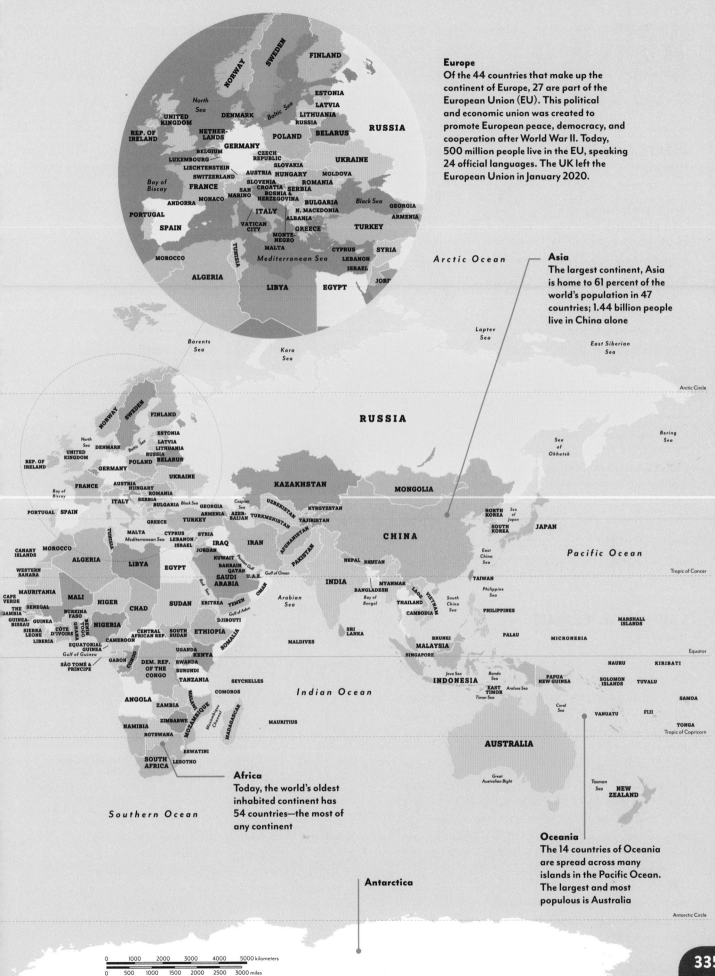

Europe
Of the 44 countries that make up the continent of Europe, 27 are part of the European Union (EU). This political and economic union was created to promote European peace, democracy, and cooperation after World War II. Today, 500 million people live in the EU, speaking 24 official languages. The UK left the European Union in January 2020.

Asia
The largest continent, Asia is home to 61 percent of the world's population in 47 countries; 1.44 billion people live in China alone

Africa
Today, the world's oldest inhabited continent has 54 countries—the most of any continent

Oceania
The 14 countries of Oceania are spread across many islands in the Pacific Ocean. The largest and most populous is Australia

Antarctica

CINDY ERMUS
Historian

What is surprising about your field?

There are so many surprises in history! For example, did you know that one famous scientist named Tycho Brahe lost his nose in a duel and had to wear a fake nose for the rest of his life?

What do you enjoy about your work?

Being a historian is fun because it is a lot like being a detective. You have to figure out what happened in the past by putting together evidence that you collect from old letters, diaries, books, newspapers, objects, and all kinds of materials. You also get to learn about the crazy things that have happened in the past. Studying history is important, because it shows us how we got to the present. History is filled with important lessons we can carry into the future.

ETANA H. DINKA
Historian

What is your area of research?

I study African history, especially the historical processes that gave rise to modern states, economies, societies, and politics. My research focus has been imperial Ethiopia, its making and survival, and its place in African history. Engaging with these themes is vital because it helps us better understand the history of humanity.

What do you enjoy about your work?

It is fascinating because historians observe how the present has come about, and have the privilege to shape how the past is understood. It requires hard work, and rigorous, sustained study for historians to serve as a bridge between the past and the present. I enjoy this mix.

TAYMIYA R. ZAMAN
Historian

What do you want to discover most?

I love reading what people from the past wrote, but usually, being able to write is something only powerful and educated people were able to do. I'm interested in how we study the lives of people who were not able to write about themselves. For instance, instead of leaving behind books, women sometimes passed down stories orally to their grandchildren, stitched quilts that remain in their family a hundred years later, or they leave behind silence, and we only know they existed because they appear as a line or two in someone else's book.

What is surprising about your field?

It's always unexpected when we can relate to someone from the past. One of my favorite people from history

is Bābur, the founder of the Mughal Empire. He got homesick while traveling, felt embarrassed around his first crush, and judged other people for writing bad poetry. At the same time, he lived in a world in which you could be crowned king at the age of 12, command an army as a teenager, and be seen as divine by the people you ruled.

Modern Times
THE QUIZ

1) The Christian kings of Ethiopia traced their families back to which Biblical figure?
   a. Moses
   b. Solomon
   c. David
   d. Abraham

2) The Ashanti Kingdom first existed in which African country?
   a. Mali
   b. Morocco
   c. Ghana
   d. Tanzania

3) Which European explorer died fighting indigenous people in the Philippines?
   a. Ferdinand Magellan
   b. Christopher Columbus
   c. Hernán Cortés
   d. Francisco Pizarro

4) Koh-i-Noor is a famous Indian:
   a. Diamond
   b. Palace
   c. Statue
   d. Mosque

5) Which Mughal emperor ordered the building of the Taj Mahal?
   a. Akbar the Great
   b. Bābur
   c. Shah Jahān
   d. Jahāngīr

6) Mughal emperor Akbar the Great owned how many elephants?
   a. 101
   b. 201
   c. 301
   d. 401

7) What is the name of the famous ship that first took English settlers to Plymouth, Massachusetts?
   a. *The Golden Hind*
   b. *The Cutty Sark*
   c. *The Mayflower*
   d. *The Flower Pot*

8) Which of the following years is often referred to as the Year of Revolutions?
   a. 1812
   b. 1830
   c. 1848
   d. 1918

9) Which country was the world's first independent black republic?
   a. Brazil
   b. Liberia
   c. Kenya
   d. Haiti

10) In 1816, French doctor René Laënnec invented the world's first:
   a. Stethoscope
   b. Syringe
   c. Anesthetic
   d. Anti-snoring device

11) The Croix de Guerre, one of France's highest military medals, was awarded to which animal for its service during World War I?
   a. Dog
   b. Carrier pigeon
   c. Elephant
   d. Horse

12) Which country was the first to give women the right to vote?
   a. Mexico
   b. Germany
   c. New Zealand
   d. Japan

13) Walt Disney's Mickey Mouse first appeared in which film?
   a. *The Birthday Party*
   b. *Steamboat Willie*
   c. *Magician Mickey*
   d. *Mr. Mouse Takes a Trip*

14) In 2018, which US company became the first to be worth more than $1 trillion?
   a. Microsoft
   b. Apple
   c. Facebook
   d. Amazon.com

ANSWERS: 1) b, 2) c, 3) a, 4) a, 5) c, 6) a, 7) c, 8) c, 9) d, 10) a, 11) b, 12) c, 13) b, 14) b

In the more than 50 years since robots started to replace human workers in factories, their uses—and their abilities—have exploded. We now have self-driving vacuum cleaners, remote-control surgery, and even digital assistants that use artificial intelligence to help us live our lives.

CHAPTER 8
TODAY & TOMORROW

At last we are here—in the familiar world that surrounds us today. Our precious planet, home to almost 8 billion people, is studded with giant cities. Satellites orbit Earth, providing us with constant connectivity. The Internet connects more than 4 billion people daily for their news, shopping, and entertainment. And researchers continually find new ways for us to live longer and healthier lives.

But such advances have come at a cost. Our thirst for everything from cars and planes to high fashion have led to plastic waste, a shortage of fresh water, and rising inequality. We are witnessing a mass extinction, our climate is warming, and our interconnected world makes the perfect breeding ground for an age-old human enemy—disease.

And so we meet, face to face, our greatest Known Unknown. What will the future hold? Will governments and scientists be able to protect us from future pandemics? Could engineers halt climate change? Perhaps it will be your generation who finds a way for both humans and the rest of Earth's precious creatures to thrive far into the future.

ONE WORLD

The global population continues to rise, from
1 billion people in 1800 to 7.5 billion today, putting
pressure on the resources of our planet. Today, we
are more connected than people have ever been.
The Internet makes it easy to communicate with
other Internet users anywhere, in an instant. Trade
flourishes across national borders. Different cultures
and people can mix easily, and ideas and resources
are often shared. However, in our interconnected
world, problems such as disease can spread across
continents quickly, too.

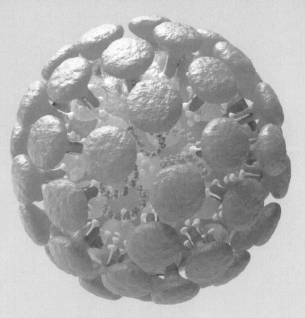

Pandemics

Infectious diseases, such as those caused by viruses, can
spread rapidly. A disease that spreads across large regions
of the globe, as COVID-19 did starting in 2019, is called a
pandemic. Governments may try to stop pandemics by testing
individuals, tracing the contacts of individual cases, and
closing borders and places where people socialize. In 2020,
the Chinese government built two new hospitals in less than
12 days to treat COVID-19 patients. Huoshenshan Hospital
(below) was built in Wuhan, the center of the outbreak.

International effort

Chinese scientists sequenced and shared the
gene sequence of the COVID-19 virus in January
2020. Scientists across the world were then able
to study the virus.

Dozens of backhoes
clear the ground for the
Huoshenshan Hospital

Millions of people
watched the
hospital being built
on live video feeds

EXPERT CONSULTANT: Charlotte Greenbaum **SEE ALSO:** Classifying Life, p.152–53; The Human Body, p.198–99; DNA & Genetics, p.200–01;
World Political Map, p.334–35; Anything, Anywhere, p.342–43; The Internet, p.356–57, The Media, p.358–59; Environmental Challenges, p.366–67

Multinational corporations

As the world has become more connected, some companies have grown to become what are known as multinational corporations. McDonald's is one of them. It is in more than 110 countries and is one of the most recognizable brands in the world. Although this sign is in Arabic, even someone who could not read Arabic would instantly recognize the golden arches.

Seeing the world

People travel for many reasons. Some are seeking sunshine in the middle of winter; others are visiting foreign cities and historic sites. Budget airlines have made flying more affordable, and domestic and international tourism has become big business.

Communication

Over 50 percent of the people in the world use the Internet. Through social media and apps, we can connect with people in other countries at the touch of a button. Video calls let us talk to people in other countries face to face without even leaving the house. Broadband has allowed Internet speeds to increase, making it possible to download ever larger files, movies, and games. But there is still work to be done to ensure that everyone has access to the Internet.

GAME CHANGER

STEVE JOBS
Entrepreneur, lived 1955–2011
US

Computer innovator Steve Jobs started Apple Inc. and helped popularize the personal computer. The launch of the touch-screen iPhone in 2007, Apple's version of the smartphone, a combination of a mobile phone and a computer with wireless Internet access, transformed how people communicated. Apple went on to become one of the most successful companies in the world.

Total world population

Graph: Billions of people (0–11) versus Year (1800–2100)

Human population growth

The number of humans on Earth has grown rapidly in the last two centuries. Better medical knowledge and living conditions have caused people around the world to thrive. However, population growth can lead to overcrowding, which puts a strain on resources like food, water, and electricity. Population scientists estimate that the world's population will stop rising and stabilize in 2100, peaking at about 11 billion.

ANYTHING, ANYWHERE

Countries sell goods and raw materials to one another. This is called international trade. Huge container ships like this one move billions of tons of cargo around the world every year. They load and unload at deep water ports with large storage areas. The invention of the shipping container, a rectangular box the size of a bus that contains the goods being transported, has made shipping faster and cheaper. Containers are easy to move between a ship and trucks and trains. There are more than 5,000 container ships in the world.

Shipping containers are moved from the dock to a ship by huge cranes. A container ship needs only about 20 crew members

About 11 percent of all the goods shipped by sea are carried in containers

At any given time, there are over 20 million shipping containers at sea

The engines can be 56 feet (17 meters) high (as tall as three giraffes) and are 1,000 times more powerful than a car engine

The containers are filled with goods, from food to televisions. Each container can weigh 30 tons—that's as much as five elephants. They are stacked on top of one another

Some containers are refrigerated and used to transport food such as fruit and vegetables

Lost at sea

In 1992, a container of plastic bath toys fell into the Pacific Ocean on the way from China to the US. Ocean currents carried the 28,000 toys, which included yellow ducks like this one, as well as red beavers, blue turtles, and green frogs, around the world. Over many years, some floated as far south as Australia, others across the Arctic to the coast of Maine and even west to Scotland.

Containers are stored in the hull, too. They slot into internal structures to stop them from moving too much when a ship is at sea

A shipping container can hold 8,000 shoeboxes. This means that the biggest ships could deliver a new pair of shoes for every person in Germany in one shipment

INEQUALITY

Not everyone in the world has access to the world's resources. In the poorest countries, many children are not able to stay in school or receive a good education, and some live in crowded conditions without access to clean drinking water. Even in wealthy countries, where most people have enough to live on, some earn very little. And income is not equally shared: 1 percent of adults own over 40 percent of the world's wealth.

Rich and poor

Some poor people live in rich countries, and some rich people live in poor countries. This photograph of São Paulo in Brazil shows fancy apartments with swimming pools next to crowded shantytowns, or favelas, whose houses have tin roofs. Some of those living in favelas don't have access to running water or electricity.

EXPERT CONSULTANT: Charlotte Greenbaum **SEE ALSO:** Education, p.230–231; Civil Rights, p.330–31; New Tensions, New Hopes, p.332–33; One World, p.340–41; The Mega Rich, p.352–53; Cities, p.354–55; Environmental Challenges, p.366–67; Stopping Climate Change, p.374–75

Equal pay for equal work

Men and women don't always get paid the same rate for their work. This is true even for tennis stars like Serena Williams and Roger Federer. Throughout modern history, women have typically earned less than men, even when they are performing the same roles. In the US, women earn on average only about 80 percent of what men earn. This is called the gender gap. It is gradually closing. Some countries, including Denmark and Norway, have come up with laws to help reduce the pay gap between men and women.

Access to health care

People in richer countries like the US have access to better health care than those in poorer countries. However, medical care in the US is expensive, and many people have trouble getting affordable care, unless they go to a free clinic (right). About 1 in 12 Americans didn't have health insurance in 2018. In some countries, such as the UK, most health care is publicly funded by taxes and delivered free to residents, whether rich or poor.

Water inequality

Many people in the world don't have access to clean water. In India, over 90 million people lack access to safe drinking water—more than in any other country. And four in ten people in India don't have a toilet they can use. This lack of sanitation facilities risks water becoming contaminated and diseases spreading. Studies suggest that access to basic resources such as water will get even harder due to climate change.

The task of fetching water often falls on women in India

A bucket is lowered down a well

Global poverty

About 10 percent of the world's population lives on less than $1.90 a day, the price of two candy bars in the US. Nearly half the people in the world live on less than $5.50 per day. However, since 1990, 35 percent fewer people in the world are living in extreme poverty.

FEEDING THE WORLD

Most people on our planet depend on farmers to provide food. But with 7.6 billion people on Earth, making sure there is enough food for everyone is challenging. More than 820 million people do not have enough food to eat, and this figure could rise. The world produces enough food for everyone, but we waste about one-third of it—in the process of transporting or storing it, and also in our homes. It is vital that we stop wasting food, but we also need to explore new sources of food as well as alternative ways of farming.

Insect eating

Humans have eaten insects throughout history. Globally about 2 billion people eat them regularly. Edible insects such as mealworms (below) are nutritious and can be farmed in large numbers. Eating insects might not appeal to us all, but they can be tasty. People say roasted mealworms have a nutty flavor, while crickets are like popcorn.

Keeping seeds safe

What would happen if some crops died out because of disease or nuclear war? How would people survive? The answer could be the Global Seed Vault in Norway that contains more than a million varieties of seeds, from corn to tomatoes. Deep inside a mountain, the vault stores the world's largest frozen collection of crop varieties.

Meat and dairy

Many of us get essential protein in our diet from meat and dairy products, but farming animals can be bad for the environment. Cows, for example, emit large amounts of methane when they pass gas and burp. Methane is a greenhouse gas that traps heat and causes global warming. If we ate less meat and reared fewer cows, we could reduce greenhouse gases and help stop climate change. For example, if every person in the US ate one fewer burger a week for a year, it would have a similar effect to taking 10 million cars off the road.

A single cow can produce up to 400 lbs (180 kg) of methane a year

EXPERT CONSULTANT: Melissa Petruzzello **SEE ALSO:** The Atmosphere, p.86–87; Climate, p.92–93; Food & Cooking, p.208–09; Inequality, p.344–45; Powering the Planet, p.348–49; Cities, p.354–55; Environmental Challenges, p.366–67; The Effects of Climate Change, p.372–73

How to Feed the Planet
LISTIFIED.

To keep the whole world fed, we need to develop more efficient methods of farming and producing food. These innovative technologies could help us achieve that goal.

1. Vertical farming Growing food in vertically stacked layers means we can produce more while using less space. This method is useful when land is not available or suitable for growing. It is also good for urban farming, where, for example, high-rise buildings can be used to grow fruit and vegetables.

2. Connected cows Farmers can remotely keep track of the well-being of their cows by attaching sensors to their bodies. For example, a sensor on a cow's ankle tells the farmer if the animal is walking too little or too much.

3. Smart farming Self-driving tractors, drones that monitor crops, and machines that accurately measure seed portions are all ways technology can make farming more productive.

4. Greenhouse technology Growers can control climate conditions inside high-tech greenhouses using artificial light and automated growing systems. This technology increases crop yield and speed of growth.

Meat substitutes

Plant-based burgers (above) with the taste and texture of meat are becoming popular. Such meat substitutes are part of the effort to produce food without harming the environment or animals. Scientists are also working on growing meat in laboratories. They grow animal cells in a bioreactor to produce lab-grown meat.

KNOWN UNKNOWN

How can we feed everyone on the planet?

About 60 percent of all calories consumed come from four staple crops—rice (right), wheat, corn, and soy. To feed everybody, we need to grow crops that can adapt to the changing climate, provide better food storage from farm to table, and not waste food at home.

Cow burps contain more methane than gas from the other end

347

ARCTIC OCEAN

GREENLAND

NORTH AMERICA

London, UK

New York, New York, US

Lisbon,
Portugal

Los Angeles, California, US

Atlanta, Georgia, US

NORTH
ATLANTIC
OCEAN

Honolulu,
Hawaii, US

Mexico City,
Mexico

Georgetown, Guyana

PACIFIC OCEAN

AMAZON
RAIN FOREST

SOUTH AMERICA

Rio de Janeiro, Brazil

Santiago, Chile

Buenos Aires, Argentina

SOUTH
ATLANTIC
OCEAN

SOUTHERN OCEAN

POWERING THE PLANET

This view of our planet at night shows places that have electricity.
From space, we can see that densely populated areas have more
light. Other places are darker because very few people live there—the
Amazon Rain Forest and Siberia, for example. Another reason some
areas look dark is because their supply of electricity is limited. That is
because some countries do not have the money to build power stations
and run electricity cables to people's homes. The Sahara and Antarctica
look pale because they are reflecting moonlight.

EXPERT CONSULTANT: Erik Gregersen **SEE ALSO:** The Sun, p24–25; Energy, p.122–23; Inequality, p.344–45; Cities, p.354–55; The Internet, p.356–57;
Environmental Challenges, p.366–67

ARCTIC OCEAN

EUROPE

SIBERIA

— Moscow, Russia

— Warsaw, Poland

Paris, France

ASIA

Rome, Italy

Beijing, China — [

— Tokyo, Japan

Jerusalem

Cairo, Egypt —

Delhi, India —

— Hong Kong, China

SAHARA

— Mecca, Saudi Arabia

AFRICA

Bangkok, Thailand

— Manila, Philippines

CONGO
BASIN

INDIAN
OCEAN

Jakarta, Indonesia —

PACIFIC OCEAN

AUSTRALIA

— Johannesburg, South Africa

Perth, Australia —

Sydney,
Australia

— Cape Town, South Africa

SOUTHERN OCEAN

ANTARCTICA

Solar-powered lights

Almost 1 billion people don't have electricity.
Seven out of ten people in Africa, for
example, live without electricity. One
solution is to harness solar power.
Global nonprofit organization Little Sun
produces lamps that store power from
the Sun in the day and light up at night.
The lamps don't require an electrical
outlet to work. That means people
without access to power can still have
some light when it gets dark.

MODERN WARFARE

The armies of wealthy and powerful countries use increasingly advanced technology to gain the upper hand in military conflicts. Satellites, drones, and advanced weapons have transformed the modern battlefield. There is also a new type of warfare, cyber war, in which nations use computers to attack other countries, perhaps by stealing military secrets or spreading false information. Cyber attacks on large private companies or government networks can damage an organization or even a whole country.

The drone is fitted with a camera and can send images back to base

This drone is a Tarantula Hawk. It can lift off vertically—straight up from the ground

This drone is light enough to be carried in a backpack

The drone's legs

Drone warfare

Drones are small vehicles that are operated remotely without a person inside them. They include devices such as unmanned aerial vehicles (UAVs), which fly over distant targets and fire missiles. People can control drones from bases that might be thousands of miles away. Soldiers use smaller drones (pictured) for aerial surveillance—viewing a large area from the air. Combat drones are sometimes used to target individual people without a soldier needing to enter the battlefield.

Soldiers can use drones as an extra eye to help spot concealed explosive devices

Fleeing war

There are about 26 million refugees in the world—people who have had to leave their homes, often because of war. They include 6 million people who fled the war in Syria. Many refugees will never be able to go home. In 2017, the Myanmar army attacked the Rohingya Muslims, driving them out of the country. In this photograph, Rohingya refugees mark the second anniversary of the violence, with a ceremony at a refugee camp in Bangladesh.

Satellites can spy on other satellites by flying near them

A laser could target a satellite and push it into our atmosphere to burn up

Satellites can be used to take images of the ground

Space warfare

Today, some satellites are used by one country to spy on another country. But with space warfare, the satellites could themselves become targets. If satellites were destroyed, it could have big impacts on Earth. We rely on satellites for services such as GPS and beaming TV signals and phone calls around the world.

Asymmetrical warfare

If a less well-equipped or smaller army fights a more advanced army, it is known as asymmetrical warfare. The smaller army might have to use older weapons such as this Kalashnikov rifle. To try and beat a strong opponent, the smaller army might resort to tactics like terrorism or guerrilla warfare, such as ambushing soldiers.

Famine as a weapon

Sometimes an army will attack food supplies to try to win a war. This often happens in civil wars—a war between different groups in a country. Limiting the amount of food available to people can lead to starvation. In Yemen (right), hunger has been used to try to stop people from supporting rebels. These people are waiting for food aid.

THE MEGA RICH

A small number of people in the world have a great deal of wealth. In fact, over 40 percent of the world's wealth is owned by just 1 percent of people on the planet. This creates great inequality. Many very rich people show off their wealth by buying fast cars, yachts, mansions, and other expensive goods, but some wealthy people use their money to help other people. This is known as "philanthropy."

The billionaires

The world has over 2,000 billionaires—people whose personal wealth is more than $1 billion. The US and China have the most. Kylie Jenner became a billionaire through her cosmetics company when she was just 21 years old. The world's oldest billionaire is Chang Yun Chung, originally from China, who is over 100 years old and the founder of a Singaporean shipping company.

Kylie Jenner was worth about $1 billion in 2020

Kylie Jenner wears a designer dress by Versace. Her jewels, diamond and purple sapphire earrings and rings, were worth $4.9 million

The Richest People on Earth
LISTIFIED.

Rich people earn their money in different ways. Here are the world's ten richest people (2020).

1. Jeff Bezos The founder of the online company Amazon.com is worth more than $143 billion.

2. Bill Gates Microsoft's cofounder gives away a lot of his $105 billion through the Bill & Melinda Gates Foundation.

3. Bernard Arnault The owner of many fashion brands, including Louis Vuitton, is worth $94 billion.

4. Warren Buffett This investor and philanthropist is said to be worth about $75 billion.

5. Larry Ellison The cofounder of the computer software firm Oracle is worth $68 billion. He is now the company's chief technology officer.

6. Mark Zuckerberg The cofounder and CEO of Facebook, Zuckerberg is worth about $66 billion.

7. Amancio Ortega One of the richest people in Europe, this fashion retailer is worth about $65 billion.

8. Steve Ballmer The former CEO of the computer company Microsoft is worth $64 billion.

9. Larry Page The cofounder of Google is worth $58 billion. Along with Sergey Brin, he invented the algorithm the search engine uses.

10. Jim Walton The youngest son of Walmart founder Sam Walton, he is worth $58 billion.

EXPERT CONSULTANT: Silvana Tenreyro **SEE ALSO:** Dress & Decoration, p.210–11; Money, p.226–27; Ancient Greece, p.268–69; The Rise of Communism, p.320–21; Boom & Bust, p.322–23; Inequality, p.344–45; The Media, p.358–59; Smart Tech & AI, p.364–65

Philanthropy

Some wealthy people give away money to good causes. For example, Bill Gates and his wife, Melinda Gates, have donated billions of dollars toward tackling poverty and improving health care, including coronavirus research. One project they are funding is an effort to rid the world of malaria. The disease is spread by mosquitoes and kills hundreds of thousands of people each year. In addition to health care, their foundation also funds education, both in the developing world and in the form of scholarships to students in the US.

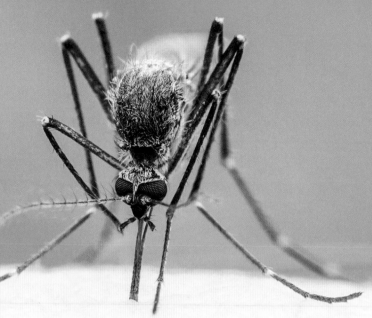

Solid gold

This gold toilet with a bulletproof seat, studded with 40,000 diamonds, was on display at a trade fair in Shanghai in 2019. Buying things to show off how much money you have is called conspicuous consumption. A gold toilet, a luxury car, or a diamond-studded pet collar are all ways to display one's status in society.

FACTastic!

It would take 200 years for the average US worker to earn enough to become a billionaire. To look at it another way, many of the super rich earn the average yearly salary of $50,000 in less than a minute.

Live like a millionaire

Some people who become very rich like to buy supercars or—even more expensive—hypercars. The Bugatti La Voiture Noire, pictured here, is a hypercar. Costing $18.7 million, it is one of the most expensive cars ever built. Often such expensive cars are just a show of wealth, or bought as an investment. They won't be driven very far.

CITIES

Cities are large, built-up places where people from many different backgrounds live and work closely together. More than half of the world's population lives in a city or urban area. Living in a city has advantages. There are more jobs, schools, shops, and cultural activities than in smaller towns and villages. Cities also have better public or mass transportation networks. But urban areas are more polluted than the countryside and can be dangerous. By 2050, two-thirds of the world's population will live in cities.

Urban sprawl

Below, you can see what the city of Manchester, England, looks like from an airplane. Many cities spread out from their centers into the surrounding area. This is called urban sprawl. Large numbers of people live in these outer areas, often known as suburbs. To get into the main city, they need to drive or take buses, subways, or trains.

Air pollution

Air pollution contains tiny particles that get into your lungs and can cause health problems. Road vehicles are the key cause of air pollution in London. The UK capital now uses electric double-decker buses (right) to help improve its air quality. The world's most polluted city is Ghaziabad in India. Air pollution kills more than a million people every year in India as a whole.

EXPERT CONSULTANT: Shauna Brail **SEE ALSO:** Fossil Fuels, p.80–81; The Atmosphere, p.86–87; Climate, p.92–93; Combustion, p.108–09; Nonmetals, p.116–17; Urban Wildlife, p.188–89; The Industrial Revolution, p.314–15; One World, p.340–41; Environmental Challenges, p.366–67

Skyscrapers

Very tall buildings are known as skyscrapers. They are often used as offices, where large numbers of people can work. Some of them are apartment buildings. Seoul, the capital city of South Korea, has more buildings over 12 stories high than any other city in the world. With 123 floors, the Lotte World Tower (left) rises above all the other tall buildings, but it is actually only the world's fifth-tallest building. The world's tallest skyscraper (at the moment) is the Burj Khalifa in Dubai, which is 2,717 feet (828 meters) tall.

Greenest Cities
LISTIFIED.
. . . .

Although many of the world's cities are crowded, their governments are taking steps to make them greener and more environmentally friendly. This can improve the health of everyone living in or near a city.

1. Copenhagen The capital of Denmark, this city has more bicycles in it than cars. It plans to become the world's first carbon-neutral capital city by 2025.

2. Curitiba This "green" city in Brazil recycles about 70 percent of all its waste to make new products or reusable energy.

3. Reykjavik This city in Iceland plans to stop using any fossil fuels, such as oil and coal, by 2050. It will do this by tapping into geothermal energy (heat energy from within the Earth) to supply the city's power.

4. Singapore This Asian country's capital city has many gardens, with some on top of buildings. One park has futuristic "supertrees"—vertical gardens that grow on huge frames shaped like trees.

5. Vancouver In this eco-friendly Canadian city, 90 percent of electricity comes from renewable sources, making it very clean. It has many green parks, too.

Crowded cities

Tokyo is the most populated metropolitan area in the world today, with more than 38.5 million people. But Japan's capital isn't actually the most crowded city. Tokyo has about 12,000 people per square mile (6,000 people per sq. km). This is its population density. Dhaka in Bangladesh is much more crowded. Its population density is more than nine times that of Tokyo.

Some of the world's most crowded cities

Approximate number of people per square mile

City	People per square mile
Dhaka, Bangladesh	106,300
Mogadishu, Somalia	73,000
Surat, India	70,900
Mumbai, India	69,500
Hong Kong, China	67,600

THE INTERNET

The Internet is a huge global connection of computers. Its invention toward the end of the 20th century changed the world. Being able to share information instantly and inexpensively transformed how people communicate, do business, and socialize. In many countries, people now spend large parts of their day online—buying and selling items, researching information, streaming shows and movies, playing games, and talking to friends.

World Wide Web

What's the difference between the the Internet and the World Wide Web (WWW)? The "Internet" is a term that describes the vast network of computers around the world that are all connected to one another, some of them by fiber-optic cables shown here as networks of light. "World Wide Web" refers to the website pages and apps you use to view things on the Internet.

EXPERT CONSULTANT: Erik Gregersen **SEE ALSO:** Artificial Satellites, p.40–41; The Media, p.358–59; Smart Tech & AI, p.364–65

The Internet
TIMELINE

1969 Early Internet begins with the ARPANET (Advanced Research Projects Agency Network). It is developed by the US military as a way for their computers to connect and communicate with each other.

1973 Different networks of computers in different countries are linked together, creating a truly global Internet.

1982 Phone lines allow networks in different countries to communicate.

1985 The first ".com" website is registered.

1991 The World Wide Web is unveiled, allowing people to view and share information on the Internet more easily.

1995 Amazon.com is founded, followed by Google in 1998 and Facebook in 2004.

2020 Around 4.5 billion people (more than half the world's population) have access to the Internet.

GAME CHANGER

TIM BERNERS-LEE
Computer scientist, born 1955 UK

In 1989, British computer scientist Tim Berners-Lee came up with an idea—then called the World Wide Web (W3)—to share information between universities and institutes. It was developed at CERN in Switzerland, the world's largest center for scientific research. The Web introduced "websites" to the world—groups of interlinked Web pages made available online by an individual or organization.

The digital divide

About three billion people in the world don't have access to the Internet. Steps are being taken to increase access to the Internet, such as installing more cables in the ground to connect different places. The people who live in Supai at the bottom of the Grand Canyon (right) were not connected until 2019. Towers on the rim of the canyon beam a signal down, allowing people in Supai Village to go online.

A minute on the Internet

This diagram shows Internet activity across the world during just one minute in 2019. Social media services such as Twitter and Instagram and entertainment channels like YouTube and Netflix now account for a large part of our time on the Internet.

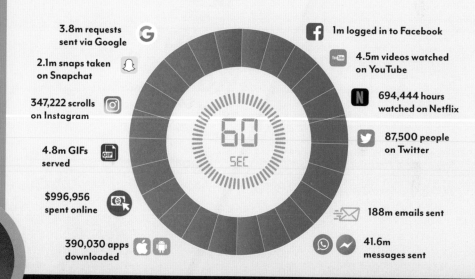

3.8m requests sent via Google

2.1m snaps taken on Snapchat

347,222 scrolls on Instagram

4.8m GIFs served

$996,956 spent online

390,030 apps downloaded

60 SEC

1m logged in to Facebook

4.5m videos watched on YouTube

694,444 hours watched on Netflix

87,500 people on Twitter

188m emails sent

41.6m messages sent

Space Internet

Several companies such as SpaceX are launching satellites that will beam Internet to the ground from space using radio waves. The idea is for large constellations of hundreds or thousands of satellites to surround Earth so that anyone, anywhere, can connect to the Internet. However, there are concerns about the project. For example, such a large number of satellites could collide with each other in orbit.

A vast satellite network would surround the Earth

THE MEDIA

Media is how we get news, information, and entertainment. It includes newspapers, magazines, TV, and video games, as well as apps and virtual reality. We interact with the media almost every day by reading articles, talking to friends on social media, or watching our favorite shows. YouTube is an example of online media; radio, books, and even billboards are examples of media we find off-line.

Headlines

Be wary if a headline uses language that makes you feel emotional or makes a promise that sounds too good to be true. Do you think it is likely that a wombat would rescue another animal? Do some research and see if you can find another source for this information before you believe it.

Quality

Be wary if the article contains spelling mistakes, slang, all capital letters, or odd punctuation. Online publishers have editors who make sure the article is written with correct grammar and makes sense.

Who wrote it?

If the author's name is given, you can find out what qualifies them to write the article. There might be a few words about them next to the article. If not, you can use a search engine to research the author and find out more about them and see what else they have written. You can learn if they are objective or biased.

Photography

Be wary if the photo looks strange and unnatural. Have you ever seen an animal with pink fur? Do some research and find other pictures of the same subject. Is this a real photo or has it been changed in some way? Responsible Web sources do not fake their photos.

cuddly n' cute

Wombats to the rescue!!!
By Our Secret Source!

Wombats save cute little animals from bushfires by herding them into their burrows. Awww!!!! Dontcha just love wombaaaats!

The only news you'll ever need!
www.cuddlyncutenews.com

Check the facts

Some Web articles say where their information comes from or give links to their sources. If the site doesn't provide this information, use a search engine to check any facts that make you suspicious.

Misinformation

Not everything you read online is true. Some news stories are false by accident. Other news stories are written on purpose to trick people into believing them. Sometimes people or organizations want to influence you, perhaps so that you will buy a product they are selling. Thinking critically about information is always important, but take extra care with online sources.

The Web address

Be wary if the Web address, known as a URL, doesn't sound serious or is one you have never heard of. Look for a link to an About Us page to find out more about who is providing the information. The site should tell you its address, who funds it, and what its purpose is.

EXPERT CONSULTANT: Heaven Taylor-Wynn **SEE ALSO:** Reading & Writing, p.218–19; Education, p.230–31; The Internet p.356–57; Smart Tech & AI, p.364–65

Print Media Firsts
LISTIFIED.

Print media includes books, newspapers, and magazines. For centuries, these were the most popular ways to read the news. Digital media is changing that.

1. The printing press is invented in about 1440 by Johannes Gutenberg in Germany. It allows many copies to be printed quickly.

2. The first news pamphlet is printed in England in 1513. It gives a report of an English victory over Scotland in a battle.

3. The first popular magazine is printed in France in 1672. It features royal news, poems, and stories.

4. The first photograph to be printed in a newspaper appears in a French newspaper in 1848. It shows a Paris street during an uprising.

5. The first full-color daily newspaper, *USA Today*, is printed in the US in 1982.

GAME CHANGER

MARK ZUCKERBERG
Cofounder of Facebook, born 1984 California, US

In 2004, a student at Harvard University—Mark Zuckerberg—came up with a unique way to socialize online with classmates. He called it the Facebook, and it would become the first true global social media platform. Facebook now has more than two billion users, and Mark Zuckerberg is one of the richest and most influential people in the world.

Television

TV is a broadcast media—it is transmitted as a signal over the airwaves. It was developed in the 20th century and remains popular today. By the late 1950s, most American homes had a TV. In 1969, some 600 million people around the world watched the Moon landing live. Today, we can use the Internet to watch TV on smartphones or other devices and choose when to watch programs.

Social media

Most people using social media share photos and information, chat with friends, or watch videos, often on smartphones. Apps like YouTube and Instagram, known as platforms, are huge brands today. This chart shows the average time people across the world spend on each platform per day. In 2019, people spent more time using social media on their phones than watching TV.

Bar chart (minutes):
- Facebook 58 minutes
- Instagram 53 minutes
- YouTube 40 minutes
- Snapchat 35 minutes
- Twitter 3 minutes

Billions of views

In December 2012, "Gangnam Style," a music video made by Korean pop superstar Psy, became the first video to be seen more than a billion times. The "Baby Shark Dance" has also been viewed billions of times. More than 200 videos on YouTube are in the so-called Billion View Club. These videos are examples of how information can spread when it is shared by many people. It's known as going viral.

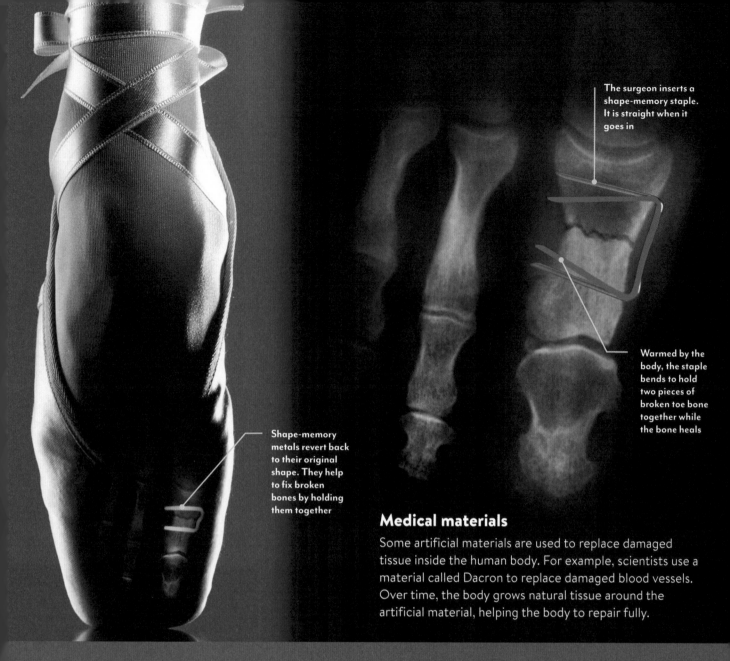

The surgeon inserts a shape-memory staple. It is straight when it goes in

Warmed by the body, the staple bends to hold two pieces of broken toe bone together while the bone heals

Shape-memory metals revert back to their original shape. They help to fix broken bones by holding them together

Medical materials

Some artificial materials are used to replace damaged tissue inside the human body. For example, scientists use a material called Dacron to replace damaged blood vessels. Over time, the body grows natural tissue around the artificial material, helping the body to repair fully.

ARTIFICIAL MATERIALS

Artificial materials are created by humans, often by changing the properties of materials that exist in nature, such as wood, coal, and clay. Plastic is an artificial material made from coal and oil. Other artificial materials include glass, fiberglass, and brick. These strong materials have varied uses. For example, fiberglass is used to make cars and airplanes, while nylon is used in many things from parachutes to the strings of musical instruments.

Soaking up oil

Wood sponge is a recently invented artificial material. The sponge is made from wood, which is treated with chemicals to strip away some of the surface. It then has an oil-attracting coating put on top. This sponge soaks up oil spills in oceans and rivers, protecting wildlife such as birds, whose feathers can become gummed up with oil (left).

EXPERT CONSULTANT: Duncan Davis **SEE ALSO:** Elements, p.102–03; Metals, p.114–15; Plastics, p.118–19; Med Tech, p.362–63; Environmental Challenges, p.366–67

New Materials
LISTIFIED.

Scientists are constantly developing new materials that could change the world. Here are some examples of exciting artificial materials being created today.

1. Carbon nanotube Super-thin graphene is made of carbon atoms. Rolling it into cylinders produces carbon nanotubes—stronger than steel but thinner than hair. They are used in such things as radios and machinery.

2. eGain Most metals are solid at room temperature, but a few, including gallium, are liquid. Gallium is used to make the nontoxic liquid metal eGain. It flows into shapes and conducts electricity, making it ideal for circuitry.

3. Metal foam This is created by making lots of tiny holes, or pores, in a solid metal and filling them with gas. Metal foam is often made using lightweight aluminum. It can be used in buildings for soundproofing and as high-impact absorbers in cars in case of a crash.

4. Metallic glass Freezing liquid metal very rapidly turns it into a material that is much stronger than conventional metals. This tough, stiff material is used in such things as golf clubs and planes.

5. Nitinol When warmed, Nitinol, made from nickel and titanium, returns to its original shape. Doctors use Nitinol in heart implants, and orthodontists use it in braces. It is also used to hold broken bones together while they heal (opposite).

FACTastic!

Scientists discovered graphene with the help of adhesive tape. Graphene is made from carbon. It is very thin and very light, yet it is 200 times stronger than steel. Researchers discovered graphene in an unusual way. They used tape to strip layers of carbon from graphite, the same material that is found in lead pencils. They continued until they had a really thin layer of carbon atoms—graphene.

Kevlar

Bulletproof vests worn by police and soldiers are made of Kevlar. This artificial material is made of fibers, or strands, of a plastic. Meshing these fibers together makes a material so strong that even bullets can't get through it. Kevlar is also thin and is an ideal material for snare drumskins (right).

Kevlar drumskins can be stretched really tightly

Fiberglass

This type of material combines glass fibers, or strands, with plastic. The result is a very strong material for its weight. It is good for both soundproofing and for trapping heat, so it has lots of uses. The fact that it is both strong and lightweight makes it a good material for kayaks.

MED TECH

Modern technology has changed the world of medicine. Doctors increasingly use new technologies to help them detect and treat illness. People also use personal devices and fitness apps to measure their heart rate, sleep patterns, and activities to make sure they are at the levels needed for good health. Scientists are continually inventing new technologies that will help people live longer, healthier lives. Already, robots are performing some delicate surgical procedures, and 3D printing is being used to make artificial body parts.

Keeping track

The most common wearable devices are smart watches and fitness trackers. They can measure how fast your heart is pumping blood around your body. Other wearables can measure things like the movement of your muscles, or even the activity in your brain.

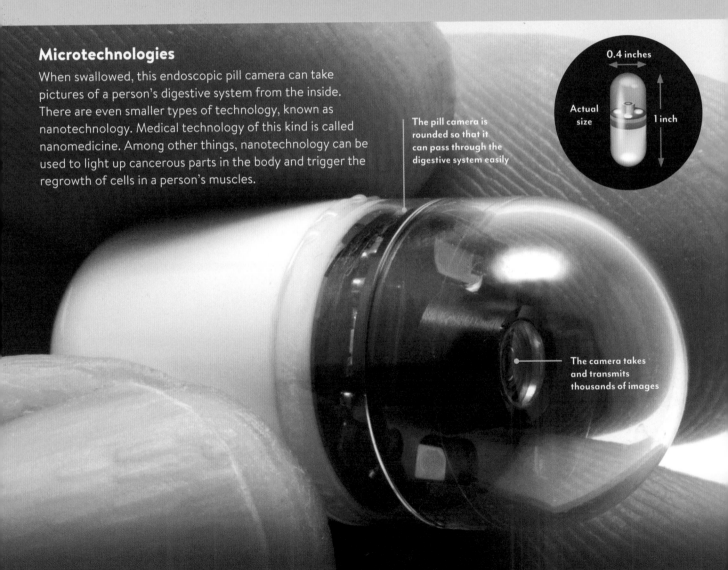

Microtechnologies

When swallowed, this endoscopic pill camera can take pictures of a person's digestive system from the inside. There are even smaller types of technology, known as nanotechnology. Medical technology of this kind is called nanomedicine. Among other things, nanotechnology can be used to light up cancerous parts in the body and trigger the regrowth of cells in a person's muscles.

The pill camera is rounded so that it can pass through the digestive system easily

0.4 inches

Actual size

1 inch

The camera takes and transmits thousands of images

EXPERT CONSULTANT: Mike Jay **SEE ALSO:** The Human Body, p.198–99; The Brain, p.202–03; Medical Milestones, p.312–13; Artificial Materials, p.360–61; Future Humans, p.382–83

Robotic surgery

Lots of different types of surgery are now performed by robots. A doctor, working on a nearby computer, controls the robotic arms. Robotic arms can be more precise than a human hand, helping a medical team perform very delicate procedures. This extra precision can also make it easier for patients to recover after surgery.

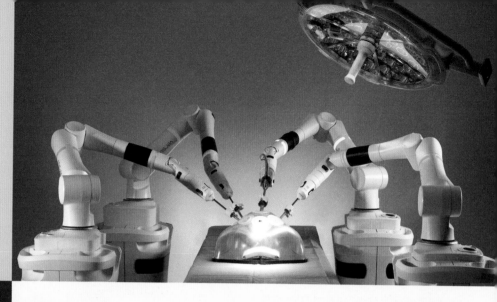

FACTastic!

The first artificial kidneys were adapted from washing machines! Our kidneys filter our blood, ridding it of toxic substances. If the kidneys stop working, people become ill. During World War II, Dutch doctor Willem Kolff noticed that the movement in a washing machine rinsed out stains such as blood. Inspired, he built an artificial kidney, using a washing machine to cleanse blood of waste products. Patients use such machines to do the work of their kidneys.

3D printing

The technique of creating a 3D object by printing lots and lots of layers is known as 3D printing. Instead of paper, it uses materials such as plastic, rubber, and metals. In medicine, 3D printing can be used to make artificial limbs. It can also make artificial organs for surgeons to practice on or to help them plan an operation. In the future, scientists think they will be able to create organs made of human cells.

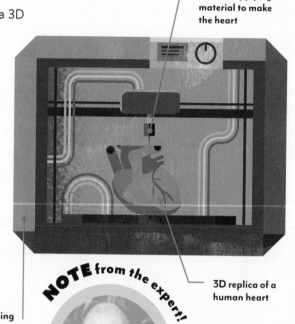

Feeder supplying material to make the heart

3D replica of a human heart

3D printers are becoming more common, as technology becomes cheaper

NOTE from the expert!

KNOWN UNKNOWN

Will we be able to wire human brains to computers in the future?

Some people think humans and machines will one day be connected, and that computers will make us smarter. This idea is being researched by South African engineer Elon Musk's company Neuralink, which hopes to boost the brain power of humans. Not everyone believes that this will work. The human brain is very complex already!

MIKE JAY
Medical historian

Mike Jay is interested in our ideas of the mind and how it works. He believes medicine has been integral to every human society in history and finds it fascinating to discover the different approaches people have taken to curing the sick through the ages.

❝ *Technology has transformed the work of doctors and nurses, but it can't replace them. Healing is an art as well as a science.* ❞

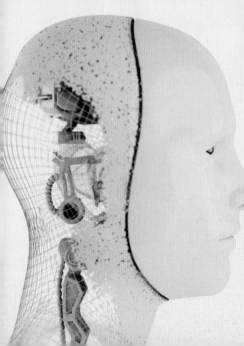

SMART TECH & AI

Smart electronic devices communicate with people and with other machines using Wi-Fi networks. We can command smart machines to perform tasks. These devices include artificial intelligence assistants such as Amazon's Alexa. Artificial intelligence (AI) is the ability of machines to think, learn, and do tasks usually associated with intelligent beings such as humans.

Smart homes

A smart home has a network of devices that communicate with each other. The refrigerator could tell our smartphone that we are low on milk, or the heating system could come on when it detects from our smartphone that we are nearly home. Robot vacuums exist today; in the future, we will have more robotic helpers.

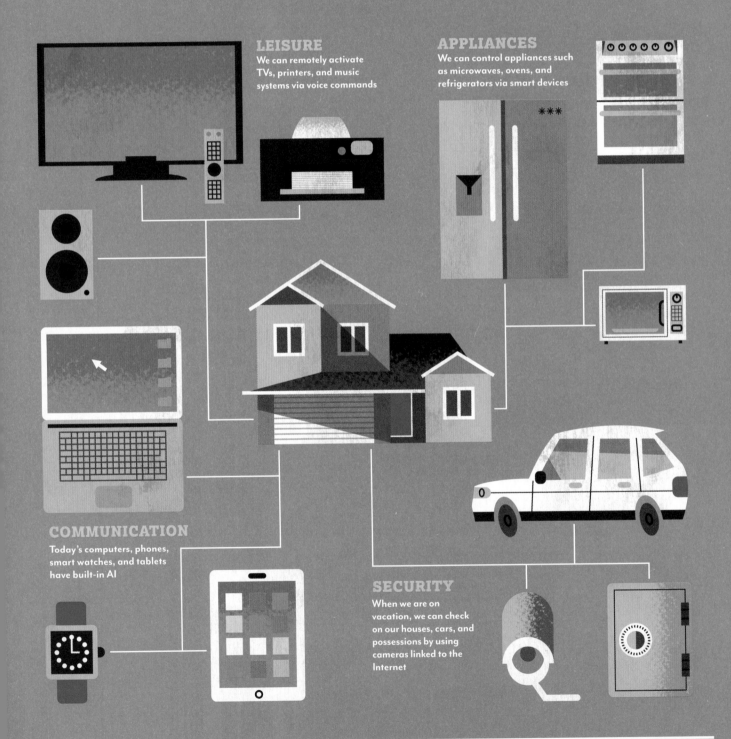

LEISURE
We can remotely activate TVs, printers, and music systems via voice commands

APPLIANCES
We can control appliances such as microwaves, ovens, and refrigerators via smart devices

COMMUNICATION
Today's computers, phones, smart watches, and tablets have built-in AI

SECURITY
When we are on vacation, we can check on our houses, cars, and possessions by using cameras linked to the Internet

EXPERT CONSULTANT: Yingjie Hu **SEE ALSO:** Earth's Riches, p.74–75; Emotions, p.204–05; Modern Warfare, p.350–51; The Internet, p.356–57; Med Tech, p.362–63; Cities of Tomorrow, p.380–81

The Internet of Things
TIMELINE

1990 A researcher develops a "smart toaster" that can be turned on and off over the Internet.

1999 The term Internet of Things (IoT) is used for the first time. IoT is the idea that our everyday devices can be connected to the Internet.

2000 South Korean electronics company LG invents the first "smart refrigerator."

2008 The number of online devices on Earth exceeds the number of humans.

2009 Google starts developing one of the first commercial self-driving cars. Car manufacturers soon follow with work on their own prototypes.

2014 Amazon releases its Echo home smart speaker. It connects to voice-controlled AI assistant Alexa.

2020 Globally, the number of devices connected to the Internet jumps above 20 billion.

Face recognition processing

This technology allows a cell phone or computer to identify a person from a photo or video. It does this by looking at patterns in a person's face and making a map of them. In some countries, the police use facial recognition cameras on streets to help find people who are missing and to track and catch criminals.

GAME CHANGER

RANA EL KALIOUBY
Computer scientist, born 1978 USA

This Egyptian-American computer scientist is a pioneer of AI and smart technology. Her main area is artificial emotional intelligence. This is technology that detects emotions in humans by analyzing or studying their faces. As part of this work, she is creating the world's largest emotion recognition database. So far, her company has examined 4.8 million face videos in 75 countries.

KNOWN UNKNOWN

Could robots ever feel emotions?

Artificial intelligence (AI) is getting smarter and more efficient all the time, but can it feel emotions like a human being? This is something researchers are not sure about at the moment. It would require machines to have thought processes more similar to humans, but those are difficult to create. So while a robot can beat a human at chess or a video game, it might be a while before it gets upset about losing.

ENVIRONMENTAL CHALLENGES

The world today is facing environmental problems caused by human activities and their effects on the planet. Our cities are growing faster than ever, and our activities are contributing to climate change, leading to rising temperatures, changing rainfall patterns, and more intense storms. With the human population set to increase to nearly ten billion people by 2050, pressure on the planet will increase even more.

Drought

Climate change is causing the world's temperature to increase. This has led to extreme weather such as droughts in some countries. Droughts happen when there is insufficient rain for a long time. It causes the ground to dry out and plants to die. Without water, animals and humans struggle to survive. Droughts can also lead to wildfires because dry vegetation burns easily. Wildfires caused by a long drought raged in Australia at the end of 2019 (pictured).

Carbon emissions

Carbon dioxide (CO_2) is a greenhouse gas because it traps heat and warms the planet. Humans produce lots of carbon dioxide, mainly by burning fossil fuels such as coal, oil, and gas. A graph called the Keeling Curve (right) plots the rapidly increasing concentrations of CO_2 in Earth's atmosphere since 1958. The increase mirrors the increase in the use of fossil fuels in the world.

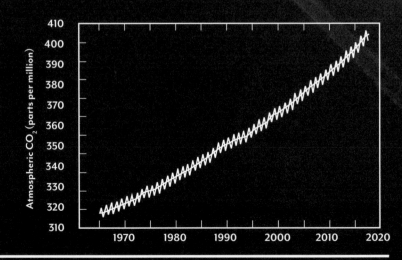

EXPERT CONSULTANT: Nicholas Henshue **SEE ALSO:** Fossil Fuels, p.80–81; The Atmosphere, p.86–87; Climate, p.92–93; Natural Climate Change, p.94–95; Elements, 102–03; Plastics, p.118–19; The Industrial Revolution, p.314–15; The Effects of Climate Change, p.372–73; Stopping Climate Change, p.374–75

Deforestation

Some carbon dioxide is removed from the atmosphere by the leaves of trees and plants that absorb carbon dioxide and give off oxygen that we breathe. When forests are chopped down, known as deforestation, we lose this natural defense against climate change.

Sometimes, trees are cut down illegally, like this timber being transported on a boat in Peru

Methane emissions

Carbon dioxide is not the only greenhouse gas. Another is methane, which is produced by farm animals, landfills, factories, and decomposing plants, and by the soil when permafrost melts. Fossil fuels such as oil also emit methane (right). Methane traps much more heat in the atmosphere than carbon dioxide, although it doesn't stay there as long. Both, however, increase atmospheric temperatures.

Chemical waste

It's not just the atmosphere that's in danger. Activities such as mining can release dangerous chemicals into nearby water sources that can harm animals and humans. Some mining produces sulfuric acid. If this gets into the water supply, it makes the water dangerous to drink.

Pollution from the Rio Tinto copper mine in southern Spain has turned the water orange

Desertification
LISTIFIED.

Human and natural activities are causing some dry areas of land around the world to become desert. This process is called desertification. Here's what is making this happen.

1. Changes in climate As the climate gets warmer, patterns of rainfall change, and there is less rain in some places.

2. Removal of trees When trees are chopped down for fuel, the soil is no longer held together by their roots. New plants will struggle to survive.

3. Excessive cultivation Growing too many crops can take the nutrients out of the soil, making it harder to grow new plants and forcing farmers to abandon old fields for new, unspoiled ones.

4. Overgrazing If animals eat too much vegetation, it can struggle to regrow. Wind and rain then erode the soil, and its quality declines.

5. Population growth As the population of a desert region increases, more people draw on the available water.

Trash

Humans produce lots of trash. Some is recycled, but a lot of it is burned or buried underground in landfill sites. The number of materials that can be recycled is increasing. It is important to follow local recycling rules and the instructions on packaging. Otherwise, items may get mixed up with non-recyclables and end up in a landfill site after all.

EXTINCTION EVENT

When many species of animals die in a short space of time, it is called an extinction event. In Earth's history, we know of five major (mass) extinction events. Each of them wiped out many living things on the planet. Many scientists say we are now facing a sixth major extinction event, caused partly by human activities and the warming climate. They believe extinctions are happening 1,000 times faster than they have for millions of years.

A supreme survivor

This fossil is of a trilobite, a sea creature related to insects, crabs, and spiders. When it emerged, around 525 million years ago, it was the most advanced life form on Earth. Trilobites varied greatly in size, from tiny to more than 18 inches (45 cm) long, weighing up to 10 lb (4.5 kg). They were the most successful early species but were wiped out in the Permian extinction.

Extinction Events
TIMELINE

444 MYA (million years ago) Ordovician A severe ice age caused rapid cooling and a fall in sea level that wiped out about 85 percent of species.

409–359 MYA Devonian About three-quarters of animal species were lost due to a number of factors, including rapid climate change, comet impacts, and nutrient runoff from land that deprived marine species of oxygen.

265–252 MYA Permian In Earth's most deadly extinction, more than 95 percent of sea life and 70 percent of land animals were lost. Causes include warming seas and huge volcanic eruptions that restricted sunlight, killing plants.

201 MYA End Triassic The loss of about 76 percent of Earth's species was perhaps due to climate change and huge volcanic eruptions.

66 MYA Cretaceous-Tertiary (K-T) A meteor or comet hit Earth and set off a chain of events that wiped out the dinosaurs.

Saving endangered populations

Endangered animals—those at high risk of extinction—can be placed in breeding programs to try to increase their numbers. Animals are bred in captivity before being released back into the wild. One successful program involved the California condor. Its numbers rose from 22 in the early 1980s to more than 500 today.

EXPERT CONSULTANT: John P. Rafferty **SEE ALSO:** Fossils, p.76–77; Climate, p.92–93; Natural Climate Change, p.94–95; Bugs, p.160–61; Ecology, p.162–63; The Rain Forest, p.164–65; Shrinking Ice, p.186–87; Endangered, p.370–71; The Effects of Climate Change, p.372–73; Stopping Climate Change, p.374–75

Doomed to extinction?

Humans are largely responsible for some extinctions. For example, hunters killed so many northern white rhinos for their valuable horns that very few animals are left. People also took over the rhinos' African habitat, using the land for farming and building. Now, only two female northern white rhinos remain.

White rhinos were hunted mostly for their horns, which were illegally sold in Asian countries for use in traditional medicines

KNOWN UNKNOWN

Are we experiencing the sixth mass extinction?

With species disappearing faster than ever before, some scientists say we are in an extinction event caused by humans. This is called the Holocene extinction. Extinction events last hundreds or thousands of years, so we still have time to reverse the trend. But we need to act soon.

R.I.P.

Bees under threat

As climate change continues to warm our planet, it has affected many different animals. Bees in particular are struggling with the increased heat. About 90 percent of the world's flowering plants depend on pollinators such as bees, so it is important that we keep them alive for our own survival.

ENDANGERED...
LISTIFIED.

A species at very high risk of extinction is said to be endangered. Climate change and human activities that destroy habitats are often to blame. Today, more than 16,000 species of animals and plants in the world are endangered or critically endangered. Below are some animals at risk of extinction. It is hard to count animals in the wild. The numbers give an idea of how few are left.

1. **Addax** Due to overhunting, fewer than 100 of this antelope remain in Africa's Sahara desert.
2. **Adriatic sturgeon** Fewer than 250 of this species of fish exist in the Adriatic Sea and the Po river in Italy.
3. **Amur leopard** This rare leopard lives in far east Russia and China. Fewer than 60 adults remain.
4. **Chinese alligator** Habitat loss, pollution, and hunting mean that very few of these alligators continue to inhabit China's wetlands. Estimates vary from 86 to 150 alligators.
5. **Cross River gorilla** No more than 250–300 of these gorillas remain in Nigeria and Cameroon. This is due to their forest habitat being cleared for timber and agriculture.
6. **Giant ibis** Fewer than 100 breeding pairs of Cambodia's national bird remain. Hunting and human activity have disturbed their wetland habitat.
7. **Kakapo** This large flightless parrot can live up to 90 years, but only about 211 of them remain in the forests of New Zealand. They are hunted by non-native mammals.
8. **Malayan tiger** Fewer than 250 of this powerful predator survive in Malaysia's tropical forests. Humans hunt them for their body parts, which are used in traditional medicine.
9. **Northern right whale** Scientists estimate only about 300–400 of these whales remain. Many have died as a result of becoming entangled in fishing gear.
10. **Panamanian golden frog** Killed off by disease, these poisonous frogs have not been seen in the wild since 2009.
11. **Saola** The population of this rarely seen, antelope-like mammal found in Vietnam and Laos may be under 100.
12. **Sumatran rhino** Fewer than 80 of these rhinos remain. The biggest threat to them is loss of their forest habitat.
13. **Vaquita** There may be fewer than ten of these sea mammals left in the Gulf of California. They are heading for extinction, unless a vaquita rescue program is successful.
14. **Yangtze finless porpoise** This dolphin species in China's Yangtze River has dwindled to fewer than 1,000 individuals.

Orangutans at risk

The Bornean orangutan lives on the island of Borneo in Southeast Asia. It has been critically endangered since 2016, due to its forest habitat being destroyed by logging. Illegal hunting also threatens its population, which has been reduced by half in the last 60 years. The most at risk group within this species are Northwest Bornean orangutans.

EXPERT CONSULTANT: Joel Sartore **SEE ALSO:** Natural Climate Change, p.94–95; The Rain Forest, p.164–65; The Taiga & Temperate Forests, p.166–67; Mount Everest, p.170–71; Shrinking Ice, p.186–87; Environmental Challenges, p.366–67; Extinction Event, p.368–69; The Effects of Climate Change, p.372–73

Orangutans have babies about once every eight years. Their populations can take a long time to recover

There are thought to be only about 105,000 Bornean orangutans left in the world

THE EFFECTS OF CLIMATE CHANGE

Burning fossil fuels such as oil and coal releases lots of gases into the atmosphere. As more fuel is burned, these gases become thicker and trap heat from the Sun. There are now more heat-trapping gases in our atmosphere than at any point in the last 800,000 years. We call this global warming.

ARCTIC OCEAN

NORTH AMERICA

PACIFIC OCEAN

SOUTH AMERICA

Worldwide effects

Some of the effects of climate change are shown on this map. Climate change causes a cascade of effects, and some of them make the planet even warmer. For example, bright white ice and snow reflect a large portion of the Sun's energy that hits Earth's surface. If ice and snow melt, the darker surface of the land and sea will absorb heat, causing further warming. A hotter world also results in more forest fires, which in turn release more carbon dioxide into the atmosphere, increasing warming.

Melting ice sheets
These cause rising sea levels and flooding

Wildfires
Higher temperatures and lack of rain lead to more forest fires

Melting ice
Losses of Arctic sea ice and the Greenland ice sheet cause sea levels to rise

Atlantic circulation
Since the 1950s, these ocean currents have slowed down. Scientists do not know yet what the effect will be

Storms
Violent storms such as hurricanes increase with heat

Drought
Higher temperatures lead to drought

Thawing permafrost
When frozen ground thaws it releases carbon dioxide and methane into the air

Dying coral reefs
Coral reefs die off as the oceans get warmer and more acidic

Rising temperature and sea level

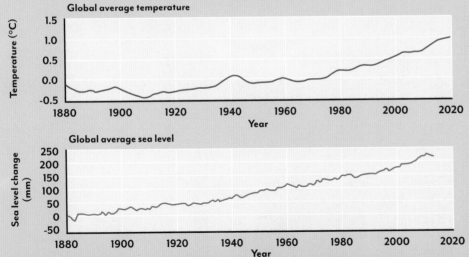

Global average temperature

Temperature (°C) / Year

Global average sea level

Sea level change (mm) / Year

Rising sea levels

The rising temperature of Earth causes sea levels to rise (left), as ice in the polar regions melts. The global temperature has already risen by 1.8°F (1°C) since 1850, and scientists think that another 0.9°F (0.5°C) will be catastrophic for some areas of the world. Low-lying coastal cities could disappear entirely because of rising sea levels. Places like Bangkok in Thailand are already threatened by rising levels in the Gulf of Thailand.

EXPERT CONSULTANT: Jaise Kuriakose **SEE ALSO:** The Sun, p.24–25; Earth's Ice, p.84–85; The Atmosphere, p.86–87; Weather p.88–89; Mega Storms, p.90–91; Climate, p.92–93; Natural Climate Change, p.94–95; Shrinking Ice, p.186–87; Coral Reef Crisis, p.178–79; The Open Ocean, p.180–81

ARCTIC
OCEAN

ATLANTIC
OCEAN

ASIA

EUROPE

PACIFIC
OCEAN

AFRICA

INDIAN
OCEAN

AUSTRALIA

ATLANTIC
OCEAN

ANTARCTICA

How Climate Change Affects Life on Earth
LISTIFIED.

Climate change will have damaging short-term and long-term effects on people, plants, and animals.

1. Flooding Flooding caused by heavy rains and rising sea levels destroys wildlife habitats as well as property, roads and transport networks, and infrastructure, including power stations and communications technology. It also leads to travel disruption and even loss of life.

2. Extreme weather Crops can die if bad weather causes drought or flooding. Food shortages and malnutrition will occur in many places.

3. Heat waves Heat waves and high temperatures cause damage to roads, buildings and infrastructure. People experience health problems such as heatstroke, difficulty breathing, and heart problems. Heat waves can cause wildfires, too.

4. Droughts Droughts affect food production, leading to food shortages and malnutrition in some countries and regions. Animals suffer, too. The 2019 wildfires in Australia, for example, destroyed many eucalyptus trees, on which koala bears (left) depend.

5. Mass migration Extreme weather events can make places uninhabitable. People may have to leave those areas and move somewhere else in order to stay safe and have enough to eat.

373

TELL THE TRUTH

Climate protests

In 2019, millions of people around the world protested the way governments were handling climate change, including these Extinction Rebellion (XR) supporters in London, UK. XR is a worldwide protest group demanding that governments take immediate action to stop mass extinction of species by reducing greenhouse gas emissions to zero by 2025.

STOPPING CLIMATE CHANGE

We know climate change is harming our planet, and we also know human beings are causing much of it. But what can be done to stop it? In 2015, an international agreement was reached in Paris and later adopted by all nations. They said they would keep global temperatures within a safe limit by reducing their greenhouse gas emissions, but progress has been slow. Now many people are demanding that more urgent and more drastic action is taken to limit the damage to ecosystems, species, and our common future.

Switch to renewable energy such as wind and solar power

Use manufacturing processes that cause fewer emissions

Eat a more plant-based diet and restore wild places

Switch to electric cars and bikes, or use public transportation

Be energy efficient

Reaching a safe limit

Scientists warn that global warming of 3.6°F (2°C) would severely damage ecosystems, human health, livelihoods, food and water security, and infrastructure. A safer limit would be below 2.7°F (1.5°C). To keep to safe limits, governments, businesses, and individuals must take action.

EXPERT CONSULTANT: Jaise Kuriakose **SEE ALSO:** Fossil Fuels, p.80–81; Energy, p.122–23; Coral Reef Crisis, p.178–79; The Open Ocean, p.180–81; Shrinking Ice, p.186–87; Environmental Challenges, p.366–67; Extinction Event, p.368–69; Endangered, p.370–71; The Effects of Climate Change, p.372–73

Fashion conscious

"Fast fashion" is bad for the environment. The term applies to clothes that are made quickly and cheaply because they will soon be replaced when fashions change. The fashion industry produces one-tenth of the world's carbon emissions. These trap heat in the atmosphere and contribute to climate change. To manufacture just one cotton shirt produces as much of these emissions as driving a car 35 miles. Imagine the effect of making a million shirts! To help the planet, buy fewer new clothes, recycle old clothes, and shop at secondhand stores.

KNOWN UNKNOWN

Is geoengineering the answer?

Geoengineering is the large-scale manipulation of Earth's natural system to reduce climate change. In theory, space mirrors (left) could be used to reflect sunlight away from Earth to decrease global warming. But doing this might not be possible, and changing our planet's atmosphere might cause other problems. Most scientists think reducing emissions is a better idea.

GAME CHANGER

GRETA THUNBERG

Environmental activist, born 2003
Sweden

Greta Thunberg is one of the most influential climate activists of all time. Through campaigning, she made climate change a much-discussed issue in 2019. Since then, she has inspired schoolchildren around the world to protest against global warming. She made powerful speeches about climate change in front of the United Nations and the World Economic Forum.

What You Can Do
LISTIFIED.

We can all help reduce carbon emissions and slow climate change.

1. Buy fewer things Manufacturing goods produces carbon emissions. The more we recycle and reuse, the more we can reduce emissions.

2. Go car-free Take the bus, walk, or ride a bike rather than travel by car.

3. Turn off computers and TVs These use electricity on sleep mode, as do gadgets turned on with a remote control. Unplug them when not in use.

4. Eat less meat Cattle- and sheep-rearing produce large amounts of carbon emissions. Favor vegetable-based dishes instead.

5. Turn the heat down And in the summer, don't turn the air conditioning up. Lower energy use means lower carbon emissions.

6. Fly less Planes release lots of carbon dioxide. Encourage grown-ups to use other forms of transportation.

375

NUCLEAR POWER

Nuclear power is a useful and clean form of energy, but it is controversial. Nuclear power stations use radioactive material that must be carefully monitored and controlled. If there is an accident, radiation can leak out and cause serious damage to people and the environment. Although rare, accidents have happened. About 10 percent of the world's power is nuclear.

How does nuclear power work?

Nuclear power is a method of boiling water to produce steam. This steam then turns big wheels or turbines that produce electricity. To produce the heat to boil the water, atoms of uranium (a radioactive metallic element) are split by a process called fission. This takes place inside the core of the nuclear reactor. A condenser linked to a cooling tower stops things from getting too hot. There are no greenhouse gas emissions to harm the environment from nuclear power because no fuel is burned.

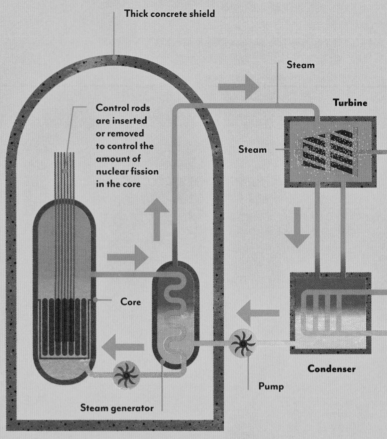

Thick concrete shield

Steam

Turbine

Steam

Control rods are inserted or removed to control the amount of nuclear fission in the core

Core

Steam generator

Pump

Condenser

Nuclear reactor

Fission and fusion

Nuclear energy can be released through processes called fission and fusion. Power plants use nuclear fission, which is the splitting of atoms. Nuclear fusion involves joining the nuclei of two atoms. It is harder to achieve but does not produce dangerous nuclear by-products. It is the process that occurs naturally at the core of stars, such as the Sun. Today, scientists are building the world's first test of a fusion reactor.

Huge cooling towers are used to remove the extra heat from the reactor. These towers can look as if they are smoking, but really they are just letting off steam from boiling water

EXPERT CONSULTANT: Michael Maral SEE ALSO: Stars p.10-11; The Sun p.24-25; The Atom p.100-01; Elements p.102-03; Radioactivity p.104-05

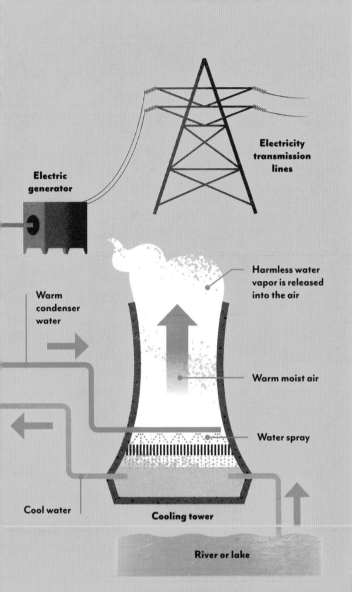

Electricity transmission lines

Electric generator

Harmless water vapor is released into the air

Warm condenser water

Warm moist air

Water spray

Cool water

Cooling tower

River or lake

5 Some effects of the radiation were detected many miles away from Fukushima

4 As the radiation spread, more and more people had to be evacuated

1 On March 11, 2011, an earthquake in the sea near Japan caused huge tsunami waves

3 People within 2 miles (3 km) of the plant were evacuated immediately

2 Reactors at the Fukushima nuclear plant released radiation

Nuclear disaster

In March 2011, an earthquake and tsunami hit Japan. This caused an accident at Fukushima Daiichi nuclear power plant. Although the reactor leaked radiation, the nuclear fuel was contained. Thousands of people left their homes. Some returned in 2017. The power plant will be dismantled when it is safe—in another 30 to 40 years.

Nuclear power in space

If we want to live on Mars or travel to distant worlds, we'll need a long-lasting energy source. Nuclear power could be the answer. It requires relatively little fuel but provides a lot of energy. NASA is in the process of developing small nuclear reactors called Kilopower systems (below) that could one day power human habitats on Mars. In the future, long-distance spaceships could run on a form of nuclear power.

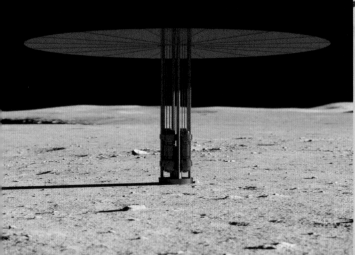

Nuclear-powered icebreaker

A Russian Arktika-class icebreaker smashes through thick ice on its way to the North Pole. Icebreakers like this work on nuclear power, so that they don't run out of fuel on their long Arctic journeys. Nuclear reactors on board the icebreakers create the power they need. Nuclear energy is also a useful way to power other vehicles, including submarines and even spacecraft.

Wind farms

Wind turbines produce electricity by using the rotation of their blades to drive an electrical generator. When it opened in 2001, this offshore wind farm in Denmark was the largest in the world. In the windiest months, it produces more than 6,000 megawatts of energy per month. Its 20 turbines produce 3 percent of the energy used by Denmark's capital city Copenhagen.

RENEWABLE ENERGY

Unlike the energy generated by fossil fuels, renewable energy comes from sources that are unlikely to run out. These include the Sun, wind, rivers and oceans, and biomass. Although biomass is burned, energy from renewables is very clean compared to that of fossil fuels.

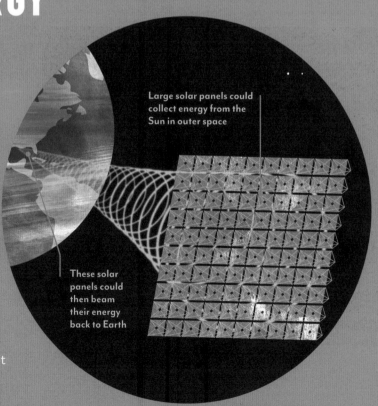

Large solar panels could collect energy from the Sun in outer space

These solar panels could then beam their energy back to Earth

KNOWN UNKNOWN

Could we put solar power stations in space?

Solar panels in space would be more effective than the ones we have on Earth because the Sun's light wouldn't be affected by clouds or the time of day. In theory, we could collect the Sun's energy and beam it back to Earth. But there is not yet a way to send the energy to the ground.

EXPERT CONSULTANT: Jaise Kuriakose **SEE ALSO:** Earth in Space, p.54–55; Fossil Fuels, p.80–81; Energy, p.122–23; Gravity, p.134–35; Classifying Life, p.152–53; Powering the Planet, p.348–49; Environmental Challenges, p.366–67; Stopping Climate Change, p.374–75; Nuclear Power, p.376–77

FACTastic!

The Sun releases more energy in one second than has been used in the whole history of humankind. If suitably harnessed, the Sun has the potential to satisfy all future energy needs. In the coming years, solar energy is expected to become much more widely used. There is an inexhaustible supply of it, and it is nonpolluting.

Geothermal 2%   Solar 6%

Biomass 46%   Wind 21%

Hydroelectric 25%

Using renewable energy

Around 27 percent of the world's electricity comes from renewable sources such as wind, water, and sunlight. In the future, 100 percent of energy could come from renewables. In the US, about 11 percent of the energy consumed in 2018 came from renewable sources. The chart above shows how much came from each of these sources in the US that year. Biomass includes biomass waste (organic waste such as scrap lumber or manure), biofuels, and wood.

Tidal energy

The ocean's tides can be harnessed to produce energy. The tides and currents move large turbines that are installed underwater, producing usable and clean electricity. Tidal current systems and tidal barrages (below) are two ways to get energy from the tides.

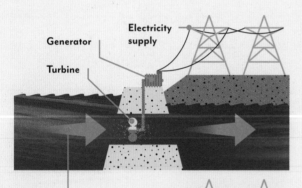

Generator

Electricity supply

Turbine

Tide going in

Tide going out

 The incoming tide pushes water past the turbine, making it turn.

 The turbine drives a generator, which produces energy.

 When the tide goes out again, it turns the turbine the other way.

 This outgoing tide also produces electricity.

NOTE *from the expert!*

JAISE KURIAKOSE
Electrial engineer

Dr. Jaise Kuriakose spends his time developing reliable zero-carbon energy that can replace fossil fuels. He is optimistic about the future, pointing out that renewable technologies such as solar panels and electric cars are getting cheaper and are being developed much faster than before.

❝ *I want to help stop dangerous climate change.* ❞

Biomass

Plants can be a source of renewable energy. For example, rapeseed is grown to make an oil used as renewable fuel. However, if large areas of land were used to produce fuel, not only would we lose biodiversity but the land could not be used to grow food. As many people do not have enough to eat, is this the right way to use Earth's resources?

CITIES OF TOMORROW

In the future, new and exciting technologies could completely change how cities look and work. "Smart cities" might have cars that drive themselves and "floating trains" that transport people in and out. Hopefully, the cities of the future will be greener and run on clean energy, producing fewer emissions and lessening their impact on the environment.

Urban jungle

The future is green! Heat from cars and air conditioners builds up in cities, making them much warmer than the countryside. But plants cool cities down. This image made on a computer shows how cities might look in the future. Buildings could be covered in plants and trees to make them more environmentally friendly. Trees absorb carbon, so having more trees would reduce the amount of greenhouse gases in the atmosphere. More trees would make people feel better, too.

Self-driving cars

Humans have been driving cars for about a century, but machines could soon take over. Self-driving cars use computers and artificial intelligence to drive, so people don't have to steer, use the pedals, or do anything. The technology is currently being tested and improved, so in the near future, many cars could be self-driving.

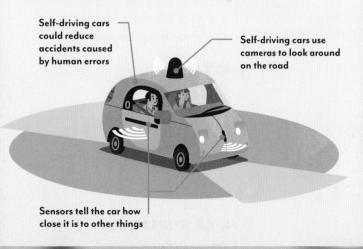

Self-driving cars could reduce accidents caused by human errors

Self-driving cars use cameras to look around on the road

Sensors tell the car how close it is to other things

The Maglev train running from Shanghai to Pudong International Airport in China is the oldest Maglev line still in operation. It takes the train eight minutes to make the 19-mile (30 km) journey

Floating trains

Maglev trains, or magnetic levitation trains, use magnets to raise the train off the rails. They have been used for passengers since 1984, but only a few countries, such as China, currently use them. They can travel much faster than regular trains, and they use up to 30 percent less energy, too.

Having some low-rise buildings allows more light and air to reach the ground

Solar panels on the outside of buildings generate electricity

Sky gardens absorb carbon and attract wildlife

The Hovenring

The Netherlands is home to the Hovenring, a floating traffic circle for bicycles and pedestrians, that is suspended 230 feet (70 meters) above the cars. This is safer for cyclists and pedestrians, as they do not have to share the road with cars.

Future Predictions
TIMELINE

2030 The United Nations predicts there will be 43 "megacities" across the world with more than 10 million people in each.

2040 It's estimated that half of all cars on the road could be electric cars. In some places, manufacturers will not be allowed to sell cars that run on fossil fuels.

2050 The world's population is projected to reach nearly 10 billion.

More than two-thirds of these people will live in urban areas.

2050 If cities continue to build upward, there's a chance the tallest skyscraper in the world could reach a mile (1,609 meters) high.

2050 Rising sea levels due to climate change mean that all or parts of some cities, including Bangkok in Thailand and Mumbai in India, could be underwater.

2070 The total geographical area of the world's cities is expected to have doubled.

FUTURE HUMANS

Some people rely on machines inside their bodies to
stay well. For example, pacemakers are implanted to
keep a patient's heart beating regularly. But one day,
machines might help us become smarter and stronger.
Already, by linking the human brain to machines, scientists
have made it possible for people to control computers,
prosthetic devices, and other machines with thought alone.

Gene editing

Imagine your parents had chosen the
color of your hair or eyes by selecting
particular genes rather than others
before you were born. The production
of such designer babies—children
with qualities their parents want—is
very controversial. However, gene
editing can also be used to ensure that
inherited diseases are not passed on.

EXPERT CONSULTANT: Cynthia Chestek **SEE ALSO:** Becoming Human, p.196–97; The Human Body, p.198–99; DNA & Genetics, p.200–01;
The Brain, p.202–03; Reading & Writing, p.218–19; Games & Sports, p.234–35; Smart Tech & AI, p.364–65; Med Tech, p.362–63; Cities of Tomorrow, p.380–81

Cochlear implants

A cochlear implant is an electrical device that allows someone whose ears don't work well to hear. It does this by communicating sounds directly to the nerve that carries sound to the brain. There are two external parts. One looks like a hearing aid and includes a microphone. It is connected to a receiver anchored inside the person's head and implanted in a part of the ear called the cochlea.

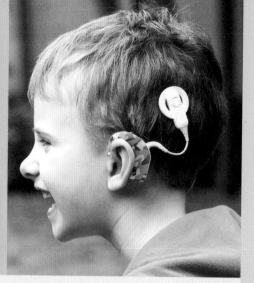

Living longer

People are living longer, but their bodies often let them down. In the near future, tiny machines known as nanobots could be used to repair organs that have stopped working or to deliver medicine to parts of the body that need it. Much further in the future, we might even be able to upload our brains to a computer. Perhaps when the body gets old, a person's thoughts could be stored and saved for future generations.

Thought-controlled artificial body parts

If people lose the use of a hand because of damage to the nervous system, they can have a "bionic" hand fitted. This is an artificial (prosthetic) hand, made of electronic circuits, not skin and bone. It's controlled by the wearer's brain.

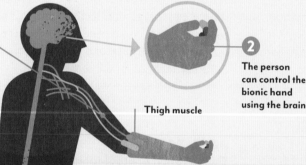

1 The muscles in the arm are reconstructed using muscles from the thigh, and the nerves are attached to the bionic hand

Thigh muscle

2 The person can control the bionic hand using the brain

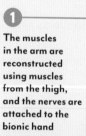

KNOWN UNKNOWN

Will people be able to speak using only their brains?

Researchers are working on technology to help people who can't speak because of illness or injury and must spell out words letter by letter on a computer, as the physicist Stephen Hawking (left) did. Scientists are taking the first steps in decoding speech directly from people's brains. In experiments, they placed electrodes on the surface of a volunteer's brain. Then, when the volunteer read a sentence aloud, a computer was able to decode it and speak the words.

ASK THE EXPERTS!

YINGJIE HU
Geographic information scientist

What do you want to discover most?
I want to find out how geospatial technologies (technologies related to computers, maps, and locations) best support disaster response and help people in need. Answering this question can protect properties and save lives. When I was a student in 2008, there was an earthquake in my home province of Sichuan, China. I wanted to use my knowledge to help the people affected by that major disaster.

What is surprising about your field?
In many countries, the field of geographic information science is under the department of geography. So, it is sometimes surprising to know that a geographer may also be an expert in new computer technologies!

What do you enjoy about your research?
We use maps on our smartphones to find the shortest routes to our destinations. But geospatial technologies are also used for finding the best location for a hospital and predicting the potential outbreak location of a disease.

SHAUNA BRAIL
Urban geographer

What is an unsolved problem in your field?
A big question that urban geographers often ask is: what makes a city grow? If we could find out the answer to this question, then all cities could be more successful. But the answer to this question changes, depending on a lot of things, like the political environment, the city's history and its location and geographic features.

What sparked your interest in your field?
I have a passion for cities. They are full of interesting people and buildings and spaces. I'm fascinated by what kinds of things most cities have in common, and what makes each one unique. I was in ninth grade when I first discovered my love of urban geography. We had to do an assignment called Locational Analysis of Home that I worked on for weeks. I still have the graded copy.

JOEL SARTORE
Conservation photographer

What do you want to discover most?
I'd like to learn how best to save the world's ecosystems and all the species that live in them. It is critically important to learn how to save all species so that we have a better chance of saving humanity in the long run.

What would you like to tell readers about your work?
I'd tell them that the most important thing is to do the kind of work you love, no matter what. If you love it, you'll be great at it. Also, become a specialist so that you're an expert in your field. That way, others will come to you for advice and assistance as you become established. That's a key to longevity in any field, actually.

Today & Tomorrow
THE QUIZ

1) **What was the world's population in the year 1800?**
   a. 100 million
   b. 1 billion
   c. 10 billion
   d. 100 billion

2) **In which year was the Apple iPhone first launched?**
   a. 2001
   b. 2007
   c. 2010
   d. 2013

3) **About how many container ships are there in the world?**
   a. Less than 500
   b. More than 5,000
   c. 50,000
   d. 500,000

4) **The Global Seed Vault in Norway contains how many seed varieties?**
   a. More than 1 million
   b. More than 5 million
   c. More than 10 million
   d. More than 20 million

5) **If everyone in the United States ate one fewer burgers per week for a year, carbon emissions would drop by about the equivalent of taking:**
   a. 10,000 cars off the road for a year
   b. 100,000 cars off the road for a year
   c. 1 million cars off the road for a year
   d. 10 million cars off the road for a year

6) **Which is the most crowded city in the world?**
   a. Tokyo, Japan
   b. Beijing, China
   c. Dhaka, Bangladesh
   d. Rio de Janeiro, Brazil

7) **When was the first .com website registered?**
   a. 1972
   b. 1985
   c. 1991
   d. 1996

8) **The village of Supai was connected to the Internet for the very first time in 2019 because it is located:**
   a. On a very remote island
   b. In the Arctic Circle
   c. In the Amazon rain forest
   d. At the bottom of the Grand Canyon

9) **What inspired Dutch doctor Willem Kolff to invent an artificial kidney?**
   a. A racing car
   b. A TV game show
   c. A washing machine
   d. A flushing toilet

10) **Swedish environmental activist Greta Thunberg was born in which year?**
   a. 2003
   b. 2004
   c. 2005
   d. 2006

11) **The printing press was created by German inventor Johannes Gutenberg in about:**
   a. 1215
   b. 1340
   c. 1440
   d. 1520

12) **Which was the world's first full-color daily newspaper?**
   a. *USA Today*
   b. *Daily Mail*
   c. *Miami Herald*
   d. *The Sun*

13) **The Keeling Curve is a graph that shows the increase of:**
   a. Sea levels
   b. Carbon dioxide levels
   c. Methane levels
   d. Seismic activity

14) **In future, tiny machines could be used to repair body organs that have stopped working. These machines are called:**
   a. Doctobots
   b. Nanobots
   c. Fixobots
   d. Nobots

ANSWERS: 1) b, 2) b, 3) b, 4) a, 5) d, 6) c, 7) b, 8) d, 9) c, 10) a, 11) c, 12) a, 13) b, 14) b

SOURCE NOTES

This book's research process was multi-layered. The authors used a wide range of reliable sources for each topic, then fact checkers used additional sources to ensure each fact is correct. In addition, an expert reviewed every topic for accuracy. The result is more sources than there is room to share here. The experts are listed on page 4, opposite the foreword. Below is a small sample of the authors' sources for each two-page feature.

Chapter 1. Universe
p.4–5 "The Big Bang Theory: How the Universe Began," www.livescience.com; Dunkley, Jo. *Our Universe: An Astronomer's Guide.* (London, UK: Pelican, 2019); Howell, Elizabeth. "What is the Big Bang Theory?," www.space.com; "NASA Science Space Place," spaceplace.nasa.gov; "The Planck Mission," plancksatellite.org.uk.
p.6–7 Cartwright, Jon. "What Is a Galaxy?," www.sciencemag.org; Fountain, Henry. "Two Trillion Galaxies, at the Very Least," www.nytimes.com; Greshko, Michael. "Galaxies, explained," www.nationalgeographic.com.
p.8–9 Hurt, Robert. "Annotated Roadmap to the Milky Way," www.spitzer.caltech.edu; Imster, Eleanor and Deborah Byrd. "New map confirms 4 Milky Way arms," earthsky.org; Taylor Redd, Nola. "Milky Way Galaxy: Facts About Our Galactic Home," www.space.com.
p.10–11 "The Life Cycles of Stars: How Supernovae Are Formed," imagine.gsfc.nasa.gov; "What is the Life Cycle Of The Sun?," www.universetoday.com. **p.12–13** Dunbar, Brian. "The Pillars of Creation," www.nasa.gov; Simoes, Christian. "Types of nebulae," www.astronoo.com; Williams, Matt. "Nebulae: What Are They And Where Do They Come From?," www.universetoday.com.
p.14–15 "The Constellations," www.iau.org; Sagan, Carl. *Cosmos.* (London, UK: Abacus, 2003).
p.16–17 "Comparison of Hubble and James Webb mirror (annotated)," www.spacetelescope.org. "Engineering Webb Space Telescope, www.jwst.nasa.gov; JWST Instruments Are Coming In From The Cold," www.sci.esa.int. **p.18–19** "Anatomy of a Black Hole," www.eso.org; O'Callaghan, Jonathan. "Astronomers reveal first-ever image of a black hole," horizon-magazine.eu; Wood, Johnny. "Stephen Hawking's final theory on black holes has been published, and you can read it for free," www.weforum.org. **p.20–21** Brennan, Pat. "Will the 'first exoplanet,' please stand up?," exoplanets.nasa.gov; "Nasa's Kepler Mission Discovers Bigger, Older Cousin to Earth," nasa.gov; Summers, Michael and James Trefil. *Exoplanets.* (Washington, D.C.: Smithsonian Books, 2018); Tasker, Elizabeth. *The Planet Factory: Exoplanets and the Search for a Second Earth.* (London, UK: Bloomsbury

Sigma, 2017); Wenz, John. "How the first exoplanets were discovered," astronomy.com. **p.22–23** O'Callaghan, Jonathan. "Voyager 2 Spacecraft Enters Interstellar Space," www.scientificamerican.com; Williams, Matt. "How Long is Day on Mercury?," www.universetoday.com. **p.24–25** Gleber, Max. "CME Week: The Difference Between Flares and CMEs," www.nasa.gov; "The Mystery of Coronal Heating," www.science.nasa.gov; "Sun Facts," www.theplanets.org. **p.26–27** Choi, Charles Q. "There May Be Active Volcanoes on Venus: New Evidence," www.space.com; Howell, Elizabeth. "What Other Worlds Have We Landed On?," www.universetoday.com; "Mars Curiosity Rover," www.mars.nasa.gov. **p.28—29** "An Interior Made Up of Different Layers," www.seis-insight.eu; "Mercury Transit on May 7, 2003," www.eso.org; Pyle, Rod, and James Green. *Mars: The Missions That Have Transformed Our Understanding of the Red Planet.* (London, UK: Andre Deutsch, 2019). **p.30—31** Mathewson, Samantha. "Jupiter's Great Red Spot Not Shrinking Anytime Soon," www.space.com; Williams, Matt. "What are Gas Giants?," www.universetoday.com. **p.32–33** Greshko, Michael. "Discovery of 20 new moons gives Saturn a solar system record," www.nationalgeographic.com; "Inside the Moon," moon.nasa.gov; "A unique look at Saturn's ravioli moons," www.mpg.de. **p.34–35** Black, Riley. "What Happened the Day a Giant, Dinosaur-Killing Asteroid Hit the Earth," www.smithsonian.mag; Starkey, Natalie. *Catching Stardust: Comets, Asteroids and the Birth of the Solar System.* (London, UK: Bloomsbury Sigma, 2018); Stern, Alan, and David Harry Grinspoon. *Chasing New Horizons: Inside the Epic First Mission to Pluto.* (New York: Picador, 2018). **p.36–37** "Dwarf Planets: Science & Facts About the Solar System's Smaller Worlds," www.space.com; "Kuiper Belt," Space.com; "The Oort cloud," spaceguard.rm.iasf.cnr.it. **p.38–39** Lieberman, Bruce. "If It Works, This Will Be the First Rocket Launched From Mars," www.airspacemag.com; "Robert Goddard: A Man and His Rocket," www.nasa.gov; "Saturn V," www.nasa.gov. **p.40—41** "ESA commissions world's first space debris removal," www.esa.int; Howell, Elizabeth. "CubeSats: Tiny Payloads, Huge Benefits for Space Research," www.space.com; "Point Nemo, Earth's watery graveyard for spacecraft," phys.org. **p.42–43** Hadfield, Chris. *An Astronaut's Guide.* (London, UK: Pan Macmillan, 2015); Tyson, Neil deGrasse, and Avis Lang. *Space Chronicles: Facing the Ultimate Frontier.* (New York: W. W. Norton, 2012). **p.44–45** "Juno," www.nasa.gov; "Space Probes," www.history.nasa.gov. **p.46–47** Clegg, Brian. *Dark Matter and Dark Energy.* (London, UK: Icon Books, 2019); Moskowitz, Clara. "5 Reasons We May Live in a

Multiverse," www.space.com; Woollaston, Victoria. "A Big Freeze, Rip or Crunch: How Will the Universe end?" www.wired.com.

Chapter 2. Earth

p.52–53 Hazen, Robert M. *The Story of Earth: The First 4.5 Billion Years, from Stardust to Living Planet.* (New York: Viking, 2012); Stanley, Steven M., and J ohn A. Luczaj. *Earth System History.* (New York: W. H. Freeman, 2015). **p.54–55** Chown, Marcus. *Solar System: A Visual Exploration of the Planets, Moons, and Other Heavenly Bodies That Orbit Our Sun.* (New York: Black Dog & Leventhal, 2016); Cox, Brian, and Andrew Cohen. *The Planets.* (Glasgow, Scotland: William Collins, 2019); Howell, Elizabeth. "How Fast Is Earth Moving?" www.space.com. **p.56–57** Allain, Rhett. "A Modern Measurement of the Radius of the Earth," www.wired.com; Choi, Charles Q. "Strange but True: Earth Is Not Round," www.scientificamerican.com; Sobel, Dava. *Longitude: The True Story of a Lone Genius Who Solved the Greatest Scientific Problem of His Time.* (London, UK: Bloomsbury, 2003). **p.58–59** "Earth's Interior," www.nationalgeographic.com; Luhr, James F., and Jeffrey Edward Post, eds. *Earth.* (New York: DK Publishing, 2013); Powell, Corey S. "Deep Inside Earth, Scientists Find Weird Blobs and Mountains Taller than Mount Everest," www.nbcnews.com. **p.60–61** *National Geographic Atlas of the World.* (Washington, DC: *National Geographic,* 2019). **p.62–63** Andrews, Robin George. "Here's What'll Happen When Plate Tectonics Grinds to a Halt," www.nationalgeographic.com; Ince, Martin. *Continental Drift: The Evolution of Our World from the Origins of Life to the Far Future.* (New York: Blueprint Editions, 2018); Molnar, Peter Hale. *Plate Tectonics: A Very Short Introduction.* (Oxford, UK: Oxford University Press, 2015). **p.64–65** Parfitt, Liz and Lionel Wilson. *Fundamentals of Physical Volcanology.* (Oxford, UK: Blackwell, 2008). **p.66–67** Dvorak, John. *Earthquake Storms: The Fascinating History and Volatile Future of the San Andreas Fault.* (New York: Pegasus Books, 2014); Taylor Redd, Nola. "Earthquakes & Tsunamis: Causes & Information," www.livescience.com. **p.68–69** Frisch, Wolfgang, Martin Meschede and Ronald C. Blakey. *Plate Tectonics: Continental Drift and Mountain Building.* (New York: Springer, 2011); "Mountains," www.nationalgeographic.com. **p.70–71** "Minerals and Gems," www.nationalgeographic.com; Pellant, Chris. *Rocks and Minerals.* (New York: DK Publishing, 2002); Zalasiewicz, J. A. *Rocks: A Very Short Introduction.* (Oxford, UK: Oxford University Press, 2016). **p.72–73** "These human-size crystals formed in especially strange ways," www.nationalgeographic.com; Packham, Chris et al. *Natural Wonders of the World.* (London, UK: DK Publishing, 2017). **p.74–75** Fossen, Haakon. *Structural Geology.* (Cambridge, UK: Cambridge University Press, 2016); Klein, Cornelis, and Anthony R. Philpotts. *Earth Materials: Introduction to Mineralogy and Petrology.* (Cambridge, UK: Cambridge University Press, 2017). **p.76–77** Hendry, Lisa. "How Are Dinosaur Fossils Formed?," www.nhm.ac.uk; Parker, Steve. *The World Encyclopedia of Fossils & Fossil-Collecting.* (London, UK: Southwater, 2016); Ward, David. *Fossils.* (London, UK: DK Publishing, 2010). **p.78–79** Brusatte, Stephen. *The Rise and Fall of the Dinosaurs: A New History of a Lost World.* (New York: Harper Collins, 2018); Jaggard, Victoria. "Why did the dinosaurs go extinct?," www.nationalgeographic.com; Osmólska, Halszka, Peter Dodson, and David B. Weishampel. *The Dinosauria.* (Berkeley, CA: University of California Press, 2007). **p.80–81** Nunez, Christina. "Fossil Fuels, Explained," www.nationalgeographic.com; Pirani, Simon. *Burning up: A Global History of Fossil Fuel Consumption.* (London, UK: Pluto Press, 2018). **p.82–83** Brutsaert, Wilfried. *Hydrology: An Introduction.* (Cambridge, UK: Cambridge University Press, 2005); Jha, Alok. *The Water Book.* (London, UK: Headline, 2015); Leahy, Stephen. "From Not Enough to Too Much, the World's Water Crisis Explained," www.nationalgeographic.com; "Our water cycle diagrams give a false sense of water security," www.birmingham.ac.uk. **p.84–85** "Glaciers and Icecaps," www.usgs.gov; Marshall, Michael. "The History of Ice on Earth," www.newscientist.com; Wadhams, Peter, and Walter Munk. *A Farewell to Ice: A Report from the Arctic.* (London, UK: Penguin, 2017). **p.86–87** "Atmosphere," www.nationalgeographic.org; Lutgens, Frederick K., and Edward J. Tarbuck. *The Atmosphere: An Introduction to Meteorology.* (Boston, MA: Pearson, 2016); Wallace, John M. and Peter Victor Hobbs. *Atmospheric Science: An Introductory Survey.* (Boston, MA: Elsevier Academic Press, 2006). **p.88–89** "Learn About Weather," www.metoffice.gov.uk; Shonk, Jon. *Introducing Meterology.* (Edinburgh, Scotland: Dunedin Academic Press, 2013); "Ten Basic Clouds," www.weather.gov. **p.90–91** Mogil, H. Michael. *Extreme Weather.* (New York: Black Dog & Leventhal, 2010). **p.92–93** Neelin, J. David. *Climate Change and Climate Modeling.* (Cambridge, UK: Cambridge University Press, 2013). **p.94–95** Cornell, Sarah, Catherine J. Downey, Joanna I. House, and I. Colin Prentice, eds. *Understanding the Earth System.* (Cambridge, UK: Cambridge University Press, 2012).

Chapter 3. Matter
p.100–01 Close, Frank E. *Particle Physics: A Very Short Introduction*. (Oxford, UK: Oxford University Press, 2004); Sharp, Tim. "What Is an Atom?," www.livescience.com. **p.102–03** Emsley, John. *Nature's Building Blocks: An A–Z Guide to the Elements*. (Oxford, UK: Oxford University Press, 2011); Gray, Theodore W. *Molecules: The Elements and the Architecture of Everything*. (New York: Black Dog & Leventhal, 2018); Parsons, Paul, and Gail Dixon. *The Periodic Table: A Field Guide to the Elements*. (London, UK: Quercus, 2013). **p.104–05** L'Annunziata, Michael F. *Radioactivity: Introduction and History, from Quantum to Quarks*. (Cambridge, MA: Elsevier Academic Press, 2016). **p.106–07** Helmenstine, Anne Marie. "These Compounds Have Both Ionic and Covalent Bonds," www.thoughtco.com. **p.108–09** Glassman, Irvin, Richard A. Yetter, and Nick Glumac. *Combustion*. (Waltham, MA: Academic Press, 2015). **p.110–11** Grossman, David. "All the States of Matter You Didn't Know Existed," www.popularmechanics.com; Miodownik, Mark. *Stuff Matters: Exploring the Marvelous Materials That Shape Our Manmade World*. (Boston, MA: Houghton Mifflin Harcourt, 2014); Silberberg, Martin S., and Patricia Amateis. *Chemistry: The Molecular Nature of Matter and Change*. (New York: McGraw-Hill Education, 2018). **p.112–13** Peratt, Anthony L. *Physics of the Plasma Universe*. (New York: Springer, 2014); Rovelli, Carlo. *Seven Brief Lessons in Physics*. (New York: Riverhead Books, 2016). **p.114–15** *The Physics Book*. (New York: DK Publishing, 2020). **p.116–17** Cobb, Allan B. *The Basics of Nonmetals*. (New York: Rosen Publishing Group, 2013); Pappas, Stephanie. "Facts About Silicon," www.livescience.com. **p.118–19** Bellis, Mary. "The History of Plastics," www.theinventors.org; Gray, Alex. "This Plastic Bag is 100% Biodegradable," www.weforum.org; Perkins, Sid. "Explainer: What Are Polymers?," www.sciencenewsforstudents.org. **p.120–21** Castro, Joseph. "How Do Enzymes Work?," www.livescience.com; Hanel, Stephanie. "Dorothy Hodgkin: The Queen of Crystallography," www.lindau-nobel.org. **p.122–23** Jaffe, Robert L. and Washington Taylor. *The Physics of Energy*. (Cambridge, UK: Cambridge University Press, 2018); Kuhn, Karl F. *Basic Physics*. (New York: Wiley, 2007). US Department of Energy. "How a Wind Turbine Works", www.energy.gov; Woodford, Chris. "The Conservation of Energy," www.explainthatstuff.com. **p.124–25** Goldsmith, Mike. *Sound: A Very Short Introduction*. (Oxford, UK: Oxford University Press, 2015); Rossing, Thomas D., F. Richard Moore, and Paul Wheeler. *The Science of Sound*. (Harlow, UK: Pearson Education, 2014); "The Science of Sound," www.nasa.gov.

p.126–27 Dwyer, Joe. "How Lightning Works," www.pbs.org; Woodford, Chris. "Electricity," www.explainthatstuff.com. **p.128–29** Feynman, Richard P. *QED: The Strange Theory of Light and Matter*. (Princeton, NJ: Princeton University Press, 2014); Kenney, Karen. *Science of Color: Investigating Light*. (North Mankato, MN: Abdo Publishing, 2015); Watzke, Megan K., and Kimberly K. Arcand. *Light: The Visible Spectrum and Beyond*. (New York: Black Dog & Leventhal, 2015); "What Is Light?—An Overview of the Properties of Light," www.andor.oxinst.com. **p.130–31** "Latest Bloodhound High Speed Testing Updates," www.bloodhoundlsr.com; McNamara, Alexander. "Land speed record: the 18 fastest cars in the world and their drivers," www.sciencefocus.com. **p.132–33** Hesse, Mary B. *Forces and Fields: The Concept of Action at a Distance in the History of Physics*. (Mineola, NY: Dover Publications, 2005); Pask, Colin. *Magnificent Principia: Exploring Isaac Newton's Masterpiece*. (Amherst, NY: Prometheus Books, 2019). **p.134–35** Clifton, Timothy. *Gravity: A Very Short Introduction*. (Oxford, UK: Oxford University Press, 2017); Goldenstern, Joyce. *Albert Einstein: Genius of the Theory of Relativity*. (Berkeley Heights, NJ: Enslow Publishing, 2014); Strathern, Paul. *The Big Idea: Newton and Gravity*. (London, UK: Arrow, 1997); Wood, Charlie. "What Is Gravity?," www.space.com; Zeleny, Enrique. "Galileo's Experiment at the Leaning Tower of Pisa," www.demonstrations.wolfram.com. **p.136–37** "Hydraulic Machinery," www.sciencedirect.com; "The Skin They're In: US Navy Diving Suits," www.history.navy.mil. **p.138–39** Burton, Anthony. *Balloons and Air Ships: A Tale of Lighter than Air Aviation*. (Barnsley, UK: Pen and Sword, 2020). **p.140–41** Inwood, Stephen. *The Man Who Knew Too Much: The Inventive Life of Robert Hooke, 1635–1703*. (London, UK: Pan Macmillan, 2003); Woodford, Chris. "How Do Shape-Memory Materials Work?," www.explainthatstuff.com and "Springs," www.explainthatstuff.com. **p.142–43** Gray, Theodore W., and Nick Mann. *How Things Work: The Inner Life of Everyday Machines*. (New York: Black Dog & Leventhal, 2019); Lucas, Jim. "6 Simple Machines: Making Work Easier," www.livescience.com.

Chapter 4. Life
p.148–49 Dodd, Matthew S. et al. "Evidence for early life in Earth's oldest hydrothermal vent precipitates," *Nature* 543 (2017); Marshall, Michael. "Fossilized microbes from 3.5 billion years ago are oldest yet found," www.newscientist.com. **p.150–51** Buffetaut, Eric. "Tertiary ground birds from Patagonia (Argentina) in the Tournouër collection of the Musée National d'Histoire Naturelle,

Paris," *Bulletin de la Société Géologique de France* 185 (2014); "Peppered Moth Selection," www.mothscount.org. **p.152–53** "Classification of Life," www.moana.hawaii.edu; Panko, Ben. "What does it mean to be a species?," www.smithsonianmag.com. **p.154–55** Biello, David. "How Microbes Helped Clean BP's Oil Spill," www.scientificamerican.com; Makarova, Kira S. et al. "Genome of the Extremely Radiation-Resistant Bacterium *Deinococcus radiodurans* Viewed from the Perspective of Comparative Genomics," *Microbiology and Molecular Biology Reviews* 65 (2001). **p.156–57** "Bee orchid," www.wildlifetrusts.org; Forterre, Yoël, Jan M. Skothem, Jacques Dumais, and L. Mahadevan. "How the Venus flytrap snaps," www.nature.com. **p.158–59** "Deep sea corals may be oldest living marine organism," www.linl.gov; Marshall, Michael. "Zoologger: A primate with eyes bigger than its brain," www.newscientist.com; Spelman, Lucy. *Animal Encyclopaedia.* (Washington, DC: National Geographic, 2012). **p.160–61** Mora, Camilo, Derek P. Tittensor, Sina Adl, Alastair G.B. Simpson, and Boris Worm. "How Many Species Are There on Earth and in the Ocean?" *PLOS Biology* 9, 2011. **p.162–63** Dorling Kindersley, Eds. *The Ecology Book.* (London, UK: DK Publishing, 2019); "Feral European Rabbit," www.environment.gov.au; "Giant Panda," www.nationalgeographic.com; Singer, Fred. D. *Ecology in Action.* (Cambridge, UK; Cambridge University Press, 2016). **p.164–65** Martin, Glen. "Humboldt County/World's Tallest Tree, A Redwood, Confirmed," www.sfgate.com; "Western Lowland Gorilla," wwf.panda.org. **p.166–67** Bachman, Chris. "Do Bears Really Hibernate?" www.nationalforests.org; Grant, Richard. "Do Trees Talk to Each Other?," www.smithsonianmag.com; "Tree Rings (Dendrochronology)," www.scied.ucar.edue; Waleed. "Siberian Tiger Facts," www.siberiantiger.org. **p.168–69** Slobodchikoff, C.N. and J. Placer. "Acoustic structures in the alarm calls of Gunnison's prairie dogs," *The Journal of the Acoustical Society of America* 119 (2006); Smith, Paul. "Giant Anteater," www.faunaparaguay.com; Suttie, J. M., S. G. Reynolds, and C. Batello, eds. *Grasslands of the World.* (Rome: Food and Agriculture Organization of the United Nations, 2005). **p.170–71** Chatterjee, Souvik. "High Altitude Plants Discovered in the Himalayas," www.glacierhub.org; Wanless, F. R. "Spiders of the Family Salticidae from the Upper Slopes of Everest and Makalu," www.britishspiders.org. **p.172–73** Hamilton, Wiliam J. III and Mary K. Seely. "Fog Basking by the Namib Beetle, *Onymacris unguicularis*," *Nature* 262 (1976); "Scorpions glow in the dark to detect moonlight," www.newscientist.com. **p.174–75** Keeling, Jonny. *Seven Worlds, One Planet.*

(London, UK: BBC Books, 2020); Riley, Alex. "The fish that makes long and short-range water missiles," www.bbc.co.uk. **p.176–77** Clark, Nigel. "Getting to the Arctic on time: Horseshoe Crabs and Knots in Delaware Bay," www.sovon.nl; *Ocean: a visual encyclopaedia.* (London, UK: DK Publishing, 2015). **p.178–79** "In What Types of Water Do Corals Live?," www.oceanservice.noaa.gov. **p.180–81** "Blue Whale," www.acsonline.org; Brassey, Charlotte. "A mission to the Pacific Plastic Patch," www.bbc.co.uk; "Sailfish," www.floridamuseum.ufl.edu. **p.182–83** Fox-Skelly, Jasmin. "What does it take to live at the bottom of the ocean?," www.bbc.co.uk; "Layers of the Ocean," www.weather.gov; McGrouther, Mark. "Spiderfishes, Bathyerois spp," www.australianmuseum.net.au. **p.184–85** Chapelle, Gauthier and Lloyd S. Peck. "Polar gigantism dictated by oxygen availability," *Nature* 399, 114–115 (1999); Egevang, Carsten. *Migration and Breeding Biology of Arctic Terns in Greenland.* (Denmark: Greenland Institute of Natural Resources and National Environmental Research Institute (NERI), 2010); "Emperor Penguins," www.antarctica.gov.au. **p.186–87** "Arctic summer 2018: September extent ties for sixth lowest," www.nsidc.org; Leahy, Stephen. "Polar Bears Really Are Starving Because of Global Warming, Study Shows," www.nationalgeographic.com. **p.188–89** Beans, Carolyn. "Lizard gets to grips with city life by evolving stickier feet," www.newscientist.com; Wiley, John P. Jr. "When Monkeys Move to Town," www.smithsonianmag.com. **p.190–91** Blakemore, Erin. "Ancient DNA Study Pokes Holes in Horse Domestification Theory," www.nationalgeographic.com; Kole, C. ed. *Oilseeds, Genome Mapping and Molecular Breeding in Plants.* (Heidelberg, Germany: Springer, 2007).

Chapter 5. Humans
p.196–97 "Australopithecus Afarensis," www.australianmuseum.net.au.; Gowlett, J. A. J. "The Discovery of Fire by Humans: A Long and Convoluted Process." *Philosophical Transactions of the Royal Society B: Biological Sciences* 371 (2016); Wayman, Erin. "Becoming Human: The Evolution of Walking Upright," www.smithsonianmag.com. **p.198–99** "Anatomy of a Joint," www.stanfordchildrens.org; Neumann, Paul E. and Thomas R. Gest. "How Many Bones? Every Bone in My Body." *Clinical Anatomy* 33 (2020).
p.200–01 Briggs, Helen. "DNA from Stone Age Woman Obtained 6,000 Years On," www.bbc.com; Fieldhouse, Sarah. "We've Discovered a Way to Recover DNA from Fingerprints without Destroying Them," www.phys.org; "What Is DNA?," www.ghr.nlm.nih.gov.

p.202–03 "Brain Basics: Genes At Work In The Brain," www.ninds.nih.gov; Kieffer, Sara. "How the Brain Works," www.hopkinsmedicine.org; Martinez-Conde, Stephen L. and Susana Macknik. "How Magicians Trick Your Brain," *Scientific American*, www.scientificamerican.com. **p.204–05** Callaway, Ewen. "Mona Lisa's Smile a Mystery No More," www.newscientist.com; Hwang, Hyi Sung and David Matsumoto. "Reading Facial Expressions of Emotion," www.apa.org; "Understanding the Stress Response," www.health.harvard.edu. **p.206–07** "Anatomy of the Eye," www.kelloggeye.org; "How Does Loud Noise Cause Hearing Loss," www.cdc.gov; Munger, Steven D. "The Taste Map of the Tongue you Learned at School is All Wrong," www.smithsonianmag.com. **p.208–09** Foley, Jonathan. "Feeding 9 Billion," www.nationalgeographic.com; "Food Loss and Food Waste," www.fao.org; Pariona, Amber. "What Are the World's Most Important Staple Foods?," www.worldatlas.com. **p.210–11** Jahangir, Rumeana. "How Does Black Hair Reflect Black History?," www.bbc.com; Keller, Alice and Terri Ottaway. "Centuries of Opulence: Jewels of India," www.gia.edu; Schultz, Colin. "In Ancient Rome, Purple Dye Was Made from Snails," www.smithsonianmag.com. **p.212–13** Armstrong, Karen. *A History of God.* (New York: Gramercy, 2004). Smith, Huston. *The World's Religions.* (New York: HarperOne, 2009). **p.214–15** Ferguson, R. Brian. "War Is Not Part of Human Nature," www.scientificamerican.com; "Medicine in the Aftermath of War," www.sciencemuseum.org.uk. **p.216–17** Jackendoff, Ray. "FAQ: How Did Language Begin?," www.linguisticsociety.org; Lustig, Robin. "Can English remain the "world's favourite" language?," www.bbc.co.uk; "What are the top 200 most spoken languages?," www.ethnologue.com. **p.218–19** Boissoneault, Lorraine. "How Humans Invented Numbers—And How Numbers Reshaped Our World," www.smithsonianmag.com; Mark, Joshua J. "Cuneiform," www.ancient.eu; Schmandt-Besserat, Denise. "The Evolution of Writing," www.utexas.edu. **p.220–21** Pettitt, P. B., et al. "Hand Stencils in Upper Palaeolithic Cave Art," www.dur.ac.uk; Vergano, Dan. "Cave Paintings in Indonesia Redraw Picture of Earliest Art," www.nationalgeographic.com. **p.222–23** "Music and the Brain: What Happens When You're Listening to Music," www.ucf.edu; "Performing Arts (Such as Traditional Music, Dance and Theatre)," www.ich.unesco.org; "William Shakespeare," www.bl.uk. **p.224–25** Longstaff, Alan. "Calendars from Around the World," www.rmg.co.uk; "Mystery of the Maya—Maya Calendar," www.historymuseum.ca; Stern, Sacha. *Calendars in Antiquity: Empires, States, and Societies.* (Oxford, UK: Oxford University Press, 2012). **p.226–27** "How Money is Made—Paper and Ink," www.moneyfactory.gov; Kishtainy, Niall. *A Little History of Economics.* (New Haven, CT: Yale University Press, 2017); "Tonne Gold Kangaroo Coin," www.perthmintbullion.com. **p.228–29** Eleftheriou-Smith, Loulla-Mae. "Magna Carta: What is it–and why is it still important today?," www.independent.co.uk.; Levack, Brian P. *The Witch-Hunt in Early Modern Europe.* (London, UK: Longman, 1987). **p.230–31** Beaubien, Jason. "'Floating Schools' Make Sure Kids Get To Class When The Water Rises," www.npr.org; "Girls' Education," www.worldbank.org; Patrinos, Harry A. "Why Education Matters for Economic Development," www.blogs.worldbank.org. **p.232–33** "Data on the future of work," www.oecd.org; Ferguson, Donna. "From Dog Food Taster to Eel Ecologist," www.theguardian.com. **p.234–35** Geere, Duncan. "Bionic Bolt: The Future of Performance Enhancing Sports Robotics," www.techradar.com; Solly, Meilan. "The Best Board Games of the Ancient World," www.smithsonianmag.com. **p.236–37** Boomer, Ben. "Ghaajj Navajo New Year," www.shamaniceducation.org; Crump, William D. *Encyclopedia of New Year's Holidays Worldwide.* (Jefferson, NC: McFarland, 2016). **p.238–39** Ebenstein, Joanna. *Death: A Graveside Companion.* (London, UK: Thames & Hudson, 2017); "Egyptian Mummification," www.spurlock.illinois.edu.

Chapter 6. Ancient & Medieval Times
p.244–45 Flood, Josephine. *The Original Australians: Story of the Aboriginal People.* (London, UK: Crows Nest, 2006); Macintyre, Stuart. *A Concise History of Australia.* (Cambridge, UK: Cambridge University Press, 2009). **p.246–47** Bottéro, Jean. *Everyday Life in Ancient Mesopotamia*, trans. Antonia Nevill. (Edinburgh, UK: Edinburgh University Press, 2001); Kramer, Samuel Noah. *History Begins at Sumer: Thirty-Nine Firsts in Man's Recorded History.* (Philadelphia, PA: University of Pennsylvania Press, 2001); Kriwaczek, Paul. *Babylon: Mesopotamia and the Birth of Civilisation.* (London, UK: Atlantic Books, 2010). **p.248–49** Hunter, Erica C.D. *Ancient Mesopotamia.* (New York: Chelsea House, 2007); Rathbone, Dominic, ed. *Civilizations of the Ancient World: A Visual Sourcebook.* (London, UK: Thames & Hudson, 2009). **p.250–51** Chippindale, C. *Stonehenge Complete.* (London, UK: Thames and Hudson, 2004). **p.252–53** Loewe, Michael and Edward L. Shaughnessy, eds. *The Cambridge History of Ancient China: From the Origins of Civilisation to 221 BC.* (Cambridge, UK: Cambridge University Press, 1999). **p.254–55** *Oxford Encyclopedia of Ancient Egypt.* (Oxford, UK: Oxford

University Press, 2001). **p.256–57** Iles Johnston, Sarah ed. *Religions of the Ancient World.* (Cambridge, MA: Harvard University Press, 2004); Lloyd, Alan B., ed. *A Companion to Ancient Egypt.* (Chichester, UK: Wiley-Blackwell, 2010). **p.258–59** Conklin, William J. and Jeffrey Quilter. *Chavin: art, architecture and culture.* (Los Angeles: Cotsen Institute of Archaeology Press, 2008); Silverman, Helaine. *Ancient Nasca Settlement and Society.* (Iowa City: University of Iowa Press, 2002). **p.260–61** Craig, Robert D. *Handbook of Polynesian Mythology* (Santa Barbara: ABC-CLIO, 2004); Lal, Brij V. and Kate Fortune, eds. *The Pacific Islands: An Encyclopedia.* (Honolulu: University of Hawaii Press, 2000). **p.262–63** Cartledge, Paul, ed., *The Cambridge Illustrated History of Ancient Greece.* (Cambridge, UK: Cambridge University Press, 2002); Speake, Graham, ed. *Encyclopedia of Greece and the Hellenic Tradition.* (London, UK: Fitzroy Dearborn, 2000). **p.264–65** Coe, Michael D. and Rex Koontz. *Mexico: From the Olmecs to the Aztecs.* (London, UK: Thames & Hudson, 2002); Foster, Lynn V. *Handbook to Life in the Ancient Maya World.* (Oxford, UK: Oxford University Press, 2005). **p.266–67** Harrison, Thomas, ed. *The Great Empires of the Ancient World.* (London, UK: Thames & Hudson, 2009); Potts, D. T. ed. *The Oxford Handbook of Ancient Iran.* (Oxford, UK: Oxford University Press, 2013). **p.268–69** Boardman, John. *The Oxford History Of Greece & The Hellenistic World.* (Oxford, UK: Oxford University Press, 2002); Konstam, Angus. *Historical Atlas of Ancient Greece.* (London, UK: Mercury Books, 2006). **p.270–71** Bosworth, A. B. *Conquest and Empire: the Reign of Alexander the Great.* (Cambridge, UK: Canto, 1993); Lane Fox, Robin. *Alexander the Great.* (London, UK: Penguin, 2004). **p.272–73** Avari, Burjor. *India: The Ancient Past, A history of the Indian sub-continent from c. 7000 BC to AD 1200.* (Abingdon, UK: Routledge, 2007); Lahiri, Nayanjot. *Ashoka in Ancient India.* (Cambridge, MA: Harvard University Press, 2015); Singh, Upinder. *A History of Ancient and Early Medieval India.* (Delhi, India: Pearson Longman, 2008); Thapar, Romila. *The Penguin History of Early India: From the Origins to AD 1300.* (London, UK: Penguin, 2002). **p.274–75** Ebrey, Patricia Buckley, ed. *The Cambridge Illustrated History of China.* (Cambridge, UK: Cambridge University Press, 2010). **p.276–77** Coarelli, Filippo. *Rome and Environs: An Archaeological Guide.* (Berkeley, CA: University of California Press, 2014); Wilson Jones, Mark. *Principles of Roman Architecture.* (New Haven, CT: Yale University Press, 2000). **p.278–79** Angold, Michael. *Byzantium: The Bridge from Antiquity to the Middle Ages.* (New York: St. Martin's Press, 2001); Mango, Cyril, ed. *The Oxford History of Byzantium.*

(Oxford, UK: Oxford University Press, 2002); Rosen, William. *Justinian's Flea: Plague, Empire and the Birth of Europe.* (London, UK: Penguin, 2008). **p.280–81** Miller, Joseph C., ed. *New Encyclopedia of Africa.* (Farmington Hills, MI: Gale, 2008); Phillipson, David W. *Ancient Ethiopia: Aksum: Its Antecedents and Successors.* (London, UK: British Museum Press, 1998). **p.282–83** Dash, Mike. "The Demonization of Empress Wu," (*Smithsonian* magazine, August 10, 2012); Lu, Yongxiang. ed. *A History of Chinese Science and Technology.* (London, UK: Springer, 2015). **p.284–85** Al-Hassani, Salim T. S., ed. *1001 Inventions: The Enduring Legacy of Muslim Civilization.* (Washington, DC: National Geographic, 2012); "The Elephant Clock," www.metmuseum.org. **p.286–87** Backman, Clifford R. *The Worlds of Medieval Europe.* (Oxford, UK: Oxford University Press, 2014). Bauer, Susan Wise. *The History of the Medieval World.* (New York: W. W. Norton, 2010).

Chapter 7. Modern Times
p.292–93 Campbell, Gordon. *The Oxford Illustrated History of the Renaissance.* (Oxford, UK: Oxford University Press, 2019); Paoletti, John T. and Gary M. Radke. *Art in Renaissance Italy.* (London, UK: Pearson, 2011). **p.294–95** "Asante Gold," www.vam.ac.uk; Sansom, Ian, "Great Dynasties of the World: The Ethiopian Royal Family," www.the guardian.com; "Wrapped in Pride," www.africa.si.edu. **p.296–97** Anderson, Maria. "5 Reasons the Inka Road is One of the Greatest Achievements in Engineering," www.insider.si.edu; Cossins, Daniel. "We thought the Incas couldn't write. These knots change everything," www.newscientist.com; "Heilbrun Timeline of Art History. Tenochtitlan," www.metmuseum.org; Mavrakis, Emily. "Ominous new interpretation of Aztec sun stone," www.floridamuseum.ufl.edu. **p.298–99** Fernandez-Armesto, Felipe. *Pathfinders: A Global History.* (New York: W. W. Norton, 2006); Worrall, Simon. "How the Discovery of Two Lost Ships Solved an Arctic Mystery," www.nationalgeographic.com; "Zheng He," exploration.marinersmuseum.org. **p.300–01** Boissoneault, Lorraine. "The True Story of the Koh-i-Noor Diamond And Why the British Won't Give It Back," www.smithsonianmag.com; "Taj Mahal Architecture with Design and Layout," www.tajmahalinagra.com. **p.302–03** Gordon, Andrew. *A Modern History of Japan.* (Oxford, UK: Oxford University Press, 2019); "Kabuki Actors: Masterpieces of Japanese Woodblock Prints" (from the Collection of the Art Institute of Chicago, 1988), www.artic.edu. **p.304–05** Machemer, Theresa. "Spanish

Conquistadors Stole This Gold Bar From Aztec Emperor Moctezuma's Trove," www.smithsonianmag.com; Pringle, Heather. "How Europeans Brought Sickness to the New World," sciencemag.org; Townsend, Camilla. *Fifth Sun: A New History of the Aztecs.* (New York: Oxford University Press, 2020). **p.306–07** "French and Indian War/Seven Years War 1754–63," www.history.state.gov; "The Mayflower Story," www.mayflower400uk.org; "The Pocahontas Archive," www.digital.lib.lehigh.edu. **p.308–09** Hochschild, Adam. *Bury the Chains: the British Struggle to Abolish Slavery.* (London, UK: Macmillan, 2005); "Slavery and Freedom," www.nmaahc.si.edu; Thomas, Hugh. *The Slave Trade.* (London, UK: Weidenfeld & Nicolson, 2015). **p.310–11** "Boston Tea Party History," www.bostonteapartyship.com; "Enlightenment," www.plato.stanford.edu; "Touissant Louverture," www.slaveryandremembrance.org. **p.312–13** Hajar, Rachel. "History of Medicine Timeline," www.ncbi.nlm.nih.gov; Hernandez, Victoria. "Photograph 51, by Rosalind Franklin," www.embryo.asu.edu; *Medicine: The Definitive Illustrated History.* (London, UK: DK Publishing, 2016). **p.314–15** Stearns, Peter N. T*he Industrial Revolution in World History.* (New York: Routledge, 2018); Weightman, Gavin. *The Industrial Revolutionaries.* (New York: Grove Press, 2007). **p.316–17** "Cher Ami," www.americanhistory.si.edu; "First World War," www.iwm.org.uk; Gregory, Adrian. *The Last Great War: British Society and the First World War.* (Cambridge, UK: Cambridge University Press, 2008); Howard, Michael. *The First World War.* (Oxford, UK; Oxford University Press, 2002); "Medicine in the First World War," www.kumc.edu. **p.318–19** Neuman, Joanna. *And Yet They Persisted.* (Hoboken, NJ: Wiley-Blackwell, 2020); "Women and the Vote," www.parliament.uk. **p.320–21** Chang, Jung and Jon Halliday. *Mao.* (New York: Knopf, 2005); Sperber, Jonathan. *Karl Marx, A Nineteenth Century Life.* (New York: Liveright Publishing Corporation, 2013). **p.322–23** "Walt Disney"; moma.org; Spivack, Emily. "The History of the Flapper," www.smithsonianmag.com; Taylor Redd, Nola. "Charles Lindbergh and the First Solo Transatlantic Flight," www.space.com. **p.324–25** Carter, Ian. "The German Lightning War Strategy of the Second World War," www.iwm.org.uk; Holmes, Richard, ed. *World War II The Definitive Visual Guide.* (London, UK: DK Publishing, 2009); "Life in Shadows: Hidden Children and the Holocaust," www.ushmm.org. **p.326–27** "Soviet Invasion of Czechoslovakia," www.history.state.gov; "The Soviet Space Program," www.nationalcoldwarexhibition.org; "Why China Rents Out Its Pandas," www.economist.com. **p.328–29** Kennedy, Dane Keith. *Decolonization.*

(Oxford, UK: Oxford University Press, 2016); Mahaffey, James. *Atomic Awakening.* (New York: Pegasus Books, 2009); Shipway, Martin. *Decolonization and Its Impact.* (Malden, MA: Blackwell, 2008). **p.330–31** Conwill, Kinshasha Holman, ed. *Dream a World Anew.* (Washington, DC: Smithsonian Books, 2016); Sampson, Anthony. *Mandela.* (New York: Vintage Editions, 2000); "Sorry Rocks," www.environment.gov.au. **p.332–33** "Malala's Story," www.malala.org; Regan, Helen and Sharif Paget. "Ethiopia plants more than 350 million trees in 12 hours," www.edition.cnn.com. **p.334–35** "Countries," www.europa.eu; "Member Countries," thecommonwealth.org; "Member States," www.un.org.

Chapter 8. Today & Tomorrow
p.340–41 Cumming, Vivien. "How many people can our planet really support?," www.bbc.co.uk; Khandelwal, Rekha. "McDonald's Global Presence and the Three-Legged Stool," marketrealist.com; Roser, Max, Hannah Ritchie, and Esteban Ortiz-Ospina. "World Population Growth," ourworldindata.org; Spence, Michael. *The Next Convergence.* (New York: Farrar, Straus and Giroux, 2011). **p.342–43** Harford, Tim. "The simple steel box that transformed global trade," www.bbc.co.uk; Statista Research Department. "Container Shipping—Statistics & Facts," www.statista.com. **p.344–45** "Demographia World Urban Areas 16th Annual Edition 2020.04," www.demographia.com; Hodgson, Geoffrey M. "What the world can learn about equality from the Nordic model," theconversation.com; The World Bank. "Nearly Half the World Lives on Less than $5.50 a Day," www.worldbank.org. **p.346–47** Reuters/ABC. "Arctic "doomsday" seed vault welcomes millionth variety amid growing climate change concerns," www.abc.net.au; World Health Organisation. "Global hunger continues to rise, new UN report says," www.who.int. **p.348–49** Firstenberg, Arthur. *The Invisible Rainbow.* (White River Junction, VT: Chelsea Green Publishing, 2020); www.littlesun.com; Quak, Evert-jan. "The costs and benefits of lighting and electricity services for off-grid populations in sub-Sahara Africa," assets.publishing.service.gov.uk. **p.350–51** "Figures at a Glance," www.unhcr.org; Firth, Niall. "How to Fight a War in Space (and Get Away with It)," www.technologyreview.com; "Hunger Used as a Weapon of War in Yemen, Experts Say," www.actionagainsthunger.org. **p.352–53** Milanovic, Branko. *The Haves and the Have-Nots.* (New York: Basic Books, 2010); "The richest in 2020," www.forbes.com; Warren, Katie. "13 countries that have only one billionaire," www.businessinsider.com. **p.354–55** "11 Most Eco-Friendly Cities of the World,"

interestingengineering.com; Broom, Douglas. "6 of the world's 10 most polluted cities are in India," www.weforum.org; Kolb, Elzy. "75,000 people per square mile? These are the most densely populated cities in the world," eu.usatoday.com. **p.356–57** "The birth of the web," home.cern; Gralla, Preston. *How the Internet Works.* (London, UK: Que, 2006); Zimmermann, Kim Ann and Jesse Emspak. "Internet History Timeline: ARPANET to the World Wide Web," www.livescience.com. **p.358–59** Hutchinson, Andrew. "People Are Now Spending More Time on Smartphones Than They Are Watching TV," www.socialmediatoday.com; Nimmo, Dale. "Tales of Wombat 'Heroes' Have Gone Viral. Unfortunately, They're Not True," www.theconversation.com. **p.360–61** Arrighi, Valeria. "Five Synthetic Materials with the Power to Change the World," www.scitechconnect.elsevier.com; McFadden, Christopher. "Inspired by Nature but as Tough as Iron: Metal Foams," www.interestingengineering.com. **p.362–63** Berger, Michele W. "A Wearable New Technology Moves Brain Monitoring from the Lab to the Real World," www.medicalxpress.com; Nawrat, Allie. "3D Printing in the Medical Field: Four Major Applications Revolutionising the Industry," www.medicaldevice-network.com; "Robotic Surgery," www.mayoclinic.org. **p.364–65** Brynjolfsson, Erik and Andrew McAfee. *The Second Machine Age.* (New York: W. W. Norton, 2016); Goddard, Jonathan. "Alumna Rana El Kaliouby named in BBC's 100 influential women of 2019," www.cst.cam.ac.uk; Reese, Byron. *The Fourth Age.* (New York: Atria Books, 2018); Shapiro, Jordan. *The New Childhood.* (New York: Little, Brown Spark, 2018); "Smart Motorways — What Are They and How Do You Use Them?," www.rac.co.uk. **p.366–67** "How Big Is the Great Pacific Garbage Patch? Science vs. Myth," www.response.restoration.noaa.gov; "Methane: The Other Important Greenhouse Gas", www.edf.org; Nunez, Christina. "Desertification, explained," www.nationalgeographic.com. **p.368–69** Aldhous, Peter. "We Are Killing Species at 1000 Times the Natural Rate," www.newscientist.com; Kolbert, Elizabeth. *The Sixth Extinction.* (London, UK: Bloomsbury, 2014). **p.370–71** "The IUCN Red List of Threatened Species," www.iucnredlist.org; Platt, John R. "Bornean Orangutan Now Critically Endangered," www.blogs.scientificamerican.com; Sartore, Joel. *The Photo Ark.* (Washington, DC: National Geographic, 2019). **p.372–73** "Could the Domino Effect of Climate Change Impacts Knock Us into 'Hothouse Earth'?," www.eia-international.org; Lenton, Timothy M., et al. "Climate Tipping Points—Too Risky to Bet Against," www.nature.com; Nunez, Christina. "What is global warming, explained," www.nationalgeographic.com. **p.374–75** Dunne, Daisy. "Explainer: Six ideas to limit global warming with solar geoengineering," www.carbonbrief.org; Gore, Al. *An Inconvenient Truth.* (New York: Rodale Books, 2006); "Is it too late to prevent climate change?," www.climate.nasa.gov; Klein, Naomi. *This Changes Everything.* (New York: Simon & Schuster, 2014); Milman, Oliver. "Greta Thunberg Condemns World Leaders in Emotional Speech at UN," www.theguardian.com; Wallace-Wells, David. *The Uninhabitable Earth.* (New York: Tim Duggan Books, 2020). **p.376–77** Humpert, Malte. "Russia's Brand New Nuclear Icebreaker 'Arktika' to Begin Sea Trials," www.highnorthnews.com; "What Is Nuclear Power and Energy?" www.nuclear.gepower.com. **p.378–79** Hartley, Gary. "What Role Does Biomass Have to Play in Our Energy Supply?," www.energysavingtrust.org.uk; Shinn, Lora. "Renewable Energy: The Clean Facts," www.nrdc.org. **p.380–81** Carr, Nicholas. *The Shallows.* (New York: W. W. Norton, 2010); Cronon, William. *Nature's Metropolis.* (New York: W. W. Norton, 1992); Demtriou, Steven J. "We Can Build Cities Fit for the Future—but We Need to Think Differently," www.weforum.org; Dobraszczyk, Paul. *Future Cities.* (London, UK: Reaktion Books, 2019); Garfield, Leanna. "These Will Be the World's Biggest Cities in 2030," www.businessinsider.com; Giermann, Holly. "Vincent Callebaut's 2050 Vision of Paris as a 'Smart City,'"www.archdaily.com. **p.382–83** Anumanchipalli, Gopala K., Josh Chartier and Edward Chang. "Speech synthesis from neural decoding of spoken sentences," *Nature* 568 (2019); Walsh, Fergus. "Woman receives bionic hand with sense of touch," www.bbc.co.uk.

GLOSSARY

abolition Stopping or canceling something—especially outlawing slavery. Slavery was abolished in the US in 1865.

acids Reactive chemical compounds that usually dissolve in water and often have a sour taste. They typically react with other substances by releasing hydrogen ions.

activism Campaigning actively for political or social change.

adaptation (1) Any feature of a species, such as a body structure, that helps it live in its environment. **(2)** The process by which species become better fitted to their environment.

agriculture Farming—the work of preparing the soil, growing crops, and raising farm animals.

alkalis Reactive chemical compounds that dissolve in water and sometimes have a bitter taste. Alkalis react with acids to form salts and water.

altitude Height above the ground, or above sea level.

amino acid One of the 20 different kinds of small nitrogen-containing molecules that are the building blocks of proteins.

ancestor A dead relation, such as your great grandmother's grandmother. "Ancestors" are also earlier generations of a whole group or tribe of people.

antimatter Matter that is the opposite of ordinary matter. It is much rarer in the Universe than ordinary matter is. Atoms of antimatter have a negatively charged nucleus, surrounded by positively charged electrons. When matter and antimatter meet, they destroy each other and produce a burst of energy.

aqueduct A structure for channeling water across a region; for example, to bring drinking water to a city. Aqueducts often include bridges to cross valleys.

archaeologist A person who researches human societies of earlier times by studying things such as coins, graves, and ruined buildings.

arm A bright part of a galaxy that spirals out from the center.

artificial Made by human beings.

asteroid A solid natural object that orbits the Sun but is smaller than a planet. Asteroids usually have an irregular, lumpy shape.

astrolabe A historical instrument for measuring the angle of stars and planets above Earth's horizon. It was used in astronomy and as a navigation aid.

astronomy The study of the Universe beyond Earth, including planets, stars, and all of outer space.

atmosphere The layer of gas around many planets, satellites, and stars.

atom One of the building blocks of ordinary matter. An atom has a small but heavy center called a nucleus that carries a positive electrical charge, around which lighter negatively charged particles called electrons orbit.

automatic A word used for describing machines that work without being directly operated by a person.

Balkans An area of southeast Europe where many different peoples and cultures have lived. It includes several modern countries such as Albania, Bulgaria, and Serbia.

biomass The total amount or weight of living organisms in a habitat, or the amount of one species or group.

biome A major type of habitat, such as deserts and rain forests, that can be found in different parts of the world where climates are similar.

camouflage Colors or patterns that help an animal disguise itself.

capitalism A system of dealing with money and wealth, where industries and businesses are run by individual companies that compete with each other, not by the government.

captivity The situation of not being free to go where you choose. A person in prison or an animal in a zoo are both in captivity.

carbohydrates Substances such as sugar, starch, and cellulose that are made of carbon, hydrogen, and oxygen.

carbon dating A method of working out how old something is by measuring the amount of a radioactive isotope of carbon it contains.

carnivorous Meat eating.

catalyst A substance that promotes a chemical reaction but is left unchanged at the end of the reaction.

cathedral A usually large Christian church, where a bishop is based.

cell (1) A small room or compartment, such as a room in a monastery, where a monk lives. **(2)** One of the millions of tiny living units that make up the bodies of humans and other living things. Skin cells and nerve cells are examples.

ceremony A formal event or ritual; for example, as part of a religion or to celebrate something.

citizen Someone who legally belongs to a particular country and has rights such as the right to live there and to vote.

civil rights The rights to individual freedoms and to be treated equally with others in a society.

climate change The situation where Earth's climate is changing overall, rather than just normal changes in the weather.

coffin A box in which a dead body is placed for burial or cremation.

Cold War A period of history between the end of World War II in 1945 and the collapse of the Soviet Union in 1991. It featured rivalry and the threat of nuclear war between communist countries, led by the Soviet Union (including Russia) and Western democracies, led by the US.

colony A city founded, or a region settled, by people from another country. Colonies are usually partly controlled by the country from which the settlers came.

coma The gases and small particles given off by a comet as it nears the Sun and heats up, forming a halo around the comet's head.

communism A way of running a country in which individual people do not own factories or land, but instead these are owned by the whole community or the government. Everyone is supposed to share the wealth that they create.

conductor A material through which an electric current can pass easily.

continent A main continuous land region of Earth. From the largest to the smallest, the seven continents are Asia, Africa, North America, South America, Antarctica, Europe, and Australia.

controversial Leading to arguments and disagreements, because different people have different opinions about what is being suggested.

conversion Changing one's views, or having them changed, so that one starts to believe in a religion, or changes from one religion to another.

covalent bonding A type of chemical bonding between atoms, where some electrons are shared between them.

crime An action that is against the law and that a country will punish you for.

crops Plants that are grown for food.

crystal A solid whose individual atoms or molecules are arranged in a three-dimensional pattern of neat rows.

dark energy A still-mysterious phenomenon that is believed to make up most of the energy in the Universe and causes its expansion to speed up.

decipher To work out the meaning of something, such as words written in an unknown language.

deity A god or goddess.

democracy A form of government in which the people of a country can freely choose whom they would like to rule over them by voting in elections.

density How much mass or weight a thing has for its size.

dictator A person who rules a country with no restrictions on their power.

dolmen A prehistoric structure made of two or more upright stones with a single large stone lying across them.

dream A series of thoughts and pictures that happen in a person's mind during sleep.

ecology The study of the relationships between living things and their surroundings or environment.

economy The overall pattern of goods and services produced and consumed in a country, a region, or the whole world.

ecosystem The living things in a particular habitat and how they interact with each other and with their physical surroundings.

electromagnetic radiation Radiation that transmits energy in the form of waves that travel at the speed of light. It includes visible light, infrared waves, radio waves, and X-rays.

electron A negatively charged particle that orbits an atom's nucleus.

electron microscope A microscope that works by detecting beams of electrons instead of light. With it, scientists can see much smaller objects than they can with a light microscope.

element A basic chemical substance that cannot be broken down into simpler substances.

emission Giving out something; for example, the radiation given out (emitted) by a radioactive substance.

energy The ability to be active or to work. Forms of energy include potential, kinetic, thermal, electrical, chemical, or nuclear. All forms are associated with motion. For example, a moving body has kinetic energy; if it is resting, it has potential energy. Energy is also a type of heat that transfers from one body to another. This is an example of thermal energy.

Enlightenment A way of thinking that began in Europe in the 1700s and aimed to use reason, logic, and science to solve social and political problems.

entropy A measure of disorder and randomness in a physical system. A chemical reaction is more likely to happen if entropy will increase as a result.

epicenter In an earthquake, the epicenter is the point on Earth's surface directly above where the rock movement that started the earthquake took place.

epipelagic zone The uppermost layer of the open ocean, from the surface down to around 650 feet (200 meters).

equator An imaginary line around Earth's surface that separates the Northern and Southern hemispheres.

equinox One of the two days in the year when day and night are the same length.

erosion Any process where land is worn away and the fragments transported somewhere else; for example, by wind or water.

estimate An approximate measurement that may turn out to be different from reality.

ethnicity The feature of belonging to a group of people with shared culture and history.

event horizon The edge of a black hole, beyond which gravity is so strong that not even light can escape, so that we can't detect anything that happens inside it.

evolution A change in the genetic makeup of a population of organisms over many generations.

extremist Somebody who has extreme views, especially about politics or religion.

famine A large-scale shortage of food leading to widespread starvation.

fasting Going without food on purpose, such as for religious reasons.

fingerprints Marks left by your fingers that show the pattern of grooves on your fingertips.

fossil A long-dead living thing (such as a plant or animal) or a trace of that living thing (such as a footprint) that has been preserved in the ground.

fossil fuel A fuel such as coal, crude oil, or natural gas that is found under the ground. Fossil fuels are the remains of ancient living organisms.

frequency For any type of wave, frequency is the number of waves that reach or pass a point in a second.

fulcrum A fixed point that supports a lever and allows it to turn.

gas A form of matter in which individual atoms or molecules move around independently of each other, rather than sticking close together as they do in liquids and solids.

gender Whether a person is male or female (or does not identify as either). A **gendered** word in a language is one that relates to a single gender—for example, "spokesman" or "spokeswoman."

gene One of the thousands of different sets of "instructions" found in nearly every cell of your body. They control how you grow and what makes one person look different from another. Half of your genes come from your mother and half from your father. Genes are made of a substance called DNA.

genetics The study of genes and their effects, including how features such as height and eye color are passed down from parents to their children.

geyser A hot spring in a volcanic region that erupts suddenly.

glacier A large, slow-moving "river" of ice that flows down from an ice cap or a high mountain range.

global warming An increase in the average temperature of Earth's atmosphere and oceans. Scientific measurements show that global warming is happening now, almost certainly due to **greenhouse gases** in the atmosphere.

gravity The force that attracts all matter in the Universe, such as the attraction between a person and Earth, or between Earth and the Sun.

greenhouse gas Any gas that contributes to the **greenhouse effect**, where heat energy that is radiated from Earth's surface gets trapped by gases, making the atmosphere warmer than it would otherwise be. Greenhouse gases include carbon dioxide and methane, both of which have increased due to human activity and are causes of global warming.

groundwater Any water under the ground that is not chemically combined into rocks and minerals.

gyre A large ocean current that circulates around a central point.

habitat Any area that is suitable for particular kinds of animals, plants, and other organisms to live in.

heir A person who is going to inherit something when another person dies. It can be a title such as king or duke, or property and wealth, or both.

hemisphere Half of a round object, such as one-half of Earth's surface.

hibernation A state in which an animal is inactive during winter, and its body processes slow down.

hierarchy Any arrangement in which some people or things are ranked as higher or more important than others. In human organizations, people further up a hierarchy often have control over people below them.

humidity Dampness, especially the amount of water vapor in the air. **Relative humidity** is the percentage of water vapor in the air relative to

the maximum amount possible: above the maximum, the water vapor starts to condense as water or ice. Warm air can hold more water than cold air can.

hydraulic (1) Referring to liquids under pressure, especially in pipes, that can be used to transmit power. **(2)** Referring to a type of cement that is able to harden under water.

hydrothermal Referring to hot water circulating in Earth's rocks. A hydrothermal vent is a place on the ocean floor where hot water jets out.

impurity An extra, usually unwanted, material; for example, in a scientific sample or in drinking water.

independence For a country or territory: having control over itself, rather than being controlled or partly controlled by another country.

indigenous people The original inhabitants of an area and their descendants.

inertia The tendency of an object to resist being moved or to resist having its motion changed.

infrared A type of radiation, invisible to the naked eye, that transmits heat.

infrasound Low-frequency sound that is below the range of human hearing.

infrastructure The structures needed to keep a modern society working, such as transport systems, water and sewer systems, and power plants. Usually, these are created by the government and owned by the public.

innovative Refers to a new and different way of doing things.

invertebrate Any animal without a backbone, such as an insect, snail, or jellyfish.

investor A person or organization who puts their money into a project, often in the hope of obtaining a profit later.

ion An atom that has gained or lost electrons, so that it has a different number of electrons than protons.

ionic bonding A type of chemical bonding in which electrons transfer from one atom to another.

irrigation Any method of channeling water across a farming region to help crops grow.

isotope One of two or more versions of an element whose atomic nuclei contain the same number of protons but different numbers of neutrons.

keystone species A species that is important to a particular habitat, so that the habitat would be quite different if it disappeared.

landfill A way of disposing of trash by putting it in large pits in the ground that are then covered over.

lava Molten rock flowing from a volcano or other crack in Earth's surface.

leap year A year in which an extra day or days are added to the calendar in order to keep it in line with the solar year (the time it takes Earth to orbit the Sun). Leap years are necessary because the solar year is 365.25 days, whereas there are 365 days in a standard calendar year. In the Gregorian calendar, used by most Western countries, a day is added to February every four years.

legend A story from long ago that may or may not be based on truth.

lens A device that bends and focuses light so that an image of an object can be seen.

LGBTQ+ Short for "lesbian, gay, bisexual, transgender, queer, plus." It is a general term for everyone whose sexual orientation or gender identity varies from the idea that the type of body a person is born with determines whom that person will love, what gender that person will be, and how that person will behave.

literacy The ability to read and write.

magma Molten rock when it is below Earth's surface. When it reaches the surface, it is called lava.

magnetism A property of certain substances, including iron, that allows them to pull other objects toward them or to push them away. Magnetism is closely related to electricity.

mammal Any animal, including humans, of which the females produce milk for their young. Mammals usually have hair or fur and give birth to live young.

mandible The lower jaw of a vertebrate. The biting parts of insects such as ants are also called mandibles.

mantle The thick rocky layer under Earth's crust, or similar layers in other rocky planets.

mass transport Transportation systems that can carry a lot of people at once, such as trains and subways.

matter All substances in the Universe—everything that has weight or mass, including every atom.

maze A puzzle where you have to find a route through a network of paths.

meditation Going into a quiet or trancelike state to calm the mind or for religious or spiritual purposes.

merchant A private individual who sells and trades goods, especially on a large scale and to foreign countries.

metabolism The chemical reactions inside the cells of a living organism that produce the energy for it to live and grow.

meteor Any small solid particle that enters Earth's atmosphere from space at high speed and produces a glowing trail. If it reaches the ground, it is called a meteorite. Such particles before they enter Earth's atmosphere are called meteoroids.

microbe A microscopic living organism, especially a bacterium.

microorganism A microscopic organism, such as a bacterium, protist, or yeast.

mineral (1) A natural substance with a definite chemical composition that is not part of a living thing; for example, a metal ore. **(2)** In biology, one of the chemical elements needed in small amounts by living things, such as iron, potassium, and zinc.

mission A group of people sent officially to do something. For example, a member of a religion sent to promote that religion.

molecule The smallest unit of a chemical compound. Molecules are made of two or more atoms joined together.

monarchy Rule by one person, usually a royal, such as a king or empress.

Monera The kingdom of living things that includes bacteria. Monera have no nuclei in their cells.

monsoon A pattern of winds in some tropical regions, where the wind blows in one direction for part of the year and in the other direction for the other part. These winds usually result in wet and dry seasons, and monsoon also means the heavy rains that occur during the wet season.

mosque A place of worship in the Islamic religion.

multicellular Having a body made of many cells. Animals and plants are multicellular, but bacteria are not.

multinational Operating in, or involving, several different countries.

mummy A dead body that has been partly preserved by special treatments to prevent decay.

myth An old story once believed to have been true, especially one involving gods and goddesses, or explaining how something came to be created, such as Earth or the sky.

mythology A set of myths belonging to a particular ancient civilization or tribe.

nationalism A political outlook that involves having a strong attachment to one's own country or people.

natural selection The process of evolution in which the most successful individuals in a species are more likely to survive, and so pass on their genes to their offspring.

neutron A subatomic particle found in the nucleus of most atoms. A neutron does not carry an electric charge.

niche The role that a species plays in a habitat—for example, specializing in eating a particular kind of plant.

nobles People assigned a higher status than others in a society, such as dukes, duchesses, and barons.

nuclear fusion A process in which the atomic nuclei of lighter elements, such as hydrogen, join together to create nuclei of heavier elements.

nucleus (plural, nuclei) The heavy central part of an atom or the central part of a cell.

nutrients Substances in food that help your body to work, such as vitamins and minerals.

Oceania The geographical region that includes all the small islands of the western Pacific Ocean. Australia and New Zealand can also be included.

ommatidium (plural, ommatidia) An individual unit of an insect's eye. Such eyes are called compound eyes and may contain thousands of ommatidia.

opponent A person who disagrees with another person's actions or opinions or who objects to an idea or a policy. It also means anyone you are competing against in a game or sport.

orbit The route of a body in space, such as a planet, moon, or artificial satellite, when it is circling a larger body under the influence of gravity.

ore Any metal-containing mineral that is valuable enough to be commercially mined for that metal.

organism Any living thing, from a bacterium to a human being.

oxidation When a chemical substance combines with oxygen. Oxidation is also a chemical reaction, where one chemical loses electrons to another.

oxygenated Provided with oxygen.

particle Usually short for **subatomic** particle—any particle smaller than an atom or atomic nucleus, such as a neutron, electron, or quark.

permafrost Permanently frozen ground; this is common in Arctic and Antarctic regions.

pharaoh A ruler of ancient Egypt, who was often worshiped as a god.

pheromone A chemical signal released by an animal to other animals of the same species, to attract mates or warn of danger.

philosophy Thinking deeply about the basic questions of life, such as what we are here for or how we can have sure knowledge about anything.

photosynthesis The process in which green plants use sunlight to make their own food.

phytoplankton Microscopic plantlike organisms floating in the surface layers of the ocean. They are the main source of food for marine ecosystems.

pictograph A picture that stands for a word or a phrase. Early kinds of writing often used pictographs.

pigment A colored substance, usually a powdery solid, used in paints and other coloring materials.

pilgrimage A long journey to visit a religious place or shrine.

plasticity The ability of a material to be molded and stretched, without either tearing or springing back to its original shape.

pollination The process in plants where pollen is transferred to the female part of a flower to fertilize it, so that seeds will develop.

polymer A very long molecule consisting of a flexible chain of small molecules joined together.

prayer Any speech addressed to a god to ask for help or offer thanks or praise. Prayers can also be made to holy individuals such as saints. The standard words spoken to a god during religious services are also prayers.

prehistoric Refers to the time period before written records. This period is different in different places.

prevailing Term applied to winds that usually blow from the same direction throughout the year. The "trade winds" that blow in warmer regions near the equator are an example.

primates The group of mammals that includes lemurs, monkeys, apes, and human beings.

probe An uncrewed spacecraft sent to explore an area of space and transmit back information.

prophet A person who claims to speak on behalf of a god and/or to foretell the future.

prosthetic A word referring to prostheses, which are artificial substitutes for parts of the body, such as artificial hands.

protists Organisms that have cells with nuclei but are not animals, plants, or fungi. Most protists are microscopic and single-celled, such as those found in ocean plankton.

proton A positively charged particle found in the nuclei of all atoms.

prototype An experimentally built machine or other device, created to test out how well it works before thousands of them are made.

province A large region of a country, often with its own culture and traditions.

pyramid In mathematics, a solid shape with a square base and triangular sides that slope upward to a point at the top. Buildings of similar shape include the pyramids of ancient Egypt and the ancient Maya.

quark One of the tiny particles that protons and neutrons are made of.

racism Treating people differently; for example, giving them fewer rights, because of the race they belong to.

radiation High-speed beams of particles or energy.

raw material A natural substance that is used to manufacture something. For example, sand is a raw material for making glass.

refraction The change of direction, or bending, of waves when they travel from one substance into another, such as lightwaves going from air into water.

refugee A person who has fled from one country to another to escape danger.

regurgitate To bring food back up from the stomach to the mouth.

Renaissance A period in European history from the 1300s to the 1500s, when art and thought advanced, partly because of a renewed interest in ancient Greece and Rome.

renewable Able to be used again and again without running out. The word is often applied to energy sources such as solar and wind energy.

replica A copy of an original object; for example, a modern copy of an ancient statue. Replicas can be used to show an object in different places, such as in a traveling exhibition, if the original object cannot be moved.

revolution **(1)** A sudden change of government, often violent and involving a rebellion. **(2)** The single completion of an orbit, such as that of a planet around its sun.

robot A machine that does tasks without the help of a person.

sacred Worshiped or regarded as special by a particular religion.

sanitation Arrangements for ensuring a clean and healthy human environment, especially by providing clean drinking water and safe ways of disposing of waste.

satellite A natural or artificial body that orbits a planet. Natural satellites are also called moons.

segregation Separating, especially using laws to separate people of different races.

settlers People who make their homes in new areas.

shrine A sacred location or object where people of a particular religion worship and pray.

siege A form of warfare, where an army surrounds a city, hoping to make it surrender when it runs out of food, water, or weaponry.

silicate Any substance, usually a rock, that is mainly made up of the elements silicon and oxygen. Silicate rocks are the main rocks of Earth's crust.

singularity A point of infinite density, where the ordinary laws of physics break down. Scientific theory predicts that singularities should exist at the centers of black holes.

smog Originally meant a mixture of smoke and fog, but now usually refers to a hazy layer of pollutants in the atmosphere that may be dangerous to health.

socialism A way to organize society to spread wealth more evenly.

solar panel A panel designed to absorb the Sun's rays to provide a source of heating or to generate electricity.

solar wind Streams of tiny fast-moving particles—mainly electrons and protons—given off by the Sun.

solstice The time of the year when the Sun passes overhead at its furthest point north or furthest point south of the equator.

Soviet Union The Union of Soviet Socialist Republics (USSR), a northern Eurasian empire that emerged after the fall of the Russian tsar in 1917. It was established in 1922 and collapsed in 1991, with the end of the Cold War.

specimen A sample for scientific examination.

stamen One of the male structures in a flower that produces pollen.

stromatolites Mounds of rock formed gradually underwater in layers by photosynthesizing bacteria.

sublimation When a substance goes straight from a solid to a gas when heated, without going through a liquid stage.

suffrage The right to vote.

surface tension The force at a liquid's surface that resists something small being pushed through it.

tarsus (plural tarsi) The end part of an insect's leg, made of several small joints.

tattoo A pattern or design marked permanently on the skin using ink or other pigments.

tax Money or property taken by law from a person to help run the country, state, county, or town they live in or belong to.

taxonomy The scientific classification of living things.

tectonic plate One of the huge geological plates into which Earth's crust and upper mantle are divided. For example, the African plate includes the whole of Africa as well as a lot of the ocean floor around it.

temperature A measure of how hot or cold something is. Temperature is measured in Fahrenheit (F or °F) and Celsius (C or °C). Under usual conditions, the freezing point of pure water is 32°F (0°C) and the boiling point is 212°F (100°C).

temple A name for a place of worship in several different religions.

tensile Referring to pulling. **Tensile forces** are forces that tend to pull a material apart, while **tensile strength** is the ability to resist these forces.

terrorism The use of fear to try to change society, including committing violent crimes to make people fearful.

theology The study of philosophical religious questions, especially within the Christian church.

toxic Poisonous.

treaty A legal agreement between two or more countries or groups.

tsunami A powerful, fast-moving sea wave created by an underwater earthquake, volcanic eruption, or a landslide. On reaching shallow water, it gets much higher and can devastate coastal areas.

turbulence Where a gas or liquid does not flow smoothly, but swirls around.

ultrasound High-frequency sound that is above the range of human hearing.

ultraviolet A kind of light that is invisible to humans but can be seen by other animals, including insects.

urban Relating to cities, suburban, and built-up areas.

vertebrate An animal with a backbone, such as a fish, bird, or mammal.

vibration A shaking or trembling motion.

viral (1) Relating to viruses. **(2)** To go viral is when a story or image on the Internet is copied thousands or millions of times.

virus (1) A tiny particle that can cause disease in people, animals, and plants. Viruses cause many diseases, including colds, flu, and Covid-19. Smaller than bacteria, viruses can reproduce by getting inside living cells and using them to make more viruses. **(2)** A piece of computer software that can spread from one computer to another, often causing damage.

weathering The breaking down of rock or soil; for example, by frost or by chemicals in rain.

wormhole A theoretical passageway that connects directly from a black hole to a distant part of the Universe. Its existence has not yet been proven.

INDEX

space programme 26, 32, 38, 39, 42, 43, 327
space race 327
women's suffrage movement 318, 319
World War I 316
World War II 324, 325
Universal Declaration of Human Rights 230
Universe 2–49
    beginning of 4–5
    end of 46–47
    expansion of 4, 46, 47, 133
    intelligent life 7, 21
    parallel universes 47
universities 230
unmanned aerial vehicles (UAVs) 350
uranium 102, 104, 376
Uranus 22, 23, 30, 31, 32
urban farming 347
urban sprawl 354
urban wildlife 188–189
Ursa Major 14
Uruk 248

V

V2 rockets 38
vaccines 312, 313, 340
Valles Marineris 29
Valley of the Kings 255
valleys 84, 95
Van de Waals forces 118
Vancouver 355
vaquitas 370
vegans 209
Venezuela 311
Venus 22, 24, 26, 27, 28, 32, 44, 55
Venus flytraps 157
vertebrates 158
Vesalius, Andreas 312
Vespucci, Amerigo 305
Vesuvius, Mount 65
Victoria, Queen 300
video calls 341
Vietnam 213, 319, 321, 329
Vietnam War 327
Vikings 257, 287
Virgo 15
viruses 154, 155
Vishnu 257
visible light 128, 129
vitamin B12 121
volcanic mountains 69
volcanoes 59, 60, 62, 63, 64–65, 66, 69, 368
    Mars 29
    Ring of Fire 60, 65
    Venus 27
voles 171, 189

volunteering 233
Vostok 1 43
voting rights 269, 318–319, 330
Voyager spacecraft 22, 31

W

wall paintings 262, 264, 277, 279
Wallace, Alfred Russel 151
Walton, Jim 352
wampum beads 226
warfare 214, 215, 273, 276, 277, 281, 287, 307
    aerial warfare 317, 324, 325
    armies 252, 266, 267, 275, 277, 287
    asymmetrical warfare 351
    cyber war 350
    guerrilla warfare 351
    modern warfare 350–351
    space warfare 351
    World War I 316–317, 322, 323
    World War II 38, 323, 324–325, 331
Warsaw Pact 327
Washington, George 310
water 52, 53, 54, 55, 81, 82–83, 106, 107, 115, 129
    arrival on Earth 83
    freshwater 81, 82, 84, 85, 174
    groundwater 81, 82
    in the human body 111
    inequality 345
    on Mars 29
    meltwater 84
    pollution 367
    pressure 136, 137, 182
    saltwater 82, 174
    tap water 375
    water cycle 82
    water security 83
    water vapor 64, 82, 110
    see also ice; snow
water bears 154
water boatmen 175
water wheels 123
Watt, James 315
weak nuclear forces 133, 136
wealth inequality 344, 352
wealthy people 352–353
weather 86, 87, 88–89, 92
    weather maps 89
    weather satellites 41
    see also climate
websites 357
Weddell Sea 184
weight 134, 136, 137
weightlessness 135

welding 232
westerlies 88
whales 124, 158, 181, 185, 186, 187, 370
wheels 142, 143, 247
white dwarfs 11
white light 128
Wi-Fi 364
Wicca 213
wigs 211
wildebeest 168, 169
wildfires 366, 372, 373
Wilkinson Microwave Anisotrophy Probe (WMAP) 5
Williams, Serena 345
Wilson, Robert 5
winches 142
wind farms 378
wind turbines 123
winds 88, 89, 90, 91, 93
    prevailing wind zones 88
    turbulence 87, 129
    wind power 378
    see also storms
witchcraft 213, 229
wolves 171
women
    astronauts 327
    education 230, 333
    equal opportunity 230
    gender discrimination 315
    Mughal 301
    queens and empresses 255, 267, 279, 283
    Spartan 268
    suffrage movement 318–319
    voting rights 269, 318–319
wood sponge 360
woodpeckers 172
woolly mammoths 151
work 230, 232–233
    division of labor 315
    see also Industrial Revolution
World War I 316–317, 322, 323
World War II 38, 323, 324–325, 331
World Wide Web 356, 357, 358
wormholes 19
worms 158
wrestling 235
Wright, Wilbur and Orville 315
writing systems 218, 247, 253, 255, 263, 264
Wu, King 252
Wu Ding, King 252
Wu Zetian, Empress 283

X

X-15 rocket plane 131
X-43A jet plane 108
X-rays 121, 129, 313, 317
Xerxes 266, 267
Xia dynasty 252
X'ian 283
Xuanzang 283

Y

Yahweh 257
Yangtze River 83
year
    leap years 55, 224
    planetary 22–23
    solar years 224
yeast 121, 152
yellow dragon robes 283
yellow dwarfs 11, 24
Yellow River 252
Yellowstone National Park 65
Yemen 351
Yenisey-Angara-Selenga system 83
Ying Zheng 274, 275
yin-yang 53
You, King 252
Yousafzai, Malala 333
YouTube 357, 358, 359
Ypres, Battles of 316
Yu the Great 252

Z

Zeb-un-Nisa 301
zebra 168, 169
zebra surgeonfish 178
zero carbon energy 379
Zeus 257, 269
Zheng He 298
Zhou dynasty 252, 253, 283
ziggurats 248
Zimbabwe 227
zinc 107
zooplankton 179
zooxanthellae 178
Zoroastrianism 213
Zuckerberg, Mark 352, 359

PICTURE CREDITS

Key: top (t), bottom (b), left (l), right (r), center (c)

br Wikimedia Commons; **p.207 cr** istock/VikiVector; **cr** istock/appleuzr; **cr** istock/Rakdee; **cr** istock/mechanick; **cr** istock/soulcid; **bc** istock/ByM; **br** istock/GlobalP; **p.208 br** Dreamstime/Chernetskaya; **p.209 tc** 123rf.com/yupiramos; **r** Clickalps SRLs/age fotostock/Superstock; **bc** 123rf.com/fuzullhanum; **p.210 tc** World History Archive/Superstock; **b** Dia Dipasupil/Getty; **p.211 tl** Science History Images/Alamy; **br** istock/master2; **p.212–13** Dreamstime/Sadalaxmi Rawa; **p.213** 123rf.com/redberry; **p.214 t** World History Archive/Superstock; **bc** Ashraf Shazly/AFP/Getty; **p.215 tl** 123rf.com/chatcameraman; **cr** ITAR-TASS News Agency/Alamy; **bcr** Encyclopaedia Britannica, Inc.; **cl** 123rf.com/Alexander Pokusay; **bl** 123rf.com/artush; **p.216 tr** istock/JohnnyGrieg; **p.217 cl** istock/Lokibaho; **cr** Image courtesy of Laura Kalin; **bl** Dreamstime/Danemo; **p.218 tr** istock/f9b65183_118; **c** DeAgostini/Superstock; **bl** DeAgostini/Superstock; **br** Jose Peral/age fotostock/Superstock; **p.219 cl** istock/coward_lion; **bc** 123rf.com/Kobby Dagan; **p.220–21** Look-foto/Superstock; **p.220 bc** Javier Etcheverry/Visual & Written/Superstock; **p.222** Robert Marquardt/Getty; **p.222 bl** Jan Wlodarczyk/Alamy; **p.223 tl** TAO Images Limited/Alamy; **cl** istock/TonyBaggett; **c** NASA; **br** Dreamstime/Kino Alyse; **p.224–25** 123rf.com/magicpictures; istock/bananajazz; 123rf.com/aratehortua; istock/AVIcons; Dreamstime/Sadalaxmi Rawa; Dreamstime/Dreamsidhe; istock/ekazansk; istock/MicrovOne; istock/appleuzr; istock/kumarworks; istock/Tatiana_Ti; istock/Drypsiak; istock/olnik_y; istock/Alexey Morozov; 123rf.com/Svitlana Drutska; istock/Photoplotnikov; **p.225 tr** World History Archive/Superstock; **p.226 l** istock/GeorgeManga; **l** istock/Bakal; **l** istock/Balora; **l** istock/Counterfeit_ua; **l** istock/-VICTOR-; **l** istock/13ree_design; **l** istock/Tanya St; **l** istock/Vectorios2016; **l** istock/einegraphic; **tr** Wikimedia Commons/Baomi (CC BY-SA 4.0 International); **p.227 tr** Dreamstime/Kwanchaidt; **cl** Dreamstime/Joe Sohm; **br** Dreamstime/Taigis; **p.228 t** istock/TonyBaggett; **p.229 cl** istock/undefined undefined; **cr** Image courtesy of Jack Snyder; **p.230 cl** agefotostock/Alamy; **tr** istock/hadynyah; **p.231 t** Jonas Gratzer/Getty; **p.232 t** Steve Morgan/Alamy; **bc** David Gee 4/Alamy; **p.233 tr** Nature Picture Library/Cyril Ruoso; **bl** istock/cherstva (chair/table); **bl** istock/Alex Belomlinsky (dog bowl); **br** 123rf.com/Ian Allenden; **p.234 tr** Jose Breton/NurPhoto/Getty; **p.235 tl** Alain Guilleux/age fotostock/Superstock; **tr** Sueddeutsche Zeitung Photo/Alamy; **bl** Warren Little/Getty; **p.238 t** istock/Solange_Z; **br** Chris Warren/Superstock; **p.239 tl** age fotostock/Superstock; **r** DeAgostini/Superstock; **bl** istock/ThamKC; **p.240** Image courtesy of Pravina Shukla; Image courtesy of Gina A. Zurlo; Image courtesy of Martin Polley; **p.242** istock/Carlos Aranguiz; **p.244 tr** Auscape/Getty; **p.244–45 b** LEMAIRE Stephane/Hemis/Superstock; **p.245 tl** Dreamstime/Rafael Ben Ari; **cr** robertharding/Superstock; **bcr** Image courtesy of Dave Ella; **p.247 tr** 123rf.com/Nicolas Fernandez; **br** istock/Species125; **p.248 tr** Peter Willi/Superstock; **c** Wikimedia Commons/Eric Gaba (CC BY-SA 3.0); **bl** DeAgostini/Superstock; **p.249 t** PRISMA ARCHIVO/Alamy; **cl** INTERFOTO/Alamy; **br** DeAgostini/Superstock; **p.250–251** istock/MNStudio; **p.253 tl** The Print Collector/Alamy; **tr** Heritage Image Partnership Ltd/Alamy; **cl** 123rf.com/Willaume; **br** 123rf.com/Anan Punyod; **p.254 tr** Stock Connection/Superstock; **p.255 cl** 123rf.com/Mikhail Kokhanchikov; **cr** 123rf.com/Silviu-Florin Salomia; **bc** Tom K Photo/Alamy; **p.256–57** Peter Barritt/Superstock; **p.258 tc** 123rf.com/Aleksandra Sabelskaia; **cr** George Steinmetz/Getty; **bl** Cicero Moraes; **p.259 tr** 123rf.com/makasanaphoto; **cr** Image courtesy of Alicia Boswell; **bc** istock/SL_Photography; **p.261 cl** Encyclopaedia Britannica, Inc.; **br** David Tomlinson/Alamy; **p.263 tr** Wikimedia Commons/Xuan Che (CC BY 2.0); **cl** DeAgostini/Superstock; **cr** North Wind Picture Archives/Alamy; **bl** istock/D_Zheleva; **br** PRISMA ARCHIVO/Alamy; **p.264 tr** DeAgostini/Superstock; **bl** DeAgostini/Superstock; **p.265 cr** Image courtesy of Elizabeth Graham; **bl** istock/Soft_Light; **p.266 l** Funkystock/age fotostock/Superstock; **cr** DeAgostini/Superstock; **p.267 cl** Philippe Michel/age fotostock/Superstock; **cr** Wikimedia Commons; **br** José Fuste Raga/age fotostock/Superstock; **p.268 tc** Granger Historical Picture Archive/Alamy; **b** World History Archive/Superstock; **p269 tl** funkyfood London - Paul Williams/Alamy; **cr** Image courtesy of Bill Parkinson; **bl** Dreamstime/Leremy; **p.271 tc** PRISMA ARCHIVO/Alamy; **p.272** istock/kaetana_istock; **p.273 tcl** Dinodia/Bridgeman Images; **cr** Dreamstime/Arindam Banerjee; **bl** 123rf.com/vectorstockcompany; **bc** Dreamstime/Adisak Paresuwan; **p.274–75** istock/zhaojiankang; **p.274 bc** istock/aphotostory; **p.276 tr** istock/Aaltazar; **bl** Universal Images/Superstock; **p.277 tr** Metropolitan Museum of Art; **cl** 123rf.com/Rusian Gilmanshin; **p.278 tc** 123rf.com/vincentstthomas; **p.279 tl** Heritage Image Partnership Ltd/Alamy; **cl** Wikimedia Commons; **br** Wikimedia Commons; **p.281 tl** DeAgostini/Superstock;**r** Gilles Barbier/imageBROKER/Superstock; **bl** Dreamstime/Fireflyphoto; **p.282 r** Martha Avery/Getty; **bl** Robert Kawka/Alamy; **p.283 tcl** Pictures from History/Bridgeman Images; **c** 123rf.com/Peng Hua; **br** Aterra Picture Library/Alamy; **p.284 r** Cultural Archive/Alamy; **p.285 tl** Christie's Images Ltd/Superstock; **cr** istock/Ghulam Hussain; **br** Dreamstime/Giuseppe Sparta; **bc** Heritage Image Partnership Ltd/Alamy; **p.287 tr** istock/a40757; **cl** istock/bubaone; **cr** The Picture Art Collection/Alamy; **bl** INTERFOTO/Alamy; **p.288** Image courtesy of Salima Ikram; Image courtesy of John O. Hyland; Image courtesy of Patrick V. Kirch; **p.290** istock/Keith Lance; **p.292 tr** JORDI CAMI/Alamy; **p.293 cr** Edwin Remsberg/Visual & Written/Superstock; **bl** MyLoupe/Getty; **br** Heritage Image Partnership Ltd/Alamy; **p.294–95** Wikimedia Commons; **p.296 cl** Lanmas/Alamy; **bl** Katya Palladina/Stockimo/Alamy; **p.297** Lucas Vallecillos/age fotostock/Superstock; **p.298 tc** istock/artisteer; **p.299 tc** Wikimedia Commons; **cr** Image courtesy of Lorenzo Veracini; **bl** Print Collector/Getty; **p.300 tc** 123rf.com/thelightwriter; **b** istock/somchaisom/Dreamstime/Cbaumg; **p.301 tl** IndiaPicture/Alamy; **cl** The Granger Collection/Alamy; **cr** Granger Historical Picture Archive/Alamy; **p.302** istock/MrsWilkins; **p.303 tl** Christie's Images Ltd/Superstock; **tr** Historic Collection/Alamy; **cr** Image courtesy of Katsuya Hirano; **bl** DEA/G. DAGLI ORGTI/Getty; **p.304 tr** North Wind Picture Archives/Alamy; **cl** Artokoloro/Alamy; **cr** istock/mj007; **br** istock/CNuisin; **p.305 cl** Pantheon/Superstock; **p.306 b** Mira/Alamy; **tr** North Wind Picture Archives/Alamy; **p.307 tl** World History Archive/Superstock; **tr** Historic Collection/Alamy; **br** istock/sharpner; **p.308 b** Wikimedia Commons; **p.309 tl** The Granger Collection/Alamy; **cr** Image courtesy of Joseph E. Inikori; **bc** Library of Congress; **p.310 tr** North Wind Picture Archives/Alamy; **b** Wikimedia Commons; **p.311 l** istock/Victor Metelskiy; **l** istock/vectortatu; **l** istock/bubaone; **l** istock/jamesbenet; **l** istock/AVIcons; **l** istock/Yuriy Bucharskiy; **bcl** Google Art Project; **cr** istock/ilbusca; **br** Stefano Bianchetti/Getty; **p.312–13** istock/lushik; istock/TSUKIYO; istock/CSA-Archive; istock/Barbulat; istock/pop_jop; istock/jamesjames2541; istock/Panptys; istock/lushik; istock/vectortatu; istock/Bismillah_bd; istock/-VICTOR-; istock/Enis Aksoy; **p.313 tr** istock/Raycat (kidney); **p.314 t** World History Archive/Alamy; **br** Science History Images/Alamy; **p.315 tcl** North Wind Picture Archives/Alamy; **bcl** istock/supanut piyakanont; **bc** Science History Images/Alamy; **r** istock/filo; **r** istock/eduardrobert; **r** istock/d-l-b; **r** istock/AVIcons; **r** istock/pepsizi; **r** istock/GeorgeManga; **r** istock/DmitryLarichev; **p.316 tr** World History Archive/Superstock; **p.317 tl** Classic Vision/age fotostock/Superstock; **c** istock/solargaria; **cr** Dave Bagnall Collection/Alamy; **bl** Granger Historical Picture Archive/Alamy; **p.318–19** LSE Library; **p.320** istock/mustafahacalaki (speech bubbles); **p.321 tl** istock/Kreatiw; **tcl** Universal Images/Superstock; **cr** Library of Congress/Getty; **bl** David Pollack/Getty; **p.322 tr** New York Daily News Archive/Getty; **b** Chronicle/Alamy; **p.323 cl** Allstar Picture Library/Alamy; **cr** istock/Shams Suleymanova (factory); **cr** istock/Ihor Kashurin (dollar); **bl** World History Archive/Superstock; **br** istock/leremy (jobs); **br** istock/bubaone (soup kitchen); **p.324 tr** Dreamstime/Micha Klootwijk; **cl** Bentley Archive/Popperfoto/Getty; **cr** © The Paul Kendel Fonoroff Collection for Chinese Film Studies, C.V. Starr East Asian Library, University of California, Berkeley; **br** istock/Irina Cheremisinova (submarines); **br** istock/bebuntoon (waves); **p.325 bl** World History Archive/Superstock; **br** Dreamstime/Alexmillos; **br** istock/supanut piyakanont; **br** istock/pop_jop; **br** istock/grebeshkovmaxim; **br** istock/Maksym Kapliuk; **br** istock/Mai Vu; **p.326 tr** Dreamstime/Vitaly Komorov; **b** Walter Sanders/Getty; **p.327 cr** istock/Shunrei; **bcl** Universal Images/Superstock; **br** Sueddeutsche Zeitung Photo/Alamy; **p.328 tr** Wikimedia Commons; **cr** Prisma by Dukas Presseagentur GmbH/Alamy; **bl** Wallace Kirkland/Getty; **p.329 r** istock/lukiv007 (compass); **cr** Image courtesy of Robtel Neajai Pailey; **bl** Dominique BERRETTY/Getty; **p.330 c** Robert W. Kelley/Getty; **br** Miami Herald/Getty; **p.331 tl** National Archives and Records Administration (NARA); **tr** istock/FiledIMAGE; **cr** istock/supanut piyakanont; **bcl** World History Archive/Alamy; **br** istock/olga_besnard; **p.332** Stacy Walsh Rosenstock/Alamy; **p.333 tl** Dreamstime/Xi Zhang; **cr** Edwin Remsberg/age fotostock/Superstock; **br** MJ Photography/Alamy; **p.336** Image courtesy of Cindy Ermus; Image courtesy of Etana H. Dinka; Image courtesy of Taymiya R. Zaman; **p.338** istock/PhonlamaiPhoto; **p.340 tr** Science Photo Library/Roger Harris; **b** STR/Getty; **p.341 tl** robertharding/Superstock; **tr** Dreamstime/Bundit Minramun; **cl** Dreamstime/Featureflash; **cr** istock/justhavealook; **p.342–43** mauritius images GmbH/Alamy; **p.343 tr** 123rf.com/Valentin Valkov; **p.344** istock/C_Fernandes; **p.345 tl** Shutterstock/James Gourley/BPI; **cr** Visions of America, LCC/Alamy; **bl** Maria Heyens/Alamy; **br** 123rf.com/yupiramos; **p.346–47b** istock/Martijnvandernat; **p.346 tr** istock/GlobalP; **cl** Nature Picture Library/Pal Hermansen; **p.347 tr** istock/NatashaPhoto; **cr** 123rf.com/Dai Trinh Huu; **p.348–349** NASA; **p.349 bc** Little girl playing with a Little Sun in Ethiopia – photo: Merklit Mersha; **p.350** UK Ministry of Defence; **p.351 tr** Science Photo Library/Alamy; **cl** MUNIR UZ ZAMAN/AFP/Getty; **cr** istock/daz2d; **br** KHALED FAZAA/AFP/Getty; **p.352** Dimitrios Kambouris/Getty; **p.353 t** istock/nechaev-kon; **cl** Imaginechina Limited/Alamy; **cr** istock/ArnaPhoto; **br** NurPhoto/Getty; **p.354–55 c** istock/Thomas De Wever; **p.354 cl** istock/Nigel_Wallace; **br** istock/pidjoe; **p.355 br** istock/smile3377 (city skyline); **p.356** istock/imaginima; **p.357 tr** US Marines Photo/Alamy; **cl** Science Photo Library/Sam Ogden; **cr** 123rf.com/artrosestudio; **cr** Dreamstime/Nanmulti; **cr** Dreamstime/Andrii Kuchyk; **cr** Dreamstime/Raffaele1; **cr** Dreamstime/Fidan Babayeva; **cr** istock/13ree_design; **cr** Dreamstime/Sandaru Nirmana; **cr** Dreamstime/Mary San; **cr** Dreamstime/Provectorstock; **p.358** istock/scanrail (phone); istock/Katharina13 (Australian animals); 123rf.com/bennymarty (wombat); **p.359 tr** ClassicStock.com/Superstock; **cl** Dreamstime/K2images; **cr** 123rf.com/artrosestudio; **cr** Dreamstime/Raffaele1; **cr** Dreamstime/Fidan Babayeva; **br** Dreamstime/Danang Setiawan; **p.360 t** Science Photo Library/Pascal Goetgheluck; **bc** age fotostock/Superstock; **p.361 tr** istock/NPavelN; **cr** istock/aceshot; **b** istock/technotr; **p.362 t** istock/Sudowoodo; **cr** Dreamstime/Viktoriia Kasyanyuk; **b** istock/Gannet77; **p.363 tr** CMR Surgical; **cl** 123rf.com/arcady31; **cr** Image courtesy of Mike Jay; **bl** istock/piranka; **p.365 tr** 123rf.com/Wantarnagon; **cl** Image courtesy of Rana el Kaliouby; **br** EThamPhoto/Alamy; **p.366** istock/petar belobrajdic; **p.367 tl** Amazon-Images/Alamy; **c** Martin Shields/Alamy; **bl** imageBROKER/Superstock; **br** istock/Nataniil; **p.368 tc** istock/ScottOrr; **br** istock/Pavliha; **p.369 bl** istock/Misha Shutkevych; **br** istock/Suzyanne16; **p.370–71** Nature Picture Library/Anup Shah; **p.372** Dreamstime/Zaur Tahimov; **p.372–73** Dreamstime/Johnpaulramirez; istock/ArnaPhoto; Dreamstime/Liudmyla Klymenko; **p.373 br** istock/GlobalP; **p.374 t** SOPA Images/Getty; **br** 123rf.com/Rosanna Cunico; **br** istock/Enis Aksoy; **br** 123rf.com/pytyczech; **br** istock/-VICTOR-; **p.375 tr** istock/PamelaJoeMcFarlane; **cl** Zoonar GmbH/Alamy; **bcl** Jasper Chamber/Alamy; **p.376 b** istock/jotily; **p.377 cr** Sue Flood/Alamy; **bl** NASA; **p.378 t** istock/imagean; **p.379 tl** NASA; **cr** Image courtesy of Dr. Jaise Kuriakose; **bl** Dreamstime/Ricoistda; **p.380–81 t** istock/3000ad; **p.380 bl** Dreamstime/Yinan Zhang; **p.381 bl** Jochen Tack/Alamy; **p.382** Dreamstime/Jie Xu; **p.383 tc** Science Photo Library/Life in View; **bl** JEP Celebrity Photos/Alamy; **r** Shutterstock/Quirky China; **p.384** Image courtesy of Yingjie Hu; Image courtesy of Shauna Brail; Image courtesy of Joel Sartore.

**BRITANNICA
BOOKS**

Britannica Books is an imprint of What on Earth Publishing, published in collaboration with Britannica, Inc.
The Black Barn, Wickhurst Farm, Tonbridge, Kent TN11 8PS, United Kingdom
30 Ridge Road Unit B, Greenbelt, Maryland, 20770, United States

First published in the United States in 2020

Developed by Toucan Books

Contributors
Edited by Christopher Lloyd
Foreword by J. E. Luebering
Cover illustration and lettering by Justin Poulter
Interior illustrations by Mark Ruffle and Jack Tite
Text by Jonathan O'Callaghan (Chapters 1 and 8), John Farndon (Chapters 2 and 3), Michael Bright (Chapter 4), Cynthia O'Brien (Chapter 5), Dr. Jacob Field (Chapter 6), Abigail Mitchell (Chapter 7), Richard Beatty (Glossary)
Expert consultants listed on p.IV

Staff for this book
Toucan Books: Ellen Dupont, Editorial Director; Thomas Keenes, Senior Designer; Dorothy Stannard, Senior Editor; Tessa Bindlove, Nicola Erdpresser, Leah Germann, Elaine Hewson, Dave Jones, Lee Riches, Designers; John Andrews, Julie Brooke; Carron Brown, Alethia Doran, Fiona Plowman, Rachel Warren-Chadd, Editors; Michael Clark, Assistant Editor; Gabrielle Handberg, Editorial Assistant; Marie Lorimer, Indexer; Susannah Jayes, Picture Researcher; Dolores York, Proofreader; Cosmographics, Maps, p.60–61, p.261, p.298, p.329, p.334–35

Encyclopaedia Britannica: Alison Eldridge, Managing Editor; Brian Duignan, Senior Editor, Philosophy, Law, and Social Science; Erik Gregersen, Senior Editor, Astronomy, Space Exploration, Mathematics, Physics, Computers, and Inorganic Chemistry; Amy McKenna, Senior Editor, Geography, Sub-Saharan Africa; Melissa Petruzzello, Assistant Editor of Plant and Environmental Science; John P. Rafferty, Editor, Earth and Life Sciences; Michael Ray, Editor, European History and Military Affairs; Kara Rogers, Senior Editor, Biomedical Sciences; Amy Tikkanen, Corrections Manager; Jeff Wallenfeldt, Manager, Geography and History; Adam Zeidan, Assistant Editor, Mideast; Alicja Zelazko, Assistant Editor, Arts and Humanities; Joan Lackowski, Fact Checking Supervisor; Fia Bigelow, Letricia A. Dixon, Will Gosner, R. E. Green, Fact Checkers

What on Earth Publishing: Nancy Feresten, Publisher and Editor-in-Chief; Natalie Bellos, Executive Editor; Andy Forshaw, Art Director; Daisy Symes, Junior Designer; Alenka Oblak, Production Manager

Library of Congress Cataloging-in-Publication Data available upon request

ISBN: 9781912920488

Printed and bound in India

10 9 8 7 6 5 4 3 2 1

whatonearthbooks.com

MIX
Paper from
responsible sources
FSC® C016779